Sod and Stubble

Sod and Stubble

The Unabridged and Annotated Edition

by John Ise

With Additional Material by
Von Rothenberger

Foreword by Thomas D. Isern

 University Press of Kansas

Published by the University Press of Kansas (Lawrence, Kansas 66049), which was
organized by the Kansas Board of Regents and is operated and funded by Emporia State
University, Fort Hays State University, Kansas State University, Pittsburg State University,
the University of Kansas, and Wichita State University

Library of Congress Cataloging-in-Publication Data

Ise, John, 1885–
    Sod and stubble / by John Ise. — The unabridged and annotated ed.
    / with additional material by Von
Rothenberger.
        p. cm.
    Includes bibliographical references and index.
    ISBN 0-7006-0774-9 (cloth) — ISBN 0-7006-0775-7 (pbk.)
        1. Pioneers—Kansas—Osborne County—Biography. 2. Ise, Rosa
Christina Haag, 1856–. 3. Ise, Henry Christopher, 1841–1900.
4. Frontier and pioneer life—Kansas—Osborne County. 5. Osborne
County (Kan.)—Biography. I. Rothenberger, Von. II. Title.
F687.O7I84 1996
978.1'21503'092—dc20   96-37221
[B]

British Library Cataloguing in Publication Data is available.

Printed in the United States of America

10 9 8 7 6 5 4

Contents

Illustrations

A Plainsman's Appreciation
for *Sod and Stubble*

by Thomas D. Isern

Any discussion of John Ise's book *Sod and Stubble* is to me a
double delight; that is, I appreciate the book for two reasons. The
first is that I feel as though this book, an ethnic, family-farm document, is my own story. (I even take secret satisfaction that on
shelves where works are lodged alphabetically according to authors' names, mine rub shoulders with Ise's.) Like the Ises, my ancestors were all Germans who settled on the agricultural frontier of
Kansas. When I look at those line drawings of Henry and Rosie Ise
that appeared in the various editions of *Sod and Stubble,* I see my
great-grandparents Adolph and Wilhelmine as I know them
through family photographs.

My favorite family photograph was taken on their farm in Bar-
ton County during the late 1890s. In the background are a frame
house and a windmill, signs of reasonable prosperity. Up front are
the three boys. Uncle Alvin is holding a draft horse by the bridle,
and Uncle Walter is holding a croquet mallet, which tells you
something about the directions their respective lives would take.
Between them, in more than one way, is my Grandfather Alfred.

Overlooking all are Wilhelmine and Adolph, and it is they
who give me pause. They have their farm, and their home, but
they look so weary, hardened, careworn. They had persevered, but
they had known failures—the failure of the peach orchard, the failure of the carp pond, and no doubt many others of which I do not
know. Was it worth it all? Maybe they should have stayed in Ohio.

Those big questions, and many of the small details, too, are
commonalities in the family histories of people on the plains. Over
the years I have been touched by the experience of leading discus-

sions of John Ise's book with public groups in many communities. One question I always ask is, What is the saddest part of the book? Opinion varies. Some say, when the baby dies; some say, when Henry dies; most say, when Rosie sells the farm and sits lost among her treasures as they are auctioned away. I never inquire too closely why people give the answers they do, because I know that the answers depend on their own personal and family histories. Those experiences are close to the surface, and I'm not some therapist who has to drag them to the surface. Everyone knows already. Although I would not have said so a few years ago, I'm willing now to say that to me, the saddest part of the book is when the family takes Henry around the place in the buggy for one last look before he goes to bed and dies. That I have made that drive in a Chevrolet instead of a buggy makes it no less poignant—for me, or for the many others I know have made the same ritual round. Commonalities.

My own sentiments notwithstanding, I also, as a scholar, revere *Sod and Stubble* as the greatest of all primary documents of the farmer's frontier on the Great Plains of North America. By a "primary document" I mean a nonfiction narrative written by someone who was there. (I know that Ise changed names and played loose with chronology, but his book is still memoir, not fiction.) No other primary document of the homesteading experience, in either the United States or Canada, matches this one. I make that statement not because of superior artistry in composition. The organization of the book is capricious, the prose style often naive. Nevertheless, the book succeeds in recording and communicating the homesteading experience. It is history of the best sort, vicarious history, allowing us to live someone else's experience.

More specifically, what is so good about *Sod and Stubble?* Here we approach a philosophical question as to what it is important to know about. When I teach seminars at university, students pick topics for individual research, and I always ask, Why do you want to look into this topic? Often the answer is, Because it's unique. Then I advise the student to pick another topic. If something is unique, then it is one of a kind, it happened but once, and so who cares about it? We need not know about what is unique, because that experience is of no use. We need to know about what is common, about the things that happened over and over. This is valuable experience we can use. We should study the things that are prosaic, common, everyday.

Sod and Stubble is a common story. That is why it is important. It is common, but not dull, and why not? Because we get to know the characters in it personally. We care about them, about practical Rosie and sensitive Henry and wild Billy and the rest of them. Over the past thirty years or so historians have made much of what they call the "new social history." By this they mean the study of the lives of ordinary people, not just the great white men featured in the textbooks of previous generations. The new social historians do their work mainly by analyzing quantitative data, such as census returns. This yields lots of good information, but the problem is that it is all so dull no one but reviewers, graduate students, and other conscripts will read it. Sod and Stubble, on the other hand, is hard to put down once you get to know the people in it.

Especially Rosie, who is the most memorable person in the narrative. How was it that a male author—an economist at that!—produced this most memorable of portraits of a plainswoman? The answer is obvious only if you know that John Ise the author is Joe in the narrative, the boy who had polio—who was unable to go to the field with his father but had to stay around the house and yard. Would it be too perverse to say that this affliction on the boy, this trial for his parents, was a blessing to posterity?

As for the lack of artistry in the book—we can turn this around and call it lack of pretense. More to the point, we can realize that pioneer life was not so simple as Laura Ingalls Wilder or Hallmark television specials would have it. It is silly to bemoan our complicated lives today and to assume that a century ago things were not so. A reading of Craig Miner's history of western Kansas, West of Wichita, makes it obvious that frontier farm life was complex as well as rude. If the events in Sod and Stubble sometimes seem pell-mell and incongruous, that is because the Ise family lived them that way.

Indeed, the unpretentious genius of Sod and Stubble is that Ise gives us a startling admixture of the formulaic and the idiosyncratic. If you gathered together any collection of old-timers—a focus group, we would call it today—and asked what things ought to be written in their story, what were the essential elements in the narrative of regional history, a list of things certainly would come

out: grasshopper plagues, prairie fires, tornadoes, eccentric bachelors—you can finish the list. That distillation of commonplaces,
however, would not replicate life as they lived it. Every life, in addition to the commonplaces, comprised countless events that were
random, some of them strange, examples of Great Plains grotesque. For every prairie fire, every interchangeable part, there was
a General Bull being gored by his pet elk, an idiosyncratic episode.
People who lived these things did not sort them out at the time
and say, "This is part of a larger pattern and is historically signifi-
cant," or, "This is just a trivial happenstance." Neither did Ise as
he composed, or rather compiled, his narrative.

John Ise was distinguished in his field of natural resource economics (as well as feared by generations of University of Kansas
students). I have a fascination with great thinkers whose intellectual attainments go far beyond the common understanding but
who, on close examination, are found to be still connected to their
roots. Such was the case with John Ise. His conservation was his
mother's thrift; his reverence for forests was her love of flowers and
trees around the place. And he, whose family knew such want and
hardship, was enraged by ostentatious wealth. I love the way he
railed against lazy bankers and smart-aleck rich kids in *United
States Oil Policy* and enjoined them to improve their minds with
good books.

Good books like *Sod and Stubble*. I used to like to think about
how this book came to be, how Ise got the manuscript together. He
did not exactly cover the tracks of his research. I knew from the in-
ternal evidence he must have looked up some things in old newspapers; surely he drew on the recollections of family members and
neighbors, as well as his own; but most of all, in my mind I saw
him sitting at a kitchen table with a yellow pad, the kind all professors make notes on, asking questions, and across the table was Rosie, telling what she remembered. It came out in episodes, all
mixed up, and then even the episodes digressed, but the notes accumulated, were set in order as much as possible, and finally the
book happened. It was no surprise, but a great gratification, when
Von Rothenberger, on the trail of *Sod and Stubble,* told me what he
had found in the Ise papers. Yellow sheets, mixed-up notes—just
the way I had imagined.

I have read the book at least six times. Although it can be read with profit and enjoyment by middle schoolers, I learn something from it every time I read it. The more you come to know about pioneer customs and life on the plains, the more you can get from the book. For instance, the tragic chapter about Nebraska Stevens and the mad wolf—it makes sense on first reading. It makes more sense when you understand what a feverish fear rabies provoked in nineteenth-century communities, and more still when you learn what a madstone was. Still, you cannot really understand the veiling sensitivity behind the passive construction, "Smothered in his own bed-tick," used by Henry to report the sad end of young Stevens, until you know how pioneer communities came together to put an end to the suffering by victims of rabies.

If you haven't read Sod and Stubble, I envy you the experience of reading it fresh. If you have read it, do it again, and this time take in the whole narrative.

Editor's Preface

In 1933 John Ise wrote to a prospective publisher the following statement: "I trust you will not consider this manuscript as a novel, or view it from the standpoint of novel writing, although it is written in the form of a story. It is the story of my mother's life in the semi-arid section of Central-Western Kansas, and is intended to be an accurate picture of that early life, embellished only as indicated in the preface."[1] That statement reflects the idea I had in mind when I first considered compiling an annotated version of John Ise's now-classic account of life on a Kansas homestead; that *Sod and Stubble* is essentially not a work of fiction but one of historical fact. Born and raised twelve miles from the site of the Ise homestead, I had long been familiar with the story of the Ise family, and the popularity of the work led me to conclude that there was an audience for a version using new material on the subject. My research began amid John Ise's papers in the University of Kansas Archives at Lawrence, which yielded not only the original manuscript of *Sod and Stubble* but also the notes and sources Dr. Ise had compiled from 1924 to 1932 while tracing his family's history. Further on-site research in the Downs region and other areas in Kansas and Iowa provided background on the book's characters (along with their real identities) as well as verification of the authenticity of Ise's notes and sources. The conclusions that I came to agreed with his assertion. *Sod and Stubble* is a work of astonishing historical accuracy; the acknowledged "embellishments" are few in number and minor in nature.

The order of the book reflects the two goals born of that early central idea. Part One presents John Ise's story as he first envisioned it. It consists of the original manuscript of *Sod and Stubble*, published here for the first time. Entitled "Breaking Sod," it includes four chapters (Chapters 1, 2, 7, and 11 in this book) that were left out of the book's initial publication in 1936. I have deviated from the manuscript in one instance. Originally, the chapters "The Hopeful Journey" and "A New Homestead" were combined. However, the length of the chapter seemed inconsistent with the rest of the work, so I elected to retain the later chapter break and left "A New Homestead" as a separate chapter. At the end of Part One, I have included a reproduction of the sale book, spelling errors and all, that was kept at the auction of the Ise homestead as described in Chapter 36. Part Two brings together the full story of the Ise family, spanning a period of approximately 180 years. The material offers enlightening background for many of the circumstances dictating the actions taken by Henry and Rosa during the *Sod and Stubble* years.

The annotations are used to present the historical evidence behind *Sod and Stubble*. Many of them are quotes taken directly from newspaper accounts or from John and Rosa Ise's original handwritten notes. Through these I have sought to reveal the sources used by John Ise in the course of his writing and to establish both the accuracy and chronology of the work. Hopefully they will appeal to both the scholar and the average reader, who may finally learn what became of old man Vietz, or who Steve Linge really was.

Von Rothenberger

Acknowledgments

Many people have provided valuable assistance during this project. A special debt is owed to the people of the Downs area and elsewhere who took the time to share their family histories, photographs, and memories. Although space does not allow for a complete list, special thanks go out to JoAnn McMichael, Beth Sharp, Doug Brush, Grace Otte, Rebecca Tetlow, and the other members of the Historical Society of the Downs Carnegie Library. I am also grateful to the descendants of the Haag and Ise families for their support and aid: Bill Haag, Lydia Haag, Frank Ise, Jr., Franklin Ise, John Ise, Jr., Ruth Muller, David Schirmer, and Marcy Wright. Many archivists and librarians assisted with the tracking down of old and new material; foremost of these were the people at the University of Kansas Archives, who showed considerable patience and courtesy.

The following people especially have offered advice and encouragement during the course of this project: Leo Oliva; James Hoy and Ron McCoy, Emporia State University; Tom Isern, North Dakota State University; Michele Thun of Kansas State University and William Keel of the University of Kansas, who assisted with the German translations; and David Readio, who assumed the "voice of the general public" and whose generosity and help make a proposed manuscript become a reality at last.

The Kansas Humanities Council provided funding for part of the research material to the Historical Society of Downs Carnegie Library, which in turn has graciously given permission for its inclusion here.

Part One

Breaking Sod—A Story of Pioneer Life in Kansas

by John Ise

To
My mother, and to the memory of my father,
who lived the story I have written here

Preface

A few years ago, as I listened one night to my mother telling incidents of her life pioneering in the semi-arid region of Western Kansas, it occurred to me that the picture of that early time was worth drawing and preserving for the future, and that, if this were ever to be done, it must be done soon, before all of the old settlers were gone. This book is the result—an effort to picture that life truly and realistically. It is the story of an energetic and capable girl, the child of German immigrant parents, who at the age of seventeen married a young German farmer and moved to a homestead on the wind-swept plains of Kansas, where she reared eleven of her twelve children and, remembering regretfully her own half-day in school, sent nine of them through college, and some of them afterward to Harvard, Yale, Columbia, Stanford, the University of Chicago, and the University of Zurich, Switzerland. It is a story of grim and tenacious devotion in the face of hardships and disappointments, devotion that never flagged until the long, hard task of near a lifetime was done.

It seemed proper and necessary to take a few liberties with the literal truth. I have changed the names of most of the characters, and have even changed the characters in many episodes; but I do not believe that the fundamental accuracy of the picture has suffered. In general, I have tried to tell the story as it was told to me, truly and without exaggeration. I spent a summer in the vicinity of my mother's old home, talking with the few pioneers still living, checking up details of my mother's story. I went through local newspaper files covering the early years, in a further effort to verify important points in the narrative. My sister, Mrs. F. E. Lindley, and

5

her husband, who formerly lived not far from the scene of this narrative, read the manuscript with great care, and she spent two weeks with me and my mother, talking over various incidents. My other brothers and sisters helped generously in many ways. And day after day, as I worked on the story, my mother sat patiently across the table, piecing together the scattered recollections of years now long past.

"Not for delectation sweet,
Not the cushion and the slipper, not
    the peaceful and the studious,
Not the riches safe and palling, not
    for us the tame enjoyment,
    Pioneers! O Pioneers!"

Chapter One

A Simple Wedding

The clear notes of a meadow lark floated across the green pasture.

"Oh, those dear little birds!" exclaimed Rosie. "What would spring be without them?"

"Pretty dull," replied Henry Ise. "I would almost rather see spring come without flowers."

"Are there any out there on your claim—any meadow larks?" asked Rosie, as she looked back at the little log house now partly hidden by the hill they were descending.

"Lots of them—more than here!" replied Henry with enthusiasm. "And they sing better than these meadow larks here in Eastern Kansas—quite a long song, twice as long as those larks sing; a song that winds up with a kind of a trill." Henry pursed his lips and tried to whistle an imitation of the song of the western meadow larks, but with indifferent success. "You'll like the meadow larks out there," he added, as he gave the horses a vigorous slap with the lines.

Henry and Rosie were going to town to be married. Looking at them, as they jogged along atop of a double-box wagonload of corn, an observer might have supposed that marriage was a rather casual matter, for Rosie's own family were not even going to the wedding. It would have been evident from the dress and appearance of the couple, however, that they were on no everyday errand. Rosie was dressed neatly in a new calico dress, green with orange and white stripes, with a full fluffy overskirt of the same cloth, and a green straw hat tied on with a veil. The man seated beside her, at least a decade her senior, was dressed in a black Sunday suit, with

9

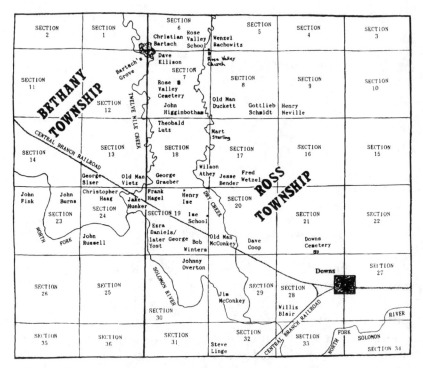

Northeastern Osborne County, Kansas. (Courtesy Von Rothenberger)

starched white shirt. His collar was yards too large, and the bow of
his black tie was pulled far to one side, and apparently on the point
of coming loose; but Henry was clean shaved, except for the beard
that brushed his shirt bosom, and under the dust of his boots was
evidence of careful polishing.

Even as they drove along, it was apparent that the pair were of
different dispositions. Rosie was wide-awake, observant, interested in everything; her eyes wandered everywhere, as if she never
could see enough of the fields, and the pastures, and the flowers
blooming everywhere, of the men and teams at work. She kept up
a barrage of questions and comments regarding the condition of
the crops and orchards and vineyards and gardens, and of the
homes they passed. She noticed every tree or shrub that had been
planted, every shed and coop and fence that had been built, and
commented upon it with enthusiasm.

Even under her veil, Rosie was a fine picture of life and health and energy. A great roll of black hair bulged out under her green straw hat, blending strikingly with the healthy tan of her face and the dark brown of her eyes. Her mouth slanted slightly downward at the corners, in an expression of resoluteness and determination that might have lent a trace of hardness to her face, but for the friendly animation of her eyes. Her hands, brown and rough from washing and scrubbing, and even harder work in the fields, were in shape the hands of a child, for Rosie was only seventeen.

Except when he was urging the horses on, Henry sat quietly, apparently absorbed in thought. When he spoke, his blue eyes lighted up with kindly interest; but he did not speak often, except in response to Rosie's many questions and observations.

Henry was in a hurry. He wanted to get to town, unload his corn, and get married, so that he could start west by early noon—start on the long drive to his new homestead in Western Kansas.[1] He slapped away diligently and called out, "Get along! Get along!" to his deliberate span of bays. Frank and Sam did not greatly mind being slapped with the lines though, for they were used to it. They quickened their pace for a few steps, and then settled back again into their accustomed slow, steady walk.

When they reached town, Henry left Rosie with friends while he drove over to the mill with his load of corn—the corn that was part of his share payment for husking he had done during the winter. It was no great fortune that he got for it, but he put it into his wallet with a smile of satisfaction, climbed into the wagon, and drove back to get Rosie. Together they went to the preacher's home, where, in the presence of the preacher's wife and one of Rosie's friends,[2] they exchanged vows of love, protection, and obedience; and then, a bit embarrassed by their new status, started back to Rosie's home—a drive of six miles.

So, on May the sixteenth, eighteen seventy-three, were united the houses of Ise and Haag, and so begins this story of pioneer life in Kansas. By what strange and devious paths do the gods sometimes bring men and women together, to start new currents in human affairs! Henry Eisenmanger, an immigrant boy from Württemberg, Germany,[3] coming in eighteen fifty-seven, had worked on a farm in Illinois four years, but joined the Union army at the outbreak of the Civil War, and at the end of the war returned to Illinois, with a new name—Henry Ise.

The marriage license of Henry Ise and Rosa Haag, issued on 16 May 1873. The couple were married in Holton later that same day. (Jackson County Courthouse, Holton, Kansas)

The captain of his company,[4] while registering his men one day at the beginning of the war, had come down near the end of the line, where the men of shorter stature were standing. "And what's your name?" the captain queried.

"Eisenmanger," replied Henry.

"Isen——what?" the captain snorted.

Henry repeated the name.

The captain, still baffled, looked down at his list, wrote "Ise——" and drew a long dash, saying, "Ise—that's enough name for any Dutchman[5] your size."

So it was Henry "Ise" who helped guard the Mississippi, fought around Chattanooga, marched with Sherman to the sea, and at the close of the war returned to Illinois, riding on the top of a freight car.[6] He soon went on west to Iowa,[7] where in three or

Wedding picture of Henry and Rosa Ise (1873). At the time, Henry was thirty years old and Rosa was seventeen. (Photo courtesy Marcy Wright)

four years he earned enough breaking prairie to buy a farm of his own; but he lost his hard-earned money—lost his wallet out of his hip pocket as he was riding to town to get his plow lay sharpened—and then decided he must move to Western Kansas and take up a free claim. This happened in the summer of eighteen seventy-one, and after a year on his claim he had driven down to Eastern Kansas, near Holton, to find work and earn money for the purchase of implements and cows. He had a vague notion too, that he needed a wife, and when he met Rosie, he was quite sure he needed one—a very particular one.

Not far from Henry's old home in Germany, in one of the peasant villages of the Neckar,[8] Rosie's forefathers had lived and farmed for generations; but her parents had come to America even before Henry came, and lost their small capital trying to farm in Wisconsin—where Rosie was born—and then moved to Eastern Kansas.[9] There for a few years they endured the most desperate poverty. Rosie's father fell ill with typhoid fever a week after he came, never to recover his health fully. The first summer there was a terrible drouth and they raised no crops whatever. They borrowed money to buy a team of oxen, but the oxen died. The next year they borrowed money again, to buy milk cows, but the cows died of black leg.[10] Deeper in debt each year, their situation seemed almost hopeless; but with true German tenacity, they persevered, and within a few years had paid their debts, bought horses and cows and implements, and were now in comfortable circumstances.

When Henry and Rosie got back home, Rosie's mother, a sad grim-visaged woman, greeted them with a kindly sincerity which needed few words. She kissed her daughter with tears in her eyes, which seemed to say: "My dear girl, what years of hard work and self-denial I fear I can see before you." But she said merely: "We'll have some dinner soon. You can get your things loaded while you're waiting"; and then hurried into the kitchen to prepare dinner.

Rosie's father, a visionary and impractical old German—more poet and philosopher than farmer—after giving them his blessing, went to the cellar to get them a drink of his best wine, then brought out and presented them a new German Bible, and explained the family register which he had written in it, in beautiful German script. In the meantime, the older boys went out to feed the horses and the cows that Henry was to take along. The younger children stood sheepishly about, until they were sent on their various ways.

In the meantime, Henry and Rosie changed their clothes, and then loaded the wagon for the journey west. First the huge box which Henry had brought from Iowa—he always called it his "scuttle box"—was packed with the more valuable articles: a few dishes, knives, forks and spoons, a tablecloth, a sheet and two comforters, two picture albums, four extra dresses, a pair of Sunday shoes and a shawl for Rosie, and a few copies of the Sunday school paper *Kinderfreund*.[11] When everything was in place, the box was lifted into the wagon and pushed to the front, where it was to serve as a seat. Henry's valise, with Sunday boots and shirt and suit in it, was then wedged in at one end of the box.

The rest of the wagon was packed with some of the modest equipment and supplies needed in the new home: several sacks of flour and corn meal, a jar of lard and one of butter, a wooden churn filled with molasses, a skillet, coffee pot, bucket and cup; and a small supply of bread, butter, bacon, lard, eggs, salt, coffee and sugar. Henry's army canteen, full of water, swung from one of the wagon bows. A sack of home-made soap was thrown in, to be taken to one of Henry's neighbors,[12] from relatives living near, and a few gifts from mother to Rosie's brother Chris,[13] whose claim was only a mile from Henry's. Enough straw was spread on top, finally, to fill the hollows and make a bed. The wagon cover was rolled up along the bows, so that they could enjoy the breeze as they drove along.

"There!" said Henry triumphantly. "I guess that will ride two hundred miles." Then he glanced at Rosie, and his enthusiasm waned, for he saw that she was not quite satisfied. "Well, isn't that all we need, Rosie? That's all we *have* anyhow, isn't it?"

"Oh, I was just wishing we could take some flowers along, somehow," said Rosie. "There will be none out there, will there? Couldn't we put some in the feed box here, on the back of the wagon—just a few things, so the home won't look too bare?" Rosie looked wistfully at the yellow rose bush that was already bursting into buds.

"Surely," replied Henry, relieved that the problem was so simple and that the solution was to be found in flowers, for he too loved flowers. "I'll find another box for the horses, while you get the flowers you want." Rosie dug up a few slips of the yellow rose bush, several marigolds, bachelor buttons, and a bunch of asparagus roots, which she packed into the feed box with fresh dirt.

Again Henry felt satisfied with his handiwork, and Rosie was happy as well. It was fine to be able to go to her new home thus, with a team of horses, with provisions to last for weeks, and even with flowers. She almost began to imagine the envy that her fortunate circumstances would arouse in her neighbors, but a sensitive conscience and native good sense stopped this foray of the imagination.

As they stood admiring the completeness of their equipment,

dinner was announced; and they went in and took their places at the long table. It was a grand dinner—chicken and noodles, potatoes and gravy, lettuce and green onions, and coffee with cream and sugar; but in spite of all the wealth of wonderful things to eat, and in spite of the efforts of the family to voice happiness and festivity, a cloud of sadness hung over them. Although only seventeen years old, Rosie had been full of courage, always ready with her capable strength, in the meager years of pioneer life in Eastern Kansas. Her Spartan mother had for years looked to her for help in caring for her husband, almost an invalid, and her large family of children, and for comfort in the disappointments that had been hers in such large measure. Now Rosie was leaving to build a home of her own on a new frontier, farther west.

Chapter Two

The Hopeful Journey

When dinner was over, Henry brought out the horses and hitched them to the wagon while the boys drove the cattle out into the yard—four red cows that belonged to Henry and three that Rosie's father had given her: Brindle, Suke, and Tulip. Rosie's cows were rather plebeian, brindle brutes, of no aristocratic antecedents, but they would make a valuable contribution to the new home out on the prairie, so they were to be driven along with Henry's red heifers.

"Goodbye! Goodbye! Goodbye, Mother!"

"Goodbye, my dear girl! Goodbye, goodbye." The horses moved out of the yard, the brindle cows in the lead, and the red cows following.

They had almost reached the main road when Rosie's mother called them to halt. As the cavalcade stopped, she disappeared into the house, and soon came out with a bed sheet, which she had taken from her own bed.

"You have only one sheet," she explained, hurrying out to the wagon and handing her gift up to Rosie, "and I can get another one here. Give our Grüssen to Chris. Leb' wohl, meine Kinder, leb' wohl. Und schreibt mir wenn ihr könnt."[1]

The wagon moved on again, and her mother walked slowly back to the house—her mother, so stooped and bent, in the dress of faded calico. Rosie looked back with misty eyes, but the log house with the dear ones waving goodbye disappeared as the wagon lurched down a steep slope to the creek crossing and into a grove of trees on the other side.

When they pulled up out of the creek and on to the level road again, they soon began to realize that a hard journey was ahead. Their motley herd of cattle proved utterly unmanageable. There were few fences along the way, and Rosie's brindle heifers refused to stay in the road.

"Hi! Hi, there! Hi, there, hi!" shouted Henry. He leaped from his seat on the scuttle box and started in pursuit of Brindle, as she ran into an enticing field of wheat. After a spirited chase, he headed her off and got her back in to the road, just as Tulip entered the same field a short distance ahead. Another race ensued, and these two trespassers were brought out again; but in the meantime the red cows had lagged behind; and while Henry was bringing them up, the three brindle heifers again invaded the wheat field. By the time he had chased them out again, he was panting and perspiring and muttering deep imprecations against his unmanageable herd.

The cows were badly assorted, that was clear. The red cows were blasé brutes, of a gentle and indolent disposition, and they constantly lagged far behind. Rosie's brindle heifers, on the other hand, were by nature active and enterprising—and enterprise is no recommendation for a cow. They displayed a speed and agility, too, that was completely baffling. It was evident that it would be impossible to keep the herd together.

"You watch them, can you Rosie, till I go back to get the boys to help us for a few miles?" asked Henry, as he circled about the herd, waving his willow switch threateningly.

"Certainly," said Rosie, with assurance, as she set the brakes and climbed down from the wagon. It required all her alertness to keep the brindle heifers out of the wheat field until Henry returned with help, but she had everything in order when he emerged from the trees along the creek, accompanied by two of her small brothers, both armed with heavy cudgels.

Each of the boys took one side of the road, while Henry climbed upon the wagon, and the procession started once more. Sometimes the brindle heifers would get so far ahead that they could make forays into the fields, but they were soon brought back; and as the miles passed and the afternoon wore on, they lost some of their energy. Henry then undertook the task of driving them, and the boys started back home, while Rosie took the lines and drove the team. Thus they moved along, Rosie slapping the lines at the lazy horses, Henry urging the red cows on, and shouting threats and warnings at the brindle heifers in the lead.

Long before sunset Henry was tired and fagged out, and Rosie then volunteered to walk and drive the cows while he drove the team. Rosie always wanted to do her full share of whatever work there was to be done, and she was accustomed to walking long distances. When but a little girl, she had known what it was to walk twenty or twenty-five miles in a day on errands for her father—perhaps carrying her shoes to avoid wearing them out—and had thought very little of it.

Thus "spelling" each other from time to time, they followed the deep ruts that served as a road, on toward the green hills and valleys that stretched ever before them—on toward the west. With young and hopeful spirits they looked forward across the miles of waving grass and scattered fields, while the wagon jolted from side to side and then rattled smoothly along. As she trudged along behind the wagon, Rosie even found time to gather bouquets of the breadroot, prairie roses and daisies that grew along the roadside.

They drove late, and the sun had sunk behind the grassy hills when they stopped for the night, on the bank of a small creek.[2] The brindle heifers were ready to drink and graze by this time; and, while Henry unhitched, watered and fed the horses, Rosie prepared the supper of bread and butter, bacon, eggs, and coffee. How good the eggs tasted, and the smoking bacon! How wonderful the aroma of the coffee! Henry picketed the horses, while Rosie spread a blanket and sheet over the straw in the wagon to make a bed. Before lying down to sleep, they rolled the wagon cover higher, so that they might better watch their livestock. Not only was there danger that the cows might stray away, but there was always great danger from that scourge of all pioneer countries—horse thieves. When a team of horses represented a small fortune, horse stealing was a rather common and highly profitable business, and movers had to be alert.

It was an eerie and lonely night, with the owls hooting in the trees above, the coyotes yelping and howling in the hills to the north, and dogs barking in reply, far up the creek. It seemed reassuring to hear the occasional sneezing of the horses as they grazed about the wagon, and Rosie was soon asleep. She did not awaken until the cool gray of the dawn spread over the hills, and peered down into the valley, and under the wagon cover.

"Where are the cows, I wonder?" she asked, even before she had looked over the side of the wagon box.

Henry roused himself and looked out. In the uncertain light of the early morning it was impossible to see very far, but there were no cows in sight.

"Probably they're down in the creek, or up along the bank somewhere," he said, as he tugged at his boots. To Rosie it sounded somewhat as if he had said: "Probably they've gone back home."

A few minutes search revealed the red cows lying in the high grass, but Brindle and Suke and Tulip were gone; and Henry started back after them, looking in the road for tracks as he went.

Rosie turned to the preparation of breakfast. She brought a bucket of water up from the creek, cut a few sticks of wood from a dead branch, and soon had a fire and a pot of coffee simmering over it. She waited impatiently, hoping Henry would not go too far back, leaving her alone there by the side of the road. A yoke of oxen appeared over the hill, and a prairie schooner trailed after, but no brindle cows followed. As the wagon rolled slowly past her she called to the driver. He stopped—a tall, lanky fellow in patched blue overalls tucked into the tops of his boots—and climbed down from his wagon to greet her.

"Any trouble, missus?" he queried.

"Did you see a man up the road there, or three brindle cows?" she asked anxiously. It did not occur to Rosie that she might fear this man, who appeared to be alone.

"Yep. I seen 'em all," he replied, turning his head to send a flood of tobacco juice over the front wheel. "Man was back a mile or so, and cows a mile furder. He'll be along pretty soon, I reckon. His cows looked a heap spryer'n mine, and they'll come fast when they do come. Right smart mornin' ain't it?" He climbed back to his seat, and cracked his whip at the oxen. As the wagon lunged down into the creek ford, Rosie saw that she had been mistaken in assuming that the man was alone. The rear opening of the wagon cover teemed with the faces of children, gaping curiously at her.

The sun was well up when the brindle heifers appeared. Rosie broke the eggs into the skillet, and had breakfast ready when Henry got back to the wagon. It was very much like the supper of the preceding evening—bread and butter, bacon and eggs and coffee—indeed, to be absolutely frank, it was exactly the same, was it not, except that the bread was harder and drier, and the butter did not pour so easily?

The morning was now far advanced. Henry finally got the horses hitched, and the cows started on ahead; and they moved on, down the steep bank of the creek ford, up the opposite side, around the nose of a jutting bluff, and on to the west, with the wagon jolting from side to side, and the meadow larks singing from every field and hill. The summer was in its green and glorious youth, and Henry and Rosie felt the hope and promise of it. Henry walked and drove the cows most of the time, but Rosie insisted on taking her turn occasionally.

At noon they stopped at a settler's cabin where there was a well, with clear, cold water to drink—a refreshing luxury after the heat and the dust of the morning's travel. In a short time after dinner was over, Rosie had the dishes washed and the dish rag flapping from a bow of the wagon; and they were on the road again, slowly but steadily plodding on toward the land of their hopes.

They passed many ox-drawn wagons—the slow-moving but irresistible tide of settlers seeking new, free lands—wagons covered and uncovered, wagons driven by single men, wagons teeming with children, many of them loaded with every imaginable sort of household utensil or farm implement, with beds and cupboards and bureaus, or with a plow, corn planter, cultivator, fanning mill, or corn sheller[3] occupying the main space, and lesser implements stacked around it, with buckets, pans, kettles and boilers hanging from the standards or bows, and crates of chickens tied onto the end or sides of the wagon, or perhaps with a pig or two appertaining to the load somewhere. A few of the wagons were loaded with lumber, some of it rough lumber sawed from the trees along the creeks, some of it fine white pine—the promise of a new house somewhere on the road ahead. Occasionally a team of horses trotted around them, drawing a wagon, or even a spring wagon, in which the aristocrats of the road sat complacently eyeing the slower and humbler transients as they passed them, perhaps speaking or waving their hands in friendly condescension. In one spring wagon Rosie saw an organ, with grain sacks tied around it, wobbling back and forth as if it were about to topple over at every log in the road.

They overtook an ox-drawn prairie schooner,[4] followed by a herd of cattle and had to drive for several miles in a choking dust. When Henry finally got past he found that Brindle was mixed in with the other man's herd, and it took him half an hour to cut her out and get started again. As the afternoon wore on, the sun beat down with oppressive heat, the horses turned black with sweat under their harnesses, and even the brindle heifers needed constant urging. At sunset all were ready for camp, which was made again on the bank of a creek where they would get wood and water.[5] This time the brindle heifers showed no signs of homesickness. They were content to drink at the creek, and graze, and then lie down until morning.

So they drove along, day after day, always dog-tired at night, but rested and refreshed in the morning, and glad to be on the road again. For Henry, the road had lost most of its novelty. He had followed this trail several times before; but as he recalled the first trip that he had made, two years before when he first came from Iowa, he could not help thinking how pleasant it was to be jogging along thus, with Rosie, and with his herd of seven cattle and generous stock of provisions. An unhappy memory, that trip from Iowa was—his savings stolen, and then the long days of his lonely drive out to Western Kansas, to make a home in a country he knew nothing about. A trip back east to Holton the next year to husk corn, a few visits with Rosie, and her consent to go out to the claim with him, another drive west to plant spring crops and put in the floor that she wanted in the cabin, then the final trip back to get her—yes, he had been over this trail so often that it was no novel experience.

To Rosie, everything was new and full of interest, and in spite of the heat and the lazy cattle, she enjoyed every mile of it. She loved to see the good, rich land along the creek and river bottoms;

and when they passed men plowing she sniffed gratefully the fragrance of the fresh turned soil, especially the smell of new sod. Rosie loved good land; she enjoyed picturing the crops that would presently grow and ripen on it. She could not help wishing that she could own every fertile farm that they passed, and wondered whether her own would be like it.

Toward evening of the fifth day, they came to the Republican River, the one stream always remembered by early travellers on the "Parallel Road."[6] It was impossible to ford it with a wagon, because of its depth and quicksands, but a ferryman carried them across for a dollar, making an extra trip for the cows.[7] They camped on the farther side of the river, along with several other movers; and from one of these Rosie heard the story of the man whose mutilated body had recently been found on the sand bar, not far from the ferry, and of the two women who had been carried away by the Indians from a nearby settlement.

Late the next afternoon, the trail rounded the face of a steep hill, and there before them lay the Solomon Valley[8]—the valley in which they would find Henry's claim thirty miles farther on! It was a level valley, a few miles wide, with ranges of hills on both sides—rolling, round-topped hills, except where their steeper sides, facing the river, broke into a frowning outcrop of white limestone.[9] Behind the first range of bluffs, several miles to the west, a distant summit rose slightly above the surrounding hills, high enough to command a view up and down the valley, and miles in every direction.

"An Indian lookout and signal point, some people say," observed Henry, pointing out the commanding elevation. "There are several of them along the south rim of the valley west of here—one of them a few miles south of my claim."

Rosie looked across at the distant hill, lonely and mysterious in the evening sunlight. How easy to conjure up stories of the Indians, who so recently had roamed there! How easy to picture tribes of feather-bedecked warriors silhouetted against the sky, signal fires burning on that lone eminence at night, perhaps broadcasting a call for help against the onrushing tide of settlers who were despoiling the red men's hunting grounds! How many a tale that solitary mound might have told, if it could have spoken of all it had

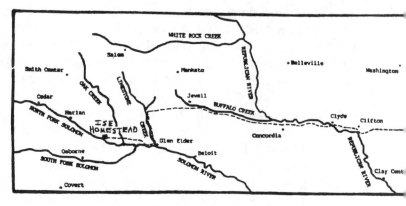

Northern Kansas, showing the route taken by Henry and Rosa Ise west to Henry's homestead in June 1873. (Courtesy Von Rothenberger)

looked down upon: of the trailing herds of buffaloes that had once blackened the hills and the valley between, of the lurking wolves that followed close, and of the tragic death-combats that marked the end of so many lordly careers; of the Indian hunts and feasts and famines, love-makings and battles and migrations!

Rosie felt the spell of those lonely hills and mysterious distances. It seemed she was trespassing upon a domain not fitly here, a domain that would always really belong to the free, wild creatures and savage men whose estate it had been for uncounted centuries, all now defeated and scattered and gone.

They drove several miles up the valley, and made camp that evening on the bank of the river near a great cottonwood tree.[10] An ominous-looking cloud loomed up in the west and there was a muttering of distant thunder. As Rosie busied herself with supper, and Henry picketed the horses and bunched the cows, the great blue cloud rose with astonishing rapidity. The thunder boomed ever closer and louder. The lower fringe of the cloud presently appeared as a long, grayish-green bank of hurrying, churning clouds, below which was a curtain of rain lighted up with incessant and intense vivid flashes of lightning. How grand, how terrible, it seemed to Rosie as it came closer! She had always seen storms through the seeming protection of trees. Here on this prairie, with

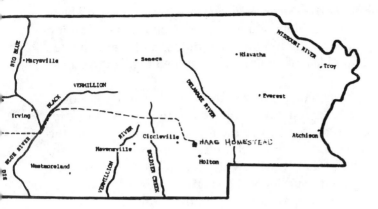

only one lone tree to obstruct the vision, the storm seemed a grander and more terrifying thing.

Henry tied the wagon cover down securely, and hung the blanket at the open end, to protect the scuttle box and its precious contents. With everything in order, they sat in their shelter, await-

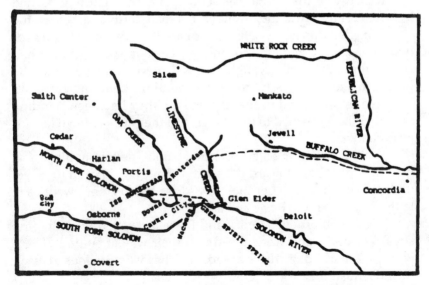

Detail of the area around Henry's homestead. (Courtesy Von Rothenberger)

ing the onslaught of the storm. As it came nearer, a cool wind blew out from the tumbling clouds, a few great drops came splashing upon the wagon cover, then more great drops, and then a deluge of rain, driven by a blast of wind that threatened to tear the canvas off the bows.

Almost frightened by the fury of the storm, yet full of curiosity to see more of it, Rosie lifted the wagon cover to peer out. A blinding flash of lightning, and immediately another lighted up the prairie, and a terrific crash of thunder shook the very earth. Through the falling rain, Rosie saw the cottonwood tree shivered to splinters by a bolt. Suddenly the wagon began to shake, and even to move, as if driven by the power of the elements.

"Whoa there! Whoa!" Henry shouted, trying to raise his voice above the boom of the thunder. "Whoa there, Sam! Whoa there, Frank!" He poked his head out around the blanket that hung at the end of the wagon. The horses had been tied to the wagon, and in their terror at the unusual stress of the wind and lightning, were trying to pull away. When they heard Henry's voice, they quieted down again, and Henry tried to reassure Rosie as to the innocence of prairie thunderstorms.

The fury of the storm was soon spent, the lightning flashed less frequently, and the thunder boomed farther away as the clouds passed down the valley to the east. The torrents of rain suddenly ceased altogether, and only a delicious coolness breathed across the valley. Henry lighted his lantern, and picketed the horses in the wet grass. After some hunting, he found the cows bunched up in a bend of the river, where they had been standing with their backs turned to the storm, and their heads down low for protection.

"Lucky they didn't start over that bank," he said to himself as he drove them back toward the wagon. They soon began to graze, for they were hungry after their day's travel; and Henry went back to the wagon, and to Rosie and sleep.

The next morning[11] Henry and Rosie awakened with the first streaks of dawn and were already on their way at sunrise. There was only a half a day's drive ahead, and they were anxious to reach their destination.

The vegetation along the way had been changing gradually as

they moved westward. The trees were now scarcer and scrubbier, excepting the cottonwoods, which grew to giant size along the creeks and the river. Flowers were more rare, yet here and there in the grass they saw the dark-red breadroot flowers; and sensitive roses spread their fluffy balls of pink on the banks and cuts by the roadside. On the hills and uplands, to their right as they drove along, were blue and white larkspurs, scattered purple blossoms of the medicine root, and occasional "bluff lilies," or yuccas, with their great stalks of waxy white bells ready to burst into bloom.

The bluegrass and bluestem had changed to buffalo grass almost everywhere, except in the creek and bottoms. They passed many prairie dog towns, where the soft, grayish-green sod was pock-marked with symmetrical mounds, on which the wary little dogs stood like statues, perhaps to dart down their holes with a warning bark as the wagon came nearer. They saw many buffalo wallows[12] along the way, in which the buffaloes had disported themselves so recently that the pits were still bare of weeds and grass. At one of the creek crossings, Henry pointed out how the bark of the trees had been rubbed smooth by the shaggy monarchs of the prairie—monarchs that had still roamed in fugitive herds when Henry first travelled that road two years before, now scattered about in the countless skulls and skeletons that lay bleaching in the summer sun.

A few log cabins they saw, occasionally some houses, and at rare intervals frame residences that seemed palatial, but oddly inappropriate to their surroundings. Nearly all of the houses were sod dugouts, most of them scooped out along the banks of creeks and draws, with sod walls rising two or three feet above the ground, with sod roofs, and protruding above each, a chimney, perhaps also of sod, or a few inches of rusty stove pipe. On a few of the roofs, gravel had been thrown, to fill the cracks between the strips of sod; and on the roof of one of the sod houses that they passed, flowers had been planted—wild verbenas, prickly pears and portulaccas.

The trail passed near the Great Spirit Spring, known far and near in Indian legend,[13] and Henry drove a little out of the way so that Rosie might see it. The spring was a perfectly round pool of brackish water, fifty feet across, and bottomless, as far as anyone knew, lying in the top of a little mound that rose thirty feet above the surrounding valley. The water ran over the top and trickled down the sides of the mound in several tiny streams that joined at the foot and ran down toward the river. Henry and Rosie climbed to the top, and tasted the water—said to be medicinal—without enthusiasm. Returning to the wagon, Rosie clambered up and took the lines, while Henry got the cattle together; and they started on again.

The trail meandered into Cawker City[14]—almost all towns were "cities" in those hopeful days—and Rosie saw the great store of the pioneer merchant, Parker,[15] with its impressive assortment of groceries, candy, tobacco, clothing, furniture, stoves, hardware, guns, lumber, implements, drugs—and whisky. The cows grazed by the side of the road while Henry went in to buy some coffee, sugar, and salt.

"Ten miles more!" he announced with enthusiasm, as he came out with his purchases. While Rosie took the lines, he drove the cows on ahead until they were well out of town, then climbed into the wagon again. The cows did not know they were near home, and did not share his enthusiasm, and that of his horses, so he had to get off frequently and drive them on ahead; but there was no note of irritation in his "Hi there! Hi! You brindle critter!" Henry was in great good spirits, and no brindle heifer could irritate him seriously.

Several miles farther on, as they passed a dugout on the bank of the road, the horses suddenly shied to the side of the road, almost upsetting the wagon. Henry pulled a tight rein, cracked the lines, and got them back into the road; but they looked back fearfully at the dugout until they were well toward the top of the next hill.

"What was that?" gasped Rosie. "I didn't see anything to be afraid of."

"Buffalo hides in the yard! Frank and Sam always act that way when they pass here. Those people always have a lot of buffalo hides on hand."

"Are they so afraid of buffaloes?"

"Scared to death. I was breaking prairie one day on the south side of that hill ahead of us, and heard a terrible rumbling and thundering. Couldn't imagine what it was, till a herd of buffaloes broke over the brow of the hill, coming right down on us. Frank and Sam just stood there and trembled—too scared to run."

"And then what?"

"Oh, nothing! The herd divided as soon as they saw us, and went thundering by, half on one side, and half on the other. Buffaloes won't hurt you, but these horses can smell a buffalo, or a buffalo hide, a mile away."

Chapter Three

A New Homestead

At a spoken "Whoa!" the horses stopped. Rosie wrapped the lines around the bow of the wagon, stepped down onto the wheel, and gathering her skirts in her hand, leaped to the ground.

"Henry, come on now!" she called out, starting back to meet him. "I'll drive the cows a while again."

"You go on ahead," he replied, flourishing his switch at the laggards in his herd. "It's only a few miles yet."

She walked back to him and took the switch from his hand. "I'll drive 'em," she said, smiling, but in a tone of finality.

A puzzled expression crossed Henry's face, then, apparently sensing the futility of argument, he climbed up into the wagon and untied the lines.

"Giddap Frank! Giddap Sam!" The horses started on, the tired cows and the young woman following.

With the new driver, the wagon moved more slowly, jogging sleepily along the ruts that served as a road; but the cows no longer lagged far behind, for Rosie indulged in no reveries. With resolute determination in every step, she not only kept the cows close behind the wagon, but found time to gather bouquets of the breadroot, prairie roses, larkspurs and daisies that grew along the roadside.

At the crest of a little knoll[1] overlooking a level valley, Henry called out "Whoa!" and pointed out a little log cabin a half mile ahead.

"There it is! That's my cabin—our cabin—and our claim. The corner is right there by the creek crossing; and it runs half a mile

30

south, and half a mile west—not a creek on it, nor a hill, nor a rock! Doesn't it look like good land?" He turned to Rosie with unwonted enthusiasm, then looked down at the little cabin.

Rosie caught something of his enthusiasm, but said nothing. She sat gazing at the picture that lay before her, shimmering in the brightness of the noonday sun: the broad, green valley with its bordering grass-covered hills on the south and north, directly across the valley, a few miles distant, a high, flat-topped hill that rose above the rest, with a steep, conical mound on either side— three sentinels guarding the landscape; the river tracing its winding course with a fringe of cottonwoods—the only trees to be seen anywhere, except a few scattered willows and cottonwoods growing along the creek or draw that ran by the nearest corner of Henry's claim. A number of sod dugouts and log cabins were scattered here and there, most of them along the river and creek, the dugouts scarcely visible above the level of the ground, the cabins standing out stark and lonely, each dwelling with its sod stable, perhaps with a team of horses and one or two cows picketed out in the yard, and with a small patch of broken ground near, green with wheat that was already heading out, or newly planted to sod corn. The rain of the night before had brought fresh green life to the buffalo grass; and here and there, prairie flowers waved their faces in the wind. Over all was the sky, washed clean by the rain, wider and higher and bluer than any sky but that of the prairie, an intensely and vividly blue background for the scattered white clouds that drifted across the heavens, casting shadows that sped swiftly along the grass.

As Rosie looked at the happy scene, tears came to her eyes; but whether they were tears of happiness or of fear and foreboding, she never could have told. She only said, "I hope it will be a good home for us. It surely looks like good land."

"It *is* good land—all of it," he replied. "I plowed a furrow all around it, and never turned up anything but black soil. In two years I can get my patent—three years off, you know, for my war service.[2] Then we can feel independent and can improve it better. I need a granary, and a corn crib—you see I haven't any granary or cribs at all—and a better stable, and some fences; and perhaps we can have a better house some day. It won't take long, if we have good luck."

"Oh yes, or maybe we can buy one of those claims next to us. It would be fine to have two quarters—bottom land like that."[3]

"Maybe—if we want to. But let's not be too ambitious. We can live well enough on one good quarter." Looking at the cabin, they saw a man step out into the yard and gaze intently in their direction for a moment, then rush back, grab something from the door step—apparently the broom—and disappear in the door again.

"I know what's the matter," exclaimed Henry, laughing. "That's Frank Hagel. He's a bachelor—been taking care of my cabin; and I'll bet he hasn't swept out since I left—just thought of it when he saw us." He turned in his seat and leaped to the ground.

"Giddap there! Sam! Frank! Only half a mile yet!" He started back, and rounded up the cows while Rosie drove the horses on ahead.

The cavalcade soon reached the Dry Creek crossing,[4] but here Rosie was brought face to face with that dark danger of all pioneer countries—high water. The creek was bank-full from the rain of the night before, apparently impassable to any wagon loaded with flour and cornmeal, or indeed to any wagon at all. They had travelled two hundred miles, and here, a quarter of a mile from their destination, they were for the first time stalled by flood waters. Dry Creek was not an imposing stream ordinarily, a mere gash across the face of the prairie, with a tiny stream trickling along its shallow bed; but today it was a raging torrent.

Rosie gazed longingly across at the cabin, then she looked at the muddy waters hurrying past with their burden of driftwood and broken sunflower stalks. Something in the dark, whirling eddies frightened her, and she would gladly have camped by the bank of the stream until the waters subsided; but she felt ashamed to express such fears. The horses stopped, obviously loth to enter the water.

Henry sat for a moment, looking in perplexity at the stream ahead, then at the contents of the wagon. Finally he jumped down from his seat, and began taking the cover off the bows. This he wrapped carefully around the wagon box and tied it firmly. He then drove the cows into the water. They waded and swam across safely.

"I believe we can make it!" he said, as he climbed to his seat again and drove rapidly into the whirling current. The water rose to the wagon box and boiled up along the sides. The wagon sank deeper—and then started to float—yes, it was floating down stream! The horses reared and plunged, but they were so nearly afloat themselves that they could get little traction on the load. Henry cracked the lines and shouted. For an instant he turned to Rosie with a look that made her grip the wagon bow tighter. He pulled out his knife and opened the blade.

"I'll cut the tugs." He stood up on the buckboard, ready to plunge into the water, when the wagon suddenly struck bottom, the horses got their footing, and with a mighty splashing pulled the wagon up the steep bank and out. It had all happened in less than a minute.

"Oh Henry, our flour!" cried Rosie, when they were safely on the bank.

"Yes, our flour, and our sorghum, and our wagon, and our horses, and our precious selves!" he replied. "I am glad enough to be out of there. I could have got you out, but I was afraid my horses were gone. It's washed since I was through there the last time."

He jumped down from his seat and pulled off the dripping wagon cover, while Rosie scratched the straw off the sacks of flour and cornmeal and examined their contents. She was vastly surprised and relieved to find that only a little water had seeped into the wagon box, and that their supplies were but slightly injured.

The team, still wet from their plunge in the water, soon stood before the little cabin. Henry vaulted over the wheel and helped Rosie down. "Home at last! Here Frank, this is my wife!"

"And Rosie, this is Frank Hagel[5] . . . lives on the claim over west, and is keeping house for me. What have you got for dinner, Frank! We're hungry as coyotes . . . drove all the way from Glen Elder this morning."

While greetings were being spoken, Rosie's eye took in the premises: cabin of hewed logs, with sod roof, apparently twelve or fifteen by eighteen—almost spacious compared with the dugouts she had seen along the way that morning—with a home-made door and three small windows; a straw stable, made of wheat straw thrown over a frame of logs and saplings; a sod chicken house; a well, with a wheel and two buckets on a rope, and a small cow lot fenced in near the stable—about the only fence she had seen in the morning's drive. The well, only a few steps from the house, was a luxury that Rosie noted with joy, for at her old home she had always had to carry the water up from the creek, a distance of a quarter of a mile. There was a corn field of a few acres south of the cow lot; and a patch of wheat and one of oats lay west of it. The corn was up, and the wheat and oats, lush and green, were beginning to head. It must be good land, to grow such crops, was Rosie's silent observation; and that was the important thing. On good land one could surely build a good home. It would be her own home too, her very own, and Henry's, she thought to herself, with solid, possessive satisfaction, as she looked around at the smooth level land and the promising crops.

Entering the one-room cabin, she could hardly feel so cheerful. On the table was a pack of cards, which she promptly threw in the stove. Henry's cabin had been the rendezvous of several bachelors living near, and they had been playing cards to pass the time—not a Christian form of amusement, Rosie thought. Frank Hagel was obviously no housekeeper; but dirt and disorder were only a challenge to Rosie, a challenge that she accepted as a confident trooper accepts the gage of battle. The cabin had a floor, as Henry had promised—she did not yet realize what a luxury this was—and was chinked between the logs with a kind of clay mortar. There was no ceiling, but there were wide cottonwood boards underneath the sod roof.

Of furniture there was little enough, and that of the most primitive construction; but Rosie appraised it all without consternation: a bedstead made of cottonwood boards, without springs, with a bed tick[6] filled with straw, a table made also of warped cottonwood boards,[7] and a tiny cook stove. Two empty nail kegs and two boxes served as chairs, and on another nail keg by the door there was a washpan, half full of soapy water. A hammer and a saw hung from nails driven in one of the logs, a coffee grinder was

screwed onto the log just below, and a few other household utensils were scattered about the room: a broom leaning against the
wall, a boiler and washboard behind the stove, and on the shelf
near the stove, a kettle, two bread pans, a few iron knives and forks
and tin spoons. There was no bureau, no cupboard, no clock, no
rug, no tablecloth; there were no curtains nor blinds on the windows, no sheets on the bed, no pictures on the walls. Rather bare
and primitive, the little cabin seemed.

"It's better though, than we had at Holton, at first," thought
Rosie, as she looked around; "and I'll soon have it looking different." A dozen plans were soon shaping in her mind for building
shelves for the cooking utensils and flower pots that she hoped to
get.

While Frank Hagel took charge of the horses and cows, Henry
brought in a bucket of cold water from the well for Rosie to wash
and comb her long, black hair. Henry then proceeded to carry in
the flour and cornmeal, the churn-ful of molasses, and the varied
contents of the scuttle box and wagon.

After dinner, Rosie set to work, and before nightfall a new
home was there: table scoured and floor scrubbed—not with a
mop, for there was no mop in the cabin, or in the country, but with
a scrap of grain sack found in the stable; a shelf was up, and on it
were several tin cans of flowers, transplanted from the feed box.
The sacks of flour and cornmeal were set in a neat row behind the
bed, and the kitchen utensils were washed and scoured and deftly
arranged on one end of the shelf. The churn, with its delectable
saccharine contents, and the lard and butter were stored away in
the small cellar under the house. Outside, two precious sheets and
pillow slips, and a few articles of clothing, were spread out on the
grass to dry. When Henry came in from the field that evening, he
marveled at the transformation; and when he sat down to supper
at the clean little table, he had no doubt that it was going to be a
good home. After supper, he made a potato masher and a rolling
pin out of two sticks of wood, while Rosie set out the rose bushes
and asparagus they had brought along.

The next morning Henry took Rosie with him on a ride around

the claim, to show her the boundaries and let her see for herself how fine and black the soil was. When they got back, he helped her plant a garden of peas, turnips, lettuce, and cucumbers in the sod at the end of the little cornfield. Henry had a few chickens, and several hens were given settings of eggs in the chicken coop.

Chapter Four

The Neighbors

In the new country there were settlers from various parts of the United States and Europe.[1] Along Dry Creek, north of Henry's claim, there was a settlement of Germans—Germans from Iowa, Germans from Pennsylvania, Germans from Switzerland, Germans from Germany, "low Dutch," "high Dutch"—all kinds of "Dutch," as the Germans were sometimes called. South of his claim, along the river, there were settlers of many nationalities and persuasions: Germans, English, Irish, Welsh, Americans—not Mayflower quality, of course—Missourians, Campbellites,[2] claim jumpers, and one Democrat.[3] Among them were men of almost every imaginable calling: doctors, dentists, druggists, merchants, lawyers, preachers, teachers, tailors, textile workers, clockmakers, painters, shoemakers, barbers, printers, carpenters, cabinetmakers, stone masons, cowboys, and horse and cattle thieves. A few of them had combined a half dozen or more of these various vocations, and some, especially among the Germans and Swiss, really wanted to farm. The New Haven and Hartford Colony,[4] up on Twelve Mile Creek west of Henry's claim,[5] represented a particularly motley assortment of talents; and many of these town- and city-bred Yankees were shortly crowded out by the thrifty hardworking Germans.

Rosie soon became acquainted with some of the neighbors. Frances Athey came over with her four children the very first afternoon to get a bucket of water and some lettuce from the garden she had planted at the end of Henry's cornfield. Wilson Athey had no well yet, and his farm was all newly broken sod, not good for a garden, so Henry had given him a patch of older ground at the end of

Wilson Athey. (Courtesy the Historical Society of the Downs Carnegie Library)

his field. Rosie let herself in for much future trouble by giving each of the children a piece of " 'lasses bread." The Atheys were from Missouri, richer in children than in worldly goods;[6] and their claim was partly second-bottom land, not as good as Henry's. They had tried to farm for a year without a team, but now had a yoke of oxen.

Frank Hagel lived on the adjoining claim, only a quarter of a mile west. Henry had lived with Frank the first winter after he filed on his claim, while he was building his own cabin, and he and Frank were always good friends. Frank was not a good farmer, indeed he had not even a team to farm with, but he was a fine honest fellow. Henry did his breaking for him, and in return Frank helped with chores and various odd jobs whenever he could.

The Graebers, who lived half a mile east, were Pennsylvania Dutch and were rather stingy people.[7] When Rosie went to see them one evening, to deliver some soap that friends at Holton had sent to them, she was surprised that none of it was given her for the bringing—she would have been so glad to get a few cakes of that soap.

The next evening after they arrived, Henry and Rosie went to see Rosie's brother Chris and his wife, Louisa, who lived on their claim a mile west.[8] Chris had come to the new country two years before—had come from Eastern Kansas the same year Henry came from Iowa. He and Henry had been good friends; and when he went back to Holton the first winter, he invited Henry to go along. Henry spent the winter there, husking corn for one of the neighbors, and incidentally getting acquainted with Rosie. Chris often joked about the way he had managed to make a brother-in-law of him.

Rosie often ran over to see Chris and Louisa after supper and on the way, she passed Jake Hunker's house.[9] The Hunkers were sad people, for only a short time before, their little daughter Katie had fallen over the creek bank and broken her neck.[10] Mary Hunker was so lonely that she was always glad to see visitors, and Rosie often stopped to see her. Jake had a binder,[11] the only one in the community, and had cut Henry's wheat and barley and oats for him; so Henry felt kindly toward him, and often went over to see him too.

As Rosie was going over to see her brother one evening, she learned something about another of her neighbors. As she was crossing the creek, she heard a splashing in the water nearby, and turned to see a man, apparently a mulatto, dressed only in a pair of trousers, dipping water with a bucket. Very much frightened, she ran up the bank and hurried on to her brother's home, looking back frequently to see if she was being pursued. When she told Chris of her fright, he laughed heartily.

"Oh, yes. That's old man Vietz. But he's no mulatto, and no nigger. He's burnt that black from never wearin' a shirt. He's an honest Dutchman and a preacher. I guess his wife and children won't come out here to live with him. They say he sometimes eats skunks, and a lot of people are prejudiced against that. He's our postmaster."[12]

And Chris laughed again at the idea that anyone would be afraid of old man Vietz.

One evening, after supper, Henry walked up to Bender's, who lived three-quarters of a mile up the creek, to grind his axe, and Rosie went along to turn the grindstone; so she had a chance to meet

Chris and Louisa Haag. (Courtesy the Historical Society of the Downs Carnegie Library)

Sketch of Steve Linge by an unknown artist. (Courtesy the Historical Society of the Downs Carnegie Library)

another neighbor.[13] She was not quite comfortable or happy with her new acquaintances, for, in spite of his friendly and voluble greeting, Jesse Bender had a treacherous gleam in his eye which she distrusted; and the affectation of leather riding pants and boots and spurs, by him and his older boys, did not raise her rating of the family. Henry had hired the Benders to herd his cows with theirs—he could not yet afford to build a fence around his pasture land—and it was to be one of Rosie's tasks to take the cows over every morning and get them each evening. So she saw a great deal of the Benders, and they were always really friendly and kind to her.

When Rosie and Henry were comfortably settled in their cabin, Steve Linge came to see them.[14] Steve was one of Henry's closest friends—a German Catholic, big, rough-spoken and hot tempered, but kindly, and honest to the point of eccentricity. Steve had "bached" with Henry during the terrible winter of eighteen seventy-one and seventy-two, and Henry told Rosie many stories of their life together. That was the winter when a three-day blizzard, with zero temperature, blew in on November fifteenth, and covered the ground with a foot of snow, which remained for weeks. A great herd of thousands of Texas cattle was being wintered along the river, between Henry's cabin and Steve's claim; and after the snow had covered the grass, these cattle ate the twigs and smaller branches off the willows as far up as they could reach, and then slowly starved to death.

On a ride over to visit Steve one day, Henry and Rosie saw many pathetic and gruesome reminders of the memorable storm of 1871.[15] Piled up at the foot of a steep bank along the river were hundreds of carcasses of cattle that had drifted before the storm until they plunged to death over the bank. Along the lower river bottom were other carcasses, thousands of them: with the flesh rotted away, and the hides still clinging to skeletons that were slowly disintegrating and falling apart. So thickly did they cover the ground that one might have walked upon them for half a mile, stepping from one to another, and never touching the ground.

A mile or two beyond Steve Linge's, in an unfinished house on the very top of the commanding hill across the valley, lived Jim Terry, an Englishman with some money and a visionary ambition to establish a baronial estate covering all the land he could see from his elevation.[16] Just before sunset, Rosie could often see the reflection of the sun in the windows of Terry's little stone castle, and she was full of curiosity about the place—could not figure out what he did for water and for a garden there on the top of the hill; but she never found time to go there until years later, when the house had crumbled to ruins. Terry never owned the valley, but he had a hill named after him.

Chapter Five

The First Months in the Log Cabin

It was a good summer, Rosie's first summer in the little cabin, with fair rains and fair crops of spring wheat, oats, sod corn and barley, with late lettuce, beans, cucumbers, tomatoes, and roasting ears for the table. There was not much of the field crops, to be sure—perhaps ten acres altogether—but five acres was sod corn that Henry planted in the sod with a hatchet. It was a back-breaking job, and the field looked big enough before he finished planting. Henry did not get a corn planter or "stabber" until two years later. Very few weeds grew in the sod corn, so there was little hoeing to do the first summer.

Prices were good at first, for what little butter and stuff there was to sell. The first butter Rosie sold brought forty cents a pound, but all prices soon began to decline, and before the end of the summer, butter was worth only ten cents a pound, and eggs scarcely worth taking to town. Some of the local politicians talked about a panic and hard times in the country, but Rosie knew only that butter and eggs were cheap.

A few weeks after Rosie came, Henry took a load of oats to Cawker City and brought back three chairs and some sugar. Rosie was proud of the new chairs, but later in the year she saw that it had been an extravagance, for they really needed the oats for the horses, and they could have done without the chairs.

In keeping her little cabin, Rosie faced difficulties that would have disheartened a less resolute soul. Her stove was so small that she could bake only two loaves of bread at a time, so she had to bake almost every day. The floor was of cottonwood lumber, which had warped so badly that it was a problem to set the bed so that all

43

four legs would rest on the floor. One day Henry bought some new cottonwood boards for a granary, and Rosie persuaded him to tear up the floor and put the smooth new boards in the house and the old floor boards in the granary; but this was only a temporary gain, for the new floor was soon as badly warped as the old had been. It was hard to walk about in the house, and Rosie often tripped on the uneven boards, until she got used to them.

There was another discomfort that developed when cold weather came. On windy days the cold wind blew a gale through the cracks in the floor, and it was almost impossible to keep her feet warm. Henry banked the house outside with dirt and straw and manure, covering even the outside cellar entrance. This made the house warmer but brought another inconvenience, for they then had to clamber into the cellar through a trap-door in the floor.

The cracks in the floor and in the log walls afforded a rendez-vous for various pests that kept Rosie in a militant mood much of the time; and the battle front between her and the bedbugs shifted back and forth, with never a decisive victory. Every day she went through the bed, tick and all, and every Saturday searched the house, with a kettle of hot water in one hand and a can of kerosene and a feather in the other. At times she thought she had the enemy beaten, but presently movers would come along and spread their bed on the floor, or perhaps it would be a preacher halting to pass the night, and then the battle had to be fought all over again.

One discomfort that some of the neighbors in sod houses al-ways complained of, she never had to endure. She never had fleas in the house, because the house had a floor with a cellar below. There were fleas in the grass, of course, and every venture out into the grass had to be paid for in considerable physical discomfort, but the fleas did not stay in the house. Frances Athey, who had no cellar, told her one day of the toad she kept under the floor, which not only rid her house of fleas but served as a pet for the children. She named the toad "Tilden"—it was the time of the Hayes-Tilden campaign.[1]

There were several tragedies in the neighborhood those first few months. Soon after Rosie came, Henry was called upon one day to help hunt for the body of a woman who had drowned, with her two little children, trying to cross the river when it was up.[2] One of the neighbors told Rosie how the poor woman, after she sank, had tried to hold her baby above her head, hoping someone might rescue it. Henry helped hunt for several days, but with no success. A week later the woman's body was found in a pile of driftwood on the State land section several miles downstream, and several weeks later the body of one of the children was found. The other was never recovered.

A few weeks afterward, a man was killed down on the river. He was hauling logs, and a heavy log rolled off the wagon and struck him, crushing him to death. For some of the sympathizing neighbors there was a touch of consolation in the fact that he was a Democrat—the only one in the community.[3]

Not long afterward Rosie was called upon to help line the coffin of a man named Tipp, who had been shot accidentally.[4] It was a sad task, for the man left his wife and six small children with very little to live on, and he had begun work on his house only a short time before he was killed. The preacher who delivered the funeral sermon made opportunity for a few pointed moralities regarding the dead man, who was not a church member, declaring that he "had not loved his Lord." To this Jesse Bender promptly objected, insisting that Tipp was a good man; and the funeral very nearly closed with a fight over the merits of the deceased. The next day the neighbors came together and finished the house he had begun, and built a stable and chicken coop too. Not long afterward, Tipp's widow gave birth to a little boy with a mark on his breast—just where the father had been shot.[5] She never doubted that the baby's mark was the result of the accident.

In July, the wife of one of the neighbors, John Sibley, died in childbirth. She was buried the next morning; and that night John called a dance.[6]

Chris drove back to the old home in August to get his cane mill, and Rosie went along. It was hot and dry, but she enjoyed the trip, enjoyed the freedom and change, sleeping out in the wagon and cooking over a camp fire. When they returned with the cane mill, she and Chris made enough molasses to last all winter, Rosie stripping the cane while Chris attended to the horse power, the machine, and the boiling pans. They worked hard, sometimes until nearly midnight; but when it was all done, it seemed good to have so much of their winter's food supply set away in the cellar.

More women were coming to the new country. Two years earlier, there had hardly been a woman within miles. Frances Athey and Lizzie Graeber had come out the year before Rosie arrived; and about the time that Rosie came, many of the married men went "back east"—which usually meant Eastern Kansas, Missouri, Iowa or Illinois—to fetch their wives out to their new homes. These women soon set about tidying up the primitive dugouts that dotted the prairie. A few brought children, others soon had them, and strings of diapers flapped from many a clothes line or covered the buffalo grass in the yards.

Frances Athey became the mother of twins soon after Rosie came.[7] Rosie went over to help, but found hardly enough clothes there for one baby, and everything so scanty and meager in the little dugout that she hardly knew how to manage. Afterward some of the neighbors induced the Cawker merchant, Parker, to give them some cloth and Rosie helped make it up into diapers and dresses for the two babies.

"Didn't really need two right now, while we're tryin' to git the oxen paid fer," Frances said one day; "but I reckon the Lord knows what's best." The Lord was destined to have a lot to account for over at Athey's.

Promising indeed the new country seemed to these settlers; and they were soon boasting of the wonderful climate, of the mildness of the winters, of the balmy spring days, of the cool nights of summer, of the healthful and invigorating tonic of the air. It was a common jest that they would never need a cemetery, that people would probably live forever in such a salubrious climate. And they knew the soil was deep and rich and productive—the finest in the world. Some of the more sanguine began to feel a sympathy for unfortunate friends and relatives who were enduring the hard life of Iowa or Illinois or Pennsylvania or Eastern Kansas; and wrote back urging them to come to the new Elysium, in the valley of the Solomon. At a party at McConkeys, one night,[8] Rosie first heard a song which was often sung that year:

> O, give me a home where the buffalo roam,
>   Where the deer and the antelope play,
> Where never is heard a discouraging word,
>   And the sky is unclouded all day.[9]

When fall came, and the little patch of corn had been husked, there was not a great deal of work to do, for they had only the two horses, a few cows, two pigs, and two dozen chickens to care for. It seemed a life of leisure to Rosie, for in her own home, even as a girl of twelve or thirteen, she had always had to do much of the house work for a family of ten and had helped her father with the corn husking and other farm work. Henry bought a half-interest in a big cottonwood tree from Chris, and he and Chris together cut a supply of wood for both families.

There were frequent social festivities to attend: Granger parties, taffy parties, surprise parties, and quilting and sewing parties for the women. Henry made a sleigh of two bent saplings, so that he and Rosie could go in style when there was snow on the ground. Occasionally there was a party in the neighborhood. Dancing to the music of the violin was not deemed a Christian form of amusement by the stricter moralists of the community; but the accordion was not thought to be to the same extent an instrument of the devil, and since Henry played the accordion, he was much in demand. Rosie had been taught that life was for work and not for pleasure, and she was never quite sure that it was right to go to any such light affairs; so she sometimes stayed at home when Henry went out with his accordion. She felt lonesome on such evenings, and even a bit hurt to think he would leave her alone; but of course Henry could not refuse anyone who wanted him to play.

The refreshments at these parties were usually simple and inexpensive, although sometimes fried cakes were served, or even pie or cake. Once when Henry and Rosie had a party at their house, Rosie served blanc mange,[10] which was thought quite an extravagance. At a surprise party at Benders, the hostess was obliged to bake corn bread and serve it with black coffee. Sometimes no refreshments were served, and to guard against such contingencies, Steve Linge sometimes took bread along in his wagon and went out between dances to eat.

Then there were literary societies to go to, spelling schools, and lectures on Mormonism; and sometimes Henry and Rosie would visit the neighbors—perhaps go in the morning and stay all day. On New Year's Eve they went up to Bartsch's, who lived two miles up the creek, to watch the old year out, passing the time with

The family of the Reverend John Bowers. (Courtesy the Historical Society of the Downs Carnegie Library)

visiting, singing and prayer. Chris Bartsch, a German with a face so full of kindly wrinkles that no child could look at him and be afraid, had filed on his claim the year before Rosie came.[11] His claim was not good land—the good land had all been taken before he came. When he brought his wife out a year later, he arrived at his sod dugout during a heavy rain, to find the roof partly caved in and a foot of water in the house. His wife had hardly expected such accommodations and refused to enter the house—perhaps not seeing any particular advantage in being there. When he had dipped the water out and got the children in, she was induced to enter and take up the duties of a homesteader's wife. She and Rosie became fast friends, and many a time, when the latter was sick, she came down to help with the work.

Religious meetings held in the various homes from time to time served as entertainment, too, and there was always a crowd in attendance. There was little in any of the new homes to afford interest or entertainment—few newspapers, or books, or magazines, or musical instruments. Many homes had none of these; and the people were glad to have a place to go where they could see each other and forget the tedium of their homes.

Most of the preachers were poorly educated, a few of them almost illiterate. The Reverend Mr. Bowers, who preached occasionally at Henry's cabin, was able to read his precious Bible only very slowly and stumblingly, but he had the spirit of evangelism in his heart, and preached with such power that neighbors a mile away could enjoy the message, and even those more than two miles away could sometimes hear him on quiet evenings when the windows were open.[12] Many of these preachers were sincere and unselfish crusaders, but some were crude and uncultured, others selfish and fleshly, and a few the worst type of rascals, impostors, or even rakes.

Whenever a preacher came into the community, a meeting was arranged at the home of one of the settlers, and someone tried to get word to as many of the neighbors as possible. People would come long distances—ten or twelve miles, or even farther—to attend these meetings, driving in their lumber wagons, or even walking—perhaps barefooted—if they had no teams. One night when a meeting was being held in Henry's cabin, so many crowded in that the floor began to sag dangerously, and in the midst of the services Henry had to ask the worshippers to step outside until he could go down into the cellar and brace up the floor with poles.

One Sunday afternoon, when there was a meeting at Henry's house, during one of the prayers the room suddenly turned dark, and on looking up, the worshippers saw the faces of Indians peering curiously in at the windows.[13] For a moment there was consternation in the little room. Henry seized his revolver and ran to the door, but at a glance he saw that the Indians standing around the cabin carried no weapons and seemed peaceful enough. They finally made him understand that they only wanted something to eat; and Rosie had to give them all the bread she had baked for the after-church dinner, spread with butter and with some precious citron butter that she had put up for the winter. The Indians seemed dissatisfied and finally made Rosie understand that they disliked the salted butter on the bread; so she scraped off what she could, and gave them bread spread only with citron butter.[14] This they took without any word or comment, and went away.

The services had scarcely begun again, when the Indians reappeared at the door, and one of them exhibited a dead chicken that had died of the cholera some time before.

"Heap good," he exclaimed, showing how the skin peeled easily from the decaying flesh. "Heap good." And he pointed to

Old man Vietz. (Photo courtesy Dorothy Viets Schell)

other dead chickens in the hands of other Indians. Henry and Rosie finally understood that they wanted to take all of these with them, and, when they signified their willingness, the noble red men started off again to their camp down by the river.

The post office was established in Henry's cabin that winter, under the name "New Arcadia."[15] Old man Vietz had kept post office in his cave in the creek bank, but Bender coveted his claim and had threatened to shoot him if he did not leave the country. One day the poor old German came up to Henry's with a bunch of letters, and asked Henry if he would distribute his mail for a few days, as he was leaving for a while.[16] Henry agreed, but Vietz never returned; and so the job of postmaster came to Henry and Rosie.[17]

The pay was small—their percentage receipts from stamps sold and cancelled amounted to only about two dollars a month— and it was a great deal of trouble, for one of them had to be at the house practically all the time. The neighbors came often for their mail—always anxious for letters and news from their old homes— and usually stayed to visit. Sometimes they stayed much too long, or even for meals. If anyone came for mail at dinner time, he was of course invited to eat. The stage driver, who came every day with the mail, usually took his dinner at a station farther up the river, but if he came at dinner time he was often invited to dinner too. Henry and Rosie, on the other hand, did not need to go anywhere for their own mail; they got a wide variety of stuff through the mail—pictures, magazines, newspapers, samples and advertisements; and they always had interesting news of the outside world from the stage driver.

One day they received a little photograph of Charlie Ross, who had been kidnapped in Philadelphia, with the pathetic request that they help to find him; and for months afterward, whenever an emigrant wagon passed, Rosie could not help wondering if Charlie Ross might be hidden away in it. She was particularly sympathetic because of a kidnapping which her father had once seen, and often told about. Her father and an old friend from Germany had just been admitted as immigrants at New York, and were walking up the street with their families, when a cab with three men in it stopped beside them, two men jumped out of the cab, seized the man's daughter—a young girl of seventeen—threw her into the cab, and drove rapidly away before anyone realized what was happening. Her father never saw her again.

Rosie and Henry once got complimentary tickets to the Ringling Brothers' Show, which was coming to Cawker, so they drove down to Cawker to see the circus. Hundreds of wagons with teams of horses or oxen tied to them stood on the vacant lots about the town; and the crowds of people completely filled the town's single business block. It was a grand circus too, one to be remembered for many long years.

Rosie herself did not read much of the stuff that came through the mails. As a little girl she had never been able to go to winter school, because she had no shoes and no warm clothes; and when a summer term was organized later, she went only half a day—to a teacher who came to school barefooted. Rosie's mother became ill that day, and she never was able to go again. Her father then taught her at home, but with all the work that had to be done, she never developed the habit of reading much—even, from her observations of housewives who read a great deal, got a strong suspicion of the habit. Yet now and then she did take the time to read some of the papers that came to them. Henry always liked to read, and sometimes lost himself in the newspaper when he should have been doing something else—lost himself so completely that he was utterly oblivious to everything going on about him.

Henry was justice of the peace, too, for several years, and the office took time that brought little money returns.[18] Whenever a case came to him for settlement, Rosie usually went down into the cellar to be out of the way. One day two men came in with a quarrel over some cattle, and Rosie went down cellar with her sewing, as usual; but when she overheard all the vile cursing and swearing of the men in the room above, she almost wished she had gone to the stable. On another occasion, a man living several miles away asked Henry to come over and "hitch him up" to the woman of his choice. Since the horses had been working all day, Henry walked over, although it was raining. When the ceremony was over and the man properly "hitched up," he asked Henry what the "damages" were, to which Henry replied that he made no particular charge, expecting of course that the man would give him something for his trouble; but the fellow only thanked him and invited him to supper. Even this Henry could not accept, for his clothes were wet, and it was getting dark, and he wanted to get home. Rosie spent most of the next day cleaning his clothes and boots. It was Henry's usual experience in such matters—and Rosie's too.

Homesick Rosie was, often, for her own people and for the hills and trees and flowers and fruits of Eastern Kansas; but Henry was kind and considerate, and appreciative of his pretty and efficient young wife. He was not a good manager or business man, and often allowed himself, and incidentally Rosie, to be imposed upon by strangers, and by a few of the neighbors. When he lent out his breaking plow,[19] or his corn sheller, fanning mill, or his horses, he never could bring himself to ask any rental; he never charged a really fair wage for breaking sod for the neighbors; and of course Rosie had to help make up for his generosity, by skimping in every way. He was generous with Rosie too, though, and never raised any question about her expenditures for herself or for the house; in fact he sometimes bought things for her that she would never have thought of buying for herself. He was a good farmer, always had good crops if anyone had; he was an ingenious mechanic, kept his implements in good working order, and fixed up many little conveniences in and about the house; and, as Rosie often said to herself, he had "good ideas" about almost everything—except money. Rosie soon learned to respect his weather predictions, his skill in treating any kind of illness, and his general information, for he had received a good education in Germany, an education which proved useful not only to her but to some of the neighbors, who often came to him for help.

Henry's manner of shaving was one of Rosie's greatest surprises. For her father, shaving had always been the rough equivalent of a major operation. His razor had to be stropped at great length, the water had to be heated to just the right temperature, the room must be kept closed, for any draught hurt his face; and even with all conditions favorable, he would grit his teeth as he plied his razor, and would puff out his cheeks and groan and grumble as if he had swallowed a stand of bees. Rosie had learned to think of shaving as a terrible ordeal. What was her surprise to see Henry get out his razor and mug, pour a little water of almost any temperature into the pan, draw the razor a few times across the strop or his boot top, and shave in a few minutes, without any fuss whatever!

Henry was like that in all matters. In the house and outside, he always had his things in order, and with no fuss or noise or irritation. He was scrupulously clean and neat in his personal habits, and gentlemanly in his language and behavior. He never came to the table without first washing and combing his hair and beard with care, he never used tobacco in any form, he never resorted to profanity, and seldom even to slang. "Ach, the deuce!" was his nearest approach to violent language.[20] Most important of all, he was invariably thoughtful and considerate of Rosie. Occasionally he even brought her bouquets of wild flowers when he came in from the field, if he found some that were unusually pretty or fragrant.

It always seemed lonely when Henry went to Russell or Hastings or Waterville. He usually traded at Cawker City only ten miles away, but Cawker City was sixty miles from the nearest railroad, and prices of goods were high there, while the Cawker City merchant, Parker, paid less for grain and butter and eggs than the dealers in the railroad towns. So Henry sometimes took his stuff to Russell, or even occasionally to Hastings or Waterville.

While he was gone, Rosie had tasks that called for all her capable energy. She had to do the chores, feed and care for the livestock, and attend to the mail. She tried to do as much other work as possible too, while Henry was gone, so she could help him when he was at home. She sorted out corn husks to make a new husk bed tick to replace the straw tick, which was getting rather hard to sleep on; she braided husks and sewed them together to make little mats for the floor; she made lye of wood ashes and then used it in hulling corn for hominy; she browned rye for coffee. Then she had sewing to do, for she was making a wagon cover, an everyday dress for herself, shirts and mittens and a vest for Henry; and, most important of all, she was making baby clothes, tiny little dresses with hand embroidery and lace, getting the cloth from one of her white skirts and her white polonaise. Rosie worked hard when Henry was gone.

And yet it was lonely, especially at night, when the coyotes barked and howled down along the river and up in the hills, and the owls hooted from the prairie dog town. Then the prairie seemed a vast and lonely place. Although Rosie was almost a stranger to fear, she barred her door, kept Henry's revolver on a chair by her bed, and a few times spent sleepless nights.

Sleeping thus alone one night she was awakened by a sound of voices in the yard. Henry had just left for Russell that morning, and she knew he could not be back so soon. She held her breath and listened. There were two men outside, talking to each other in low tones. Presently the silhouette of a bearded face darkened the little window across from her bed. For what seemed a long time the face peered into the cabin, while Rosie sat up in her bed, too frightened to think of the revolver that lay on the chair beside her. Presently the face moved from the window and a moment later she heard a footfall on the door step; a cautious hand fumbled the latch and tried to push the door open. The lock held, and Rosie began to hope that the insistent visitor had gone, when the face appeared at the window, and a hand slowly raised the sash. For a moment she sat there too frightened to move or cry out; but when the intruder started to push his head into the window, Rosie searched for the revolver, aimed above the figure wedged in the opening, and fired. At the report the intruder jerked his head back with such force as to break the window to slivers, and disappeared in the darkness. Very soon she heard a wagon driven rapidly out of the yard. The next morning she saw the wagon tracks left in the grass, but she never knew who her intruders were. They had stolen nothing from the barn or chicken house, but Rosie enjoyed no sound sleep again until Henry returned.

"I'm certainly glad," she said, when he got home, "that you don't have to go down east to work every winter, like Steve Linge. I don't know what I'd do if I had to stay here alone all winter."

The next day after this incident, two passing tramps, perhaps the same ones who had tried to get into Rosie's cabin, outraged the wife of one of the settlers, and this frightened some of the young wives of the neighborhood. Some of them stayed with neighbors when their husbands were away from home; but when Henry, the next time he went to Russell, suggested that Rosie stay with Chris and Louisa, Rosie declared that there was too much work to do, and she thought she could take care of herself. She kept the revolver within easy reach, studied all callers critically, and once had to threaten with the revolver a man who persisted in coming into the house without invitation.

Chapter Six

The Mad Wolf

When great herds of buffaloes roamed the prairies, packs of wolves followed them, hamstringing and killing stragglers—the old, infirm, sick or crippled; but the buffaloes were almost all gone before Rosie came, and the wolves with them. Yet on still nights she could sometimes hear wolves howling from the woods along the creek, or up in the hills to the north—a wild, long-drawn, lonely howl that made the dog creep close to the door, and caused her own blood to run cold.

One crisp, sunny morning in December, as Henry and Rosie were sipping the last of their breakfast rye coffee, a man on horseback rode into the yard and reined up at the door.

"Hello, Henry! Hi there!" he called, in a voice like the roar of a lion. It was Mart Starling, a settler living several miles over toward Oak Creek, a man with a stentorian voice which neighbors a mile away could hear easily on quiet evenings.[1]

Henry stepped out into the yard. "Hello, yourself. Don't you know enough to come in where it's warm!" But Henry quickly saw that his levity was out of place, for Mart Starling looked very serious.

"They've got some trouble up on Oak Creek," he said, "and I wonder if you would have time to help a little."

Henry usually had time to help the neighbors. "Surely. What's the trouble?" He stepped out, closing the door behind him.

"It's Nebraska Stevens, the boy that was bitten by a mad wolf a while back.[2] He went mad yesterday, and chased his folks out of the house. Some of us will have to help take care of him."

56

"Oh, I hadn't heard about it; I knew they had a bad scare up there a while back."

"Worse than a scare, a hell of a lot worse, Henry. He was down at the south ranch, heard a great noise and commotion in the chicken house one night, and went out to see what was wrong. Must have been afraid of a wolf—people had been talking about a mad wolf coming down the creek somewhere, so he took his gun along; but when he got to the door of the chicken house, the brute jumped out and chewed him up before he could raise his gun."

"Couldn't they get him to a mad stone?"[3] asked Henry.

"Took him to Saint Joe, but the doctor couldn't find a stone big enough to cover the bite. He came on home—for a while thought he was all right. But yesterday he was down to the creek to get a bucket of water, and had a fit when he saw the water."

"Have they got a doctor?"

"No use getting a doctor. A doctor would be afraid to come near him. He went back to the house and told his mother. His father and John Wise are taking care of him now; but somebody will have to take a turn today. Hasn't bitten anybody yet, but when he gets a fit they just run outside, and hold the door on him. I saw him last night. It's terrible, terrible." Mart looked away for a minute, and then reiterated: "Terrible!"

"I'll be up as soon as I can. Shall I bring the missus?"

"Nothing for her to do. No place for a woman anyhow. No place for anybody, really." Mart turned his horse and was gone.

Henry went back into the house to tell Rosie of his errand, and after feeding his stock, he struck across the prairie toward Oak Creek. At every step his feet slipped on the frost-covered buffalo grass; but the clear, crisp air gave him energy that made the miles short, and in an hour he could look down into the valley of Oak Creek and see the sod house in which the doomed boy was being held. There were two wagons standing in the yard, with horses picketed near. Smoke was rising in a thin column from the chimney.

When yet a long way from the house, Henry heard the sound of a voice, high, raucous and hysterical, apparently in angry protest at some wrong. As he came nearer, the complaints turned to suffocated sobs, and just as he reached the house, the door was suddenly thrown open, and two men rushed out into the yard, slamming the door after them.

"Can I help a little here!" asked Henry.

"Take Bill Stevens' place," said John Wise, "so he can take his wife away. This is no place for her." John Wise was one of Henry's best friends, although he lived several miles away, up on Oak Creek.[4]

The knocking and commotion in the house ceased, and they opened the door again. There on the dirt floor, with clothing torn and soiled, lay the boy, almost a young man, panting and exhausted, his eyes staring wildly from their sunken sockets.

"Water, water! Won't you give me a drink?" he moaned, reaching out his hands in anticipation. "I want a drink!"

John stepped into the other room, and returned with a tin dipper of water. "It won't do. But, God, to hear him beg! Get to the door, boys. I'll give it to him."

The boy rose and sat on the edge of the straw tick. He reached for the cup with both hands, a look of pitiful hope, yet of terror, on his face. No sooner had he raised the cup to his lips than he fell into a suffocating paroxysm of sobbing and coughing, and the water splashed to the floor.

Henry turned his face away, and stepped through the door into the next room. Hearing a sob behind him, he turned. There was the mother, standing by the single little window, with her face buried in her hands, as if to shut out the sounds that came from the other room. In a few minutes the boy's paroxysms ceased, and then the piteous begging for water could be heard distinctly through the closed door.

John presently appeared at the kitchen door. "Come on, mother," he said. "The team is ready. You and Bill will have to go. We'll take care, the best we can."

The mother permitted her shawl to be thrown over her shoulders, but she must see her boy again; and, refusing to be led out to the wagon, she opened the door into his room.

"You have to go, don't you, ma," the boy said hoarsely, looking at her with abject terror in his wild eyes. "I can't help it. But I won't bite this time. Kiss me, anyhow, before you go away."

She stepped toward his bed, but Henry grasped her arm and

held her. "Don't do that!" he said, with a world of kindly sympathy in his voice. "You better go, before . . . before he gets worse."

"I won't hurt you this time! Surely I won't!" pleaded the boy. He rose from his bed and took a step toward her, but reeled and fell heavily against the wall, crumpling to a pitiful heap on the floor. She reached down to help him up, but Henry again held her back and himself lifted the boy up onto his bed.

"Please come now," he said. "You can't do any good, and you ought not to be here."

She paused a moment, looking back at the helpless figure on the bed, and then suffered herself to be led from the room and out to the wagon. With Henry's help she managed to climb up over the wagon wheel and into the seat. He picked up the shawl that she had dropped and handed it to her.

"We'll do the best we can, and I'll send for you, if there's anything you can do."

"Oh yes, let me come back . . . let me come back when I can. And if you could only give him some water!" She looked at him imploringly.

"I'll try it again. We'll do all we can." Henry watched the wagon roll out of the yard and down the road, the mother sitting with her head bent over and hidden in her heavy black shawl.

Mart Starling presently came, and John went home. The day and night passed, and another day, filled with such experiences as Henry would never banish from his mind. He slept part of the second night, wrapped in a horse blanket, on the kitchen floor.

Toward morning the sick boy called again for a drink.

"No, better not drink now," said Mart. "It will only make you worse."

"Water! water! Just a little drink!" pleaded the boy in a hoarse whisper. "It won't hurt this time."

"Let's give him some," said Henry. "It can't hurt much. I told his mother I would."

"You do it, if you want to," said Mart, turning to the door.

Henry got a dipper of water from the kitchen, and held the boy's head up with one hand while he raised the dipper to his lips. This time there were no paroxysms. The boy drank deeply, and fell back on the bed and slept. Henry threw the blanket over him and returned to his comrade in the kitchen.

"I wonder if he could get well?" he questioned. "Do they ever get well?"

"Never heard of such a thing. But anything is better than— than to see him try to drink."

The next night Henry went home, carrying a stout club all the way—an unusual thing for him to do, for he generally did not know what fear was. As he entered the yard he began singing "Stille Nacht," so that Rosie would know no intruder was coming, and the door was open when he reached the step.

"How is he?" asked Rosie.

For a minute he made no answer, but occupied himself with lighting the lamp and poking the smoldering embers in the little stove. As he put another stick of wood on the fire he said simply: "Smothered in his own bed tick." And those were the only words Rosie ever heard him utter regarding his days and nights with the mad boy.

The death of Nebraska Stevens was soon known to all the settlers roundabout. The mad wolf bit a man farther down the creek and infected a number of dogs, cows, and horses, and wild animals before it was killed. The man did not yield to the infection, but there was an epidemic of hydrophobia among animals of all kinds. Mothers feared to trust their children out of doors. Dogs were watched with the greatest anxiety, and many were killed at the first suspicion of the disease. Several cows went mad and bellowed themselves to death. Pigs and horses were not immune. Steve Linge's horses were bitten by a skunk, and he had to shoot one of them when it developed the dreaded symptoms on the way home from Russell. Having only a light load, he hitched his remaining horse to the doubletree and drove on. A few miles farther on, the animal began to rear and froth at the mouth, but by driving between fits he managed to get home before it died. Henry stopped all the holes in his stable carefully, and kept the door shut when the horses were in, lest some rabid animal should get in and bite them; Rosie cast an anxious eye up and down the road whenever she ventured far from the house.

Wild animals became unusually dangerous. One evening Henry and Rosie were sitting at the supper table they heard a scream outside. Almost immediately the door flew open Lizzie

Graeber stumbled into the room, slammed the door after her, and crumpled to a dishevelled heap on the floor.

"A skunk! A mad skunk!" she screamed, as Henry stooped to lift her into a chair. The animal could be heard threshing about, scratching and biting at the door. Sensing the danger to his livestock if the animal should invade the corral or should get into the barn, Henry grabbed the revolver from the shelf, opened the door an inch or two, and shot the insistent and unwelcome visitor. Lizzie had been visiting the Benders and had been chased by the skunk on her way home.

Another danger was seldom out of mind, in dry weather—prairie fires. With most of the land still in grass, fires had a clear sweep of the land, and would sometimes travel a hundred miles. When Henry saw the sky lighted up in any direction, he saw to it that the rain barrel was full, and watched anxiously.

Chapter Seven

Horse Thieves

There were horse thieves in the vicinity, and Henry never knew when he might return from a visit to the neighbors, or might awaken in the morning, to find his horses gone, to find himself without any means of cultivating the land he had homesteaded. To lose his horses would have been worse than to lose his claim, indeed, for while he might easily take another claim or buy a relinquishment from someone else,[1] he could have found it very hard to earn enough to buy another team.

Several horses were stolen one night from some of the settlers living up the creek, and Henry set himself seriously to the task of making his own possession more secure. His first thought was to build another stable directly against the house, as several of the neighbors had done, so that he could watch the horses better at night, but after talking it over with Rosie he dropped this idea. It would cost something to build a stable, and then the horses would be unpleasant neighbors. He then tried to work out some scheme for running a rope from the stable to the house, so that any opening of the stable door would give the alarm in the house, but this had to be abandoned, as the distance was too great. Finally he decided that it would perhaps be sufficient to get a heavy bolt and lock for the stable, and keep the dog in the stable at night. When he left home at night he almost always drove the team, even sometimes when he would rather have walked. Thus by watching the horses day and night, by unremitting care and vigilance, Henry managed to keep his team. He even began to hope that danger from thieves was past, and permitted himself an occasional relaxation in his accustomed vigilance; and this presently brought serious consequences.

It happened early in March on the way home from Russell,[2] where Henry had gone with a load of wheat. He had taken Steve Linge along because Steve was a good companion and wanted to buy a few supplies for himself. On the way home they camped by the roadside at night, cooked and ate their supper—Henry was really a good cook—hobbled the horses and turned them loose to graze, and lay down under the wagon to sleep.[3]

Henry always slept lightly, and he presently found himself wide-awake and listening. Some unusual sound had awakened him. He sat up and peered through the wagon spokes on either side, but could see nothing unusual. In the darkness he could not see the horses, but perhaps they were down in a nearby ravine. He listened . . . nothing disturbing . . . yes, there was the sound of horses galloping over toward the road. There was something wrong about that, for his own horses would not be able to run, hobbled as they were.

He turned to Steve and shook him vigorously. "Steve, the horses are gone. Wake up!"

"Oh, damn the horses," Steve drawled, less than half awake.

Henry jammed him in the ribs again. "Steve! Wake up! Somebody's after the horses!"

"Oh, hell!" Steve rolled over on the other side and would soon have been asleep again, but Henry grabbed the corner of the blanket that he was sleeping on and rolled him over again.

"What in the devil's gone wrong now?" grumbled Steve as he finally came to as near a sitting position as he could manage under the wagon. "What do you want to get up for?"

"The horses are gone. Come on!"

Henry slipped his shoes on as he spoke and was gone. Steve followed close on his heels, for Steve wore no shoes and his complete toilet consisted in throwing his blanket off.

They struck the wagon trail and ran in the direction of the noise Henry had heard, but found nothing. Presently Henry stopped to listen. Not a sound broke the stillness, save the occasional "ku ku" of a prairie dog owl in the distance. A breath of wind from the north brought the faintest sound of hoofbeats—yes, horses galloping, miles away.

"Those are not my horses!" said Henry.

"How do you know?"

"Frank can't gallop—can't even trot so you can tell it on him."

"Then they ought to be around here somewhere—in the ravines maybe." Steve proceeded down in the direction of the nearest ravine, feeling his way gingerly in the darkness, to avoid running into cactus. After what seemed a long walk, he stopped.

"What's that?" Steve pointed toward a dark object on the side of the opposite hill, vague and indistinct in the darkness.

"That tree?"

"No tree up there! Listen."

They listened intently. Suddenly a horse sneezed and stamped. Henry dashed off across the ravine and up the hill.

"It's Frank," he shouted back to Steve. Sure enough, it was Frank, but his hobble had been cut, and his halter was gone.

"Something wrong here," he said to Steve as Steve came up. "I'm afraid Sam's gone." He thought a minute and then proceeded: "They probably tried to take them both and left Frank when they saw he couldn't keep up."

"Mebbe Sam strayed off."

"No, he never would have left Frank, unless he had to. Poor Sam!" It was like Henry to think of his horse rather than of himself.

"Poor Henry, you better say, if you got to buy another horse now—your best one too. Damned thieves!"

"No use hunting now. Let's go back to the wagon—before they get that," and Henry led the way with Frank, back to the wagon.

The next morning they wandered about the hills and ravine looking for Sam, but he was not to be found; and finally Henry found his hoof print on the trail. He knew it by a V-shaped piece cut out of the front of the hoof. Sam was headed north, evidently with several other horses, perhaps the horses that the thieves were riding.

There was nothing to do but wait until someone came along who would take them the rest of the way home. About noon two freighters came along, who tied Henry's wagon on behind their own and hauled him and his stuff home. It was a sad homecoming that night, without Sam.

Early the next day Henry set about to get together a posse to

give chase. The news that horse thieves were active again spread
like wild fire, and so many of the neighbors had lost horses that
when the sheriff called for volunteers from the Vigilance Committee, he got more men than he could use to advantage.

On the night that Sam disappeared several other horses were
stolen farther up the creek, and this directed suspicion immediately to the Oldacre boys, the boldest and most aggressive gang of
claim-jumpers, thieves, and bandits in the country. Their mother
was said to have helped to deliver Jesse James when he was born.
They had a ranch along the creek, with a hidden dugout along the
stream where they hid stolen horses until they could get them out
of the country. This ranch was reputed to be one of several stations
in a great chain horse stealing organization reaching eastward all
the way to Atchison and southward to Hays; and it was commonly
believed that certain businessmen in Atchison were interested in
the organization. Whether this was true or not, there were certain
members of the gang who travelled back and forth, stopping for a
while at one station or another, stealing a few horses at one point
and at night taking them to another where they could be disposed
of; and they always had pocket money and good lawyers to defend
them when in trouble.

It was an angry and determined but motley mob of men that
rode up the creek and quietly surrounded the Oldacre dugout. The
sheriff stepped forward and announced in a loud but rather unsteady voice that he had a warrant for the arrest of Green Oldacre,[4]
Am Oldacre, Bill Hicks and Jack Hunter, and demanded that they
surrender in the name of the law. A voice from the dugout told him
to go to hell, and go damn quick. The sheriff precipitately retreated
to a safe position behind a neighboring hay stack.

With three other men and a boy named Mart Rychel,[5] Henry
crossed the creek, swollen with a recent rain, and ran for the
horses which were tied a hundred yards down the creek. Just as he
did so the outlaws bolted from the door of the dugout, and in a fu-
sillade of shots swam the creek, guns in hand, and followed. As
they neared the horses they leveled their guns and ordered Henry
and his men to drop their guns.

"Damned if I will!" shouted the boy Mart, and raised his rifle.
As he did so a shot from Hick's gun struck the chamber of his car-
bine, exploding every shell except the one in the barrel and tearing

a bloody path along his arm and into his side. Undaunted, the boy raised his gun again and sighted, but the horse he was holding reared and almost pulled him over. He braced himself and sighted again, and at the report Hicks, who had turned to run, pitched heavily into the mud. Henry's shots at the other men went wild, and in an instant Hicks regained his feet and disappeared above the bank, spitting blood as he ran.[6]

Henry dropped his gun and ran to the wounded boy, and soon bound up his wounds with strips torn from his shirt. In the meantime the sheriff ventured out from his position behind the hay stack, and the rest of the posse came across the creek to help, rather sheepish and ashamed of their marksmanship and little inclined to give chase to the retreating bandits, since they now had the stolen horses. Henry thanked the men for their help, mounted Sam and started homeward, happier than he had been in many a day. He had found not merely his horse, not merely a valuable chattel; he had found again his faithful friend and comrade; and they ambled off down the creek in a state of great mental contentment.

The horse thieves, unabashed and unafraid, remained in their creek rendezvous for a year or more. Occasionally one of the settlers' horses would disappear, and there was always a suspicion that the Oldacre boys and their gang were still at work, but nothing could be proved. A year or two later they sold out and moved farther west, where there was a better field for their operations.

Chapter Eight

The Bright-Eyed Baby

It was the friendly springtime, time to dig in the ground, to hoe and rake and burn the dead stalks and leaves, time to plant things; and this spring Henry and Rosie were planting trees. Henry dug up a wagonload of seedlings down by the river, and he and Rosie spent several days planting a big grove of cottonwoods along the north side of the claim. Then they planted some apple trees and grape vines that Rosie's father had sent, and a white rosebush that her mother had put in the package. Rosie conjured up splendid visions of shade and fruit and flowers as she dug in the soft, mellow ground and poured buckets of water around the new plants. Every tree would help, too, to bring the change in climate which all of the settlers looked forward to.

The work was barely done soon enough, for it was time for the baby to come. There was of course no doctor. No one thought of calling a doctor for so casual a matter. Mary Bartsch came down to help,[1] and afterward one of the Bartsch girls came and stayed for a week.[2] Then Rosie resumed her work, with the added task of caring for her bright-eyed baby.

What bright blue eyes he had—so bright that when he was lying on his mother's lap, she could see the buttons of her dress reflected in them! And how Henry enjoyed playing with him, holding the little fellow and letting him pull at his beard! There is nothing like a baby to give life a real meaning. They called him Albert, after Rosie's youngest brother, who had died in infancy.[3]

Rosie hardly suspected that the first danger that should threaten her baby would be one of the buffaloes that were disappearing so fast. One day, as she was on her way up to see Mary

Bartsch, carrying Albert in her arms, a lone buffalo appeared over the hill, charging directly toward her. The poor animal had been chased until it was wild with fright and fatigue, and seemed to see nothing as it plunged ahead. For an instant she stood terror-stricken, but when she saw that it was headed straight for her she ran to the side, and the big brute tore past her, its head down, its eyes wild and blood-shot, apparently taking no notice of anything.

Henry too saw the buffalo, and mounted Sam quickly to join in the chase; but several of the neighbors were ahead of him, and Wilson Athey overtook and shot the animal several miles up the creek. Of course Henry got a piece of the meat, but he did not reach home with it until after dark. In the meantime, Rosie had been worrying about him, for she had no idea as to what might have happened. Sam was so afraid of buffaloes.

In June, the weather became distressingly dry, and the wheat never headed out. This was discouraging, but Henry had only a small patch of spring wheat, and the new corn crop had a promising start. At a Fourth of July picnic held in Stone's Grove, up on Twelve Mile Creek,[4] there was much talk among the neighbors about the fine prospects for corn, and much hopeful planning of new houses, new barns, new dresses, and trips back east to see the home folk.

The weather remained persistently dry, however, and the corn began to shrivel. In July came the long-remembered sixteen days of hot winds that fired the corn before the tassels had a chance to develop, burned the grass to a dull brown, and blasted even the sunflowers that grew along the edges of the fields. Some of the leaves fell from the little trees that Rosie and Henry had planted in the spring.

The baby did not thrive. Healthy and vital girl that she was, Rosie had far more milk than the baby could use at first, and her breasts caused her great discomfort and pain. She tried various expedients to secure relief, but without much success. One day Lizzie Graeber suggested that if she would heat a bottle in live steam and hold the opening of the bottle to her breast, the cooling of the bottle would drain the surplus milk. Rosie tried this, but scalded her nipples so badly that she could no longer nurse the baby at all. She would have been willing to endure the pain, but the nipples festered until the baby would not have them. So she had to feed him on cow's milk, which soured quickly in the steady heat, even in the cellar or when they hung it down in the well. With no screens on the windows, there was contamination from flies and dust, and the baby fell sick with indigestion and dysentery. Not skilled in baby dietetics, Rosie boiled the milk, which promptly turned the baby's dysentery into constipation, and finally into cholera infantum.

He cried a great deal, day and night. Rosie cared for him in the daytime, but at night she and Henry took turns carrying him back and forth, trying every imaginable way to quiet him. Rosie searched her medicine cabinet for something that would bring him relief. She appealed to the neighbor women when they came for their mail; but, although most of them had medicines and nostrums that they thought would work wonders, none of their remedies did Albert any good. He grew slowly weaker and more emaciated—at last almost too weak to cry.

One morning, after a long and anxious night, Rosie took him over to the door, and held him up to the light.

"Henry," she said, "you will have to go and see the doctor. Our little boy can't last long this way."

Henry stepped to the door and looked down at the child, who moaned weakly in his utter misery, more wasted and emaciated than Henry had realized before. He lifted one of the little hands and was frightened to see how thin were the tiny fingers—how unlike the chubby fingers that used to pull at his beard.

"I better go right now, don't you think?"

"Oh, yes! go quick—just as quick as you can!"

Without a word Henry hurried out to get the horses from their pickets. In a short time he had them harnessed and hitched to the wagon, and was gone along the winding trail that led to Cawker City, ten miles away.

Rosie rocked the baby in her arms as she watched the wagon shrink to a tiny spot on the horizon—so slowly it moved that it seemed scarcely to move at all—and then saw it disappear. How helpless she felt, how helpless and alone, with the miles of prairie stretching about her, with no one near to help, and her little baby moaning out its life! If her mother were only there! Her mother would surely know what to do—or even Henry. Henry always had good ideas. She almost wished he had not gone, for she dreaded what might happen before he returned. Across her mind flashed a wild impulse to follow him, to overtake him and drive with the baby to the doctor; a glance down at the frail mite of humanity in her arms showed how truly wild this idea was.

How long would Henry be gone? She tried to figure it out, as she looked fixedly at the point where the wagon had passed out of sight. Three hours—no, four hours at least, for Frank could not trot. Five hours, more likely, even if the doctor was at home, and longer than that if he was out. It would be past noon before he could possibly get back; and then he would bring medicine only, not the doctor. If she had only told him to bring the doctor!

She sat down on the bed a moment to rest, but the child moaned and struggled convulsively in her arms, and she rose and resumed her walk. Back and forth she dragged her aching feet, from the stove to the door and back again to the stove, to and fro, brushing the flies from the thin little face, pausing at the open door each time she passed, to look hopelessly across the prairie. The rising wind, already searing hot in midmorning, blew intermittent clouds of dust and broken corn leaves up from the field and corral. She closed the door against a particularly dense cloud; but without the breeze the room was too hot, and she opened it again.

Oh, the incessant, wearying wind! How it knocked and pounded at the windows and at the sod roof, scattering dust and pebbles over the floor, flapping the curtains, the towel hanging on the door, and the sheet that hung down over side of the bed, rattling the saw that hung on the wall, banging the door back against the wood box, pulling and twisting the flower plants on the window shelf! If it would only quiet down for a while, or blow cool from the north again! The hot, implacable wind that had taken the growing crops—now must it take her baby?

As Rosie paced back and forth in the little cabin, Mary Hunker appeared in the door. Mary had come for her mail.

"Oh, dear Mary," exclaimed Rosie, hurrying to her with the baby, "what shall I do for my little boy? I'm afraid he's worse, worse this morning. See his eyes—his eyes are not right!" Rosie held the baby up to the light.

Mary held out her arms. "Let me carry him anyhow, while you sit down a minute. What kind of medicine do you give him?"

Rosie showed her the bottle from which she had been getting

Mary Bartsch. (Courtesy the Historical Society of the Downs Carnegie
Library)

medicine. "It is some that we got from the medicine man the last
time he was here. It's good medicine, but it hasn't helped him. Oh,
I'm so afraid! His eyes were all right this morning, and now see
how they stare!"

"Let's try again," suggested Mary. While she held the baby,
Rosie poured out a small spoonful. With some difficulty she got it
into his mouth.

He choked and vomited and fell into convulsions. Rosie took
him again and walked about the room, rocking him in her arms

and crying, "Oh, my poor little boy, my poor little boy." The baby's convulsions were followed by weak and plaintive crying.

"Let me hold him anyhow, while you make your bed," Mary suggested. Rosie handed him over helplessly, and turned to spread the covers of her bed; but a sharp cry from the child arrested her. He had turned his face toward her and was holding his hands out appealingly. This time there was recognition in his bright eyes.

Oh, yes, he was better! He looked like himself again. She took him again in her arms and looked out across the prairie for Henry—hopefully this time.

A movement of the child made her look down. He was in convulsions. His tiny, clinched hands pulled at her dress. His eyes, so bright a moment ago, stared unrecognizingly past her. He writhed a moment in agony, and then lay quiet.

When Rosie realized that all was over, she hugged the little body to her and sobbed: "Oh, my poor little boy! My poor little boy!" She looked out across the prairie—but there was no longer any use. There would be no help from there now, no medicine that could cure, no doctor whose services would avail. "My poor little boy," she moaned; and, forgetting Mary and all the world, she resumed her walk up and down the room, from the door to the stove, and back to the door, to and fro, back and forth, burying her face in the little white dress that she had just put on fresh and clean that morning.

Presently she stopped at the door. "I wonder where Henry is?" she asked. "He ought to come back. It's no use, no use, no use now."

"I'll run home and get Jake to go after him," volunteered Mary. Tying on her bonnet she hastened out of the door and down the wagon trail toward her home.

Rosie turned to the bed, laid the body of the child down, covered it with the corner of the sheet, then sat down on the edge of the bed, and surrendered to her utter grief and loneliness.

An hour later she was awakened to the world by the distant sound of a horse galloping. It was Henry, coming rapidly up across the prairie on Jake Hunker's horse. He dismounted quickly and hurried into the house. A glance at the bed, and at Rosie sitting there, told him all. For a moment he stood looking down at the bed, as if trying to understand it, then sat down beside Rosie and threw his arm around her shoulders. He could not speak the words with which he would gladly have comforted her, but in the touch of his hand Rosie felt the healing sympathy of an understanding heart in their first great sorrow.[5]

Chris and Louisa and other friends soon came to help, and there was need of it, for there was no cemetery, no undertaker, no coffin, and no preacher to conduct a funeral. It had never occurred to Rosie that there might be need for such things. It was finally arranged that Frank Hagel should dig the grave, in a corner of the yard; that Wilson Athey should make the coffin; and, since Rosie insisted that there be funeral services, that George Graeber should read from the Bible and preach the sermon. Chris Bartsch offered to lead in the singing of a hymn.

That night Henry and Rosie, worn out by many sleepless nights and by the tragedy of the day, slept the sleep of utter exhaustion in the same room with the body of the child and the neighbors who had volunteered as watchers; and the next morning they did not awaken until the watchers were gone, the sun was up, and the wind already blowing hot and dry from the south.

When they had done the milking, and Rosie had taken the cows over to Benders for herding, Wilson Athey came with the coffin, a little oval-shaped box, made of cottonwood boards, tapering to the foot, and scraped with glass until it was smooth. There was no lining in it, but Rosie tore up a white underskirt and folded the pieces into the coffin.

The funeral was held at ten o'clock, with such decent dignity as the circumstances permitted. The neighbors came in lumber wagons, and tied their teams to the corral fence. In the house Henry had placed boards along the walls on supports of chairs, boxes and nail kegs; and those who could not find room on these boards sat on the bed. When all were seated, George Graeber took his place in the door, and read a brief passage from Matthew:

"Then were there brought unto him little children, that he should put his hands on them, and pray: and the disciples rebuked them. But Jesus said, 'Suffer little children and forbid them not, to come unto me: for of such is the kingdom of heaven.'"

After a simple sermon and a hymn, two men took up the coffin, and the rest followed out to the grave. There, with the wind blowing clouds of dust over from the corral and tugging at the women's skirts and bonnets, a short prayer was offered, and the little coffin was lowered into its shallow grave—one of the few graves of those days that were never lost in the years to follow.

When the funeral was over, and the last wagon had rattled out of the yard, Henry and Rosie returned to the house, carried the board seats out, and set the few articles of furniture back in place. Rosie gathered up the soiled baby clothes and put them in the washtub, and folded the clean clothes away carefully in the big box that served as a dresser.

How quiet, and how empty, seemed the little room now! Rosie's steps seemed almost to echo from the ends of the room, as she busied herself with setting things to rights. Henry sat on the edge of the bed, staring vacantly at the floor.

Rosie stepped to the door and looked up at the sun.

"I guess it's about time for dinner," she said.

Henry seemed not to hear.

"Will you get some milk, the milk on the south end?" she asked, as she set out the bowls and spoons on the table.

Henry went outside and into the cellar, brought up a crock of milk which he put on the table, and sat down at his place. The dinner of bread and milk was eaten in silence; then Henry rose and started out to feed the horses.

Chapter Nine

Grasshoppers

Already during the funeral, Henry and Rosie had noticed a great many grasshoppers flitting about; and after the people had gone, Rosie saw that the cypress vine which grew up over the window was covered with them, eating the leaves greedily. As Henry stepped out of the door, he noticed a peculiar cloud in the west, too light in color to be rain, or even dust. He called Rosie to the door to look. The cloud came nearer, drifting higher, until it obscured the sun. Like a cloud of glistening snow flakes it was, but the flakes were alive, eddying and whirling about like the wild, dead leaves in an autumn storm; and soon the flakes came down, circling in myriads, beating against everything animate or inanimate. Grasshoppers—millions, billions of them—soon covered the ground in a seething, fluttering mass, their jaws constantly at work biting and testing all things, as they sought what they might devour, their wings fluttering as if with some irresistible impulse of motion, making altogether a low, crackling, rasping sound, like the approach of a prairie fire.

For a few minutes Henry and Rosie stood looking at the miracle in astonishment, but when the pests flew into their faces and lodged in their clothing, they began to realize that this visitation was a serious matter. Rosie went back into the house and closed the door and windows, while Henry stood watching from the doorstep.

The swarming insects flitted about, covering the ground and the house and the fence and the well curb. Crunching them under his feet at every step, Henry hurried out to the garden. There they swarmed over the onion, cabbage and tomato plants, on the few melon and cucumber vines that had survived the drouth, and on the weeds along the edge of the garden. Not a green leaf or stem could be seen, so thickly they swarmed. Out in the cornfield they covered every green leaf and stalk. It was clear that what fodder had been left by the hot wind would soon be gone. Henry hurried back to the house.

"They're eating the garden and the corn!" he exclaimed, bursting open the door.

For a moment Rosie stood confused and aghast. Then her natural self-reliance returned. "Well, let's go out and cut what we can," she said. She grabbed her bonnet from a nail on the wall, shook the grasshoppers out of it, and in a minute was ready.

Henry had only one corn knife, so Rosie took the butcher knife, and they hurried out to the field, where they found the few green leaves fast disappearing in the grasshoppers' voracious maws; but they set bravely to work hacking the stalks and standing them up in neat shocks.

The butcher knife proved a poor tool to work with, for Rosie had to stoop low for every stalk, and it began to tire her, so they decided that Henry should cut the corn, and Rosie would carry it over to the shock—it was not heavy fodder and was growing lighter every hour. In the heat and dust and wind, they worked steadily all afternoon, and at sunset had two rows of shocks standing in defiance of the omnivorous insects—not entirely successful defiance, to be sure, for the grasshoppers immediately swarmed over the shocks, but they could eat only the outside.

Covered with sweat and dust, and oh, how thirsty, they came in from the field at sunset. While Henry fed and watered the horses and pigs, Rosie went over to Benders to get the cows. It was dark before the last of the cows was milked and the supper of bread and milk had been eaten. Soon afterward Henry and Rosie were again out in the corn field, where they worked until midnight.

Worn out though she was by all that had happened during the day, Rosie slept uneasily that night. Several times she started from her pillow with a vivid dream that she had heard that plaintive cry in the little bed beside her, only to remember, with a tightening at her throat, that it would never awaken her again.

Early in the morning they went out to the field to cut corn

again, but the remaining stalks had been stripped bare and were no longer worth cutting. The hungry insects had not only eaten the leaves, but they had eaten the pith out of the stubs, even down into the ground. As Rosie passed the garden she saw that every green plant was gone. Even the weeds had everywhere been stripped, and an old bonnet which had been left hanging on a post was eaten to shreds.

When Henry went to the stable, he found some of the ropes cut through, and the sweat-soaked parts of the harnesses were badly eaten. He carried the harnesses to the house to save them. The wagon was covered with the pests, and the paint had been eaten off in places. The water in the well swarmed with them. The little cottonwood trees that they had planted in the spring were stripped bare of all leaves, and even the bark was etched in places. A hoe handle leaning by the door of the cabin had been etched where the sweat had soaked in.

Many of the ubiquitous pests had crept into the cabin. They flew into the water, into the milk pans, and into the kettles cooking on the stove. They ate holes in the curtains on the windows, and in the clothes hanging on the wall. They stripped Rosie's house plants bare. When the windows and door were closed, the house was dark and unbearably hot; and Rosie had to keep them open as much as she dared.

The next day Henry started to draw the water out of the well, but he soon stopped, for as fast as he got the insects out others flew in. He tried covering the well with a buffalo robe, but they immediately began to eat the robe, so he had to take it off.

The unwelcome visitors stayed about a week, apparently trying to fly on eastward, but the wind remained persistently in the southeast for several days, and they seemed unwilling or unable to fly against it. When the wind turned, blowing from the west, they flew away as suddenly as they had come.

As soon as they were gone, Henry started to draw the water out of the well. He worked hard, and by evening had the water almost all out; but the next morning when he drew the bucket up, he found almost as many of the pests as there had been the day before. Many of them were still hidden in the wall, unable to fly out, and as they grew weaker fell down into the water. The water smelled to heaven, but it was all there was to drink. Rosie tried making rye coffee each meal, and that was better, although even in coffee the grasshopper flavor was merely diluted. It was weeks before the water was really fit to drink.

After the pests were gone, the drouth and the heat continued unabated. Occasionally the wind shifted to the north, for a day or two of cool weather; but it soon veered around to the south again, and blew hot and dry across the dead grass and leafless stubs of corn. Henry tried to plow for wheat, but he could hardly hold the plow in the ground, and the soil came up in great, dry chunks; so he gave it up, and waited for rain.

Henry was more fortunate than many of the neighbors. Those who had only shallow wells found themselves out of water, and were forced to haul water from the creek or river. The farm wagon loaded with barrels became a familiar sight, rising above the dugouts and stables of the neighboring farmyards. And when water had to be hauled, the cows often went thirsty, bawling and milling around the empty water troughs.

In spite of drouth and pests, Henry gained a new neighbor that year—Fred Wetzel, Pennsylvania Dutch, who bought the Bender place when Bender moved onto old Vietz's claim.[1] Wetzel was an undersized little man, but amazingly active and industrious, with sharp, cruel blue eyes and a high voice that broke into falsetto whenever he became excited. He worked his horses half to death, using a stick with a sharp nail in the end for a whip, and drove his children unmercifully, to get money to give to the church. In threshing, his daughters even worked at the tail of the straw carrier—the dirtiest job—and when one of them fainted one day, he laid her out in the shade until she revived and sent her back to work again. Yet he was honest, and always very kind to Henry and Rosie, and his wife, who was a midwife, later helped Rosie with two or three of her babies.

Chapter Ten

Two Letters

One day the stage driver brought a letter, a letter from Iowa, and Henry sat down by the table to read it.

August 12, 1874

Dear brother Henry:

Your letter came so long ago that I am ashamed that I have not answered it before; but we have had the threshers, and are building a new barn, and there is always so much to do. It is too bad you have been having such hot winds. George says several people that left here for Kansas when you went are coming back this fall—Nungessers and Stecks and Schirmers[1]—I guess you knew them. I don't know how it will work out for them. It is not good to move too much; but if you think it would be better to come back here, Brietzes want to sell out. They want a thousand dollars for their quarter, and I could let you have the money.

We were so sorry to learn about the baby. As mother used to say, "Das vergisst man nicht."[2]

We are sending a box with a few things that we didn't need here. Perhaps they will be good this winter. And if I can help you in any way, you know how glad I will be to do it. Everything is doing fairly well here. We had another rain yesterday, and George thinks the corn is about made if it does not frost too early.

As ever,
Kate[3]

Henry read the letter several times, and then sat staring at it until Rosie looked up from her sewing. She was patching a pair of overalls.

79

"From John?"[4] she asked.

"No, from Kate." He hesitated a minute, and then continued: "She says everything is fine in Iowa." Henry handed her the letter and sat picking with his thumbnail at a splinter in the table while she read it.

"If I just had the three hundred dollars that woman stole in Iowa!" Henry said, when Rosie had finished reading the letter. It was unusual for Henry to bring up unhappy bygones.

"I've always thought perhaps some day she might be sorry, and send it back to you," she answered, "but such things don't ever happen, I guess, except in the story books."

"If I had even that much, it might be better to go back to Iowa. It's a good country, and that Brietze farm is about the best farm around there—only a little corner cut out by the creek. I broke the land on it in 'sixty-five, when I got back from the war. I could have bought it then for three hundred dollars in greenbacks—had a hundred dollars, and could have borrowed the rest, but they wanted fifteen per cent interest. Thought it was too much." Henry looked out of the door across the devastated patch of what had been his corn, and an air of settled dejection came across his face. He had seldom complained, even when Rosie had felt almost ready to give up, and now she saw that it was her turn to bear a cheerful countenance.

"Oh, well, it will surely rain one of these days," she said. "I remember how it was fourteen years ago at Holton—worse than this, I believe. That was our first year there, so mother and father didn't know what kind of a country it was going be."

"Eighteen sixty. Yes, that was bad in Illinois too, but not like this." Henry's eyes turned to the devastated corn field again.

"Oh, worse, at home! I don't remember much about it, but it was worse than this, except we had no grasshoppers." Rosie laid her sewing down as she spoke. "No rain from May until November, no wheat, no corn, no rye, or anything! We had no money that winter. Father was sick, and we had nothing to eat—*nothing* to eat—even our corn meal was giving out. Poor mother!" Rosie's eyes filled with tears, as she looked out beyond the open door that knocked back against the wood box with each gust of the wind, beyond the corn field on the other side of the corral, back into the dim recollections of early childhood. For a time she forgot herself, and only came back to reality when Henry turned in his chair to see what had happened.

"That winter," she continued—"about Christmas time it was—she saw that we couldn't get through till spring and must have help. Mother hated to beg, and the neighbors were about as poor as we were. But she heard that there was aid in Atchison—it was thirty miles away—and there were Germans there who could understand her. She started to walk to Atchison one morning, with her poor shoes and ragged old striped shawl and coat. We had no team then—not even oxen. At noon a blizzard came up and, oh, it got terribly cold. The snow piled up high around our old house and drifted across the bed, where the wind blew in around the window sashes, and through the cracks between the logs."

"Almost sounds good, a day like this."

"Yes, but it wasn't good. It was terrible. And mother didn't get home for a week."

"She wasn't out in it all?"

"Oh, no, but we thought she was. And one day father called us girls, Minnie and me,[5] and said, 'Now, girls, mother is gone and I won't have time to bother with combing your long hair, there will be so much to do'; and he got the scissors, and cut our hair close. I remember how sad we all felt that day, although I didn't really understand it all."

"You were only about four or——"

"Five. But I knew it was very serious, because father was crying, and I had never seen father cry before. And a couple of days afterward a man drove in with a team and wagon; and there on the seat beside him was mother he was bringing home! How happy we all were; and mother cried and cried and hugged us!"

"Where had he found her!"

"On the road, over in the Indian reservation. It was getting dark, and she was worn out with wading through the deep snow drifts. She told us all about it, said she just wished she could lie down in one of those snow drifts and go to sleep—she hadn't had anything to eat since she left home, you know. But she thought of us at home waiting for her, and went on. And then she saw a light ahead, and pretty soon a team came along behind her, and the man took her to his home where the light was. They thawed out her hands and feet with snow, and brought her home as soon as they could. Oh, we were so glad to see her!"

"And she got no help?"

"Not then. But later they brought some supplies in from Atchison. So we got through the winter, and the next year was such a good year."

"It might be good here next year. I suppose we can get through the winter if the neighbors can. Several are going back, though," said Henry, then added, "the ones that have money to get away. Wise said last Sunday that he had bought some pigs from a fellow up in the hills for twenty-five cents each, and chickens for a penny, and a pile of corn for two dollars. If we had money we could buy some more stock cheap—but I don't know what we'd feed them."

"There are surely a lot of movers going east. That was such a sad woman here last night. She said they had nearly three hundred dollars, besides their team, when they went out to Gaylord two years ago; and now they are going back to Illinois without anything."

"The great trouble is that we would lose our homestead rights," said Henry, whittling down a rough corner of the table with his jack knife as he talked. His mind was still on Kate's letter.

"Oh, foolishness!" exclaimed Rosie, picking up her sewing again with a decision which showed that in her mind the matter was settled. "We have no place to go, and nothing to do anywhere but here. A thousand dollars of debts would worry me to death. Mother always said when everything looked worst, that was the time to hang on. And everyone seems to think our rain will increase, just as it did at Holton. Let's just get along the best we can, and stay in our little home. It's ours, and there's no mortgage on it. We can surely manage somehow."

Henry rose from his stool, took his hat from a nail, and started out; but he had scarcely got out of the door when he called back in a voice Rosie had not heard for long days:

"Rosie, come out here!"

Rosie gathered up her scissors and thread, and stepped out into the yard.

"Look there!" Henry exclaimed, pointing to the west. There was a great blue bank of clouds, its fleecy white edge gradually covering the sun, casting a cooling shade that spread like a bene-diction over the earth. Rosie looked at the cloud with interest, but without great confidence or enthusiasm. During the past weeks she had seen several clouds much like this thin out and disappear, and she was now thoroughly skeptical. Yet she always had great confidence in Henry's weather predictions, and asked, even hope-fully: "Do you really think it will come this way?"

"It looks favorable," said Henry. "The wind has been from the south for several days, and it's in the east now. There was a big ring around the moon last night, and the flies have been bad on the horses today."

Henry and Rosie sat down on the wagon tongue to watch the cloud come nearer. It came rapidly, the blue turned to gray, and the rain curtain emerged clearly from the wide cloud expanse. The lightning flashed in the distance, then closer, and the thunder growled and grumbled, and presently boomed triumphantly. The wind turned cool—how deliciously cool—as it shifted to the north-west and blew a few great drops of rain down from the overhang-ing clouds.

Rosie and Henry forgot themselves completely until the first drops fell in the dust at their feet. They scarcely had time to get the clothes off the line and close the windows before the torrents of rain poured from the heavens, splashed against the windows in fit-ful gusts, and started rivulets of muddy water down through the sod roof. It took most of the pans on Rosie's shelves to catch the water, and she was busy for the next hour shifting the pans from one place to another, as the rain found new leaks in the roof.

The wind died down, and the rain settled to a steady drizzle as evening came on. Henry took his shoes off and rolled up his overalls to go after the cows. When he came back, and was slipping and splashing about in the mud of the stable yard, Rosie could hear him whistling snatches of tunes with spirit and gusto. It was dark before the milking was done, and Henry came in for supper, drenched with rain and covered with mud. By the light of the lamp, with the cool air pouring in through the open door, they ate the supper of eggs and biscuits that Rosie had prepared while Henry was milking, with coffee—real coffee. And then, to the sound of the gentle falling rain, two tired people slept a restful sleep they had not known for a long time.

The rain was too late to help crops, even if the grasshoppers had left any crops, but the pastures and the volunteer wheat came out green, and the cows that had been drying up soon gave more milk. So Henry and Rosie had plenty of milk, with wheat and corn bread, hominy, and even occasional delicacies—eggs, dried corn and apples that Rosie's mother sent, wild currants, citron butter, and molasses. They killed the little pigs that they could not feed, and occasionally bought buffalo meat from the hunters who came through from the west. They often longed for something green, for fruit or vegetables, and Henry's stomach bothered him a little some times—a trouble he had had since the Civil War—but they got along, and did not need to accept any charity that winter.

One day they went to Cawker City to do some trading—an all-day trip, with Frank and Sam. At late noon, as she was making the modest purchases permitted by her butter and egg credits at Parker's store, Rosie began to feel very hungry, and was nearly tempted to buy some cheese and crackers she saw on the counter. She always liked cheese so well. For some time she wrestled with herself, as she eyed the tempting delicacy; and was on the point of buying a nickel's worth, when it occurred to her that a nickel would buy a spool of thread which she needed for patching. That settled the matter. She bought thread, and waited until she got home that evening for her dinner.

Rosie's shoes were badly worn, and she and Henry were finally tempted to drive up to Sid Chapin's,[6] where relief supplies were handled, to see if they could get a new pair. While they were searching through a pile of shoes lying on the dirt floor, a number of people came in to get flour or beans or clothing, and Henry noted among them several who had never seen the grasshopper invasion at all, but had come weeks after the grasshoppers were gone. Quite disgusted, he whispered to Rosie:

"Kind of a sponging business, for some of those fellows. Let's go home."

Rosie hadn't found anything to fit her anyhow, and she readily assented. She managed to get along with her old shoes the rest of the winter.

Probably Rosie did not sense the exact meaning of her words when she so often declared herself thankful because there were "many who were worse off." Some indeed were worse off, in that they had not enough food; and many suffered from the lack of variety in their diet. There were a few cases of scurvy in the neighborhood, and one of the Athey girls died as a result of eating hominy from which the lye had not been washed with care.[7] Many of the settlers lacked decent clothes. George Graeber came to see Henry dressed in two pairs of overalls, one of which he wore with the seat in front, so that the holes would not fall in the same place. Steve Linge wore trousers that his wife had made of grain sacks. Many a one wore clothes that had been patched with every imaginable kind and color of cloth, and shoes so badly worn that they had to be tied on with twine. A few children never knew the feel of shoes that winter, or underclothes, or coats or mittens. And, as usual under conditions of poverty, the livestock suffered worst of all.

In December, a letter—written in German—came to Rosie from her father:

My dear children:

I should have answered your letter sooner, but Eugene[8] and mother were busy just then, getting ready to go to Leavenworth. Mother had got together about two hundred pounds of butter, and some eggs, and took them to Leavenworth, hoping to get the tax money with them. They got home yesterday, with some supplies for the winter: a coat for Eugene ($5.00), a shawl for Minnie ($1.25), a shawl for me (75¢), some shoes for me ($2.00), a shawl for George (75¢), thirty-six yards of shirting ($4.00), a box of soap—sixty pounds ($3.00), coffee, tea and sugar ($5.00), eighteen yards of calico ($1.50); and $25.00 she brought home in money. But that is not quite enough for the taxes, and I will have to add a little to it. Minnie wanted to work out for a while, to earn a shawl herself, but the pay is only $1.25 a week, and she has been working too hard. Eugene has bought mother an album for Christmas. We are well, and very happy, and thankful to God that we are so well cared for, when so many people are not.

In your letter, Rosie, you told us how hard it is to forget the little baby boy. Yes, my dear child, I know how it is, but we must resign ourselves. What God does is well done, and we have the further consolation that we know certainly that such a dear child is in

Heaven. If you will read Samuel 1, Chapter 1, verse 8, you will find consolation.

Affectionately your father,
Christopher Haag

That night, Rosie read the verse from Samuel and the rest of the chapter and book; but when she laid the Bible aside, and looked across the room at the bed where she had so often put little Albert to sleep, she felt more utterly lonely than she had felt since the day he was buried.

Chapter Eleven

Grasshopper Relief

In spite of the hardships of that winter, there was a great deal of sociability. The settlers had little to do but care for their small herds of livestock, and so had much time for festivities. There were many surprise parties, where the neighbors got together and drove in their wagons, or perhaps in only one or two wagons, to the house of the host and hostess, walked in, and took possession. They played various games until late at night, when the host was supposed to furnish refreshments.

One cold night, Henry and Rosie were taken to such a party at the Russells, across the river.[1] George Graeber drove his team, and gathered up a wagonload of the young folk, including Henry and Rosie. A noisy and hilarious crowd it was that rattled across the snow along the trail to the river, cracking obvious and boisterous jokes that set the women laughing dutifully. The river was frozen over, so that they did not have to go to the crossing, which would have been a mile out of the way.

As they finally pulled up the bank on the other side of the river, a little log cabin appeared—people on the river had timber, so they did not have to live in dugouts—and the crowd quieted down, because it was to be a surprise party. The horses were quietly un-hitched and tied to the wagon, and the crowd moved up to the house.

The surprise was not a complete success, for the dog heard them, and came bounding out with savage warning, and, by the time he had been pacified, the host was out in the yard with his gun. When he found out that his guests were not much-dreaded

George Graeber. (Photo courtesy Norris McComas)

horse thieves, but friendly neighbors, he laughed apologetically and invited them in.

It was a snug little one-room cabin, furnished much like Rosie's own home. There were not enough chairs for all, so the host brought in some cottonwood blocks from the woodpile, and set them around the wall. Sitting on these, and on the bed, the neighbors talked of the cold winter, of the chances for a good crop the next summer, of the settlers who had gone back east, and of their own difficulties in trying to eke out the winter and feed their livestock on what the grasshoppers had left. From this, the conversation drifted to the subject of relief.

"Well, I don't know but we're all fools mebbe, to stick around here any longer," said one bearded little man, George Sizer.[2] "If this weather hangs on a few weeks longer, my horses will have to go. I'm on my last row of fodder now, and can't buy any more. Couldn't even if I had the money. Fink[3] is the only man who has any extra, and I guess it's all promised."

"Fink told me that old Preacher Forester[4] had been giving

The family of George and Eliza Sizer. (Courtesy the Historical Society of the Downs Carnegie Library)

away some relief money, and a lot of clothes and grub—mostly to his special friends, I guess," said George Graeber.

"Or else he kept the best," piped up his wife, from her corner on the bed. "One of the girls said they had enough good clothes to last the rest of their lives. I expect she talked a plenty; but they all do seem to wear nice clothes, since he came home from the East."

"Yes," chimed in Lydia Sizer,[5] "and I remember when he used to wear old ragged underclothes outside, instead of an overcoat, when he drove out in the winter. I remember one day over on Kill Creek, when he came into the meeting and began to take off the underclothes. Mary, you were there with me. Don't you remember how some of the people snickered?"

"You wouldn't snicker now, I guess," answered Mary Russell, from a precarious seat on a cottonwood block, "if you saw him and all the kids marching in with nice new shoes and coats and caps, the like of what you've never worn since you've been out here."

"That's just the trouble," exploded Jesse Bender indignantly. "The people that need help the worst ain't got any time to go around beggin', and they wouldn't get nothin' if they did. The best goes to the high mucky-mucks that already have more'n they need. I never heard about Colonel Altman havin' any great lot of money, and now he's back from Philadelphia and talkin' about buildin' a new hotel;[6] and old Bascom certainly never made any big fortune preachin', and now he's gettin' rock out for a big new house."[7]

"Yes," Mary replied, "and his girls have been bragging, too, about the fine clothes they've got, and about the coffee they have every morning, with sugar in it—all they want to put in."

"Didn't he get an inheritance from somewhere?" asked Henry, who always found it difficult to believe ill of any man. "He says he got some money from his folks in Pennsylvania."

"Grasshopper inheritance very likely," retorted Bender. "Nobody ever heard about him havin' any rich relatives before, did they? Why didn't they take care of him then, and not let him live the way he's been livin' down there—and him a'tryin' to preach?" Jesse laughed uproariously at the idea of Bascom's preaching, and from the way in which the contagion of his mirth spread, it was evident that many of those present had heard the Reverend Mr. Bascom preach the gospel.

"He's not the only one that's been doing well on grasshopper relief, anyhow," insisted Rosie, whose training precluded all criticism of preachers. "Didn't Jim McConkey[8] buy some cattle as soon as he got home from Boston? I remember when he went away, he said he was going to get some help for his neighbors, and when he got home he helped them by buying their cattle for next to nothing. I never heard that he had any rich relatives back in Iowa, either; and he certainly never earned any money by working."

"Nothin' but his mouth," rejoined Jesse, with emphasis, "and that won't work for Jim, no more than it is for Bascom; and Bascom's no worse than that preacher up on Oak Creek, that ran away with three hundred dollars, and the wife of one of the neighbors."

Two or three of the women began to look a little embarrassed at this rather wholesale denunciation of the spiritual guardians of the community, and Rosie was glad when the host suggested that the room be cleared for a few party games. The bed was knocked apart and carried out, and the chairs and cottonwood blocks were soon piled up outside the house. Only the stove was left in the room, because it was too cold to dispense with it, and because the hostess had to prepare refreshments while the rest were dancing.

When the room was cleared, half of the crowd took the floor, while the other half stood along the wall singing and occasionally clapping their hands or stamping their feet, to emphasize the rhythm. There was no musician in the crowd, and no musical instrument to play, but no musician was needed for such tuneful melodies as "Weevilly Wheat," "Old Dan Tucker," "Buffalo Gals," "Miller Boy," "Old Brass Wagon," "We'll All Go Down To Rousers," "My Father and Mother Were Irish," "Old Man's Dead," "London Bridge," "The Needle's Eye," and "Granny Will Your Dog Bite."

To the ringing music of their own voices, the young people danced up and down the little room until far into the night, when the hostess announced that, if they would go out and get their stools, she would give them something to eat. With merry yells of approbation they rushed out, and each came back with something to sit on. A lunch of fried cakes and coffee was passed around. The host had just butchered a hog that day and had lard for such an extravagance.

When the refreshments had been eaten, and the coats and shawls and mittens sorted out and distributed to their owners, goodbyes were said; and a happy bunch of merry-makers filed out of the house and down to the wagon, where the horses stood shivering in the cold north wind. The men had hitched up and were ready to go when Henry suddenly paused and exclaimed:

"Wait a minute. That won't do. We left that bed out in the yard. We'll have to help him put it up again."

"Sure we will," agreed Jesse, but the horses were rearing and plunging to go, so he added, "George, you drive the horses around, until we can get the bed back. The women can go with you, or they can come and help."

The women all chose to help, so while George drove the team around the house, the rest of the crowd went back and helped get the bed back into the house, nailed it together, straightened out the tick and covers, and carried the stumps out to the woodpile. With everything again in order, they climbed into the wagon, and were soon down across the river and rattling along the trail homeward. The full moon sailing high shed a cold light on the snow as they drove along, while occasionally from the hills to the north they could hear the lonely howl of a wolf, as it called to other wolves on other hills and along the creek. It seemed a wild and lonely world, after the light and warmth and merriment of the evening, and Rosie was glad when they reached home, and could start a fire in her own little stove. A trip to the stable proved that the horses were there, much to Henry's relief, for the country was still infested with horse thieves. Some of them, he had reason to believe, did not live far away, and might even know that he was away from home this night. After warming their hands and feet by the stove, they blew out the lamp and went to bed, where they were still sound asleep the next morning when the sun peeped above the banks of drifted snow.

Surprise parties were not the only amusement indulged in by Henry and Rosie this winter. There were literary societies, ciphering matches, spelling schools, and meetings whenever a preacher came along, and always there were visits with their special friends among the neighbors—sometimes they would go in the morning and stay all day. On New Year's night they went up to Voglers to watch the old year out, passing the time with visiting, singing, and prayer. The Voglers were very religious people.

At one of the literary society meetings, up at the Green Ridge School,[9] there was excitement enough to provide material for gossip for many a week. A young smart Aleck named Fate Norton[10] had once spoken disrespectfully of the teacher, Harriet Dedham,[11] saying that he could go out with her anytime he wanted to, and the teacher planned to punish him in a dignified way by giving him a horsewhipping before the assembled society.

The schoolhouse was packed to the very aisles, for word had gone out that the teacher was going to put on an interesting little play of her own. When young Norton walked up to the platform to make his speech, a sister of the teacher followed him up the aisle. A sudden hush fell upon the audience as she drew a revolver from under her coat and, pointing it at him, told him to "Stand there!" Just then the teacher, who was sitting behind him, rose from her chair and, pulling the whip from beneath a fold in her skirt, began to rain blows upon him.

For a brief moment pandemonium reigned. The young man grabbed the revolver and tried to wrest it away from the girl, firing it directly into the audience. Girls screamed and men shouted. Some stampeded for the door; others rushed to the front of the room to disarm the participants in the affair.

One man was slightly wounded, and young Norton's dignity was seriously ruffled, but otherwise the encounter brought no grave result, and the debate proceeded. It all turned out very happily. She was fined two dollars and a half for assault and battery, but some of the boys chipped in and paid the fine; and she did give him a whipping later. It was a bit too rough for Henry and Rosie though, and they did not go again. When nothing worse happened, the exercises were often disturbed by rowdies from town, or perhaps hoodlums cut the harnesses from some of the horses standing outside. Always there were men who spit tobacco juice all over the floor, much to Henry's disgust.

Spring broke early. The snow melted in the warm sunny days of the latter part of February, and the hungry cattle and horses that had so long stood hunched up on the south side of stables and straw stacks were able to get out and graze on the dried buffalo grass that had lain under the snow. When the grass began to turn green in March, Rosie was able to make butter to sell, so that they could buy some sugar and real coffee, and some cloth for baby clothes, for another baby was expected in June.

Chapter Twelve

The Great Menace Again

Following the combined disasters of grasshoppers and drouth came a hard winter, with snow in December and a howling blizzard early in January that drove the temperature far below zero, and covered the grass with snow. The cattle could no longer graze, and Henry started feeding them his precious fodder, anxiously wondering, as he hauled it up to the stable each morning, whether the few shocks that he and Rosie had saved would last until the snow was gone.

One bright morning in April, as Henry was drilling wheat in the corn sows, he noticed an extraordinary number of tiny white insects in the soil. He picked up a handful of the dirt and studied it for a minute, then scooped up another and looked at it for a long time. Finally he took off his hat, filled it with dirt, and turning his horses out of the corn rows, started off toward the house, slapping the lines with wholly unwonted vigor.

"What's the matter, Henry?" asked Rosie from the doorway, as he drove into the yard. "Why are you coming home so early?"

Without pausing to reply, Henry hurried up to the door with his hatful of dirt.

"Look there!" he exclaimed, holding the hat out toward her and turning the dirt over with his fingers. "What's that?"

Rosie looked intently at the contents of the hat. "Grasshoppers!" she cried, and picked up a handful of the dirt. There was no room for doubt. The insects had no wings yet but their resemblance to the pests of the summer before was unmistakable.

"The ground's full of them—just like that," said Henry. "George Graeber told me the other day that he had seen some in

94

his potato patch. There are enough in that dirt there to eat a whole field of wheat."

"Are you going to stop drilling?" asked Rosie.

"What's the use? Those things will be big enough to begin eating just about the time the wheat is up. They won't be able to fly yet, and they'll just sit there and eat. Perhaps they will come out later. Last year they came in July—the twenty-fifth, you remember."

Henry stood for some time looking vacantly down into the hat. "Another year like last, and—!" He never finished the sentence, but stood looking around at the little log cabin and the meager farmstead, then slowly poured the dirt out of his hat, slapped the dust out over his knee, and turned again to his drill. Rosie followed him out.

"Have you talked to any of the other neighbors, to see what they think?" she asked.

"None but George."

"What did he say?"

"He didn't say much about them. He's drilling some wheat himself, and so is Wilson and Steve. Chris said he was putting in ten acres. Most everybody seems to be going ahead."

"Well, why not finish what you've started, anyhow?"

"There's only a day's work left. I guess I might as well"; and Henry turned his horse toward the field. He was soon at work again, plodding back and forth behind the drill, with his eyes on the ground, occasionally stooping to pick up a handful of the soil and examine it as he walked along.

Fortunate it was that Henry finished his drilling that day, for early the next morning he was awakened by the sound of a steady drizzling rain. The wind had shifted to the northeast; and several days of cold rain and mist followed.

Unable to work in the fields, Henry pottered around with chores, oiled the harness, tacked new soles on his shoes, shelled some of the corn he had bought, and sat by the little cook stove reading the *Bottschafter*.[1] When the neighbors came for their mail they usually sat down by the fire long enough to dry their clothes and talk a while—mostly about the grasshoppers, and the probable effect of the cold and rain on the young that had hatched out in the soil.

After several days of cold, damp weather, the clouds parted and the sun beamed again upon the muddy fields. Henry rolled up his overalls and walked barefoot out to the wheat field to see whether the little grasshoppers had survived.

He dug up handfuls of mud here and there, and examined them carefully; then started for the house with a double handful from the end of the row. When he reached the house he bolted in without even cleaning his muddy feet.

"They're dead, I believe!" he exclaimed, holding his batch of mud out for Rosie to examine. "Look here! Come to the light!" He stepped over into the sunlight at the door, with Rosie following. "See that one right there? Isn't that dead? Pour a little water over it and see if it isn't."

Rosie brought a dipperful of water, and poured out enough to wash the insect clean. There was no sign of life.

"Let's see if warming it will revive it," she suggested. She put the mud in a pan and placed it in the oven a few minutes. When she took it out there was still no sign of life.

"They're dead, I believe," reiterated Henry, "and the wheat is sprouting. We may have some wheat yet, and maybe some corn. Maybe we won't have to go back to Holton, or Iowa, or anywhere. That was surely a great rain!" And Henry started for the stable in high spirits.

The whole world seemed to be in good spirits: the roosters that crowed from their stations on the straw pile, the hens that cackled their contented soliloquies as they scratched in the straw on the sunny side of the stable, the prairie chickens that drummed from across the prairie, and the meadow larks that sang everywhere. A few flies were out, buzzing cheerfully about in the warm sunshine. All nature seemed contented and friendly, as if anxious to make amends for the tragedies of the year that was past.

Chapter Thirteen

The Prairie Smiles
Once More

Lengthening days of warmth and sunshine followed each other, and in a short time the brown and gray of winter gave way to the brilliant light-green of early spring, on the prairie and wheat fields and along the roads. Tiny green leaves appeared on the hardy little cottonwoods that Henry and Rosie had planted the year before. This was a happy surprise. The trees had been stripped bare by the grasshoppers, and it had seemed doubtful if they would recover and flourish again; but the kindly spring sun and rain soon brought out crowns of shiny leaves that flashed green in the sun, and rustled in friendly companionship when the winds blew in from the south.

Early in June, Mary Bartsch helped usher the baby into the world, a little girl this time.[1] It was an awkward time to be in bed, and Rosie was soon at work again, hoeing in the garden. There was no one else to do it, and in the warm spring weather the call to gardening was irresistible.

The days of summer came and went, with the sun and heat and rains, rains that came whenever the winds threatened the growing crops. The wheat crop that Rosie helped to harvest early in July was one to be talked of for years afterward—forty bushels per acre, altogether two hundred bushels from Henry's five-acre field. Fifty bushels were enough for the year's bread and for seed, so there were one hundred and fifty bushels which could be hauled to Russell and sold.

The day after the harvesting was done, Henry and Rosie drove to Cawker City to celebrate the Fourth of July, taking their month-old baby for her first ride in the wagon. Everybody was there; and it seemed good to see the crowds of happy people jostling each other on the noisy board sidewalks, talking and laughing, boasting about the climate, the size of the wheat crop and the prospects for corn, and having a good time generally. Some of the men were somewhat the happier for having refreshed themselves from the whisky jug in Parker's store, and there were even a few fights, but generally the crowd was orderly enough. Most of the women were red-faced and tired from carrying their babies up and down the short block of sidewalks, and trying to keep them quiet during the "speaking," but they carried out their part in the celebration heroically, and even cheerfully. After many weeks in the drab little dugouts and cabins they were glad to get out and see the metropolis, as it throbbed with the life of the hopeful frontier.

When the wheat had been cut, the hot winds blew across the stubble for several days, and the corn leaves began to curl. Then, one day, when Henry went out to cultivate, he saw grasshoppers swarming over the corn—little grasshoppers, like those of the year before! There were not so many this time, yet enough to ruin the corn in a few days—the corn which had been so fine and green. In a fit of desperation, he pulled off his hat and started down the row, waving his hat about him and shouting, as if he might thus frighten away the devouring horde. Like a man bereft of reason, he circled about in the field, waving his hat and shouting his helpless imprecations, while his horses stood looking wonderingly at him; then, suddenly sensing the futility of it all, he stopped, walked slowly back to his horses, turned them out of the row, and started to the house to tell Rosie about it. With her baby in her arms Rosie went back to the field with him; and they deliberated a long while as to the best way to meet the impending disaster. They finally agreed that it would be best to wait a day or two, anyhow, before starting to cut the corn.

In the meantime, as the hot days followed each other, Rosie's thoughts turned back to another tragedy of the summer before, and she began to fret about the baby. She noted every symptom of illness with apprehension, worried when the baby seemed to be sleeping too long, even sometimes awakened her to make sure she was perfectly well.

But fortune was kind, this time. Most of the grasshoppers soon disappeared as mysteriously as they had come; and the rain came to cool the winds and save the corn. All that summer, rain came when it was needed, and the corn grew tall and strong and green—a dark, rich green. Great ears grew and bulged out of their inadequate husks and finally turned down with their growing weight, often two on a stalk. When the first frost came, early in October, the ears were made and matured, although they clung to mighty stalks which were still alive and green.

This year Henry tried planting wheat in the fall. There was much discussion of winter wheat, many of his neighbors claiming better yields and better quality than from spring wheat; so he planted a few acres before he started to husk the corn.

Henry and Rosie cut and shocked part of the corn, and husked the rest. Rosie helped, because she always wanted all farm work done promptly. She remembered years at her old home when her father had failed to get the corn out in time, and the snow and sleet had come and buried some of the ears until they molded.

Husking corn was not an easy task with a five-month-old baby to care for; but Rosie solved the problem by dressing the baby carefully in warm blankets, and placing her in the feed box on the rear of the wagon. Indeed, this was a most happy scheme, for the thump, thump of the big ears as they struck the bump board and rolled back into the wagon provided excellent diversion for little Laura. When she tired of this, Rosie put ears of red and yellow corn in the box with her, and she played contentedly for hours at a time as they moved slowly back and forth across the field. When Laura got hungry, dinner was there too, and Rosie would sit down in the corn row and let her nurse.

Working together in this way, Henry and Rosie had the corn out before Thanksgiving, and its wealth of red and yellow and mottled ears piled high in the crib that Henry had built of poles and saplings. How rich and fine it looked, too—feed for the stock and chickens as well as for themselves; and some could be sold to buy shoes and stockings! A few weeks later, Henry hauled up from the river several loads of wood that he had cut—generous warmth in the little cabin for the rest of the winter, and fuel for cooking all of the next summer. How different the world seemed after only one short year! Even the hurt of little Albert's death was slowly healing as time passed and as little Laura grew more and more into their hearts and lives.

The mild sunny days of the prairie winter followed each other, until long past Christmas, even after New Year's Day; and in late February the flies were buzzing around in the sun on the south side of the cabin, confident that the winter was over. During these fair days Henry built a fence around a part of his pasture land, using smooth wire and cottonwood posts he had cut on the river. When the fence was finished, he hauled two loads of wheat to Russell, and bought a hand corn planter, a cultivator, a drill, a rake,[2] and some sugar, soap, kerosene and Arbuckle's coffee. A little later he traded some potatoes for a clock.

The mild days of winter were followed by milder days of spring. Early in April Henry and Rosie set out a quarter of a mile of hedge and a large patch of wild plums, getting the little plants up in the hills where the land had not yet been homesteaded. Rosie helped plant the corn that spring, using the new hand corn planter. It was a tiring job for her, one that left her with aching shoulders for days; but nothing seemed really hard when the future seemed so full of promise.

Not all was to be happiness, for one day in May brother Chris came over to tell Rosie that he had traded his claim for a herd of cattle, and was going to move back to his old home in Eastern Kansas.[3] It was sad news for Rosie, for it had always been a great comfort to have one of her own people near.

A few weeks later several of the family came out in the wagon to help Chris move—mother, brother George, and sister Jennie.[4] His cupboard Chris gave to Rosie, and on June fifth he loaded the rest of the movable goods onto the two wagons and started on his two hundred-mile journey, mother driving one wagon, his wife Louisa the other, and George and Chris and Jennie driving the cattle. Rosie felt so lonely as she waved goodbye to them. Two weeks later she learned that in crossing a creek her mother had fallen from the seat, and the heavily loaded wagon had run over her, causing injuries from which she was destined to suffer for years, and never to recover entirely.

Another summer of timely rains and good crops followed, and in the fall the crib was again piled high with its treasure of red and yellow corn. Rosie again helped with the husking and luckily, as she said, was able to finish the job a week before her third child was born.

The day after the last load of corn was hauled out of the field, Rosie was doing the washing, when she began to feel very unwell. After calling Henry in from the stable she lay down on the bed for a rest.

"I'm afraid you will have to wring those clothes out, and then go for Mary," she said apologetically, as Henry entered the door.

"Hadn't I better get Mary first?" asked Henry, glancing at the tub of clothes. "Oh, no. There's no hurry, and the water will get cold. Just wring the clothes out and hang them on the line. I guess that last pile of overalls will have to wait until—until afterward. It's too bad too. I had the water hot, such nice hot water," said Rosie in a tone of dejection. Wasting firewood in heating the water over again was a sin that she usually avoided.

Henry wrung the water out of the clothes and went out to hang them up. Somewhat awkward at such work, he was gone some time; and when he came back into the house there was Rosie, pouring the hot water into the tub, with the evident intention of finishing the washing!

"Better not do that, Rosie," he urged. He reached out to take the kettle from her, but she waved him away.

"I guess I'm all right. It must have been a false alarm. Anyhow you can go to your work, and I'll finish this washing,"

Rosie finished the washing, and that afternoon she ironed. The next day she baked a great boiler-full of bread. When her time was come, and Mary Bartsch had to be called, everything was in order—wood was stacked behind the stove, the floor scrubbed clean, the clothes ironed and neatly piled away in place, and a little pile of baby clothes lay on the foot of the bed. Out by the well she had a barrel of well water "breaking" in wood ashes, so that there would be soft water for use until she could be about again. The baby was a big boy, and he grew healthy and fat and strong.[5] A few weeks after he was born, Henry took more wheat to Russell, and got ninety-five cents a bushel—enough altogether to buy a mower,[6] which he needed badly.

It seemed evident that the climate was changing, and that dry summers like that grasshopper year would not likely come again. The Solomon River and the creeks flowed deeper and more steadily than ever before, and fish were plentiful, even in the smaller creeks.

The country was booming. Four hundred and fifty new settlers filed on the last tillable lands in the county. A real estate office established in Osborne was soon doing a thriving business in sales, relinquishments, and doubtless in less ethical transactions. A few men went up to the Black Hills, where a gold strike was reported, but those who stayed were buoyantly hopeful about the country. Day after day a stream of covered wagons moved westward, into Rooks, Phillips, Graham and Norton counties. Almost every night movers built their campfires along the road by the cottonwood grove, and came in to get milk or eggs or something from Rosie. A few of the neighbors built new houses or barns, and many of them began hopeful planting of shade and fruit trees, and eager testing of various new crops. Hopeful of a coming silk industry, a man at Osborne put out two hundred mulberry trees—the silk worms were to come later. A company was promoted to make salt from the water of the Great Spirit Spring, beyond Cawker, and there were reports of coal discoveries in several places in the country.[7] The probable extension of the railroad westward from Waterville was a favorite theme for talk and for editorials in the Osborne paper, and there were even rumors that this had been definitely decided upon; while the settlers up north in Smith County held meetings to discuss the question of voting bonds to help build the Rock Island westward. In the meantime, as a hint of the character of the politics at Topeka, the Santa Fe was giving the legislature a free trip to Colorado.

The editor of the Osborne *Farmer* was impressed by the speed and stress of the life of the time: "We are living in a fast age. We have fast women, fast men and fast farmers. . . . We have all the modern improvements it seems necessary to have to do fast work; but brains are needed to make farming a success in such an age as ours." This, in eighteen seventy-seven!

Chapter Fourteen

The New House, and a Trip Back Home

When Henry had hauled another load of wheat and two loads of corn to Russell, he had a large wallet of greenbacks, which he hid in a cranny in the cabin wall until they should decide how to spend it—there was no bank near. There were many hours of planning for the use of this money, and many schemes were brought up as Rosie and Henry talked over the dinner dishes. Henry needed another team, to break more of his grass land. Frank and Sam were getting old and now moved more slowly each year. Rosie approved the idea of another team, but she also saw that, with two babies growing into childhood—and perhaps others would follow—the little one-room cabin would soon be crowded. Indeed it was already crowded, a fearful congestion of boxes, firewood, dishes, tubs, pots, buckets, pans, kettles, garden and carpenter tools, flower plants, garden seeds, nails, patent medicines, sacks and cans of flour, corn meal and other foods, carefully treasured newspapers, calendars, pictures cut from advertisements, Sunday clothes and baby clothes.

Rosie did her best. She kept everything as neat as anyone could, but there was no way of keeping all this stuff in a fifteen by eighteen room without crowding, and without some order. The big bed occupied a fair share of the floor space, and the baby bed covered half as much more. Several sacks of flour took one corner, the wash pan, a bucket of water and a towel another, the stove a third, and the opening of the door spoiled the only remaining corner. There was left a space of perhaps eight by ten feet which had to serve for cooking, washing and ironing, dining, entertainment of visitors, and for the postoffice. In warm weather, she did much of her work out of doors. When the weather permitted, she washed out in the yard, on the shady side of the cabin, and the wash pan was moved out by the steps; but even so, there was surely need of more room, and Rosie ventured to hope that, after the necessary team horses had been bought, there might be enough money left for an addition to the house, and a trip back to see her mother, who was still in bed from her injuries.

After many days of planning, a happy solution of the problem was worked out. Rosie would send part of the money to her father, and ask him to buy two young colts. These would be able to do farm work in two or three years, and, since they could be bought for much less than grown horses, there would be enough money left to build an addition to the house. The colts would have to be brought out from Holton, so a trip down there would be a necessity and not a luxury; and a load of wheat or flour could be taken, saving a sixty-mile drive to Russell. It seemed good to be able to plan so much, all in one year. They decided to wait until fall to take the trip home, but Rosie sent the money for the colts immediately, and the house plans were soon made.

The new addition was to be of stone. Cottonwood lumber would not do because it warped so badly. Pine boards would have to be hauled from Russell and would be entirely too expensive. Logs had become scarcer and more expensive, and logs harbored bedbugs. Rosie hated bedbugs. Stone seemed the best material and, since Henry could help to quarry it, not too expensive. There were quarries of soft white limestone in the hills, where it could be obtained with little trouble, and Henry was soon at work with drill, feather and wedge, crowbar and stone axe. Every noon and every evening he came home with a load of stone, which he piled up around the cabin.

The new house was to be one room, built near enough to the old so the two could be joined by a hall, making a two-room house.

Some supplies were hauled from Greenleaf, ninety miles east—the Central Branch Railroad had now been built that far west.[1] Henry drove down and got a load of planks and shingles, windows and doors, hinges and nails, as the return load when he took some wheat to market. "Native lime"—a sticky mud of clay and sand—was to be used for mortar, except for pointing, and for that, real lime was brought from Russell.

There was to be no ceiling in the house, but for five cents a yard Henry bought a bolt of muslin to tack onto the rafters. In his generous enthusiasm he also bought Rosie some blue calico for a dress; but Rosie did not look well in blue, and when one of the Bartsch girls expressed a great admiration for the cloth, Rosie traded it to her for two weeks' use of her sewing machine.

The building of the new house meant two extra hands to be housed and boarded, one to do the stone work and another to work in the field, for Henry had to work on the house. So it was a busy season for Rosie, with all the baking, cooking and washing, and the care of the babies that were growing daily more active and harder to look after. She even had to superintend the building of the house, when Henry was gone. The stone mason often found her watchful eyes upon him when he rested too long on the job. He was getting seventy-five cents a day, and Rosie thought he ought to work hard for such wages.

Early in May the house was done. How fine it looked, with its smooth white walls, its white plaster pointing, yellow shingle roof, and two large windows—double windows, that could be opened at top or bottom! Two doors it had, one opening into the log cabin, the other facing the road; and the floor was of soft pine, grooved and tongued and fitted tight. Such a floor would seem warm, after the rough, ill-fitting cottonwood floor of the old house. It was a luxurious home now, and with boundless happiness and enthusiasm Rosie and Henry moved part of their furniture, including the bed and chairs, into the new room. Little Laura sensed the importance of the event and ran from one room to the other, carrying shoes or sticks of wood or whatever she could pick up, in a child-like desire to be helpful and join in the general commotion. Even Billy seemed to understand that it was a great day, and crowed with delight when he was laid on the bed in the new room. Soon after they moved in, Henry bought several yards of mosquito netting for the windows, but the wind soon whipped it to shreds. Rosie always kept one piece of it, though, to throw over the baby when he was asleep.

A few weeks later another great wheat crop was harvested. Henry had two very painful felons on his hand and could not stack the wheat, and the hired hand botched the job so that the rain soaked into the stacks, spoiling some of the grain. Yet there was enough sound wheat to fill the bin that Henry built in a corner of the new house, after one load had been hauled to Russell. The price was nearly a dollar a bushel—it was the time of the Russian-Turkish War[2]—and the one load of wheat brought enough money to buy several needed articles, including a new bed to replace the cottonwood bed, a bed with springs.

In September, after he had the wheat sown, Henry loaded his wagon with flour that he had ground at the mill, and he and Rosie started to Holton to get their colts, hoping to make something on the flour to pay part of the cost of their trip. Jake Hunker was to care for the stock while they were gone, and in return for this, Henry was to bring back a horse for him too.

They were on the road only two or three days when they saw that the railroad was coming westward. Surveying parties were at work, grading gangs busy, new boom towns were being laid out, where lots were advertised for sale—the railroad company got half the land in every town it went through. At Clyde they saw rails being laid, and a little farther on locomotives were puffing back and forth. The prospect of a railroad out home and of a town nearby was cheering and, with the perfect fall weather, made their trip a pleasant one.

On their first drive along this road, four years before, they had camped by the road; but this time, with two little children—the youngest only ten months old—they usually slept in the houses of settlers, spreading a blanket or two on the floor, and covering themselves with another. Laura slept at their feet, Billy between them, and they managed to keep warm even on the chilliest nights.

They spent nearly two weeks visiting with friends and relatives, so busy every day that the time slipped by before they realized it. Rosie's family were getting along very well indeed. They had completed payments on the home place and had just bought another quarter section. They had a new barn and a cattle shed, several new farm implements standing in the yard, and more cattle than Rosie had ever seen on the place. Her brothers and sisters seemed much older, and wore better clothes than they had ever worn when she was at home.

A pleasant two weeks it was, but the frosty days of October reminded them that the corn had yet to be husked, so they loaded

Jake and Mary Hunker. (Courtesy the Historical Society of the Downs Carnegie Library)

the wagon with apples, got their colts and the horse for Jake Hunker, and started home, with gifts from the home folks—two pictures from Mother, and a glass water pitcher from Chris and Louisa. In the wagon they also put a bunch of little maple trees, wrapped carefully in wet sacks. Henry and Rosie were always trying out new kinds of trees and plants at their new home.

The trip home seemed long and tiresome. Neither of the colts would lead behind the wagon, so either Henry or Rosie had to walk all the time and lead them, while the other drove the team. They were glad when they at last looked down upon the little cabin from the top of Bender's Hill.[3]

When they got home they stored the apples in the cellar—all that they did not give to the neighbors—and buried the roots of the little maples for the winter. Henry worked for a week repairing the braces and supports in the stable, and banking it with fresh straw. It was a mild and pleasant winter. Christmas Day found him husking corn in his shirt sleeves, and by New Year's Day the husking was done, without Rosie's help.

The next spring Henry proved up on his claim, and got his patent—with the signature of President Hayes on it.[4] He might have done this two or three years earlier but delayed as long as he could, because when he got his title he had to begin paying taxes on his land.

So many fine things could be had after two good years! Henry bought a new wooden harrow[5], to take the place of the brush harrow he had been using, and a wheat drill—broadcasting did not make an even stand. He bought a "cow's worth" of apple trees, and set them out west of the house. They grew for a while, but before the end of the summer, all but one had died. He also set out some choke cherry trees, and more plum trees; and these thrived much better. Later he traded another cow—a breachy cow that he could not keep in the pasture—for a sewing machine for Rosie.[6] Rosie had long wanted a sewing machine, for hand sewing was slow and tedious, and she had a great deal of sewing to do. She made all her own clothes, Henry's overalls, shirts, jackets and mittens, and all the children's clothing. Often she sat and stitched away far into the night to get her sewing done.

It had been impossible to rent or borrow a sewing machine. The Bartsches had the only one in the neighborhood, and it was about worn out. Once, when Rosie was making a dress with bias folds on the skirt, Henry suggested that she let him take the dress up to Mary Bartsch to have Mary sew the bias pieces on with her machine. Rosie readily assented, but the machine puckered the folds so badly that the dress was hardly fit to wear. She paid fifty cents for the work, too—a cent a yard for the stitching.

Rosie was delighted with her machine, and soon had neat little piles of clothing made for the children and Henry, and a new dress for herself; but she presently found that the machine was a nuisance in one respect. It was the only good one in the neighborhood, and neighbors from every direction brought their sewing to her. Most of them did not know how to operate the machine, so she found it best to do the work herself. Some of them offered to wash dishes or do other work for her in return, and of course some of them had done her many a kindly turn, but it was often inconvenient to drop her work and do someone else's sewing. The sewing machine was in a real sense a community institution.

Horse thieves were still active in the community. The Oldacre boys had moved out to Wyoming, but the Miller boys were suspected of several thefts, and a posse of men caught them and hung them to a tree, but let them down before they were dead, with a warning that they should leave the country. Instead of doing so, the victims sued the members of the posse for assault with intent to kill, and they were all convicted and fined heavily—realizing on the witness-stand, for the first time, that they had no proof that the Miller boys were really guilty.[7] With his usual preference for orderly procedure, Henry had refused to go with them.

Chapter Fifteen

Dangers of Pioneering

Rosie always thought the children would be less trouble when they could walk and play by themselves; but when they began to run about in the yard she found a new reason for anxiety. There were still a great many rattlesnakes about. She herself killed several in the yard and garden, and a few people in the neighborhood, mostly children, were bitten. One little girl was bitten while picking wild currants, and was later found down in the creek bed, bathing the wound in the mud. She had torn her clothes almost off in her agony and died a few hours after she was found. One of the Graeber girls was bitten by a rattler when she went down into the cellar after potatoes; but her parents gave her whisky, then cut open the breast of a live chicken and put that on the wound, and after days of suffering she recovered.

Henry and Rosie were seldom troubled with snakes in their own house, but they once had a rather embarrassing experience at one of the neighbors'. One Sunday they went up to the Rachowitzs for dinner.[1] The Rachowitzs, who were from Bohemia, lived a couple of miles up on Dry Creek, in a very primitive dugout—one with a sod roof, resting on straw, which was in turn supported by small willow switches laid across the beams. Just as they sat down to dinner, there was a rustling above in the straw, and a big bull snake plumped down onto the table. It had evidently been chasing a mouse, and had worked up too much momentum.

Poor Minnie Rachowitz surely had a hard life. Her husband was not very well, and she had to do much of the farm work, as well as her own. When they needed a well, she did the digging, while her husband pulled the dirt up. When she had butter and eggs to sell, she carried them to Cawker, twelve miles away, for her husband had no team to drive; and with all her other work, she kept her little dugout neat and clean—as neat and clean as any dugout could be kept. She lived bravely, and even preserved a rough sense of humor through all her hardships. Once her neighbor Higginbotham's bull invaded her premises and got her cow with calf; and Higginbotham tried to collect a service charge for it.

"Why I pay that yet?" she demanded of Rosie one day when Rosie was there visiting. "Why I pay that, when I no ask him over? It was anyway no work for Higginbotham."[2]

Another dooryard pest proved almost worse than rattlesnakes. One day Rosie went down to the corn field to get roasting ears for supper, leaving Billy in Laura's care. She had snapped half a dozen ears and was looking about for more to fill her apron, when she heard the baby crying as if in great distress. Her first impulse was to hurry back to the house, but on second thought she decided to finish her task first. The cries of the baby continued though, louder and more insistent and piteous. She finally snapped off a few more of the most accessible ears and started on a run to the house.

As she emerged from the corn field and rounded the stable, she saw the horrible truth. The baby had crawled into an ant heap! There was a large red ant heap only a few feet from the door, which she had repeatedly dug up in an effort to drive the dangerous pests away; and there he was in the hole she had dug, covered with the poisonous insects—body and neck and arms and hands and feet and legs, and even his face, screaming and waving his hands helplessly in the air!

Dropping her roasting ears, she seized him and ran into the house, tearing off his clothes as she went. Her first impulse was to pick the ants off with her fingers, but this was slow; and often she succeeded only in pulling them in two, leaving the heads with the tenacious mandibles fastened in the child's soft flesh. In a sudden inspiration she grabbed the butcher knife and began scraping them off with that, as fast as the baby's incessant and spasmodic motions permitted. Even when she had them all off, many of the poisonous pincers still remained in the child's flesh, and she tried to pick them out with a needle, but without much success. His screams changed to convulsive sobs as she worked, and his arms and legs and hands and neck swelled to grotesque proportions.

Henry came in from the fields, and Rosie left the baby a moment to call him. From her voice he sensed the seriousness of the occasion, and ran to the house, leaving his team standing by the stable.

"What's the matter?" he asked, as he entered.

"Ants! He crawled into the ant heap! He was covered when I got back!" Rosie picked up the baby and showed Henry his swollen arms and legs and body.

"Mud! Put mud on him, mud and bluing!" Henry seized the water bucket and a bottle of bluing from the shelf and ran into the yard. In a moment he was back, with a mixture which he spread thick over the child's body and arms and legs.

But there was no relief for the tortured infant, who sobbed and cried in his misery. Supper time came, but no one thought of supper. Night came, and the lamp was lighted; but there was no cessation of the piteous crying. Henry went out to do the chores, and when he came back, he was greeted by the same plaintive cries, only weaker; and the baby no longer waved his arms about. Rosie was bending over him, dampening the mud with a wet rag. She turned when she heard Henry's step at the door.

"Henry, I'm afraid we better have the doctor. This isn't doing any good. Just look at those legs!" Rosie wiped the mud from one leg, to show how swollen it was. "He's been crying since five o'clock."

Henry remembered a time when he had started for the doctor too late. Yet a ride to Cawker City would take much of the night, and perhaps the doctor would not come so far anyhow. It was not even certain that the doctor would know any more than any one else. He was turning all this over in his mind when he heard a step outside and a rap at the open door.

"Hello, Henry! What's the trouble? Baby not so well?" It was Higginbotham, the local jack-of-all-trades, who had come to get his mail. John Higginbotham lived a mile north. He was a doctor, dentist, preacher, druggist, tailor, lawyer, politician, and perhaps also something of a farmer, although most of his farming was done by his wife and children. He was handsome and well-mannered in public, with a gift of speech which could hardly have been used to full advantage on the horses in the field; and his various talents often proved useful to Henry and Rosie, as to others in the vicinity.

"Hello, John! Come in." There was no mistaking the look of relief in Henry's face at the sight of his neighbor, or the cordiality of his greeting. "Come and see this baby. Crawled into an ant heap this afternoon, and they chewed him up like that. Do you think Doc Johnson could help him? I was just going to get him."

Higginbotham stooped over the bed and examined the crying child carefully.

"What's the mud for?" he asked.

"To draw the poison out," answered Henry.

"All right. But haven't you any good salve to put on now— Smith's Arnica Salve, or something like that?"

Henry stepped to the medicine shelf and took out several boxes of salve. John looked them over and after smelling them carefully selected one.

"There, that ought to do. No use going for a doctor. All he'd do would be to give you some salve and charge you fifty cents for it. Just wash that mud off and put this on. He'll be all right in the morning."

Higginbotham started to go, but turned at the door. "Oh, I forgot my mail. Is there any here for me, or for Bartsch?"

While Rosie washed the mud off, Henry sorted out the letters and gave them to his neighbor, who departed, happy with the prospect of news from back east. The salve was applied liberally and the baby put back on the bed. His cries changed to a plaintive moan, which gradually grew weaker and, about ten o'clock, he went to sleep. Rosie watched him for a while, but when she saw that his breathing was regular, she finally got supper and then went to bed—to dream of ants crawling on her arms.

One fall day, Rosie drove the wagon with the two young colts to Bartsch's, two miles up the creek, to get a barrel of molasses, taking the two children with her. On the way home she took a short cut across the prairie, which led her to a gate that she must open to get out to the main road. When she had driven the horses through, she hesitated a moment, trying to figure out how she could get the gate closed without leaving them. It occurred to her that she might turn the wagon around and hold the reins while she closed the gate; but the horses were standing quietly, and it hardly seemed necessary to go to so much trouble. So she pulled the lines tight, tied them to the front standard, and with an anxious eye on the horses, ran back to the gate. She had scarcely reached it when they started off on a gallop.[3] She ran after them, crying "Whoa" at the top of her voice; but they sensed her fright and helplessness and tore down the road at top speed, the wagon rattling, the molasses barrel bouncing from side to side, and the children screaming in their fright.

Henry and the hired hand had come in from the field, and were eating supper. Knowing she might get home late, Rosie had set a cold supper on the table for them. "She's certainly driving like a prairie fire," said Henry, as he heard the wagon rattling in the distance.

"Sounds like Johnny Overton—when he's got something besides molasses on board," said the other.[4]

As the horses approached, the screams of the children were audible above the rattle of the wagon.

"A runaway!" cried Henry, dashing out of the door just in time to see the horses turning the corner into the lane.

By a miracle the molasses barrel did not upset and crush the children sitting on the floor of the wagon. The horses ran to the stable and stopped.

"Get the children!" Henry shouted, and started down the road after Rosie, uncertain what might have befallen her. He saw her a quarter of a mile away, running as fast as her long skirts would permit. When she came closer he shouted: "All right! Children all right!" Hearing the good news, she stopped and panted until he reached her.

The children were unharmed, although a bucket of molasses skimmings had upset in the wagon, smearing them from head to foot. Rosie did not so much mind washing them as she regretted the loss of the skimmings, which she had expected to use in making vinegar.

Henry and Rosie were never bothered much by the Indians, although occasional stragglers came through the country, begging or pilfering.[5] Rosie was always afraid of them, especially if they came when Henry was away from home; and the children were frightened out of their wits at the sight of an Indian.

One day when Henry and Rosie had gone to Cawker City,

leaving Laura and Billy in the charge of Frank Hagel, a big buck Indian came along begging for something to eat. Frank had a great deal of sympathy for the Indians, and invited the fellow in to have dinner, although the children were so frightened that they both crawled under the bed and refused to come out until he was gone. So frightened were the children that they became sick, and vomited on the floor, much to Frank's disgust. When Rosie got home she scolded him roundly for feeding her scanty supplies to an Indian, and for giving the children such a scare; but when another red man came not long afterward, Rosie treated him generously.

One thing Henry never had to fear. He never had to be concerned about claim jumpers. After Jesse Bender chased poor old Vietz off his claim on the creek, there was no threat of lawlessness in the immediate neighborhood.

Across the river there were several cases of claim jumping and of violence. A poor widow who had filed on a claim on the river and was living with her daughter in a dugout there was set upon one day and beaten severely by a ruffian who wanted her claim. She recognized him and had him arrested; but the fine imposed by the judge—five dollars and costs—hardly seemed calculated to discourage this form of banditry.

One day the whole neighborhood was thrown into wild excitement by the news that a young German named Kutchell, living two miles down the river, had been found murdered near his dugout.[6] Henry mounted Sam and rode down to the scene of the murder. There were dozens of people there, walking back and forth from the dugout to the place where the body had been found, examining clues and footprints—and unwittingly making other footprints to confuse the sheriff—standing about in groups, discussing the question of the probable perpetrator of the deed. One side of the dugout had been blown out, apparently by an explosion in the stove. A wagon thimble was found in the debris, and a bloody scythe blade a short distance away. The body of the dead man had been found a hundred yards from the dugout, with gunshot wounds in the head and back, and the head beaten into the soft earth.

Suspicion immediately pointed to a well-to-do neighbor named Knox, who had contested Kutchell's claim.[7] The Land Department had decided in favor of Kutchell, but Knox had still insisted that Kutchell was jumping his claim and had made various threats against him. A few hours after the murder, the sheriff found Knox's hired man—Soules—with bloody clothes, a black eye, and one finger cut off.[8] Soules explained that he had fallen and hurt his eye, and that he had got blood on his clothes in killing a lamb; but he was jailed for further questioning. The next day a neighbor, Tom Kenton, was arrested, charged with complicity in the crime; and he turned state's evidence and told his story of the murder.[9]

When the evidence was all pieced together, it showed a most brutal murder of Kutchell by four men—Knox, his son Charlie,[10] the hired man Soules, and Kenton, who dropped a wagon thimble filled with gunpowder down the chimney, while the other three waited in hiding with their guns. The explosion blew the door open, and Kutchell ran out, grabbing a scythe blade as he ran. Soules shot but missed. He seized Kutchell, but Kutchell, who was a powerful man, knocked him down with his fist. Fearing to shoot, lest they kill their accomplice in the dark, the other three men came to his rescue with fists and clubbed guns; but for a while Kutchell wielded his scythe blade with such desperation as to hold them all off, cutting his own fingers to the bone while doing so. Seeing the hopelessness of this contest, Kutchell dropped his scythe and ran, but had gone only a short distance when the Knoxes shot him in the back and head. He dropped, and overtaking him they battered his head into the ground with their gunstocks. Then they went home and arranged a story to tell the public if suspicion should point their way, as they knew it probably would.

At the trial, Knox, who was the superintendent of one of the Sunday schools and an active church worker, called upon God to witness his innocence; but probably his half dozen lawyers were his main reliance. They got him off with a twenty-five year sentence, and seven years later Governor Martin—for reasons which will never be known—set him free.[11] His son got fifteen years and was also out in a few years, while the hired man served only two years. The trial was not over when the Secretary of the Interior handed down a decision reversing the local land office and giving the claim back to Knox. The murder had been for nothing.

With medical science still primitive, and most of the doctors poorly trained, certain diseases presented a serious danger. Not a few of the neighbors, down along the creek and river, were troubled with malaria during the early years, but this was not very serious; and Henry's claim, without any stream or stagnant water, seemed to be free from malaria. There were other diseases, however—especially diphtheria and typhoid fever—that occasionally took a sad toll of life; and Henry and Rosie dreaded them. When Alpha Neville died of typhoid fever, her mother, who had seen her suffer so long, never entirely recovered her mind.[12] Rosie helped line the coffin.

Chapter Sixteen

Henry Signs a Note

One evening, as Henry was sitting on the step of the old log house, watching a rain cloud scatter in the west, a man rode into the yard on an underfed little roan pony, dismounted, tied his pony to the hitching post, and came up to the house. Henry recognized Jake Hardtarfer, one of the neighbors living across the river.[1] He knew little about him, except that Jake seemed a very plausible and likable fellow.

"How are you, Jake?" Henry greeted him cordially, as he greeted everyone. "Come in."

"No, thank you, Henry. No, thank you. Thank you very much. This is fine right here"; and he sat down on the other end of the step. His manner was friendly and ingratiating. "Well, how are all the folks, Henry?"

"All well. And how's your own?" Henry sat down again.

"Oh, tolerable. Tolerable only, but I guess it's no use complaining as long as we can worry along. The best we can do is the best we can do, as the saying is."

"Any of the folks sick?"

"Oh, no, Henry, not sick, not at all. But it's hard to do much farming out here in this country without a team."

"Pretty hard, I should say. I thought you were going to buy Willis Blair's team.[2] Graeber told me something like that."

Jake pulled a chunk of tobacco out of his hip pocket and offered it to Henry, who refused with thanks.

"Don't chew, Henry?" Jake took a generous bite, and rolled it appreciatively in his mouth. "It's one thing to talk about buying a team these days, and another to find the money. You know how

118

that is, Henry. A bird in the hand is worth two in the bush, as the saying is."

"Worth a dozen, generally."

"You're just right, Henry. You know how tight everything is. Unless a man has the cash right in hand, nobody will look at him." Jake squirted a stream of tobacco juice in the general direction of the stable, but it fell short a yard or two. Apparently relieved, he continued:

"It's hard, Henry, to get a start without a team, and it's hard to get a team without a start. I tell you it's a hard proposition."

"If I could just get a little backing for a while, it would all go along nicely," Jake resumed; "but there's the rub, Henry! There's the whole difficulty. If I could just get some good neighbor to stand behind me for a while, till I could get a start. I could make it fine, just fine."

At this Henry began to see a little more light, but he still did not quite grasp the purpose of Jake's visit. His reply was a non-committal: "The start's the thing, that's true enough." Then he added: "I remember how hard it was to raise the money for my team back in Iowa."

"Yes, Henry, you've been through it, and you know how hard it is; and, Henry, I wonder if you would mind signing my note, just for the money for a team. I can pay it off before long, and then I'll have a team to work with; and I can get something done. And I would surely appreciate your help, if any man ever did."

The appeal to Henry's own hard experience was shrewd, and it struck him where he carried no armor. An opportunity to do a generous and neighborly act was always hard for him to resist, and without any further inquiry, he replied:

"Oh, I suppose I might do that much for a neighbor." Jake produced a note for two hundred dollars, and Henry took it into the kitchen, signed it, and brought it back, without a trace of misgiving in his mind.

"Thank you, Henry. That's certainly a great accommodation," said Jake. He took the note, folded it into his wallet, and started off to his horse.

"I'm afraid, Henry, that our rain is blowing over," he called out, as he mounted his pony.

Jake Hardtarfer. (Courtesy the Historical Society of the Downs Carnegie Library)

"Yes, it looks pretty thin there now," replied Henry, and turned back into the house.

A moment later, Rosie came hurrying in from the garden, carrying the hoe in one hand and the baby in the other. The baby had been playing at the end of the row while she worked. She leaned the hoe up against the door casing, set the baby on the bed, and turned to the stove.

"I'm afraid supper will be late," she exclaimed, as she reached into the wood box for cobs to start a fire with; "but I wanted to finish that row of tomatoes."

The cobs blazed up, and she threw several cow chips into the flames.

"Who was that just rode away?"

"Oh, that was Jake Hardtarfer."

"Hardtarfer? What was he looking for?" Rosie often showed

an uncanny insight into the motives of people. "I suppose he wanted to borrow the team, or the wagon, or something!"

Henry had enjoyed a warm glow of satisfaction in his act of neighborly kindness, but there was something in Rosie's question, and in her manner, which sent a chill over him. He would have been glad to escape any further discussion of the matter; and his answer was somewhat equivocal: "Oh, no, he was just telling me some of his troubles."

"What troubles does he think he's got!" Rosie was not to be diverted.

"He hasn't any horses yet, and I guess it's pretty hard, farming without a team."

"Oh, yes; but don't you think you've got to help him. He can get help from his own people, and his own neighbors. There are a lot of people over there that can loan him horses and stuff easier than you can." Rosie had had experience with Henry's loans to the neighbors.

"He didn't want to borrow anything. He just wanted me to help him get a team—just wanted me to go on his note to buy a team from Willis Blair."

"Go on his note!" Rosie dropped the stove lid with a clatter. "You didn't sign his note, did you?"

"Oh, surely he's good for two hundred dollars, as long as he has the horses." Henry's voice lacked every trace of enthusiasm. He had not the heart to answer her question directly. How different his neighborly kindness looked now!

"He's good for nothing, I'm afraid. Oh, dear me! You're in for it now! I'll bet you'll have to stick for it. It'll take every cent we can scrape up for the next two years to pay that. I won't pay it. He's no good, or he wouldn't have to come all the way over here to get somebody to help him. And you get no thanks for it, I'll just bet. You'll only get hard feelings for all your trouble and worry and expense. I just know how that will be, because it always turns out that way. When it's all over, you've lost your money, and you'll have to work yourself crooked making it back, and he won't even speak to you. Likely as not, none of his people will either."

Whenever Rosie was particularly discouraged, she worked with a desperate, driving energy that made tasks melt before her;

and as she talked, the pans and kettles and skillets clattered to their places, and supper was soon cooking on the stove.

"Why didn't he go to Graeber!" she asked suddenly, turning from the stove for an instant. Before Henry could answer, she continued: "George knew him back in Pennsylvania, and his people too. Why didn't he get George, or Mrs. Miller, or John Hege, or some of the Stegimans?[3] They all knew him before he came here. Oh, I'm afraid we're stuck for it sure enough." Tears came to Rosie's eyes as she pictured the trouble ahead.

Henry sat by the table in silent dejection as Rosie outlined the position in which his mistaken generosity had placed them. He had thought of himself as doing a neighborly act, but now it seemed clear that he had only piled up a mountain of trouble for himself and for Rosie. It had happened thus so often. Henry could never say "no" to anyone, friend or stranger, worthy or unworthy; and it was something he was never to learn. His weakness in this respect was to bring troubles that would follow him to the very grave.

When Rosie saw his utter dejection, her heart softened, and she tried hard to appear more cheerful.

"Well, we'll just have to make the best of it. Perhaps it won't turn out so badly; but you keep your eyes open, and watch every chance to get it straightened out. You better see Willis Blair as soon as you can, and see if he won't hold Jake for at least all he's worth. It'll be none too much at best."

Rosie was right. Proof of that was not long coming. The very next day Henry learned from George Graeber himself that Jake had tried to get him to sign the note, but George had refused; and he grinned and chuckled audibly when he learned that Henry had signed it.

Most men will pay their debts if it does not require too much self-denial—if they can eat their customary good food, wear the kind of clothes they are used to, if they can have all the comforts they are accustomed to, and still have enough to pay with. But few and far-between are the men who will cut their expenditures to the irreducible minimum, who will wear rags and eat bread and molasses rather than fail in their obligations.

Jake was certainly not that kind of a hero, and times were hard. The first summer was hot and dry, and his crops were poor, even a little poorer than the average in the neighborhood, for he was not an industrious farmer. The next summer the note was due, but Willis Blair gave him another year's time, to avoid making Henry assume payment. Willis was one of those really kind, helpful and generous neighbors so plentiful in stories and so rare in actual life. He was even willing to run some risk himself, rather than subject Henry to such a loss.

That fall one of the horses died. Then indeed did the matter seem serious, for Jake had to use all he made that summer to buy another horse; and the note, overdue, stood at its original figure. But Willis Blair still refused to look to Henry for his money. He never once let Jake get the impression that he was looking to anyone but himself for payment, and gave him another year. When the next year brought another crop failure, he persuaded him to give Henry a mortgage on his team. This seemed reassuring, until the price of horses dropped so low that the team was no longer security for more than half the face of the note.

Thus years passed, and the note was still unpaid. It had brought so much trouble and anxiety that Henry sometimes wondered if he would not have been wiser to pay it in the first place and drop it from his mind. Such trouble so irked him that he would doubtless have done just that, but Rosie would hear of no such thing. It was not easy to make two hundred dollars.

Finally, under steady pressure and even threats from Willis Blair, Jake managed to get together enough money to pay; and he promised to meet Willis and Henry at the bank on a certain day to take up the note. The day was cold, bitterly cold, with a cutting wind blowing from the northwest, but Henry was at the bank at the time agreed upon—ten in the morning—happy in the hope that his troubles were about over. Willis came soon afterward, and they sat down by the big stove and chatted as they waited for Jake. But Jake did not come, and finally Henry decided he would drive up and see what was the matter. It was a six-mile drive—more than an hour's ride in the wagon—directly against the wind; but Henry was resolved that he would get the matter settled if it took all day. He found Jake at home, cocked back in his chair behind the stove, smoking his pipe contentedly as his wife cleared away the dinner dishes.

"Come in," he called out at Henry's knock, without rising. Henry opened the door and stepped in.

"Come on in, Henry. Come right in and have a chair. Wife, hand us a chair, won't you? Sit down, Henry, and warm yourself. It's a mighty cold day, a mighty cold day, Henry. Have a chair."

"No, thanks, Jake. I tied my horses out in the cold and can't leave them long." Henry stepped up to the stove and held out his numbed fingers.

"We've been waiting for you, Jake," he added, with scarce a trace of anger or impatience.

"You don't say, Henry. Now that's too bad; but it's just too cold to drive so far today, really. Do you mean you've been to town and back here?"

"Surely. I told you I'd be there at ten."

"Well, now, that's too bad, to have you go to all that trouble, Henry. But it's awfully cold, don't you know, cold enough to freeze the sun dogs on the fence posts, as the saying is."

"It's not so cold, when you once get out and get used to it. Come on, wrap up, and come with me; and we'll go down and get this fixed up. We'll take my team."

"Oh, it's too cold, Henry, and my coat's awful thin. It's too cold. We'd freeze coming home."

"No, I've got two good blankets out there, and you can wrap yourself up all you want to." Henry would only too gladly have gone home to get dinner, for he was hungry and chilled through; but he was determined to get the note paid before Jake had a chance to spend the money for something else—he sometimes spent a great deal for whisky.

Jake finally agreed, and the two climbed into the wagon and drove back to town, detouring a mile out of the way to pick up Willis Blair. It was late in the afternoon before the note was paid and the mortgage release forwarded to the county-seat. Henry was obliged to pay the costs incidental to the business, but he felt fortunate to get off with so small a loss and he took Jake all the way home. It was almost dark when he got there.

In the meantime, Rosie had troubles too. Henry was scarcely off to town before the cows began milling around, bawling for water, and horning each other into the fence. The well was near the house, and someone always had to turn the cattle out and herd them up to the trough to drink; but the water had frozen solid in the trough, and there was no use turning them out. Rosie never neglected anything about the place, but she expected Henry back at noon; so she stayed with her house work. After noon the cows broke out of the lot and came up into the yard, where they bawled and fought around the water trough until Rosie saw that she must attend to them. She put out the fire in the stove with a dipperful of water, propped the baby up in the bed with chairs and pillows, and with a severe warning to the older children to let matches alone, she sallied out to the well to draw water, barehanded, for Henry had taken the only pair of mittens. The water froze in the trough almost as fast as she could pour it in, and her fingers soon grew numb as she lifted the dripping buckets over the well curb. She stuck doggedly to her task, warming her hands occasionally by holding them under her arms; but she was crying bitterly as she pulled at the squeaky well wheel, when she hear a voice behind her.

"Guten Tag, Rosie. Was fehlt?"[4]

Surprised and abashed, Rosie turned from her task, to see Steve Linge standing there. He was afoot and had come so quietly that in her distress she had not heard him.

"Was fehlt, Rosie? You got a cold job, nicht wahr? Wo ist der Henry?"[5] Steve often mixed his German and English freely when he was speaking to friends who understood both languages.

Rosie at first tried to hide her tears and to dissemble her utter misery, but with no success.

"Oh, I don't know where he is!" she cried. "He went to town this morning, with our only pair of mittens, to get the miserable note fixed up—that miserable note that has been nothing but trouble for five years. You told him he was stuck, and I told him, and everybody could see it but himself; and we've had nothing but trouble since—nothing but trouble, and worry, and expense!" Rosie's sense of wrong and injustice swelled as the words poured forth. "So busy helping out the worthless whelp all the time, that he has to leave the cattle to me, with the children and everything, take the only pair of mittens, and the good coat; and likely as not he won't get home till dark."

The tears coursed down her reddened cheeks as the hot words

flowed; but when she turned again to her task, Steve stepped up to the curb and took the rope in his great mittened hand.

"Geh ins Haus und mach dich warm, Rosie,"[6] he said, in a voice so gentle it seemed to come strangely from his giant body. "I finish this job. Henry certainly got himself in ganz[7] trouble, but if he gets out today he's lucky enough yet. Henry never could say 'no' when he ought to."

Rosie thanked him with a genuine gratitude she would never forget, not in half a century, and hurried into the house, where she found the baby crying lustily, while Laura tried in vain to pacify her by shaking a string of spools before her. Rosie wiped the tears from her eyes, made a fire in the stove again, and then, after quieting the baby, turned to her bread which she had set to rise on the back of the stove. In a moment she had it in the oven, and a brisk fire burning. As the blood flowed again into her numbed hands and fingers, and the chill of her body yielded to the warmth of the stove, she lost much of her bitterness and self pity.

When the bread was finally baking in the oven, its crusty fragrance filled the room and further augmented her good humor. She looked out through the window, to see how Steve was getting on with the cattle, but he had finished and gone.[8] She had expected to invite him in, give him a piece of fresh bread and a cup of coffee, and have him dry out his mittens by the stove. She felt guilty to think that she had let him go without any further notice.

As evening came on, and Henry did not return, all resentment melted into anxiety; and when she finally heard the rattle of the wagon on the frozen road, she quickly threw more cobs into the stove, put on the coffee pot, and set busily about preparing a warm supper. When Henry came in from the stable a half hour later, stiff with cold and hungry to the point of weakness, there was only the kindest welcome for him, a wash pan full of warm water to wash his hands in, and a piping cup of coffee to drink while he warmed his feet in the oven. And then they moved the table close to the stove, and ate their supper of dumpling soup and fresh bread. When it was over Rosie declared with feeling: "It surely seems good to have that note out of the way!" Henry said nothing, but it was clear that he fully agreed with her.

Chapter Seventeen

The Coming of the Railroad

With the coming of the railroad in eighteen seventy-nine, a new town, named Downsville—after one of the railroad officials, and later changed to Downs—was built only three miles away.[1] Like everyone else along the line of the new road, Henry and Rosie had mildly hoped that their place might be made the site of the new town—they already had the post office—but the railroad company owned half of the land three miles east, and put the town there. It was fine anyhow to have a town and railroad so near, after years of driving sixty miles or more to Russell, Hastings or Waterville, with every load of wheat or corn or hogs; and on the day when the first train was to arrive,[2] Henry and Rosie went to town. It was a noisy and expectant crowd that stood about the station awaiting the coming of the train; and when the great engine rounded the curve and whistled its way slowly into town, Rosie heard a woman behind her exclaim, "Mine eyes have seen the coming of the Lord!" Soon afterward Henry received orders to turn the mail over to the new postmaster at Downs.[3] For a while he and Rosie felt rather lonely without their mail business; but with three little children to care for—there was another baby now[4]—they found quite enough to do.

On the last day of May—a still, sultry afternoon—a dark blue bank of clouds loomed up in the west—the usual afternoon rain promise of the prairie country. Rosie was too busy with her ironing to pay much attention to it, until she heard the rumble of thunder and noticed that the room was turning darker—so dark that she could not see clearly. She opened the door for more light, and looking out, saw above the cottonwood grove a mighty cloud drama that for a moment almost made her heart stand still. The great black cloud masses in the background were moving forward heavily but rapidly, sending out intermittent flashes of lightning that made the background only darker. Fleecy clouds beneath raced along madly, dipping low and rising again, twisting and whirling and scurrying this way and that, as if in a veritable panic. As Rosie stood looking in awe at the vast commotion, she saw Henry hurrying in from the field. He pulled the harnesses off the horses at the stable door, turned them into the corral and started on a run to the house.

"Better get to the cellar with the children!" he exclaimed, quite out of breath. "I'll shut the windows. I'll be down, if it comes too close."

While Rosie poured water on the fire in the stove and took the children to the cellar, Henry closed the windows, then stood on the doorstep watching the coming storm with his arms folded— Henry so often stood that way, with his arms folded across his breast. The rain curtain beneath the scurrying clouds presently turned a luminous green, against which the trees and the stable stood out in spectral silhouette; a deathly quiet intervened, the leaves on the trees stirring tremulously, in weird contrast to the vast commotion overhead; then the clouds over to the northwest circled and rushed together, and a black funnel dropped toward the ground—the dreaded cyclone!

A few great hailstones came hurtling down and bounced along the ground, vivid streaks of lightning flashed from the outlying clouds, while the great, black cloud stalactite moved relentlessly forward, writhing and bending sinuously, reaching down menacingly toward the ground, then rising again, as if loth to begin its work of desolation.

Rosie was calling insistently from the cellar, and Henry closed the door and went down to join her. He gathered the family together on the lower steps of the outside cellar entrance, where a collapse of the cabin would be least likely to crush them; and there they sat waiting for the blow to strike, Rosie with the baby in her arms, Henry with his arms protectively about Laura and Billy. A long wait, it seemed to those huddled together in the darkness. Then the wind suddenly struck, the cellar door creaked, and the cabin shook above them. Henry hugged the children closer to him as he peered up at the cracks in the cellar door. For a few minutes the wind raged, and then slowly died down. Henry climbed up the steps, lifted the cellar door and looked out. The sun was shining bright and serene! He threw the door wide open and stepped out. The stone house was still standing, and the stable, and the chicken house. The storm had missed them! He called Rosie and the children up and they stood about the doorstep watching the towering black mass of clouds, capped with billowy white, as it retreated slightly north of eastward with vivid flashes of lightning and steady, sullen rumble of thunder.[5]

Anxious about the fate of neighbors up north, Henry hitched the horses to the wagon and took Rosie and the children up to Bartsch's. Half a mile on their way they found the ground white with hailstones, trees stripped of their leaves, and even of branches, wheat and corn pounded into the ground. Chris Bartsch's promising wheat was completely ruined by the hail, dead chickens lay scattered about the yard, and the backs of some of his horses and cattle were covered with blood; but Chris' smile was unchanged. He was thankful it was no worse. The next day came news that the cyclone had left a ghastly path of ruin eastward. Irving, a hundred miles away, had been torn to kindling.[6]

That spring Henry and Rosie bought the Frank Hagel quarter adjoining them.[7] The new railroad ran diagonally through Frank's claim; and when the appraisers allowed him only fifty dollars damages, Frank was so angry and discouraged that he offered his place to Henry for seven hundred dollars. Henry was not enthusiastic about buying more land, but when he told Rosie of the offer, she urged him to take it.

"Don't let that get away," she insisted. "That land is good, and will always be good. And anyhow, I don't want anybody living right across the corner there, under our very noses, with his turkeys feeding in our hog lot, and his chickens eating the new wheat, and his hogs out, and his children running back and forth. George Graeber's turkeys and Athey's children are all I can stand. Father will let us have seven hundred dollars, I am sure."

Father lent them the money, and they bought the place the very next week. It seemed fine to have so much good level land, although they were several years paying off the loan; and they often missed Frank Hagel after he had gone.

Poor, lonely bachelor! He had no horses or oxen, no cows or chickens—nothing but his claim, with a little cabin on it. He was lonesome in his little shack, and sometimes actually hungry, so he often came over to visit, and was of course welcome at the table. Rosie even did his washing, ironing and mending, but he paid her for it—ten dollars a year.

When he was invited to eat with them, Rosie could sometimes see a pathetic struggle in his mind, between his hunger and his honest desire not to impose upon his hosts. One morning he came over early to hear Henry's Bible reading, as he often did, and afterward was invited to stay for breakfast.

"Oh, no, I guess I better not. I'm not so very hungry this morning," he replied, with some hesitation.

"Well, better sit up anyhow, and have a biscuit and a cup of coffee," Henry urged.

Protesting weakly, he sat down to the table—and ate nine biscuits, with butter and eggs and gravy, and drank three cups of coffee. The poor fellow was nearly starved.

Perhaps because of his meager living, his health was poor and he took S. S. S. all the time.[8] Some of his neighbors thought his professed ill health was only laziness, but Henry and Rosie knew how honest he was, and were always kind to him.

Frank was an impractical fellow, utterly unfitted for the task of building a home under the hard conditions of the frontier. One winter he had conceived the idea that he would try to write a novel, a love story, and so make enough money to buy a team. His own shack was not really habitable in winter, and he had no lamp, so he asked Henry if he might work in his house. Henry consented, and for weeks Frank stayed there every night, writing by lamplight, in the same room where Henry and Rosie and the babies were sleeping. Of course, nothing came of his efforts.

After he had sold his claim, Frank stayed a while and took organ lessons of Anna Wetzel.[9] Since he had no organ himself he had to do his practicing on Anna's organ, but, being without any social graces, he soon found himself unwelcome. So he made a dummy keyboard and tried to practice at home on that, but with little success. Old man Wetzel got the payment for a full term of lessons in advance by borrowing from him, but Frank found it wise to stop before he got all he had paid for. Soon afterward he went

down to Brown County to live with his brother, where he died a
few years later of a paralysis which had been creeping up on him
while he lived on the claim.

The new farm meant added work for Rosie, cooking and
washing, for now they had to keep a hired hand most of the time.
After Henry got part of the land fenced,[10] Rosie had to take the cattle to pasture every morning too, and then had to go down to the
river, at the foot of the pasture, to clean out a place along the bank
where they could drink. This meant a walk of more than two miles
every morning. Laura, age four, was left in charge of her smaller
brother and the new baby Alice—a very good baby, little given to
crying.

The building of the railroad west across the Hagel farm meant
still more work, for two foremen of the construction gang wanted
to board with Henry and Rosie. Henry did not want Rosie to do so
much extra work, but Rosie insisted on doing it. Every addition to
the cash income would help them to pay their debt a little sooner.

Hope and optimism were in the air, and the people began to
indulge in occasional luxuries. That winter many of the neighbors
gave parties, and Henry and Rosie gave an oyster supper on the occasion of Henry's birthday. Several of the neighbors bought
sleighs. George Graeber flashed past Henry's one day with a new
set of sleigh bells, and the next spring he began work on a new
house.[11] Within the next year or two, Downs made a brave start toward metropolitan size and dignity with a dozen or more new
business buildings—wooden boxes with the traditional wooden
roofs sticking out in front, over plank sidewalks—with new houses
going up all over town, and lot subdivisions running far out into
the prairie dog towns. Merchants mostly rather new to the business sold general merchandise, hardware, meat, bakery goods,
millinery and drugs—"pills, pukes and purgatives," as advertised
in the local paper. There was a hotel, too, and a monopoly lumber
yard, a barber shop, a dam and grist mill, two wagon makers, a
plow maker, and a lawyer. Two new churches for the women, half
a dozen lodges for the men, and a new school house testified to
the spiritual, social and intellectual ideals of the people; while the
thriving business done at the drug store indicated that their interests were not entirely spiritual. Fred Wetzel gave six hundred dol-

lars to the Congregational Church—precious money he had taken out of the hides of his poor horses, and out of the lives of his girls.

"Land lookers" came in on every train, seeking relinquishments or scattered, unoccupied land up in the hills; and a steady stream of movers jogged slowly along the road on their way westward. Eastern money began to trickle in, now that the settlers had title to their land and could mortgage it. Agents and peddlers came along every few days, with packs of clothes, trees, barbed wire or lightning rods. The lightning rod agents, hyenas in human clothing, operated in cahoots with some money lender or banker, who bought the farmers' notes at twenty-five per cent discount and, as innocent purchaser, could collect regardless of frauds in the transactions. Rosie warned Henry against these swindlers, and he never bought lightning rods, but he could not always resist the tree agents. There was much discussion of the new self-binders, and Henry bought one. It did not tie all of the bundles properly, and the wire used in tying was expensive, and a great nuisance in threshing; but it saved a great deal of labor, and now with his own binder, Henry did not need to wait on any of the neighbors to cut his wheat.

There was considerable political excitement in the late seventies. Temperance lecturers were scouring the country, exhorting frail men to sign the pledge and vote for prohibition. Some of the local bibbers who could "take it or leave it alone" usually decided to take it, every Saturday—all they could buy with their wives' butter and egg money, perhaps going home late at night to beat their wives and children, and salving their consciences with the business-like slogan, "You can't have a good town without booze." Prohibition was debated at every country school house, and when debate failed to bring a satisfactory meeting of minds, the debaters occasionally proceeded to fight it out with bare knuckles. Downs was splitting into two factions on the question, while Cawker— "ancient cesspool of iniquity," as one of the temperance lecturers called her—had two breweries and drank their product without serious qualms. As the Osborne paper expressed it: "Reading makes a full man, but the Cawker boys rely mainly on 'Old Crow' and 'Brakeman's Delight.'" Parker always had several jugs of whisky in his store too, for the refreshment of customers.

With his general aversion for all sorts of unseemly disorder,

Henry never took sides in the temperance squabble. He liked a glass of beer or wine, but seldom allowed himself an indulgence which would have cost as much as the candy that he took home to the children.

The recurrent proposal to move the county-seat came up again. The gossip was that the railroad official, Colonel Downs, owned half of the lots in Bloomington, and was trying to get the county-seat moved there; but after considerable acrimonious debate and discussion, the agitation died down.[12]

Misfortunes and tragedies there were in the vicinity. Henry and Rosie and the children suffered a siege of "pink eye," which almost blinded them for several weeks. Little Billy's eyes swelled completely shut, so that he could not see at all. Rosie used camphor as medicine, but the children seemed to prefer pink eye to Rosie's remedy.

While the Athey twins were still babies, all of the Athey children came down with scarlet fever, and Rosie had another job at nursing and carrying clothes and food back and forth. Luckily she did not get the fever, and the children all recovered. Not long afterward, Henry was called upon one day to help care for Gottlieb Schmidt, who was very sick in his cabin a couple of miles up the creek.[13] Henry had a quiet and kindly way with sick people, and knew something about medicine, so he was often called upon for such services. He found the man suffering fearfully, in convulsions which pulled his head and heels back until they almost met, while his pretty little wife fluttered around him with a cup of medicine.

"Poison!" Henry exclaimed, with a quick glance at the stricken man. "What's he been eating?"

The wife, dry-eyed, shot a frightened glance at him.

"He has no poison! He's been sick all week. I thought he was getting well—till today."

"Warm water and salt!" he ordered, scarcely hearing what she said. "Maybe we can make him vomit."

Without another word the woman hastened out to the wood pile to get wood and kindling and soon had a fire built, all the time eyeing Henry suspiciously; but before the water was warm, Gottlieb Schmidt, with his jaws locked, slowly relaxed, straightened out, and lay still.

At home that evening Henry could eat no supper, and Rosie feared he was sick again.

"No. I'm well enough," he said finally, "but there's something wrong about that business up there. That man was poisoned."

"Oh, surely she wouldn't do such a thing—such a nice little woman, and so neat and clean."

"I don't know where he got it, but it looked like poison to me. I never saw a sick man suffer so."

Henry and Rosie finally decided that there was nothing they could do about it. Some of the neighbors began to whisper their suspicions too, but the young widow had her husband embalmed, and took his body back to Iowa for burial. A few years later, the news came back that she had poisoned her second husband in Iowa; and then Henry knew what was the matter with Gottlieb.

In October, eighteen seventy-nine, Henry and Rosie drove over to Bull City—later named Alton—to attend the funeral of General Bull and two other men, who had been killed by Bull's pet elk.[14] The animal had been thought quite tame, but one day it charged Bull when he came into the pen, knocked him down, and gored him to death in a trice. Another man, Bricknell, armed with a club, tried to rescue Bull, but he was also riddled with holes by the sharp antlers. A third man, Nicholas, came to the rescue, but was caught on the brute's antlers and thrown over the fence. A fourth man, Sherman, was similarly thrown over the fence—dead, with sixty-four wounds in his body.[15] When the animal was finally shot, Bull was found to have forty-four wounds, some of them penetrating the body. Only Nicholas escaped death, and he was horribly wounded. Bull was a famous character, and two thousand people attended the funeral.

Henry's neighbor, Griff Lytle,[16] was almost killed by an outlaw bull not long afterward, but two neighbors who happened to be making hay across the road finally rescued him.

Chapter Eighteen

A Prairie Fire

The latter part of the summer of eighteen seventy-nine was very dry, and the corn had to be cut in August. The fields were too dry to plow, so Henry could put in no fall wheat. As the lumber wagons moved along the roads, they raised clouds of dust, which on still fall days hung in long streams across the landscape, drifting slowly into shapelessness. At last came the rain, in middle October, too late to do any good except to bring water back to the wells and creeks, and clean the air.

Nearly all the neighbors stayed, even those who had lost their faith in the future of the country. There was nothing else they could do. As George Graeber once expressed it: "When we have rain and crops, we don't want to go, and when there ain't no crops we're too poor to go; so I reckon we'll just stay here till we starve to death." Henry had given up the belief that the breaking up of the sod and the planting of trees and crops would change the climate; but he had so many hostages to fortune in the new country that he never dared to think of going. He was able to live anyhow, and even to help out a few of the neighbors. Toward spring Wilson Athey ran short of corn meal, which had been about the only food he had for his family—served alternately as corn mush and corn bread—and Henry lent him enough to last until spring.

That spring Henry broke out five more acres down in the south field, and fenced in more of his pasture—the end of live stock picketing. He built a good fence of barbed wire, although it was not yet determined whether horses would be safe with barbed wire fences. Henry was always indignant at the means used by a couple of the neighbors to keep their cattle from breaking through makeshift fences. Bender cut two slits in the hides of some of his cattle, at the withers, and inserted the wire bail of a small tin bucket under the strip of hide, so the animal would not crawl under the fence. Tommy Meierhoffer[1] tied tin buckets over the heads of several of his calves, so they would not seek weak places in the fence; and Fred Wetzel sometimes used his shot gun, loaded with fine shot, on cows that were guilty of trespass. Almost everyone, including Henry himself, regularly used pokes on the most aggressive fence jumpers. The prairie dogs had been taking more and more of Henry's pasture, so he borrowed a tank wagon and tried to drown them out, but with little success.

Two luxuries that Henry bought for Rosie one day were destined never to be forgotten—a can of lye, and a mop.[2] The lye saved her a great deal of time in "breaking" the hard well water; and the mop—well, the mop was the end of one epoch and the beginning of another. Later Rosie often declared that she would insist on having a mop earlier if she were living her life over again.

Another baby boy joined the family in March—Danny, they called him[3]—and this made some additional work, and even a little expense, for Rosie came down with a high fever afterward and had to hire Annie Bartsch to do her work. Henry had to go to Osborne on jury duty, to be gone more than a week; and while he was gone Rosie was often worried and frightened at the behavior of the hired hand. McAllister was a floater, a stranger in the community, a big, lazy yokel, evidently a man of little intelligence or character, sneaking and furtive, and always very greedy at the table. Several times Rosie caught him stealing cookies and sugar from the cupboard. He always put two or three teaspoonfuls of sugar in his coffee, although when he had first come to ask for a job, he had refused sugar altogether—like most of the neighbors, Rosie seldom used sugar because it was so expensive. She could not dismiss him, though, for spring work was pressing, and hands were scarce. She was greatly relieved when Henry got back from Osborne, and they could dispense with the man's services.

It was a dry spring, and night after night the skies were lighted up with prairie fires, in one direction or another. Although he had fire breaks plowed and burned around his home and his haystack, Henry always studied the sky apprehensively at night before he went to bed; and he kept the water barrel full. Steve

Linge and several other neighbors were burned out, lost all their cows, pigs, chickens, hay and corn, and even the clothing and beds and provisions that were in their homes! Henry had been one of the privates in the fight against several such fires, and had seen the black desolation that followed them.

The morning of April first was clear and balmy and serene, with the meadow larks singing down in the pasture, and the kill-deers answering from the field where Henry was plowing. Scarcely a breath of wind stirred, although little eddies of dust, like miniature cyclones, whirled up here and there and zagged across the quiet fields. The hens cackled contently as they scratched about in the mellow earth, seeking some venturesome and indiscreet bug or worm for dinner, and cocks crowed cheerily, occasionally scratching up an insect and calling the hens to come and share it, or even—what rogues these cocks will be—calling them sometimes on the false pretense of having found something. The hogs grunted lazily as they rubbed against the sides of the troughs, or wandered about, rooting up corn cobs or greening sprigs of grass or weeds; the cattle grazed on the new wheat, one of them now and then lowing to her calf shut away in the weaning pen.

Across the quiet fields came the imperious "Caw! Caw!" of the crows perched challengingly in the trees down on the creek and river, while along the road by the schoolhouse, a lumber wagon rattled complacently on toward town. The earth seemed contented and half asleep in the warm sunshine.

About ten o'clock, as Rosie stepped out to the well for a bucket of water, she saw a brownish, copper-colored cloud rolling in from the hills to the southwest, boiling up for an instant at one point and then at another, rolling like a mighty wave over the quiet landscape. For an instant she stood awestruck by the spectacle, but she recovered her thoughts and started on a run to call Henry. He had seen the cloud too, however, and soon appeared around the stable with his team on a trot, hanging on to one handle of the plough to keep the nose out of the ground.

"To the cellar! Get the children to the cellar!" he shouted. He rammed the plow into the ground, and started the team in a circle around the stable. A few furrows of fresh earth might mean a great deal in a prairie fire.

Rosie turned and ran to the house. She soon had the children in the cellar, where she put Laura in charge, and darted out to the well for a few buckets of water. The smell of burning grass was strong in the air, and the storm struck as she set the last bucket on the floor and started for the stable.

"Turn the hogs out!" shouted Henry, as he made the last turn around the stable and headed his team toward the house. With the wind whipping her skirts about her, Rosie opened the gate and chased the hogs out into the open lot, where there was not enough grass to carry fire. This done, she ran to the house, where Henry was following out his V-shaped fire guard, urging his horses on with shouts and cracking of the lines.

"The cows! Shall I turn the cows out?" called out Rosie against the rising storm.

"No, the lot's the best place! To the house!" and Henry plied his lines with growing vigor. His team, trembling with fright at the smell of fire and smoke and the roar of the rising wind, strained at their harnesses, the cows bellowed, and the other horses snorted and ran nervously about in the pasture.

The sun grew dim in the flying dust and smoke. A sudden gust took Henry's hat off, and an instant later he saw the roof of the chicken house torn from its supports, to crash to the ground fifty feet away. He turned to see if the fire was approaching, but the dust and sand blinded his eyes. When he could open them again, he saw the house still standing. A guarded look into the wind proved that the fire was not yet upon him, so he plowed on, back and forth, until he was sure that no fire could cross. The straw stable would not be a safe place in a prairie fire so he unhitched the horses and led them behind the stone house, where he stood holding them, waiting for a lull in the wind.

Rosie sat on a bench in the cellar beneath the log house, with the baby in her arms and the other children clinging to her, listening to the din and clamor of the wind, and the creaking of the joists in the cabin above her. She wondered whether the fire had reached the stable, or perhaps even the house; and at the thought of being caught there, with a burning house above her and her children, she handed the baby to Laura and stepped to the door, just as the roof of the chicken house crashed to the ground outside. She yanked the latch loose. In an instant the wind drove the door wide open, pushing her back as if she had been a child. She tried to close it, but her utmost strength was unavailing. Leaning against the wind, she ran out of the door and up the earthen steps.

"Henry! Henry!"

"All right" came from around the corner of the house, and Henry stepped into view. "Run back to the cellar!"

"The fire! Where's the fire?"

"Not here yet—" and the rest of his reply was lost in the roar of the wind.

Rosie stumbled back into the cellar, and after much tugging and pushing got the door shut. She took the baby again in her arms and reassured the other children, who were crying with fright and consternation.

For an hour the wind blew with little abatement. Occasional lulls were followed by renewed blasts that made the house quake and tremble; but then it gradually subsided in fitful gusts, as if in sullen resentment at the resistance the sturdy little cabin had offered. By two o'clock it was quiet enough for Rosie and the children to venture out of the cellar.

It was a weird world they came into as they emerged. The sun shone with a sickly light through the dust and smoke that lingered in the air. Smoke there was certainly, and an unmistakable smell of burning grass, yet there were no signs of fire near. Later in the day, as the air cleared, the hills to the south appeared black. The fire had stopped at the river.

It was far past dinner time, and the children were ravenous, but the problem of getting dinner was no easy one. Dust was everywhere. Every dish in the cupboard was full of it and had to be washed before it could be used. The table and chairs and beds were covered, and through the cracks around the door, piles of dust had drifted like so much snow. In the cellar the crocks of milk were powdered so thickly that they had to be skimmed before the milk could be used. Nevertheless, Rosie soon had bread and butter and milk on a clean table; and as she dipped her crusts into the milk she spoke with feeling:

"Oh, how many poor people there are up in those hills who haven't anything like this to eat!"

Chapter Nineteen

The Road Fight

With drouth and hot winds and crop failure, there was enough to worry about; but added to all this, a neighborhood quarrel split the community into two hostile camps, and brought Henry and Rosie endless grief.

Some of the settlers wanted a new road opened northward from the west line of Henry's farm.[1] The old road, half a mile east, crossed the creek a half-dozen times in a mile, and of course the culverts were poor and often out of order. A new road would enable some of the people up north to avoid the creek in flood times. On the other hand, those who lived on the old road wanted to have it improved, rather than have a new road opened. Henry was not deeply interested either way, but he could see how much some of the people needed the new road, so he was disposed to help them get it.

He soon found himself with strange comrades in this fight. There was George Graeber, who, although pretending neighborly friendship, had often tried in sneaking ways to injure him. It was George who had stolen Henry's weigh bill at Beloit once, when they hauled wheat to the elevator there—at any rate Henry was always certain that it was George. George had slept with him under the wagon that night, and months later, after George had come for his mail one day, the bill reappeared in one of the mail boxes in Henry's cabin, too late to be of any value, as the elevator had failed. Although it had profited the rascal none, for he was afraid to try to cash the bill, it was a heavy loss to Henry.

George and his wife Lizzie were perfectly matched; indeed it would have been difficult to tell which was the meaner of the two.

140

Henry told Rosie of the time when Lizzie Graeber had bargained to buy some goods and make him two shirts, if he would give her his wagon cover, and had skimped the sleeves so that he could scarcely bend his arms. He also told Rosie of the time he took Lizzie to Cawker City with her eggs. Lizzie was sitting on the seat beside him with a bucket of eggs on her lap, when the horses happened to shy suddenly, throwing her in a somersault backward over the seat. Although she was riding with him by his courtesy, she made him go back home and hunt around in his own chicken coop and stable until he found enough eggs to make good what had been broken.

It was George and his wife who, whenever they went to Cawker City—before the new town, Downs, was established— would angle a half mile out of their way to avoid going past Henry's house, lest they be asked to bring something home for him, although they often asked him to bring coffee or sugar or flour or tobacco for them when he went to town. Henry always noticed too, that they never bought any stamps of him, but got all their stamps at Cawker City. Henry got a percentage on the stamps he sold, and in the meanness of his small soul, George begrudged his neighbor every penny of this.

In the road fight, nevertheless, George Graeber was one of Henry's new associates, along with other neighbors of more genuine character. On the other side were ranged some of his best friends; but it was no new circumstance to find Wilson Athey against him.

Both sides hired the best lawyers they could get and for months the case dragged through the courts. There were hearings, demurrers, continuances and citations, repeated trips to Osborne—those trips always took the whole day, for it was twelve miles to Osborne—until Henry was sick of the whole business. While the case was dragging through the courts, Wilson Athey planted a row of hedge trees along the edge of his field, right where the road would have to be located. George Graeber pulled them up, and this precipitated another lawsuit, for Wilson was never slow to "take the law to" offending neighbors. This lawsuit cost George fifty dollars and court expenses. As the road fight grew more bitter, it threatened to break up the church. Some of the participants ceased going altogether, while others went but refused to have anything to do with the members of the opposing faction. The communion service had to be abandoned for a while, because neither faction would take communion with the other. Thus the church became a rather peculiar institution for the worship of the God of love, and even failed to some extent in its function as a social center. Henry and Rosie managed to preserve the amenities with most of the church members.

The quarrel got into the school, and this fell hard upon Laura and Billy, about the only children in their school belonging to the new road faction. It was Billy's first year at school, and he and Laura were most awkward and helpless in the face of the older Athey children, especially since the teacher was allied with the Atheys. The teacher was wont to take the smallest Athey girl upon her lap and shower her with flattering attentions and "dears" and "honeys," while she referred to Laura as the "dirty little Dutchie." And Laura came home crying about this, and because the other children would not play with her, Rosie began to wonder if the road fight was not quite too expensive an affair. She resented particularly the insinuation that her child was "dirty," for Rosie was always most scrupulous in the matter of the Saturday night bath for every member of the family. She could only reassure Laura, ask her not to mind but be a good girl, and tell her she would get a cookie when she came home.

But worse trouble came, and Billy was the victim. There was only one privy at school, for the use of thirty pupils, boys and girls; and frequently at recess the big boys would sally out and take possession, so that the girls and smaller boys could not get in. Once there, they would hold possession with tenacity worthy of a nobler cause, perhaps the whole of the recess, although there was nothing in the condition of the place to explain their fondness for it as a rendezvous.

One day at recess Billy ran out to the privy, only to find it already held by the big boys, with the door barred tight. He waited a few minutes, then banged at the door with his little fists, but to no avail. Then, with a fine resourcefulness, he proceeded to utilize a crack in the door.

Of course, one of the Athey boys told the teacher, who promptly promised that Billy should have a whipping proportioned in severity to the enormity of his offense. That evening he was kept after school, and all of the other children, including Laura, were ordered from the room, while the teacher took out her hedge switch and gave him a severe whipping. For some time Laura, listening at the door, had to hear not only the strokes of the whip and the cries of her little brother—he was only five—but the laughter and jibes of the Atheys, who were standing around the steps enjoying the occasion hugely. When the teacher was through, and Billy came sobbing from the room, Laura got his cap and they started home across the pasture, speeded by the jibes of one of the Athey children: "Goodbye, little dirty Dutchies."

The Atheys received a further accretion to their dignity and importance when the road fight was finally decided in favor of the old road crowd.[2] It cost the new road faction a year's savings to pay lawyers' fees and all the incidental expenses of the trial; and twenty years later the bitterness stirred by the quarrel was still remembered.

There was much petty rivalry among some of the neighbors anyhow, rivalry as to who should have the first house, or the best house, or cart, or buggy, or driving horse, or the first organ. Perhaps this rivalry was worst among some of the young girls, to whom dresses, hats, music lessons and "fellers" meant so much. If God is very sensitive as to the inner thoughts of His children, when He saw some of the girls appraising each other's hats and dresses at church, He must have been none too comfortable. This was at its worst some years later. Even at this time, there was some rivalry among the men in the church as to who should start the hymns. Chris Bartsch, the best of the men singers, usually led the singing, often starting the hymns too high, but others tried it sometimes. Henry ventured to start a hymn once in a while, but Rosie often laughed about the way some of the others would steal the lead from him before he got well started. Henry usually started the hymns too low. This was all good-natured rivalry; but later when a faction grew up in the church that wanted an organ to use in the services, there was considerable acrimony in the discussion that ensued. Some of the conservatives believed it more fitting to sing to the Lord without an organ, and they stood their ground stubbornly.

The road fight was not the only reason for the hostility, which amounted almost to a feud, between the Ises and the Atheys. This had its origin before Rosie came out. When Henry was "baching" on his claim, it was his habit to bake enough biscuits in the morning to serve for dinner and supper, and when Frances Athey came over to hoe in the garden he had allotted her at the end of his field, she often took some of his biscuits. When he came in late for dinner or supper and found his biscuits gone, it was inconvenient to have to make a fire and bake again. He had never complained about it, for Henry was far from harboring ungenerous thoughts, but he remembered this as a rather small trick. And, for ten years afterward, Wilson Athey was a perennial nuisance, with his borrowing of almost everything Henry and Rosie had. He borrowed nails and stamps, and he borrowed the hammer, and the axe, and the saw, and the awl, and the flatirons, and the pitchfork, and the hoe, and the wagon, and the hayrack, and the plow, and the rake, and the doubletrees, and the fanning mill. He borrowed corn, and corn meal, and bran, and flour, sometimes not even asking for what he wanted, but taking it as of right if he could find it, and not infrequently failing to return it. More than once, when Rosie wanted the axe to cut a little wood for the stove, she had to go over to Atheys to get it. In Wilson's manner was ill-concealed contempt for the "Dutch," whose modest accumulations he envied, but whose industry he had no desire to emulate.

He disliked Rosie, because she was not so easily imposed upon as Henry was. Even before Rosie came, Wilson had been in the habit of borrowing stamps and nails and various things from Henry, and frequently he neglected to return them. When Rosie came, she put this business on a stricter basis. Whenever Wilson borrowed stamps, she set down the amount in a little book, and insisted on settlement of the whole account occasionally. Of course, he disliked this very much and always tried to see Henry when he wanted anything.

Wilson's horses, cows, pigs and calves, of the poorest grade and frequently half-starved, usually roamed at large, because he could not afford fences; and much of the time they hung around Henry's premises, eating hay and fodder, drinking the water Rosie had drawn, upsetting the swill buckets and milk cans, tearing down the clothes line, and making nuisances of themselves generally. One hard winter, Henry had two of these horses and several hogs around most of the time; and of course he got nothing for it all.

The hogs, nosing around the kitchen door, upsetting buckets and cans, and rooting up the grass in the yard, caused Rosie endless trouble and annoyance; and one day, in a fit of exasperation, she threw a bucket of hot water out of the door, scalding one of them severely. Of course this precipitated a row with Wilson, but the hogs were kept at home for a while.

While the road fight was still raging, another quarrel developed with the Atheys. Wilson's calves got out and trampled Henry's wheat field and garden, and Henry's calves broke out one day and roamed over the Athey premises for some time. Thus far there was a measure of equality and reciprocity in the matter, and Henry made no complaint; but when Wilson's hogs got out and rooted up half of his promising wheat field, Henry demanded a settlement. Wilson acceded to this, and paid Henry a small sum of money, asking for receipt "in full," which Henry innocently gave him.

"Now I have a receipt in full for the damage my live stock has done," he said, leering out of his little blue eyes. "Now I want you to pay me for the damage your calves have done."

"But your calves did as much damage as mine did," replied Henry. "At *least* as much."

"But I have a receipt *in full* for the damage my livestock did, and I want a fair settlement for the damage your live stock did. You see, I have a legal receipt *in full*." Wilson emphasized the words *in full*.

Henry was puzzled. "You paid me for the damage your hogs did, as you know, and on the calves we are about even. If anybody owes anything on the calves, you owe me. Your calves did fully as much damage as mine, or more. You know that as well as I do." Henry was beginning to get angry, and Wilson hesitated a moment before pressing his demand further, as he had seen Henry angry once, and he did not care to be on the other side of an argument when that temper was thoroughly aroused. He knew that Henry always tried to avoid legal difficulties, however, and in an instant his assurance returned.

"No, as a matter of law, I have paid you for all the damage my live stock did. I have the receipt right here, with your signature— good before the law."

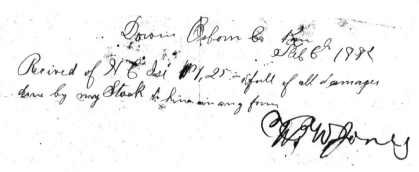

The receipt given to Henry Ise by Wilson Athey (whose signature appears by his real name, W. W. Jones). Dated 6 February 1882, it acknowledges that Henry paid Athey $1.25 for damages by Henry's livestock to Athey's land. (Courtesy Von Rothenberger)

"That's for the damage your hogs did, and nothing else."

"It says live stock."

Henry really was afraid of the law, as most men are who have been burned a time or two, and he hated trouble. He hesitated a moment or two, and then handed back the money that Wilson had paid him.

"Now, give me a receipt." Wilson fumbled in his pockets for a piece of paper, but found none.

"Well, give me back that one," demanded Henry, and Wilson handed back the receipt, with a smile of triumph on his face.

"And now," continued Henry as he tore the receipt to bits, "this will be the end of our dealings. As you live there"—looking over at the dugout on the hill—"we will have to be neighbors, but I don't want your horses or cattle or hogs or anything else on my place, and I don't want you over here borrowing anything again. You stay on your place, and I'll stay on my place, and we won't have any further trouble."

His smile of triumph fading, Wilson turned and started home. Ten years later, when one of the Athey girls was sick, Laura bought three bananas and took two of them over to her—the first friendly gesture since Henry's trouble about the calves and hogs. The other banana Laura divided among the children and Henry and Rosie, so that each might have a taste.

Chapter Twenty

The Retreat of the Defeated Legion

The wheat was poor in eighteen eighty, and the corn burned to short fodder in the hot winds of late July. After the corn was ruined, good rains came, which brought out grass for fall pasture and put the ground in shape for wheat sowing. Farther west the drouth was even worse. There had been no rain out there since the preceding summer, and the hard-pressed settlers of the western counties sent out appeals for aid. Many of them filed application at Washington for leave of absence from their claims, sold their starving cattle for whatever they could get, packed their meager household possessions into wagons and started back to their old homes in the East. In late May, after one of the few rains of that arid summer, a settler living down on the Solomon saw a wagon and a dead horse floating along on the swollen waters of the river; and the next day a man was found a few miles up-stream, the only survivor of the tragedy in which his wife and four children had drowned. He was on his way east from Rooks County, and had under-estimated the depth of the river at the ford.

All that fall, the discouraged settlers trekked out of the drouth-stricken country. Day after day they passed by, grizzled, dejected and surly men; sick, tired and hopeless women often with children who were cheerfully unconscious of the tragedy of moving, or even happy in the novelty of their adventure.

Many of them stopped for water or hay or corn meal or flour, or perhaps to stay all night; and at first they were always hospitably entertained. Henry never had the heart to turn people away at night, although the entertainment of these movers cost Rosie a great deal of extra work cooking and moving beds and furniture, and perhaps a big job of cleaning afterward. Sometimes the movers wanted only the use of the stove to cook their supper on, but when the cold weather set in they often needed a warm place to sleep. Then beds had to be made on the floor, and sheets hung up to provide a measure of privacy. In the morning the beds had to be torn up again, breakfast for two families had to be cooked on the little stove, and the visitors' dishes washed and dried. And, worst of all, not infrequently an aftermath of such visits was a long job scrubbing up pools of tobacco spit, or a siege of bedbugs that kept Rosie busy until the next invasion.

One slovenly wayfarer who stopped with them wanted supper, and then asked to be allowed to sleep in the stable or straw stack, but Henry would not permit this. He was afraid the man might start a fire, or perhaps steal something and disappear before morning, so he and Rosie fixed up a bed on the floor and allowed him to sleep there. Long before morning they regretted their hospitality, for the poor fellow, apparently afflicted with the itch or with vermin, scratched and thrashed out so violently that he kept them awake most of the night.

Some of the movers who stopped had no other idea than to sponge their way. A big fat fellow came along one day, rattling his money in his pocket as he asked for dinner, to show that he intended to pay. Rosie got dinner for him, making special effort to get him a good meal, since he was to pay for it. She even gave him a big piece of custard pie, and he ate appreciatively, to put it mildly. When he was nearly through, she stepped into the other room a minute to attend the baby. Hearing a great commotion in the kitchen she came back, to see the rascal running out across the yard at full speed. Several times, men offered to pay with a ten dollar bill, which of course Henry could not change. One such cheat thus got not only free supper, lodging, and breakfast for himself, but feed for a dozen horses.

Occasionally movers would steal corn, hay, chickens, anything that they could pick up. One fellow who had been allowed to sleep on the floor borrowed Rosie's skillet to fry his meat in the next morning, and while Rosie was out milking, he packed the skillet in the box with his own things. She did not notice it until he was gone.

Almost as much of a nuisance as thieves were the sponges

from various towns up and down the road, who made it a friendly habit to stop over night and for a meal or two every time they came past. It was hard to resist their overtures.

One crisp evening in October, a little after sunset, a mover wagon rolled into the yard, and the man in the front seat called out to Henry, who was just emerging from the stable:

"Hello there, neighbor! What's the chance of getting a bit of supper and a place to sleep tonight?"

Henry had lost a horse blanket to movers only a few nights before, and several bushels of corn—the precious grain that he was fortunate enough to have saved from the previous year—and he and Rosie had just about decided that they would have nothing further to do with movers. Noting that he hesitated, the man developed his appeal a little further.

"It's this way, neighbor. We've got a papoose along here that ain't doin' so well, and it would be a great accommodation if we could have a place to sleep."

"Well, I guess we can fix up something for you," said Henry, immediately softened by the man's reference to his sick child. "I'll go and see what the wife says." He started to the house, while the man stood by his horses, with his hand expectantly on the tug. In a few minutes Henry came back with word that they might stay; but when the wagon began disgorging its cargo of humanity, he rued his complaisance. Two other grown men got out first—rough, ill-favored men—then two slatternly women, and two small children, one of whom had to be awakened and began to cry lustily. Henry's chores were done, and he told the women to go to the house, while he got some hay and grain for the horses. As he looked at the poor brutes and noted the pitiful corrugation of their ribs, their heads hanging dejectedly down over the neck yoke, thin and red and dispirited, he wished that he might turn the creatures loose in the crib; and, but for their sakes, he would have wished again that he had not agreed to take these people in. It was a maxim of Henry's that one could always tell a man's character by the condition of his horses; and on that theory there was surely little that could be said for his guests. Two half-starved dogs, and a couple of guns hanging on the side the wagon, served as corroborative evidence of the character of the men.

They had their own food, except milk and eggs, which Rosie

gave them. One of the women cooked supper and they all ate greedily. Even the sick child ate so ravenously that Henry and Rosie more than suspected that the illness was the result of hunger. When they had eaten and the women had washed the dishes, Rosie cleared the kitchen floor and made two beds for the women and children—the men agreed to sleep in the wagon.

Before lying down to sleep that night, Henry and Rosie held a whispered conference regarding their guests. Rosie's almost unerring intuition told her that these men were thieves, worse, and she suggested that she and Henry take turns watching through the night. Henry finally dissuaded her from this, but agreed to keep the axe at the head of his bed and to sleep as lightly as he could. Rosie knew how easily he was awakened by unusual noises, and finally agreed; but she slept only fitfully that night, and, after some hours of alternate wakefulness and frightening dreams, suddenly found herself sitting bolt upright, listening and peering into the dark.

"What's that?" she whispered, seizing Henry's arm.

Henry awoke with a start. "What?"

"Listen!"

Henry sat up in his bed and listened. Presently they heard a chicken squawk.

"They're after the chickens!" Rosie whispered.

Henry slipped out of his bed, and, grabbing the axe, started for the chicken coop in his bare feet and undershirt. As he rounded the corner of the coop, he almost ran bodily into a man and woman, each carrying an armful of chickens. Embarrassed to meet a woman in his state of undress, his first impulse was to retreat, but the pair saved him the necessity by dropping their chickens and disappearing around the other end of the coop. For a moment Henry stood dumbfounded, then started back to the house to dress for further investigation. As he neared the house, a man and woman and the two children came running from the kitchen door, with arms full of bed clothes. They were upon him before they saw him, and shied around to the wagon at top speed.

When Henry got to the house, Rosie refused to let him go out again.

"Suppose they do steal a few chickens," she argued; "I guess we can get some more. They have guns and you are only one, and you have nothing but that axe. Don't you go!"

Not long afterward, and still long before daylight, they heard the wagon rattle out of the yard and down the road, and the next morning found several chickens' heads in the yard.

How much else had been stolen they could only guess.

"Well, I think we've learned our lesson," said Rosie at the breakfast table. "We'll just let some of the neighbors keep the next gang of chicken thieves. I'm getting tired of it."

One evening, not long afterward, just as Henry was washing for supper, a team of small, fagged horses turned into the yard, dragging a covered wagon that seemed far too heavy for them. Henry stepped out into the yard, but as he walked over to the wagon, he was still resolved to take in no more movers.

The driver of the wagon looked hesitatingly at a few big flakes of snow, as they circled in the air and fell gently to the ground. "Good evening, my friend," he said at length, in a voice so full of discouragement that all Henry's firm resolves faded in a moment. "I suppose you have enough to do, with your own folks, but I wonder if there's a chance to get a place for a woman to stay who isn't feeling right well. We can sleep in the wagon—my wife and I and the children—but the woman with us isn't so well."

"Oh, I guess so," said Henry, immediately touched. "I'll go and see the wife about it," and Henry went back to the house, where Rosie had been watching the negotiations through the window. In a short time he returned with permission to camp and to come to the house for supper. The man remonstrated a little at the latter, as involving too much trouble, but finally consented to come in, on condition that he be allowed to bring some of his own supplies along as a contribution to the meal. Two women and two small children appeared from the depths of the covered wagon, wrapped in ragged coats and shawls, and were assisted to the ground. Henry directed them to the house while he and his guest unhitched the horses.

"It's too cold for horses to stand out. I'll make room in the stable for them," Henry insisted; and the man acceded without remonstrance. When his horses were fed and bedded, he returned to the wagon, pulled out a long box, and, hoisting it upon his shoulder, followed Henry to the house.

As Henry entered the house and saw his guests in the lamp-light, he was glad he had not turned them back on the road so late in the evening. One of the women, apparently the man's wife, was helping Rosie prepare supper; and a friendly patter of conversation was passing between them, while the other, a thin, gray-haired woman with an air of resigned sadness, sat aside by the wood box, with her arm around one of the children and the other child in her lap. Ever so faint a smile came to her face and threw wrinkles around her great blue eyes, as Henry entered; but immediately her face resumed its settled melancholy. Henry and Rosie presently learned that she had lost her husband in the massacre at Sappa Creek, in Decatur County, and had suffered almost worse than death herself at the hands of the Indians.

When the grub box had been set on the floor, the busy woman opened it and took out a can of cookies and one of sugar, a glass pitcher of clear white syrup, a glass of jelly, sack of prunes, and lastly a sack of candy, and placed them all upon the table. Such a wonderful display of goodies and sweets made little Laura and Billy open their eyes wide with wonder and hopeful anticipation.

The Hutsons—that was the name they gave—were people of more than ordinary means, or had been such at one time; and before supper was over it was evident that they were people of character and refinement quite unusual in the new country. The children were quiet and well behaved, and spoke scarcely, a word during the entire meal; but when supper was over they soon struck up a friendly game of hide and seek with Laura and Billy.

Supper over, Rosie and the two women set to work to clear up and wash the dishes, while Henry brought in an armful of wood. They had a good visit with their guests that evening, and listened with interest to Hutson's story of the Sappa Creek massacre. The man had not only lost his brother in the massacre—the husband of the woman who seemed so sad—but had lost all his money also in two years in Decatur County and was going back to Iowa to start anew. Henry and Rosie were glad they had taken him in for the night.

In spite of drouth and destitution, the people who remained in Henry's neighborhood carried on, much as usual. Downs acquired a bank, a creamery, an "ice cream saloon," a school house, a race track, and voted bonds for a bridge across the Solomon.

Some of the town's aristocrats were much interested in fine horses and horse-racing. There were a few men in town who suffered little from the general depression. The lumberman always made money, some of the railroad men managed to live well—on much more than their salaries; and with the coming of prohibition the druggist became a citizen of much importance. At first the probate judge in Osborne got a fee for filing medical applications for liquor, and was reported to be making three hundred dollars a month in this business; but the druggist presently learned to change the figures in the applications, saving most of this profit for himself, and could afford one of the fastest horses in town. The seasoned nobility of Cawker City had not only race horses but a new pigeon shooting club to help pass the time. A singing school was organized at the Rose Valley school house, up on Dry Creek, and Henry and Rosie went a few times; but Rosie never got the hang of the Do, Re, Mi. She and Henry gave a party one night and broke into the society column of the Downs *Times* by serving ice cream. Not to be outdone, Fred Wetzel gave a party too, and was rewarded by a full account of it in the paper, with the complimentary statement that Wetzel had "three pretty daughters and a hundred and fifty dollars worth of lightning rods on his house."

The perennial search for minerals went on, with coal discoveries reported at several points in the county, and a gold craze at Bloomington, where a bit of the yellow metal was found at the bottom of a well.[1] A proposal to build a woolen mill at Osborne was discussed hopefully, while a college was built at Harlan—Gould College, a United Brethren institution.

Chapter Twenty-one

Unkind Seasons

Winter set in early, the winter of eighteen eighty, with a blizzard a week before Christmas that drove the temperature to twenty-two degrees below zero. Such a winter was to be endured and not enjoyed, a time when the family hugged the little stove and longed for genial spring. The children had shoes and flannel underwear, and Rosie made them each a pair of mittens; but they were never so warmly clad that they could enjoy playing long out of doors. Sometimes they went out to play, but always came back in a little while to warm themselves by the fire. Even in the house, the floors were so cold that unless they were running about they had to sit by the stove and toast their feet much of the time. Playing in the house, they mussed up things terribly in the crowded little rooms, and added heavily to the work of housekeeping; but Rosie had a generous understanding of child nature and allowed them to romp about with reasonable freedom.

It was too cold to cut wood, and the wood that Henry had stacked up in the yard was used sparingly, with cow chips gathered in the pasture. Thin, hungry cattle, with snow melting on their backs, stood hunched up on the south side of the stables and straw stacks, in dumb and stolid misery, which for many of them ended in the snow drifts that the next blizzard piled up around them. Henry's cattle lived, but they grew thin on poor fodder and straw. He butchered his little pigs because he had nothing to feed them. They were so thin that, as Rosie said, "You could almost hang them on the clothes line."

The snow and cold drove the wolves to depredations on the poultry and livestock, and many of the neighbors lost chickens and calves. Cattle and horse thieves were busy too, although Henry lost only one cow—to a local cattle buyer, he always believed. Early in February the last sticks of wood were gone and Henry went out to chop more. He had been at work only a short time when, by some mischance, his foot slipped, wrenching his back so severely that he had to crawl back to the house and get Rosie to lift him into bed.

Help was needed. Luckily Annie Bartsch was there that day, and she rode Sam home to get her brother Ford.[1] Unmittened and poorly clothed against the biting wind, she froze her fingers and toes before she was halfway home, and had to stop at one of the neighbors to thaw them out; but she finally reached home, and sent Ford down to help with the chores. It was two weeks before Henry was able to do his work again.

In April Rosie went back to Holton to a family reunion—her first ride on the new railroad—taking all of the children with her.[2] There were four of them now, none old enough to have to pay railroad fare. Before she left she had a neighbor girl come for a few days to help with the work, so she could make some clothes for the children. This later brought her some embarrassment, for the girl had lice in her hair; and Rosie had scarcely reached her old home when she noticed that the children had lice, and nits too. She saturated their heads with coal oil and combed their hair carefully into a newspaper, but it took several days to get entirely rid of the vermin. The ride back home a week later seemed long and tedious, with four tired children on her hands, but the conductor was very kind to her—something she appreciated deeply. Rosie had never read about Malthus,[3] but she was always a bit ashamed of the fact that she had so many little children.

Even in the hardest times, the festive days must be remembered. May the nineteenth was the eighth anniversary of Rosie's wedding; and Henry bought her a half-dozen glass goblets—about the first glassware she had ever owned—and her mother sent her a glass of tomatoes. It seemed a fine opportunity to entertain, so Rosie invited the Higginbothams down to help eat the tomatoes.

She felt under special obligation to the Higginbothams. Not long before, when she and Henry were there late one Sunday afternoon, the Higginbothams had insisted that they have supper before they go, and had served cake at supper—a cake that Annie

Higginbotham[4] had baked. They had scarcely finished supper when Annie came home with her beau, and she was obviously disappointed when she found that there was no cake left for the young man. Rosie was much embarrassed to think that she had eaten cake intended for someone else; and as soon as she got home that evening she opened a can of peaches—the only can of fruit that she had in the cellar—and gave Laura part of it to take up to Higginbotham's as a contribution to supper, for Annie and her beau. Laura got there too late for their supper and Rosie decided that she would do something for the Higginbothams just as soon as an opportunity came.

Another dry, scorching summer followed. Henry and Rosie hoed the corn with particular care, but it burned and shrivelled to fodder in the steady hot winds of July and August. The grist mills along the Solomon that stopped grinding in March because high water washed out the dams closed down in August because of low water. Some of the settlers now argued that Osborne County was not a farming country and should be abandoned to grazing. Again the train of mover wagons moved east along the dusty road, again nightly campers along the road by the cottonwood grove came in to get water and milk and eggs, again Henry and Rosie began to wonder whether it would ever be possible to rear their growing family decently in the new country; but, as before, there seemed to be nothing to do but stay. There were so many farms for sale that land was worth little, and they had little but their land.[5]

"We'll just have to stay, and manage somehow," declared Rosie grimly. "There'll be good years again, and some of these neighbors will be back again, wishing they hadn't gone."

So they stayed, gathered all the buffalo bones and bones of starved cattle that they could find along the creek and river, and sold them to the junk dealer in town for enough to buy shoes and clothes. They even added to their household equipment at some of the sales that were held in the neighborhood. Henry bought a churn, a cupboard, a chair and a boiler. Mary Hunker had once borrowed the boiler and had burned several holes in the bottom. Rosie pulled rags through the holes and made the boiler serve for several years, but she needed a new one. In a characteristic moment of generosity, Henry bought Rosie a cooking range too—a range with six lids and a reservoir. Rosie failed to clean some of the second-hand furniture carefully, and as a result was soon fighting an invasion of bedbugs.

In January another baby was born.[6] He was very fat, Robert was, no prize winner for a beauty show, but Rosie declared he was "lieb."[7]

Chapter Twenty-two

Good Years and the New House

Good years came again. In eighteen eighty-two there was a good crop of wheat, and some corn, in spite of a blazing hot September. Wheat prices rose above a dollar, and land buyers of early spring paid for their farms with the first crop. Prairie schooners moved west again, and several neighbors who had left the year before came back, bought livestock for twice what they had received for their own, and settled down to farming, resolved never to leave again. Jesse Bender sold the Vietz farm before the rains and moved to Wyoming, where the hunting was better.[1] Kansas was becoming too tame for Jesse and his boys. Henry and Rosie prospered moderately. From the sale of wheat and hogs, Henry got enough to pay the seven-hundred-dollar note that he owed to Rosie's father, and to buy a horse-drawn corn planter.

In the bitterly cold winter that followed, a few of the neighbors lost cattle, and several of Henry's hogs froze to death; but late February brought the warm sun and the hopefulness of spring. Henry had sixty acres of wheat—not too much to handle now, with his binder—and the yield was thirty bushels per acre; and corn was the best in years. Garden crops were plentiful too, with big watermelons—for the family, and for the neighbor boys, who stole many of them. The wild plum trees Henry and Rosie had planted a few years before began bearing great quantities of small red and yellow plums, of which they made a kind of plum butter—corrosively strong and sour, but for many years about the only fruit or spread the children had to eat on their bread. Rosie put it up in jars, jugs and kegs—glass jars were yet almost unknown—and sometimes it worked up sufficient pressure to blow the bungs out of the kegs, with a detonation that sounded like light artillery in the cellar. Henry was once carrying up a keg of this when the bung blew out, missing his chin by an inch or two and spraying plum butter all over the wall and ceiling of the cellar. That spirited design in plum butter could be traced on the cellar wall for years afterward.

Once when a keg of plum butter fermented too badly to be used, Henry took it out to the hogs. Pretty soon some of the smaller pigs began to show signs of intoxication. Several of them started away from the trough, wobbling unsteadily on their feet, then lay down and went to sleep. Others that had perhaps not eaten quite so much became very bellicose and chased the dog out of the pen, then squirmed through the fence and chased him right up to the kitchen door—a much puzzled and astonished dog. The ducks ate some of the stuff, and soon they were on a spree too. Some lay down and went to sleep, others flapped their wings and tried to fly and sing and do all sorts of things scarcely proper for barnyard ducks. Rosie saw some of this strange behavior from the kitchen door and could not imagine what was the matter, until she happened to remember the fermented plum butter.

With melons and plums ripe, Rosie had a great deal of company that fall; and few came in vain. If Rosie could not give them a bucket of plums, she at least cut a melon for them—generous slices always, even for people who had no watermelon themselves because they were too lazy to hoe them.

The country was booming again, and land buyers from the East hammered poor little livery horses over the backs looking around for choice farms. Gould College, at Harlan, added dormitories to its modest plant; and talk of a woolen mill was resumed— this time to be built at Gaylord—while a townsite was laid out at the Great Spirit Spring near Cawker, and plans were drawn for a big hotel.[2] Indefatigable diggers still searched for coal at several points. The farmers were building houses and barns, and buying buggies and organs with their money; and the Downs *Times* reported three pianos in the growing metropolis. Now that the people had money, there were parties and festivities, with oyster suppers and taffy-pulls quite the style.

There were, indeed, a few flies in the honey. The county treasurer ran away with twelve hundred dollars of county funds.[3] Luckily, Henry was not one of the signers of his bond. There was much complaint about "county-seat cussedness" of all kinds anyhow. It was the custom of the county treasurer, when personal taxes were not paid, to send the sheriff to serve notices,[4] and to charge each taxpayer for the entire trip to the county-seat, even though the sheriff might deliver a dozen notices on the trip. There were some sarcastic remarks about the sheriff's horse, which, by the county records, often travelled as much as four hundred miles a day. Graft in the use of passes, in the county printing, and in hiring lawyers to prosecute county suits was freely charged; and again there was talk of moving the county seat from Osborne to a town where the moral tone was higher.

There was much complaint about monopoly, and an Anti-Monopoly party arose, with the local line creamery as the special devil to be slain. When the creamery came, some of the farmers went into milk production, and the price of cream soon tumbled. The creamery manager said his reductions were forced by declines in the Kansas City price, but the farmers insisted that they had been enticed into the business just to be skinned. They held meetings, and passed resolutions, and called for subscriptions to a cooperative creamery; but nothing more was done.

On July twenty-seventh, the birthday of Downs, Henry and Rosie took the children down to the celebration—the "annual drunk," as the Osborne newspaper truthfully but unkindly called it. Five thousand sweating celebrators, from the country and from the towns up and down the valley, milled about the streets, spending hard-earned money on ice cream, bad lemonade, and balls to throw at negro dolls. Laura and Billy and Alice and Danny took little interest in the speeches by Governor Glick and Senator Ingalls;[5] but the foot race was not bad, and the ice cream Henry bought for them was something to be talked of for days afterward. When evening came—chore time—they were tired out and slept all the way home, untroubled by the fact that they were missing the grand ball at the St. James Hotel. Altogether the celebration was a grand success, in spite of the fact that, as the Downs *Times* reported, there were only two fights all day.

Not long afterward, Freddie Lutz, the little son of one of the neighbors living up on Twelve Mile Creek, was drowned—drowned in the creek as he was on his way to meet his father coming in from the field.[6] Henry and Rosie went to the funeral, taking the children along, of course. When Billy saw the body in its little casket, he exclaimed:

"Er ist wirklich tot! Ist schwartz!"[7] The body had already turned very dark. Someone had decorated it with zinnias, set in a row along the inside of the coffin.

When Carrie Howell, a little girl in Downs died,[8] a friend contributed the customary poem, which was printed in the *Times:*

> They have folded—sadly folded
> The death-shroud o'er her breast.
> They have clasped her white hands softly
> And laid her down to rest.
> They have parted back the tresses
> From her young and lovely brow.
> And the seal—the fearful seal—
> Is on her sweet lips now.
>
> Like the half-unfolded rose-bud,
> Like the leaflet's verdure hue,
> Hath she drooped in childish beauty
> And faded from the view.
> Let the tears flow down in silence,
> Let the stricken spirit moan,
> And the broken heart-strings quiver
> With a wildly plaintive tone.
>
> O we weep, that ne'er the eyelids
> Their heavy droopings ope,
> That to the deeply yearning gaze
> Comes back no answering hope.
> The pale cheek, with its death hue,
> Forevermore is chill,
> The sweet lips, with their tenderness,
> Forevermore are still.
>
> Long years of weary mourning here
> May wait the grief-touched heart;
> And clouds may shroud the darkened sky,
> But joy shall bid them part.

A seraph smile shall lure thee on,
Where angel voices ring,
And deep notes from the starry world,
A soothing balm shall bring.
Though cold the lips, whose dying breath
Caused thee thus to weep,
A hovering spirit o'er thee broods,
Since Carrie fell asleep.

These "lines" were so generally satisfactory and popular that when one of the women in Downs died the next year, they were published again with changes appropriate to the occasion.

Old Frank died in September, from eating too much wheat out of the chaff end of the straw stack. While Henry was digging the grave, Sam stood near, looking on sadly, as if he understood that he was to be alone thereafter.

Henry and Frank and Sam! How many acres of sod they had turned under, in their years of breaking prairie together! Several years in Iowa they had done little else, and since coming to Kansas, they had broken sod, not only on Henry's claim, but for many of the neighbors. Henry understood the operation of a breaking plow as no one else in the country did—could set it so that it would run a long way without any guidance or attention—and Frank and Sam had the knack of the business too. He never could do so well with any other team.

Not long after Frank died, little Joe died of distemper. Little Joe was the friendliest and most playful little colt the children had ever had, and it was a time of genuine sadness when Henry and Billy dug the grave—Billy helping with all his strength, as if it were a service he owed his little pet. When the grave had been covered, Laura and Alice sang a hymn and put a bouquet of flowers at the head. There were heavy hearts around the table that evening, and for days afterward.

Several other horses got the distemper about the same time, but Rosie made hot egg soup for them, and they finally recovered.

When the first frost came in October, Henry loaded the children into the wagon one evening after they got home from school, and drove out to the garden to gather the yellow pumpkins, squashes, beets and carrots, and a few late watermelons that clung to the dead vines. Rosie had a notion that frost-bitten watermelons were not safe to eat, but the children didn't worry much about that. There were two wagon loads altogether, and it was great fun for the children to help load them into the wagon, with spirited rivalry as to which could find the biggest pumpkins. The children carried the pumpkins and squashes and melons into the cellar, and then Henry buried most of the beets and carrots in the garden pit, for use later in the winter. This winter there would be plenty of vegetables to feed the hungry little mouths that were becoming so numerous around the table.

After the corn was husked, Henry had enough money to build a new granary, not of cottonwood boards, but of fine white pine, a granary with four large bins, and a shed for the new Peter Schuttler wagon.

The school district built a new schoolhouse across the pasture that fall.[9] The old log schoolhouse, with its board-and-sod roof—like that of Henry's cabin—had seemed good at first, when school was moved out of Dave Coop's dugout;[10] but it was really a very crude affair. The floor was full of holes, and under it were mice, snakes and rabbits that the pupils sometimes watched more intently than they attended to their lessons. To serve as desks, there was a line of cottonwood slabs running around the room, resting on sticks driven into holes bored in the walls. For seats, there was another line of slabs on legs—really a line of benches. All the pupils sat on the benches, but only the larger ones used the desk, as it was not long enough for all. The smaller pupils sat on benches and held their books and slates in their hands—if they had any books and slates. All the pupils faced the wall, and of course the light was poor; but that did not make much difference, for they studied very little anyhow. The main purpose of the school was that they should learn discipline. The first teacher had been driven out by the rowdies in the school, and Wilson Athey had finished the term with an axe lying on his desk to suppress possible revolts.[11]

When the pupils wished to get out of their seats in the old schoolhouse, they just swung around, lifting their feet over the seat—perhaps innocently kicking their next neighbor in the rib if the teacher was not looking. As the number of children increased,

The home of Fred Wetzel. (Courtesy the Historical Society of the Downs Carnegie Library)

it was necessary to have a larger schoolhouse; and of course the new building was better in every way, with real desks and seats.

Henry's house, even with the stone addition, was beginning to seem small for a family of eight—there were six children now, including the new baby; but it was not only the inconvenience of living there that forced Henry to think of a new house. The family was growing so gradually that he and Rosie had time to get accustomed to their increasingly cramped quarters. Four of the children could still sleep crosswise in one big bed, one in the baby bed, and the baby slept with Henry and Rosie—three beds were enough for all. A parlor would all be very fine, to be sure, but they never had one, and it is not hard to do without what one has never had.

Several of the neighbors were building new houses, however; big story-and-a-half houses, with pine lumber siding, with six or seven rooms, screens and shutters on the windows and jigsawed brackets in the cornices. George Graeber had built a new house and a barn several years before, and had painted on the barn in big letters, "George Graeber, Farmer and Stockman." Then he had bought a surrey, and with what a lordly air did he drive past Henry's place, with his horses checked high and buggy whip in hand! A new house for Henry and Rosie seemed almost a necessity, if they were to preserve their self-respect and their standing in the community. So they began to save and plan and hope.

The next year opened auspiciously, and after some days of planning, Henry staked out the new house—on May the sixth. He had two stone masons come out from town to lay the foundations, and they made a great deal of trouble. One day they found a toad and, after spitting tobacco juice over it, plastered it into the wall. The children did not tell Henry about it until it was too late to get it out, but Henry and Rosie were very angry and indignant. The next day, when the five o'clock whistle blew at the round house in town, Henry saw one of the men drop the stone he was lifting up on to the wall, even though he had the mortar spread for it; and with unusual spirit, he discharged both of them. He then got another man to finish the job.

How splendid the house looked, as the gleaming rows of white pine studs rose above the rock foundation, to the cheery accompaniment of the hammers' tattoo, the raucous scritch, scritch of the saws, and the merry cries of the children as they played about, building little houses with the blocks that dropped from the carpenters' saws! What visions of palatial spaciousness and comfort as more studs were erected, and the rooms at last took definite form! Rosie was busy with plans for furnishing the house long before the plaster was dry, and the children had many a noisy debate as to the room that each should sleep in. How they did enjoy boasting of the new house to the Athey children—the Atheys still lived in a half-dugout!

The new house was a story and a half high, with six rooms—big rooms—and a pantry, and two porches, one of which had pillars and a balustrade and a portico above; and there were brackets in the cornices, and a bay window with three sashes. Two chimneys, one for the parlor and one for the big kitchen, rose high above the roof. In the parlor, there was a raised plaster circle in the center of the ceiling, and a hook in the center of that where the lamp was to hang, when they could afford a hanging lamp. There was a cellar under most of the house, with an inside and an outside entrance. Then there were screens in most of the downstairs windows. No need to hang mosquito netting over the windows and doors, as they used to do in the old house, or to build smudges around the door on summer nights to keep the mosquitoes out! No need to shoo flies from the dinner table any longer.

To more sophisticated eyes, the house and its surroundings would have seemed none too friendly or homelike. The house itself stood out, stark and bare and white, like a great monument, on a foundation much too high. The back porch rested on stone pillars high enough to form a shelter for the dog and chickens on hot summer days. There were no trees close enough to afford shade, no shrubs of any kind to soften the barrenness of the walls, no walks anywhere, nothing but hard-packed dirt about the old house and the new, barren of grass and even weeds. Beyond the hitching post, where the wagon stood when not in use, there were patches of buffalo grass, purslane, rag weeds, knot weeds, and horse nettles; and around the stable sorrel dock and sunflowers grew high and thrifty.

It was impossible to finish the entire house with the money in the bank, and Henry wanted to borrow enough to finish it, but Rosie would not agree to that.

"We'll get along without plastering the upstairs for a while," she declared, "rather than borrow money. If we get a few bad years, we will be glad we are not tied down with a mortgage anyhow."

She did not realize how prophetic those words were, but Rosie had a habit of saying prophetic things. She usually planned for the worst that could possibly happen. Then if fortune frowned, she was prepared for its worst blows; and if the future proved better than she had expected, it was easy to come adjusted to happier circumstances. Rosie was not calmly philosophical in her pessimism, indeed she met adversity with far less serenity than Henry did; but she was learning the only practical way to manage in a country where there were more lean years than fat, where optimism pointed the way to debt and disaster. So the upstairs was left unfinished, while, as a compensation, a new luxury was provided from the left-over lumber, a luxury that Rosie had been hoping for since she first came—and one that few of the neighbors had—a neat little privy, which was built out behind the choke cherry trees.

There was even a carpet for the parlor, a rag carpet that Rosie's mother had made when she heard that there was to be a new house—dear mother with nothing else to do, of course. When this was laid over a heavy mat of straw it made a carpet so soft and luxurious as to trip an occasional unwary guest.

But most wonderful of all was the new organ that Rosie's father sent—a great, high organ, so high that its ornate top reached almost to the ceiling, covered all over with little jigsaw gimcracks and figures and designs and knobs and scroll work.[12] On the stops, in handsome, elaborate letters, were grand insignia: Bass Coupler, Melodia Forte, Diapason, Viola, Celeste, Celeste Forte, Melodia and Flute. Wouldn't it be grand when Laura learned to play! None of the children but Laura were allowed to play it, and she was not allowed to pump the pedal too fast, lest she injure the bellows. Rosie almost dreaded to see the preacher come, because when he played he always pumped so fast.

Another luxury, almost more important to Rosie than the organ, was a new kind of tablecloth she got in town one day—they called it "oil cloth." It was glossy and almost as easy to wash as china. Rosie was looking for a wedding present for one of the Hunker girls when she found this new oil cloth, and after buying two yards for the wedding gift, she could not resist the temptation to buy two yards for herself.

Even before the house was completely done, the beds and stove and a few pieces of furniture were moved over from the old house, which was soon partly filled with corn from the south field. It was another great corn year.

In all her happy planning for the new house, Rosie never realized how hard it would be to leave the old one; and when she got her last armful of dishes and pans from the old log cabin, she turned for a moment at the door to look back. A chapter in her life was now closed, a chapter of buoyant hope and modest realization. How the pictures thronged before her as she stood at the doorstep, looking back into the little room with the pile of yellow corn in the corner! Scarcely a dozen years ago it was, when she first scrubbed the floor and set the sacks of flour against the wall, fixed the shelves, and washed and set the dishes to rights. There, by the door, only ten years ago, she had stood with little Albert in her arms and watched the light fade in his bright eyes—it seemed an age since that day. And there the little stove had stood, radiating its kindly warmth on winter days. How often she had sat there with a baby in her arms, talking over problems with Henry! How lonely and deserted the house seemed now, even though every nook and corner was peopled with the images and recollections of those busy and hopeful years!

As she stood lost in memories of the old house, Laura came running up from behind.

"Mamma, they want to know where to put the bed, up in the preacher's room. Can you come and show them where?"

Rosie wiped away a tear with her apron, and, taking Laura's hand in her own free hand, walked slowly over to the new house. As they entered the spacious kitchen, Laura burst into enthusiastic comments:

"Isn't it nice, Mamma, and big and fine? Don't you think we'll like it over here?"

Rosie paused a moment, and answered quietly, "I hope so."

Soon after they moved into the new house, they decided that they must have yet another extravagance—a well for the cattle, down by the corral. The old well, near the house, was some distance from the corral and from the stable, and the watering of the livestock every morning and evening meant a great deal of work and trouble. Someone had to open the gate, herd them into the yard and up to the well, watch them all the time lest they run away, and finally drive them back into the corral again. Sometimes strays and laggards failed to come up with the rest of the herd, and later demanded a special dispensation. The cattle trampled out the grass around the house, sometimes even invaded the garden, on a few occasions tore Rosie's clothes down; and always, Rosie believed, they left many flies at the house. Then too, there was usually a mud hole around the trough, as long as the cattle drank there. With the new house Rosie and Henry were anxious to get grass growing in the yard again; so Henry hired a man to help him, and together they dug a well down by the corral. He did not put a pump in for several years, but the new well saved many steps, and the yard soon looked better too.

It was a good year for everyone, 'eighty-four was. Henry was not the only one to build a new house. Some of the neighbors built houses and barns too, and bought barbed wire, new implements, and blooded live stock. Steam threshers were coming in, cutting the labor of threshing about half and releasing horses from the kill-

The Big House, home of Wilson Athey. Built in 1892, the two-story structure boasted fifteen rooms and a huge kitchen—but no closets. (Courtesy the Historical Society of the Downs Carnegie Library)

ing drag of the horse power, where horses sometimes died on hot days. Wind power was being used more, and a neighbor across the river built a windmill with a wheel thirty feet across, to grind feed and crush cane. The Cawker Mining Company reported a coal discovery at three hundred seventy feet, and made plans for mining. If coal discoveries and reports of coal discoveries could have been burned, the settlers would not have needed to burn corn that winter. A man at Cawker also reported the finding of a bed of potters' clay, but no one seemed to know what to do with it. There was talk of a street car line from Cawker to the new town at Waconda Springs; and the Downs *Times,* in an outburst of enthusiasm, declared that Downs needed a cheese factory, a canning factory, a woolen mill, a paper mill and a sugar mill. Two of the local promoters built a skating rink, where roller skating became a fashionable sport, and where magic lantern shows and phrenologists' and ventriloquists' exhibitions were held. With prosperity came the rise of a new aristocracy, and the Downs Social Club was organized to sift out and put the stamp of approved excellence on the genuinely fit people of the town. Henry and Rosie read of their euchre parties in the *Times*, but only two and a half miles away, they knew almost as little of that life as they knew of the doings of the Russian nobility.

Education was not neglected in the general enthusiasm. Gould College, at Harlan, boasted of an attendance of fifty-eight students and reported the organization of the Alpha Beta Society, to give tone to the life of the college; while Beloit offered to raise twenty thousand dollars, if the Methodist Church would build a college there. Education in Henry's home school suffered from an epidemic of prairie itch,[13] which made it necessary to close the school for several weeks.

Chapter Twenty-three

Trouble for the Little Children

In the new house there were many troubles, from the very beginning. Even before it was completed, baby Louise,[1] only a year old, was nearly killed by a fall from the second story—a sheer fall of eight feet to the floor below. One of the older girls had dragged her up the steps to see the wonders of the up-stairs, and had then forgotten about her, whereupon the little baby, in a fine spirit of inquiry, proceeded to crawl over the edge of the stairway, landing on her head on the floor below.

Laura picked her up while Billy and Alice raced out to tell Rosie, who was stripping cane in the west field. Rosie dropped her stripping stick and ran to the house. She took the still unconscious child that Laura was holding helplessly in her arms, carried her out into the yard, and blew into her face, but no sign of life appeared. She tossed her up in the air, again and again, then listened for the sound of breathing, but there was none.

"Run and get papa! Quick!" she cried to Laura, who was standing by, wide-eyed with fright. Laura was gone in a twinkling, running as fast as her legs would carry her, down to the field where Henry was snapping a load of corn.

Rosie took the baby into the house and laid her on the bed, ran out to the well for a bucket of fresh water, and set to work bathing her face and head with a wet cloth. Soon Henry came running up past the stable, and he tried rather awkwardly to help her. After a while they saw the baby gasp, then breathe ever so faintly. The livid blue color of her face turned to bloodless white and she began to cry plaintively. A half hour later she sank into a sleep that was as much a stupor as a real sleep. Rosie and Henry took turns watching her the rest of the day, and into the night.

The next morning a great blood boil had risen on top of her head, and Henry and Rosie promptly took her to the doctor. He lanced the boil, and the baby recovered. How tenacious to life are these soft and tender little beings, sometimes!

Other troubles were in store. The plastering on the house was not yet dry when the family moved in, and the dampness brought several of the children down with colds and croup. One night, about midnight, Rosie was awakened by Danny's violent coughing and choking. She arose quickly, lighted the lamp, lifted the child from his bed, and wrapped him in the bed clothes.

"This room's too cold," she said to Henry, who was reaching for his boots. "Go and make a fire in the kitchen, as quick as you can."

Henry rushed out into the kitchen, while Rosie held the struggling boy in her arms. When the fire started burning, she took him into the kitchen and sat down by the stove. Henry got a bottle of skunk oil from the chimney cabinet and rubbed the boy's chest energetically with it, then covered it with a woolen cloth, and wrapped him again carefully in his covers. He next gave him a spoonful of coal oil. For minor cases of colds and croup, Rosie used a mixture of honey and coal oil—when she had honey—but this case seemed too serious to admit of any temporizing, and a dose of pure coal oil was forced down Danny's throat.

Still the child's breath came wheezingly, and the effort brought beads of sweat to his little round face. Then his breath was halted completely, his fingers clutched awkwardly at his flannel gown, and his eyes started fearfully from their sockets. Self-reliant as she was, Rosie always turned to Henry in such crisis as this. She handed the boy to Henry, who dropped into a chair, turned him over on his stomach, and thrust his finger down the boy's throat. The boy vomited, gasped and choked again, then lay limp and motionless on his father's lap.

Rosie snatched the boy up and hugged him to her:

"The doctor! Go quick and get him! Oh, it's too late! But get him anyhow!" She scarcely knew what she said; she only knew that her little boy was going from her.

Henry jerked on his clothes with a few swift motions and was gone. He ran to the stable, fumbled about in the dark until he found the bridle, and started down through the corral to the pasture, confusedly wondering how far he would have to go for Fannie. In the starlight he could see that none of the horses were up near the corral. He ran on, past the stubble field corner that jutted out into the pasture, on toward the schoolhouse that stood at the lower corner. He heard a horse sneeze, and following the sound soon saw them grazing near the fence, at the very foot of the pasture. As he approached, one of the horses snorted and started off at a gallop, the rest following—all but Fannie, God bless her, who stood quietly while he came and put the bridle on. He mounted and started back at a fast gallop—Fannie seemed to know that there was trouble, and she needed no urging as she raced past the stubble field corner and up through the corral. Henry had left the gate open, and they ran on past the stable and up to the house. As he reined up for an instant at the door, wondering whether he should stop to see Rosie before he went on, the door opened and Rosie called out to him:

"Wait! Wait a minute, Henry!"

He jumped down from his horse, his mind running vaguely back to another time, years before, when he had been stopped on a trip to the doctor. He dreaded to enter the house. As he set foot on the step, Rosie spoke again:

"Come, Henry, he's better!" Her voice carried unmistakable cheer, and he saw in the lamplight the hope that lighted her face. She led him over by the stove, where she had put three chairs together to make a little bed. On it was Danny sleeping quietly.

Henry took Fanny back to the pasture, brought in an armful of wood, and then moved one of the beds into the kitchen. The boy was put into it and covered up warm. An hour later, the first lusty cock announced the dawn of another crisp fall day, and the low-burning lamp was turned out; but Danny still slept peacefully in his bed.

What a glorious morning it was! Henry's simple prayer at the breakfast table sounded an unusual depth and sincerity of gratitude.

Danny's troubles were not over, though, for he developed an abscess in his ear which caused him intense pain, and kept Rosie up night after night, and left a serious defect of hearing from

which he was not to recover for many years. Henry and Rosie decided that they would take no more risks. They moved the beds
into the kitchen, and all of the children slept there the rest of the
winter. It was crowded, but not much more so than the old house;
and in the morning Henry took care to have a roaring fire in the
little heating stove before the children got up. They always had
spirited rivalries there in the morning, to see which could get
dressed first.

Chapter Twenty-four

A Happy Day, and an Anxious Night

Laura and Billy and Alice were out in the garden picking potato bugs. Each carried a tin can, into which the bugs were thrown—Billy had his can fixed up specially with a wire bail.

"You're not pickin' your row clean," scolded Laura, examining a vine Billy had just passed. "Look there! You left four bugs on this one vine."

"I guess they're just little bugs, those soft little bugs," said Billy, rather sheepishly, yet with no apology in his voice. "I'll bet you left some too." He stepped over to inspect some of the vines behind her.

"I'm going to tell mamma on you." Laura always thought of herself as her mother's agent in dealing with the younger children.

"All right, go ahead. I'll tell her you stepped on that melon vine."

"I couldn't help that," she snapped. "That vine was in my way, so it was."

"Well, you stepped on it, anyway, and broke it off, so it won't have any melons on. It's worse to spoil melons than potatoes, because it would be worse to get along without melons than without potatoes. These potatoes won't grow, anyway, if it don't rain. I heard papa say so last night."

"I wish we didn't have any potatoes," said little Alice, who had been trying to find some way to get the bugs into the can without touching the loathsome things. Alice was fastidious and utterly opposed to soiling her fingers. "These nasty bugs will be right back on the vines, no matter how many we pick off. We just

175

pick and pick and pick, and they always come back. Not the same ones, maybe, but just as many."

"And more too," declared Billy, throwing a bug into the can with a vengeful swing. "A lot more. I got a lot more in this can right now than I had last time."

"Wouldn't it be nice not to have to pick potato bugs, or hoe corn, or herd the cattle, or anything, like town people?" said Alice wistfully.

"Not any town kids have to pick potato bugs, I bet," declared Billy. "Or hoe, or feed the calves, or herd the cattle, like we do all the time when school is out." Billy stood erect as he spoke, and his tone revealed clearly the pity he felt for himself in his unhappy estate.

"No, but all the country kids have to do such things. All of 'em do." Laura thought it time to bolster up the morale of her workers. "Atheys and Minnie Graeber and Bartschs and everybody—all the country kids—because they live in the country where the potatoes are. You couldn't herd cattle in town, anyhow." Laura delivered this argument with telling force, and for a few moments the conversation lagged.

"Look, there's a buggy coming!" cried Billy suddenly, as he stood looking over toward the Dry Creek corner. "And two horses. I bet it's Graebers been to town."

"I guess they think they're smart," said Laura scornfully, bending to her task. "They think they're awful smart since they got a buggy."

"Nope, it ain't Graebers' horses, nor their buggy neither," announced Billy, as the team drew nearer. "Their buggy don't have that kind of a top. Wouldn't you like to ride in a buggy with a fringe top like that! And black horses! And look at that harness! And celluloid rings, and everything!" The magnificence of the general outlay was too much for Billy, and he dropped his can of potato bugs, spilling part of them on the ground. He quickly scooped them into the can again, with a liberal mixture of dirt.

"It's Uncle John!" exclaimed Laura, as the surrey turned into the driveway. "It's Uncle John and Aunt Minnie, I bet! Mamma said they were coming some day."

"Let's go and see," suggested Billy, vastly pleased with the prospect of something more interesting than picking potato bugs.

"All right. Let's run, but don't spill your bugs," warned Laura, and set off through the weeds and briers at a great speed, followed by Billy and Alice at paces according with their respective capacities.

Sure enough, it was Uncle John, and Aunt Minnie, and Johnnie, and Freddie, and Rosie,[1] and Grandmother—quite a surrey-load for a two hundred mile drive! There were many cheery greetings and kisses and how do you do's and how are you's and when did you start and how did you leave everybody and how is the baby—Rosie had another baby, two weeks old—and if there isn't our little Rosie and Freddie and Johnnie and Laura and Billy and Alice and Danny and Robert and Louise; and a thousand questions of small significance except to express the affection and goodwill of everybody. Then too, there were cousins Johnnie and Freddie and Rosie to play and quarrel and fight with, and cake and pie and good things to eat at dinner, since company was come. Of course, Grandmother and Uncle John had brought oranges and cookies and candy, as they always did, and Billy had nearly eaten his orange before Rosie noticed that he had forgotten to wash his hands. Then, when the oranges and candy had been eaten, there was the new surrey to inspect, with its shiny nickel lamps on the sides, its soft leather seats and fringed top—quite the most regal turnout the children had ever seen. They promptly took their places in the seats and, whip in hand, had a grand time driving imaginary horses at unimaginable speeds. It was a wonderful day surely, and the potato bugs were quite forgotten in the general happiness and excitement.

That night Henry suddenly became violently ill. The hardships of the Civil War had left him with a poor stomach; and after the war, while breaking prairie in Iowa, he had once become very sick from eating soured apple sauce from a tin bucket. He was baching in his wagon at the time, far from all friends, and the next day was found lying under the wagon, unable to speak or to move. Sick for many days, he was always thereafter subject to attacks of what doctors called cholera morbus.[2]

Illness came this time from drinking wine and milk. Grandmother brought a bottle of wine—a rare luxury for those days—and Henry drank some of it. Not long afterward, in skimming the milk for supper, he was tempted to drink a cup of clabbered milk, of which he was always fond.[3] This caused no immediate distress, and he ate a hearty supper afterward and was in bed before he felt the first violent cramps coming on.

For a few moments he could not imagine what was the cause of his trouble; but then he remembered the wine and the milk and realized what was ahead of him. When another attack came, he wakened Rosie and told her what he feared. Rosie soon had a fire in the kitchen stove, and a pan of bran warming in the oven; but in spite of the hot bran sacks piled around him, Henry grew rapidly worse. At times his knees were drawn up almost to his chest by the violent spasms that pulled at his vitals. He vomited, but no relief followed. Far into the night, Rosie sat by his bed and piled the bran sacks about him.

Long after midnight, she heard him groaning. She knew then that his condition was very serious, for Henry seldom complained—never made a fuss about trifling aches and pains. She leaned over him and listened.

"Henry, are you feeling worse?" she asked.

Only mumbled and half audible syllables came in reply.

"Oh, Henry! Shall I get the doctor?"

The same mumbled and inarticulate grunts were again his only answer.

She felt his hand. It was cold. Surely he was not dying! No, that could not be! Not Henry, who had been at her side these many years, so kind always. She would get the doctor. She would have him there soon, and the doctor would help.

She turned from the bed and opened the door to call upstairs to Sister Minnie, when it occurred to her that Minnie would be of no help, and Uncle John was a cripple. She took up the lamp, ran into the bedroom and roused Laura from her sleep.

"Laura! You will have to run over to Wetzel's and tell Dave[4] to go for a doctor. Papa's terribly sick. Get your clothes on, and go as quick as you can."

Laura rubbed her eyes in perplexity, but immediately caught the spirit of her task, and was dressed in a moment.

"Run as fast as you can! And hammer at the door, and when they answer tell them Papa's sick with cholera morbus, and will Dave go for a doctor. Quick! Go as fast as you can!"

Laura was only a little girl, ten years old, but without a moment's hesitation, she opened the door and was gone. Rosie turned to the bed again. She could still hear Henry's labored and unsteady breathing. After each inhalation, his throat closed, almost with a click, and he held his breath a long time, then blew it out suddenly. He could not speak. None of Rosie's questions elicited an articulate reply. She busied herself with hot bran sacks, and waited, waited for the doctor. Laura came home and was put to bed, and then Rosie sat by the bedside, watching each breath, each movement, each straining spasm of pain, fearing and dreading the next change in the condition of her patient. Once she thought she heard a team coming—the horses galloping in the pasture. Again she thought she heard the sound of a buggy approaching, but it was only the creaking of one of the beds upstairs.

At last she heard the doctor coming. Yes, there was no mistake this time—the horses trotting rapidly in the distance, and then the rattling of the buggy as it came nearer. Rosie was at the door to meet him, with a lamp in her hand to light him up the steps.

The doctor sat down by the bedside and watched the sick man for a few minutes, then rose and got a box of pills from his satchel. These he dissolved in water and after much difficulty, got Henry to swallow the liquid. In a short time he repeated the dose, and this time Henry was able to swallow with less difficulty.

The first gray tints of the dawn were coming in the east, and the cool morning breeze rustled in the cottonwoods, when the doctor rose from the bedside.

"I believe he's doing better now. Keep him warm, and give him some of this medicine every hour; and if any trouble develops, call me. I believe he'll be around in a few days." And the doctor started back to town.

Henry was better, but in the morning other trouble appeared. When Rosie went out to do the milking, she left the baby with Grandmother; but the baby was sick too. Mother's milk under such conditions of strain and anxiety was hardly a fit baby food, and little Joe was sick. He cried constantly, as if in great pain. Grandmother carried him in her arms, back and forth across the kitchen floor, as long as she could, trying to quiet him, but all in vain; and the crying baby finally burst his navel. When Grandmother saw the damage done, she quickly sent Laura out to get Rosie. Rosie, who was nearly done with the milking, hastily stripped the last cow and hurried back to the house, dressed the baby's wound, nursed him again, and finally got him quieted and to sleep.

But there was no sleep for Rosie herself, after that night of anxiety. Henry and the baby both needed attention all day; Grandmother could do little, for she was ill with asthma; Sister Minnie, never really strong, was in bed after the long drive; John was barely able to get around at best, and there were ten children and five grown people to cook and wash dishes for. So Rosie found herself too busy to snatch even a moment's rest during the day; but at night she was so tired that even the crying of the baby did not awaken her. The next day Minnie helped with the work, and a day or two later Henry was able to be out of bed, and even to do some chores.

Sickness and doctor bills are easily forgotten when fortune smiles; and 'eighty-five was a good year. There was a fair wheat crop, and a great crop of corn; but, as the fates would have it, a disastrous epidemic of hog cholera ran through the neighborhood that fall, and most of Henry's hogs died. Corn was so cheap that some of the neighbors burned it in their stoves, but Rosie would not think of such waste. Henry sold some of the corn, and invested the money in stock in a cooperative horse company, a company chartered to buy two expensive imported stallions.[5] The cooperators thought these sires would help to grade up the horses in the community—and Lucifer and Richmond were really magnificent animals[6]—but Henry's investment in the horse company was destined to bring him many gray hairs.

The new country was enjoying its fourth drink, and was almost in a mood to forget that there had ever been such a thing as a serious drouth. Land prices rose to new heights, and some speculators sold farms for twice as much as they had paid a year or two before. With good crops and prosperity, horses doubled in price too, and a good team was now worth more than two hundred dollars. Movers' wagons rolled steadily westward, and the western counties reported a rapid increase in population; Stockton had twenty-four real estate agents to handle the incoming rush of land buyers, and other towns were quite as well provided; but there were not enough good farms for the growing population and many sought other kinds of work. In Norton County there were fifty-

The six older children of Henry and Rosa Ise. In front, left to right: Laura, Louise, and Alice; In back: Robert, Billy, and Danny. (Courtesy the Historical Society of the Downs Carnegie Library)

four candidates for the office of register of deeds, and Phillips County had her choice of forty-seven candidates for sheriff.

The building of new houses and the operation of new industries required a great deal of labor. Downs and Osborne added a hundred houses each during the year, while the new brick plant at Osborne called for a large number of wood cutters to provide fuel. The Farmers' Alliance[7] built a new elevator at Downs, and an enterprising business man established a soap factory to utilize the carcasses of hogs that died of the cholera. A charter was granted to the Kansas Silk Association, "to grow, manufacture and sell silk"; but fortunately the charter represented the promoters' only investment. Tree agents scoured the country, and many of the farmers, forgetting earlier drouths, bought fruit trees. Henry bought enough peach trees to set out a small orchard east of the new house.[8]

The winter that followed was long remembered for its severity. Early in December the worst dust storm in years blew in from the northwest, with a roaring wind that sent the temperature down to zero and piled drifts of dust on the south side of every corn shock. There was much cold weather for a month, and on the night of January sixth, a terrific blizzard struck, with a temperature far below zero. With no thermometer, Henry did not realize how cold it was until he froze his face while feeding the cattle. The wind died down the second day, but the paralyzing cold hung on for several days more, and many cattle and hogs in the neighborhood were frozen. Quails froze to death in the hedge rows, and even rabbits succumbed to cold and starvation. Henry had a great many quail on his place because he never permitted any hunting of quail. Few drivers ventured along the snow-blocked roads, and for nearly two weeks no mail trains reached Downs from the east. The country seemed dead, as if all life had been frozen, like the water in the creeks and river.

When the weather turned warmer, the people, bored with their weeks of hugging the stove, dug out of the snow drifts and went visiting. One night Henry and Rosie even went to town to hear Blind Boone, the famous blind negro pianist;[9] and they sometimes attended the literary society meetings at the Rose Valley schoolhouse, where the two parties in the society—the "Prairie Stampers" and the "Pumpkin Canaries"—debated fundamental questions of the day: "Resolved that intoxicating liquors have caused more misery than everything else combined"; "That popularity elevates a person more in society than merit"; "That this is the age of humbuggery"; "That a liar does more harm in a family than a thief"; "That the Red Jersey pig is more beneficial to the country than the patent attachment harrow"; "That bachelors are a public nuisance and that their immigration should be prohibited"; "That the mind of woman is equal to that of man"; "That a dirty, good-natured wife is better than a neat, scolding wife." Henry was not much of a debater, for he had no "gift of gab," but sometimes he joined in the discussions in a rather embarrassed manner.

The summer that followed was of the kind that turns hopeful men's hearts sad and sour.[10] Dry weather early in June burned the oats yellow, and the wheat filled with shriveled kernels that were barely worth the cutting. Corn began to fire before Rosie and the children had finished hoeing, and did not even make fodder, except in the river field. The pasture dried up, and in the late summer and early fall the cows had to be herded along the road and along the railroad right-of-way—a steady job for Laura and Billy and Alice. Some of the mover wagons that had jogged westward in April were on their way back in September. Times were so hard that, as the Downs *Times* said: "The Lord's Supper, with the original cast, would not draw a full house in any town in the West."

Chapter Twenty-five

A Sick Baby

It was August, and a busy time for everyone, for threshers were coming in the morning. Rosie was working at top speed, paring potatoes, churning and working the butter, baking bread and pies, and cleaning chickens—for threshers had to be fed well, according to the tradition of the time. Little Joe, just learning to walk, was sick and fretful, toddling around after his mother, hanging to her skirts, and crying almost incessantly.[1] Once he got a stick and threatened to whip her if she did not stop and take him up; but the work had to be done, and Joe was allowed to follow around as best he could.

Next day the threshers came, and again there was little time to bother with cranky children; but Cad Winters came up to help, and she was given the task of taking care of the sick boy.[2] Uncle Bob and Aunt Kate Winters with their three children had come to the neighborhood only a few years before and lived on the farm just south of Henry's.[3] The Winters were kind and generous to everyone, and wherever there was need of help, one of them was pretty certain to be on hand. Joe was unmistakably a sick child, feverish and irritable; but he always liked Cad and made little serious trouble. The threshers stayed all that day and the next, and in the bustle and hurry of cooking and waiting on the men and shooing flies from the table—even with screens, there were always flies in the house—and then washing dishes and cooking again, Joe was not the center of interest, except at night, when he kept his parents up much of the time.

The next day was Sunday, a blazing hot August day, but Joe did not cry much, and Rosie began to hope that he was getting better. Mary Bartsch came down after church, and suggested that perhaps the boy was only suffering from teething, and that it was nothing to be particularly frightened about. Rosie felt greatly relieved to hear this, especially as the child became much quieter toward evening.

After supper, the threshers came again, to be ready in the morning; and later, after church, the preacher came with his wife and four children, to stay all night. It was late before Rosie had beds made for all—some of the children had to sleep on the floor. Joe was quiet, apparently much better, and Rosie lay down and went to sleep.

She and Henry were up before daybreak the next morning, and dressed by lamplight, for a busy day was ahead. Little Joe seemed to be sleeping soundly, but when Rosie reached over to turn out the lamp, she happened to look closely at him. His brown eyes were partly open, staring with the fixity of death! She called Henry, and for long minutes they stood looking down at the child, whose scarcely perceptible breathing belied the counterfeit of death in his face.

Henry passed his hand before the staring eyes, but Joe paid no heed, seeing nothing. He stroked the soft brown hair back from the little forehead, but the child seemed insensible to the touch of his hand. Henry took one of the hands in his own. It was warm, but limp and utterly lifeless, and when released, fell like a rag to its place again. He took up the other hand, and the fingers closed weakly around his thumb—yes, there was life there! He lifted the little bare feet and moved them this way and that, but there was no sign of life or vitality. Yet the child was breathing faintly.

"What if it should be . . . ?" He could not say the dreaded word.

"Oh no, . . . not paralysis . . . we haven't been where that was!"

"That's what Nauheim's baby[4] had . . . and Linge's, you know."

"Linge's girl . . . was she like this?"

"No, not exactly . . . not really . . . still she was like this too, in some ways . . . from what he told me . . . a fever, and fretful for a couple of days . . . and then she got . . . like this."

"She died."

"Yes . . . the next day."

They stood for a moment looking helplessly down at the stricken child, then Rosie took him up in her arms.

"Oh, Henry, you must go and get the doctor! Surely the doctor will know what to do! Surely he can do something! Oh, right now!" Rosie hugged the inert little body to her. "I'll watch him till you get back. But go as fast as you can!"

Without a word Henry hastened out to the door, snatching his hat from a nail as he passed through the kitchen; but in a moment he came back.

"Wouldn't it be better to take him to the doctor? We could get there before he could come out."

"Oh, yes. And as soon as we can—as soon as we can get ready."

Henry hurried out to get the horses up from the pasture, while Rosie awakened the children. It was not long before everyone was up. The noise and stir awakened little Joe from his stupor and he began to cry plaintively, but scarcely moved a muscle of his arms or legs. Rosie hurried back and forth, from her breakfast preparations to his bedside, a score of times, in that stiff plodding but resolute and unaccountably swift walk that covered so many miles and so many tasks each day. Breakfast was ready at sun-up, breakfast for the family and the threshers and the preacher's family—twenty-four people altogether—and when they had eaten, Henry hitched the team to the wagon, and they took Joe to town to the doctor. Rosie carried a parasol to shelter him from the sun—already hot in the early morning—and the jarring of the wagon made him sleep much of the way.

The doctor greeted them heartily as they entered his office,[5] but his heartiness faded when he saw how tired and troubled they were.

"Is the baby sick?" he inquired kindly. "This is bad weather for babies."

"I'm afraid he's awfully sick, doctor—cross and feverish since Thursday; and now he can't move either foot." Henry took one of the baby's shoes off and moved the foot this way and that. It seemed utterly lifeless.

The doctor looked on intently, then took a pin from his coat, and pricked the bottom of the foot. The baby cried, but moved not a muscle. The doctor's face turned grave.

"Henry, I wish you would take him to someone else."

"You can do something for him surely, can't you?"

"I'll do my best; but I'm afraid—" The doctor paused a minute to pick up in turn each of the little hands and feet, and move them in various ways; and the boy, mistaking all this for play, laughed back at him, but moved only one arm. "I'm afraid it won't be much—not if it's paralysis."

"You mean you think he won't get—get better?"

"He may get somewhat better, but that won't be my work, or to my credit." Doctor Poole was honest as well as kindly. "Just about learning to walk, I suppose?"

"Just a few days ago."

"I'm afraid, Henry—he will never walk again."

There was no reply. Crushed and numbed as the words struck down upon them, Rosie and Henry stood dumbly looking at the boy in Henry's arms. The doctor's conscience smote him as he saw the cruel force of his frank words, and he tried to speak more encouragingly.

"He might get much better though. He seems hearty and strong, and might overcome it partly." He turned and took down a large bottle from his cabinet.

"Give him a teaspoonful of this every couple of hours," he said, as he poured part of the liquid into a smaller bottle. "Bring him down every day for a while. Give him plenty of good, nourishing food—try to build up his general health and strength. That's the only thing we can do."

They were in the wagon again. Not a word was said, but as they jogged along the dusty road, Rosie milled over and over in her mind the problems that now faced them.

"Never walk again!" The words rang dully in her ears. "Never walk again!" Her little boy, who had walked only so haltingly a day or two—so happy, proud and triumphant at his new feat, laughing aloud as he toddled across the kitchen a few times, and once out into the yard—a greater adventure than he would ever know again—now to creep and crawl, to be carried and wheeled about all the years of childhood and youth, and into helpless age; her little boy, only last week so active and healthy, slowly to shrivel and twist into pitiful incompetency! They could care for him as long as they lived, but when they were gone what could he do? Sell pencils and shoestrings on the streets, as she had seen so many cripples do? Or beg—oh, God forbid that he should ever have to do that! He could hardly hold a county office, for Henry had no political influence. They would try to give him an education, anyhow. Perhaps he would be able to get along.

In the black and jumbled confusion of these disordered thoughts, her little brother's death, years before, came back to her so clearly. She remembered how in his cruel suffering he had pulled handfuls of hair from his head, and how her mother shouted with a fanatical joy when the chubby hands at last lay quiet at his side. Rosie had not understood it all. Even less could she understand, now, how her mother could have felt a great religious joy at such a time. Yet perhaps it might be better if her own boy could go like that; better that he should sleep beside little Albert under the elm tree, than be always a helpless and hopeless burden to himself and everyone else. Life like that, only half alive at best, seemed almost worse than death. And yet how tenaciously do such unhappy victims of the injustice of things often cling to life—life, the last poor thing that can be given up! A glance down at the face of the sleeping child brought a flood of shame and remorse at the thoughts she had harbored. No, in her great mother's heart, she could not give him up, so helpless, so dependent on her love, not while a shred of hope remained. The measure of his helplessness must always be the measure of her love.

Faith in the goodness of God had been her mother's comfort, but it was no help here. The God the preacher talked about, the God of goodness and kindness and justice, how could He visit such a sentence upon a mere baby, still innocent of any fault or wrong—the God who loved children? He could not do it. There would be no fairness in that. No man, not even the harshest man, not the meanest man, could ever do so unkindly. Yet the doctor had said her boy would never walk again.

Little Joe slept peacefully in her lap, oblivious of the hot winds blowing his brown hair about his forehead, oblivious of the joggling of the wagon and the occasional slapping of the lines, unmindful of the occasional tears that fell upon his face. Vaguely, Rosie was at least thankful that he could not know what had been measured out to him. He would find out soon enough. When he wanted to run and play with the other children, then he would know.

Her task, and Henry's, was set. She had no wish to evade or shirk, but it seemed almost beyond her power to do it well. She could care for the other children, even when the dry years came, but here was an added burden of care and expense. There would be a big doctor bill, at least, and perhaps it might be necessary to take Joe to a specialist somewhere. It was at least possible that a specialist might know more than Doctor Poole. They must not risk any chance that a crippled and helpless child should live to accuse them of neglect.

A trip to Saint Joseph to see a doctor would cost several hundred dollars though; and there was no way of getting so much money this fall, with the corn searing in the wind, the pastures brown and dead, and the milk cows drying up day by day. There would be no more than enough for shoes and stockings, books and slates for the children in October, and some flannel to make underclothes. It would cost not less than three or four dollars each, for clothing alone, even when she made everything herself—by washing their underclothes while they were in bed, she could get along with one suit each for Laura and Billy and Alice. At least twelve dollars must be saved for clothing—the price of more than a hundred pounds of butter, at ten cents a pound; and the cows were producing only twelve pounds of butter a week. Eggs, there were only enough to eat, sparingly. Sugar and coffee they could do without, and new dresses and extravagances; but the barest essentials would take everything that could be scraped together. Then there would be medicines to be bought, and perhaps expensive appliances for Joe, even if they did not take him away.

Rosie was still engrossed in her calculations when the wagon rattled into the yard and stopped at the kitchen step. The baby awakened and looked inquiringly about, but did not move or cry. As Henry helped them down from the wagon, he spoke the first words since they had left the doctor's office.

"Well, Rosie, we have a home for him, anyhow."[6]

"Yes, it's our own home; and he can be here as long as we are here," and she carried the baby into the house.

Every day for the next three weeks, Henry hitched up the

team, and Rosie took Joe to the doctor for treatment. And he did improve, slowly. First a finger moved a little, then a toe, then another finger or a wrist or elbow. Hopefully, anxiously, day by day, Rosie and Henry watched for each new sign of life. Even the children took great interest in watching the baby, and every evening, when Henry came in from the field, they had new discoveries to relate to him, of reviving strength and activity. This improvement continued for several months; and the little patient recovered the use of his arm and of one leg, but the other leg remained persistently useless. One night Rosie noticed one toe moving slightly. She awakened Henry to look at it, and together they spent an hour trying to get the child to repeat the movement. When they finally succeeded, they went to sleep more hopeful than they had been in months. For days they watched the little toe anxiously, and at first hopefully; but there was no further improvement.

They tried every kind of patent appliance that was suggested to them, tormented the child with electric currents and belts and harnesses until he cried at sight of such instruments of torture. The doctor gave them medicine for him, nasty, bitter medicine that ate his teeth to black stumps. For a while they were able to bribe him to take it, by giving him a spoonful of apple butter as a reward for each dose swallowed; but finally, wiser than the doctor or his parents, he stubbornly refused to have more of the stuff.

The next summer, although well again in most ways, he still could not walk. The doctor said he would probably never get any better, but Rosie and Henry always hoped that something might turn up that would do what the doctor could not do.

One day a neighbor told them of a doctor in Saint Joseph who had performed wonderful cures—Doctor Bishop, a great specialist in all diseases of children. At this story, the hope that had sunk to embers flamed up once more, and Rosie and Henry were again busy scheming to find the money to take Joe to Saint Joseph.

It was a hard year, though, the most discouraging since grasshopper years. Dry weather set in early. The wheat clung tenaciously to life through April and May; but early in June, the chinch bugs invaded the fields, and in a few days the beleaguered stalks crumpled to the ground. Henry had hoped to mow it for cattle feed, if it did not make a crop worth harvesting, but it was completely ruined before he realized what was happening. From the wheat fields, the chinch bugs wandered over into the corn, already fired with the hot winds; and soon the stalks were dead and bare, and the dry leaves blowing about in the fields, or piling up along the fences and hedge rows.

The garden wilted before it got a start. Hungry for greens in the spring, Rosie always planted lettuce in late March, but the lettuce wilted and died; and second and third plantings fared no better. The potatoes and cucumbers and melons peeped out of the ground, and proceeded to curl up and die. Pastures were brown in June, and the cows roamed about, bawling and breaching the fences—even the new barbed wire fences—wherever a missing staple offered an opening. Henry put pokes on several of the worst of them, but still they managed to get out of the pasture.

Misfortunes came, "not single spies, but in battalions." Billy, an awkward overgrown boy of ten, liked to ride Big Joe, one of the big gray colts that had grown up on the farm; and one day his saddle pinched the animal and set him to bucking furiously. For a moment the boy stuck to his seat, but a sudden tremendous lurch of the great brute threw him high into the air. He landed flat on his back, and lay motionless as the horse ran back to the stable. The hired hand, who was working at the stable, saw the boy fall, and ran to his assistance; but when he stooped to lift him from the ground, and saw the blood ooze from his mouth, he turned to call for help. Henry had seen it all too, though, and was already there. The two carried the limp body into the house, and laid him gently on the floor. At sight of the white face covered with blood, arms and legs dangling helplessly as they brought him in the door, Rosie herself crumpled to the floor; but she was soon revived by a dash of cold water from the dipper, and set to work bathing the boy's face, and trying to get breathing started again.

Henry suggested that he go for the doctor, but Rosie thought he would do better to stay at home and help her care for the boy. It seemed there was little a doctor could do anyhow. Hours later, consciousness returned to Billy, and the dark eyes spoke recognition to those about him; but it was hours more before he was able to speak distinctly. That evening Henry decided to get him into bed, but when he tried to lift him, the boy cried out in such pain that he had to let him lie on the floor. With much cautious pulling and lifting, Henry and Rosie and the hired man managed to slip a heavy comfort under him, and then Henry threw a pillow down on the floor and slept beside him that night. Henry could always sleep so lightly that the slightest sound would awaken him.

The next morning Billy's face was deathly pale, his breath still came in short gasps, as if it hurt him to breath deeply; and he moved only his arms and hands, as Rosie observed with more anxiety than she dared express, even to Henry. Feet and legs that did not move—she had seen such a condition once before! Henry managed to raise the boy's head so that he could drink a cup of water, but Billy would eat nothing, Rosie sat beside him most of the day, while Henry and the hired hand were at work. She sat watching his labored breathing, his hands lying helplessly on the comfort beside him, or pulling weakly at his suspenders. Late in the afternoon, she saw him bend his knees, pull his feet up, and then straighten his legs again; and a load of anxiety rolled off her mind. At any rate he would not be a helpless cripple. When Henry came in that evening Rosie thought Billy was better; and when Billy asked for something to eat, they knew he was better. After supper Henry and the hired man shifted him onto a wide board and carried him into the bedroom, where he soon began to mend. In a few days he was able to sit up in the rocker, and even walk about the house, and in a few weeks he was strong enough to do his work again—the work of a man, at many tasks.

Billy was still in bed when old Sam had to be killed—Sam who, with Frank, had pulled the breaking plow so many long miles in Iowa, had brought Henry in his lumber wagon along the rough roads and trails to Kansas in eighteen seventy-one, and two years later had brought Henry and Rosie out to their new home in Western Kansas. All that is loyal and faithful he had been, and now that he was too old to work, he had been allowed to wander about the place at will, enjoying an old age of leisure. This hard year, though, as the pasture dried up and the feed became scarcer, it seemed evident that Sam might have to go. Neither Rosie nor Henry dared to say it, as across the dinner table they talked over the critical problems of ways and means. Neither had the heart to suggest outright that they should kill the faithful brute; but when all of the horses began to grow thin, and Sam himself began to look gaunt and hungry, standing at the stable door much of the time, patiently supplicant for the doles of fodder and oats straw that were sometimes available there, then the problem took on a new aspect. Life was no boon to such a hungry and decrepit animal, tormented by the heat and flies, and they finally decided to kill him. Henry led him out to the field, tied a gunny sack over his eyes so he might not see, and killed him with an axe. That night supper was eaten in undisguised tears, and in almost reverent silence.

There seemed no end to trouble and grief. A few days later, Fanny, the family pet mare, was found dead in the cornfield. Too small for most heavy farm work, she had been the children's pet, and was so kind and gentle that Rosie always knew that the children were safe if they had Fanny along. To let them mount her, she would lower her head to the ground so they could climb up by holding onto her mane; and there seemed to be no limit to the number of children that could ride her safely at once. Fanny had been sick all summer, and like Sam had been given the freedom of the premises, no one paying much attention to her as she wandered about up to the water trough and back to the field—wherever she wanted to go. On a scorching day in August, one of the children said that he had not seen Fanny for several days. No one had seen her, although no one had thought of it before, and Henry started out to search for her. He found her down in the cornfield, where she had died several days before, after beating down the corn stalks about her, in vain efforts to get upon her feet. The faithful animal, who had never for a moment neglected any of the children given over to her care, had been forgotten for days by all of them in her final distress, in the heat of those August days without feed or water or care.

Rosie was sick with pleurisy[7] that summer, and was expecting another baby in August. Her stomach bothered her a great deal because she had no vegetables or greens to eat—not even lettuce, which she almost always had in her garden.

One day Martha Hunker[8] brought her a basket of lettuce. Martha lived down on the river, about a mile away; but when she heard of Rosie's condition she picked all the lettuce she could find in her garden and walked over with it. On the way over, she found the creek impassable from a rain up north, and had to go two miles out of the way to find a crossing; but she brought the lettuce just the same. Martha was no Venus. She always pinned her scanty hair in a little knot on the back of her head, pulling it so tight that it hurt one to look at her; but she was the kind that would walk four or five miles to bring you lettuce.

Rosie feared that she might not have the strength to pull through the ordeal. In spite of her illness, she had managed to make up a lot of clothes for the children; and one day she took Laura, aged twelve now, into the bedroom, where the clothes were laid out in eight neat piles—one pile for each of the children.

"Laura, I don't know how I'll get along," she said, "but if anything should happen, here are the clothes for the children. They ought to last them most of the winter, if the children are careful. I hope everything will be all right; but if not, you will just have to take hold and do the best you can. You have always been good to do that. It may be you won't need any of those"—she pointed to a pile of white baby clothes—"but if anything should happen to me, and the baby is all right, you might need them."

A few days later, a terrible thunder and rain storm came to break the long drouth; and in the midst of the thunder and the lightning and wind and rain, the baby was born.[9] In the long-drawn pain of her labour, Rosie could not help recalling the birth of her youngest brother many years before; when her mother, sick with typhoid fever, had several times given up hope and had called the children to her bedside to bid them bye. Yet her mother had come through her ordeal safely; and with Rosie "Everything was all right," finally; and Laura did not need to assume her responsibilities. The baby, a healthy, saucy little girl, was not unwelcome, in spite of the cares already piled high. Rosie grimly declared that more babies were not what was most needed, but she would "make the best of it and manage somehow." And with two babies on her hands—Joe was still helpless—she "made the best of it," worked a little harder, a little earlier in the morning, and a little later at night. Laura and Alice were getting old enough to help more—one of them usually took care of the baby and of Joe. Billy now took the place of a hired hand at many tasks, and even Danny, at seven, was old enough to hoe corn, help feed the calves, herd cattle, and get in the wood and cobs.

The rain brought the grass out fresh and green again, and the cattle had pasture for the rest of the summer; but there was only an old straw stack to carry them through the winter. It was clear that it would be necessary to buy feed, if any could be found in the neighborhood. Milk was a major part of the food supply of the family. Butter had to be sold to buy the essential clothing of the family, yet it was sometimes eaten sparingly, too. So the cows provided much of the family living, and it seemed suicidal to sell any of them now, when they were so cheap. Henry and Rosie decided that it would be better to buy feed for them, if they could borrow the money somewhere.

Chapter Twenty-six

More Hard Years and Hard Problems

In all the worry about the general family finances, the trip to Saint Joseph was not forgotten. It was a bitter disappointment that this year, of all years, when there was so imperative a need for money, their work should be so barren of reward; but Rosie was determined that somehow the money must and should be raised. About three hundred dollars would be needed.

Rosie first wrote her father. His reply was that he had no money to spare, but that he would borrow it for her if she could not get it otherwise, and would gladly help her if she wished him to do so.

"I guess we can borrow it here as well as in Holton," she said to Henry when she read the letter.

Henry next went to see John Wise. John got a pension from the government and usually had money to lend, but this year the drouth had struck him too, and he had no money to spare. Finally Henry went to a money lender in town and found he could get three hundred dollars, at fifteen per cent interest, by putting a mortgage on the farm.[1] It seemed a high rate of interest so he drove on to Cawker City to see if he could find someone there who would lend on better terms; but after a whole day of discouraging interviews, he gave up and drove back home.

It was dark when his wagon rattled into the yard. Rosie was in bed with the sore feet that had troubled her all summer. Her bed had been moved into the kitchen, in order that she might better direct the work, and help as much as she could. Henry finished the chores before he came in; and when he entered, Rosie was sitting up in bed, with the lamp burning low on the table where Laura

196

had put some bread and butter and clabbered milk and sugar for his supper.

"You're terribly late, Henry. Where in the world have you been?" she asked.

"To Cawker," he answered, as he poured a dipperful of water into the wash basin. He plunged his face into the cool water, then dried his face and hands, and combed his hair and beard with his usual care before he turned to say more. "I was all over town, and Cawker too; but nobody seems to have any money."

"Couldn't you get any at all?" asked Rosie.

"Oh, yes. At fifteen per cent."

"Fifteen percent?"

"With a mortgage."

"A mortgage on the home here?"

"On both places, and the interest taken out at the beginning."

"You mean forty-five dollars taken out—and leave us only two hundred and fifty-five dollars?" Rosie's voice rose in indignant remonstrance.

"He won't lend any other way, and he says he can keep all his money out at fifteen per cent."

"Armstrong?"

"Yes."

"He won't take twelve per cent? Surely that's enough!"

"No. I don't think so." Henry sat down to the table and ate in silence, while Rosie pondered over the harsh terms that had been offered, with a look that curiously combined hopeless dejection and grim determination. Henry had almost finished his supper when she first spoke.

"It's no use. We can't do it." There was a decisive ring in her voice that made Henry turn from his bowl of milk. "You can't make fifteen percent," she continued. "Twelve per cent is hard enough. It's all you can make. How father and mother and all of us worked to meet the payments, that terrible year at Holton! And it nearly took all we had, too, when the cows got the black leg. You can't do it."

"No, I guess not, unless you have reasonably good luck."

"And you never have good luck. It's always bad luck. Anyhow, that's what you have to figure on. If it isn't hot winds, it's chinch bugs, or grasshoppers, or black leg, or cholera, or distem-

per, or something you didn't expect. Interest is a terrible thing anyhow, a terrible thing, the way it eats and eats, due twice as often as
it ought to be, and always at the hardest time. I never saw interest
come due when it was easy to pay, never."

"No. I guess that's right. Rachowitz's mortgage was only four
hundred, and now they're gone."[2]

"Yes, and I remember how she cried when she told me they
would have to give up their home. And if they had kept it a year
longer, the next crop would have paid the whole mortgage."

Henry pulled off his boots and set them behind the stove. "I
wish we could have seen Doctor Bishop though," he said. "It
might possibly be that he could do something."

"If I thought he really could! But fifteen per cent is too much.
If we can't get the money for less, we will just have to sell a few of
the cattle, and depend on Poole for Joe. Mortgage the place, and
then lose it—that wouldn't be any way to help Joe." Rosie turned
to look at Joe, who was asleep on the bed beside her, his face so innocent and untroubled, even almost smiling, one hand holding
the doll she had made for him, of a worn-out sock.

"It would just be taking a chance." Henry sat for a long while
looking down at his bare feet; and then he arose, wound the clock,
and started to the bedroom. As he reached the door he stopped.

"Can I get anything for you?" he asked.

"No, unless you could put a cup of water and a couple of clean
diapers on this chair for the children, if they wake up."

Henry slipped his boots on and went out to the well for fresh
water. A cool breeze blew up from the south field, and the full
moon poured down a flood of light that covered the parched and
blasted fields and pasture with a deceiving charity. He stood for a
moment with his hand on the well rope, listening to the distant
faint rustle of dried corn leaves in the field behind the stable, and
the sighing of the wind through the cottonwoods, vaguely con-
trasting the peace of the night with the perturbation of his own
troubled mind. He drew a bucket of water, and as he saw the fresh
coolness splash over the edge he was tempted to tip the bucket and
drink. Then he poured the water into the barrel, drew another
bucket, dipped out a cupful, and went back to the house.

"Perhaps we ought to go ahead anyhow, Henry," said Rosie,
as he set the water down on a chair by her bed. All the stubborn-

ness was gone from her voice, and it was the mother who spoke. "Surely we can manage somehow, if it's what we ought to do."

Henry stood looking down at her, and at the babies sleeping beside her.

"When could you get the money?"

"Any time."

"Tomorrow?"

"I suppose so."

"Then perhaps you better do that tomorrow morning. If we are to take Joe away, the sooner the better."

"All right, Rosie. I'll see to it in the morning. Good night." He stooped and kissed her gently, turned out the light, and walked slowly into the bedroom.

"Good night," and Rosie was left with her thoughts and plans and hopes and forebodings. Since Rosie could not get around at all, Henry had to bring Armstrong out next morning to get her signature to the mortgage. When he ushered him into the kitchen, Rosie was sitting up in bed, paring potatoes, with the baby and Joe on either side of her as usual. She pushed the pan of potatoes down toward the foot of the bed, wiped her hands on a dish cloth, and greeted the capitalist with scarcely concealed hostility. When the papers were handed to her, she signed them with a resolute mouth, but with tears coursing down her cheeks.

So they had the money. Aunt Kate Winters helped to make some little dresses for Joe; and a few days later, Henry took him to Saint Joseph.

Henry and Rosie did not know, could not know, that the famous doctor was only a heartless charlatan, who waxed fat preying on the ills of ignorant and unfortunate people; that they might better have thrown their precious money into the well. And of course they could not know that no doctor, however wise and skilled, could ever help their child.

The doctor prescribed more nauseating medicines and electrical tortures, charged seventy-five dollars for his services, and sent Henry back home. For months Henry and Rosie administered the vile medicines faithfully, at first hopeful but gradually less and less sanguine, until in the spring they saw that the treatment was worse than useless and stopped it.

Unable to walk, Joe was soon crawling everywhere—out in the

yard and in the plum thicket, where he made valiant but futile efforts to catch the chickens, and even out to the stable, where he sometimes found his way into the stalls where the horses were tied. Laura cared for him much of the time; but when Laura was at school, Rosie had to watch over him as best she could. She worried whenever he ventured out of sight; and it was one of her chores to go out and find him once in a while, bring him in and give him a bath and clean clothes, for he soon soiled his clothes terribly. It was hardest of all for Rosie to see Joe hurrying out to meet Henry when Henry came home from town. Henry usually brought candy, and when the rattle of his wagon was heard beyond the cottonwood grove, the children always staged a grand race to see which one could get to him first, with Joe in the rear, churning up the dust as he scrambled along. Sometimes Rosie would run out and pick him up, and race to the wagon with him, to see that he got his share of the candy—or, more likely, a little more than his share.

A few years later Joe learned to hobble about a little, but never was able to walk well.

Among the hardest problems during these lean years was the problem of providing for the festival days, Christmas and Easter and the "Twenty-seventh." The "Twenty-seventh" of July was the birthday of the new town, entirely surpassing the Fourth in importance.

Easter was not a difficult problem. Eggs Rosie usually had, which she dyed by boiling them with onion and walnut shells. Cookie rabbits were easy to bake, and she had to buy only some cheap candy, and perhaps a few apples. In later years, Rosie once bought some bananas for Easter—a treat that the children talked about for days afterward, discussing with each other the best way to eat the new fruit to get the most taste out of it. The children looked forward to Easter anxiously; and when that happy morning dawned, and they had all been washed and combed and dressed up in their Sunday clothes, they were allowed to go out and hunt for their plates of rabbit eggs and goodies. These were usually hidden in the grass or in the plum thicket, or even as far away as the straw stack; but once in a while, when it was raining, the plates had to be hidden about the house somewhere. It was something of a problem to insure the smaller children a fair chance in the hunt; and as the family grew larger, Rosie had them form in line, Billy leading with the smallest child on his shoulder, the next smallest just behind, and the rest trailing along according to size. Someone usually hauled Joe in the little wagon. Thus in military fashion they marched about the premises until someone spied the hidden treasures; or if they failed, they would come back to the house and ask Rosie or Henry where they thought the eggs might be hidden. Somehow Rosie and Henry usually seemed able to give them good suggestions.

The Twenty-seventh celebration was a harder problem, because the children had to have a little money to spend for lemonade and candy, and in later years, for rides on the merry-go-round. Each year the financing of the celebration became more difficult, as the children grew older and more numerous.

Christmas was always a festive season for the children, with its preparatory popcorn stringing, singing practice and learning of "pieces," and with the final glittering glory of the candle-studded Christmas tree at the little schoolhouse where church services were held. For Rosie it was an occasion to worry about for weeks ahead. She had to get a few goodies for the children, whatever the cost; and always had to make a fair contribution to the Sunday school Christmas tree. Rosie had never seen a Christmas tree in her own childhood, and she wanted her children to fare better than she had. Then she sometimes exchanged gifts with a few of the neighbors. One year Rosie wanted to get something for Mary Bartsch, and had no money to buy it with, so she gave Mary a dressed chicken. For her contribution to the Christmas tree fund, she gave the due bills she got at the store for butter and eggs. The stores did not pay cash.

Once, when the Christmas program was held at Chris Bartsch's home, Rosie noticed three little guns hanging on the tree, and made out the names of two neighbor boys, Frankie Graeber and Johnny Wise,[3] on two of them. Billy, aged five, had wanted a gun, had talked of nothing else for weeks before Christmas, and had written several letters to Santa Claus asking for a gun—for a gun and nothing else. As he sat there with a group of other boys, Rosie saw him eyeing the little toys hungrily. Through all the tedious preliminary declamations and songs, the poor boy sat with his eyes riveted on those guns; and when the superintendent began distributing the presents, Rosie found herself staring almost as anxiously as her boy did, hoping that he would get one of them. If he did not—she hated to think what a Christmas it would be for him. Billy and Frank Graeber and Johnny Wise were about the same age—it seemed likely that the third gun might be for Billy, yet there were several other boys not much younger. Oh, she would have given her due bills for a month to have a gun there for him!

The superintendent reached for one of them. "Frankie Graeber!" he called out, and handed it down to Frankie, who reached for it with face beaming with happiness. "Johnny Wise" was next! Billy's eyes almost started from their sockets and Rosie could see him twisting about in his seat. Only one gun left. The superintendent took it down and scrutinized the name for a minute—no, it was an age. Billy's hands were already outstretched for it when the man sang out "Billy Ise." Blessed words! Blessed Chris Bartsch, who had put it on the tree! If he had never done another kindly act in his life—and he did a million such things—Rosie would always have remembered him gratefully.

Occasionally the embarrassment would come in another way. Once Rosie had some apples in the cellar, a few of the larger of which she had set aside for use at Christmas. One day when visitors came, she asked Laura to go down and get some apples, explaining carefully that she must get the smaller ones. Laura soon came up with the dutiful report to all that she had "got the very smallest she could find."

On another occasion, when the preacher came unexpectedly for dinner, Rosie privately cautioned the younger boys not to take more than one cookie each, as there were only enough cookies to go around. When the cookies were passed at the dinner table later, the preacher took two. Danny was watching the plate very intently as it went around, and when he saw the preacher take more than his allotment, he could not restrain himself. "Ma," he roared, "he's takin' two at a whack!"

With all the meagerness and hardship of the times, there was always much to lend interest to the lives of the children. Each year there were two or three little colts for pets, and little pigs and calves and chickens; and almost every year there was a little baby—live pets that the toy makers have never been able to equal. Usually the children had one or two prairie dogs around too, but some town folk came along one evening when most of the family were gone and traded one of the little children a marble for two little dogs. It was several years before they found others small enough to tame.

The children made play houses in the corn shocks, or sometimes made them of sunflowers. Once they made a little dugout in the yard, where they had merry times for a few weeks. It was large enough so they could all get in, by crowding a little, and deep enough so they could stand up. It had a little fireplace in the side, where they roasted onions and occasionally tried to boil eggs. It seemed a wonderful play house, for a few weeks, but when the heavy rains came the walls crumbled, and the children had to abandon it.

Most of their playthings they made themselves—stilts, corn stalk fiddles, sunflower spears or javelins, bows and arrows, shingle darts, whistles from maple or willow twigs, yarn balls from outworn socks, buzzers—small flat pieces of wood on the ends of strings, which made a buzzing sound when swung around rapidly—button buzzers made by running a string through a big button, corncobs with a heavy nail in one end and a couple of feathers in the other, which made it revolve when thrown, teeter-totters, rope swings, and merry-go-rounds made with a plank on a tree stump. Sometimes when Henry was not about, they would slide down the granary roof—Danny once broke his knee-cap at this business. One Sunday when the neighbor boys came to visit, the boys played "butcher"—erected a little derrick and butchered the mice they caught in the granary. Playing in the wheat bins was always great fun, since it could be combined with the somewhat hazardous sport of catching mice. Sliding and rolling down the straw stacks was sometimes indulged in, despite the beards and chaff; and the older children often went swimming.

Most of the children enjoyed reading, as they grew older. There were not many books in the house, but these were read and re-read, over and over again. Henry bought two big illustrated books from peddlers—"Columbus and Columbia," and "Footprints of the World's History"—and these were in constant use for a while. The children had various pacts and treaties and agreements as to who should have them at different times.

The older children sometimes amused the younger ones by singing or reading to them, or by telling stories. "Poor Babes in the Woods" was the favorite song, and "The Lone Swan" the story they most enjoyed. One or the other was always demanded by the little children, when they had been put to bed. While they listened, they would cry briny tears at the sad fate of the babes, or the lone swan—no matter how many times they had heard it before—and then they would fall asleep, happy and contented.

During the tree-climbing years of childhood, the children played a great deal in the trees, especially in the "seat tree"—a maple with sprawling branches that afforded a seat for each of them. On summer evenings, when the chores were done, they would climb up into the tree, take their respective seats, and sing, or more likely, stage a contest to see which could yell the loudest. The first evening they engaged in this pastime, Henry came running out to see who had been hurt; but he did not scold about it when he found they were just shouting in fun.

The Sunday school picnic became an important event a few years after Rosie came, and the children rated it right along with Easter and Christmas. For Rosie it meant a tremendous amount of work, and even some expense, especially in later years, when clean clothes had to be provided for so many children, and a whole tubfull of chicken, pie, cake and other delicacies had to be provided for the dinner. More than once Rosie worked far past twelve on the night before, sewing and patching, washing and ironing and baking, so that everything would be ready in the morning; and the next morning she was up before daybreak, as all of the children were too. On this festive occasion there was no difficulty getting them out of bed; and while they did the chores, Rosie packed the various delicacies into the tub and laid out the clothes for all of them, so that they could dress quickly. Everyone worked fast, with no quarrel as to who should milk the "toughest" cows; and at eight o'clock the wagon stood at the gate, ready to be loaded with provisions, swing rope and board, sack of corn for the horses, and last of all with children, who sat on board seats behind Henry and Rosie. Henry clucked to the horses, and they drove off, everyone in very good humor.

The picnic was always held in Chris Bartsch's grove,[4] up on Twelve Mile Creek, where there was shade and where there were trees high enough to serve for swings. At nine or ten o'clock the wagons began to roll down into the grove. One of the men always brought lumber for the seats and tables, another brought ice, another brought the church organ, another a barrel of water, several brought swing ropes, and almost all brought tubs or clothes baskets bulging with good things to eat. Everyone was very busy for a while, the men making plank seats, the women spreading table cloths on the long plank table, the boys hanging swings in the tallest trees. The woods echoed with the strokes of the hammers and the shouts of the children.

At eleven, the Sunday school superintendent rang a bell, and all the people came in to the seats, the children from their swings and games, the men and women from their various tasks; and the services began. There was singing by some of the classes, by the entire congregation, and sometimes by a selected quartette. There were dialogues and pieces by some of the children—not by the bad little children who neglected their Sunday school classes and went fishing on Sundays, but by the good little children who came every Sunday and learned their pieces conscientiously. Then the preacher or the Sunday school superintendent made a talk that always seemed too long, but doubtless had a chastening and uplifting influence on the children, whose eyes and minds were wandering surreptitiously over to the long table standing near. Finally, the inevitable collection was taken; and with another song by all the congregation—the singing sounded strangely beautiful out in the timber—and with a final prayer that no one really heard, the tedious preliminaries were over. The real business of the day was then undertaken. On several occasions, it was discovered when the services were over that smart Alecks from town sneaked into the wagons, which were left some distance away, and had stolen food, not only taking what they wanted to eat, but throwing biscuits and pieces of chicken about on the grass.

At last came the dinner: many kinds of cakes and pies, chicken, cold ham and beef, potato salad—of little interest to the children—pickled eggs, bread and butter and jelly for the older folk. Perhaps never did the smaller boys so keenly regret their limitations; but they performed heroic feats of gastronomy, washing down their cake and pie with lemonade from the barrel. When the children and men had eaten, the women, who had been waiting on them, sat down to the second table. After dinner, the women cleared the table while the men sat around, talking about the weather and the crops, and even occasionally about politics; and the young folk went back to their swings, which were kept going all afternoon. The prettiest girls usually got more than their share of swinging, but favors were distributed with some justice; and even the older women were sometimes given a swing. Some of the younger boys wandered down to the creek, where they caught minnows and tadpoles and got their clean clothes gloriously soiled. In a later decadent age the boys played base ball, but for some years this was not thought quite proper. By four or five o'clock usually, the lemonade was gone, and the picnic was over. The horses were then hitched to the wagons, which were loaded with empty tubs and baskets and tired children and rattled out of the grove and on toward home—where the milking and other chores waited to be done. The chores out of the way, the boys spent the evening describing and discussing the various delectable cakes and pies they had sampled at the dinner, while the girls made a critical appraisal of the quantity and quality of the contributions of each of the neighbors. For a week afterward the children were busy scratching and doping their chigger bites with salty butter; but they had had their day, and the next summer they were happy when the time approached for another picnic.

Chapter Twenty-seven

Henry Buys a Windmill, and Sells Some Cattle

The winter of eighteen eighty-seven and 'eighty-eight was a cruel winter—the winter after May was born—thirty below zero in January. Some of the neighbors lost cattle from cold and starvation, but Henry had good shelter, and enough feed to keep his livestock in fair condition. Night after night, Rosie and the children had to catch the chickens that roosted in the trees and throw them into the chicken coop. Every night Rosie carried live coals into the cellar to prevent the vegetables from freezing, and put hot bricks in the children's beds. In March there was enough pleasant weather to tempt the box elder leaves out, and to bring birds back from the south. Then, on March the nineteenth, a raging blizzard rode in from the north; and when spring finally came, the children found quails, robins, snow birds and meadow larks frozen to death along the hedge rows.

The interest on the mortgage ran on, and there was no money to pay on the principal that year. Henry often thought of a bit of doggerel that was widely printed at the time:

> A chattel mortgage in the West
> Is like a cancer on your breast.
> It slowly takes your life away,
> And eats your vitals day by day.
>
> A cloud by day, a fire by night,
> It keeps him in a dreadful plight;
> And haunts him in his dreams and sleep,
> While salt tears trickle down his cheek.

The sorghum lapper, tired and poor,
Sees "Bank" in gold above the door.
And when the threshold once is crossed,
The trap is sprung—the lapper's lost.

His team, his grain, his cow, his hog,
His bed and breeches, wife and dog,
Upon the altar of three-per-cent are tossed,
Time rolls on and all is lost.

But Henry borrowed a hundred more in August to buy a windmill. One hot, still day, when he had gone to town, Rosie was drawing water for the cattle. The thirsty animals crowded around the trough, fighting the tormenting clouds of flies, the "boss" cows horning the others against the trough and fence. Rosie was almost in despair. Pull as she would, she could only keep the bottom of the trough wet. As she struggled with rope and bucket, along came John Wise in his buggy.

"Hello, Rosie," he called out, as he drove up to the well. John always liked Henry and Rosie, and there was unfeigned friendliness in his greeting. "I'm afraid you have a steady job there."

"Oh!" Rosie turned with her hand on the well rope. "I'm afraid so. They seem to drink as fast as I can draw—and get thirsty doing it. But put your horse in the stable. Henry will be home, and I'll soon be done here, and we'll have dinner."

She turned to her task, but he stopped her.

"You go on to your dinner. I'll finish this when I put up my horse."

Rosie went to the house, picking up an armful of wood on the way; and presently, through the kitchen door, saw John pulling up bucket after bucket of water, which splashed refreshingly as he poured it into the lead trough.

A half hour later, as the last of the cattle turned away from the trough and started down to the pasture, Henry drove in; and he and John soon came up to the house for dinner.

"Henry, you ought to have a windmill," said John, as they seated themselves at the table. "You have too many cattle to be drawing water by hand."

"Yes, I guess so—but the way things look now we'll soon be lucky to have any cattle to draw water for."

"Too much work! Too much work, Henry! You can't afford to draw water. I'll let you have a hundred dollars if you want it, as long as you want it. Pottsburg[1] will put you up a windmill for a hundred dollars—a Dempster, and it's a good windmill."

"That's good of you, anyhow, John. What do you think, Rosie?"

"Oh, it would be fine, if it would really pay. Sometimes we draw water when we wouldn't be doing anything else that counts; but sometimes the hired hand does it, and that costs money, right out of our pockets. We wouldn't need to hire so much, would we, if we had a windmill?"

Henry had not thought much of this angle of the problem, but he agreed it was so.

Rosie's eyes lighted up with genuine enthusiasm as she saw a possibility of release from the chore of drawing water—release that could be justified financially.

"And if we didn't have to hire so much," she continued, "we wouldn't need to spend quite so much for sugar and coffee and stuff. We always have to cook more when we have a hand. Just how would all that balance up?"

Rosie got a pencil and piece of paper, and with Henry's expert help made some rough calculations of interest and principal, against savings in labor and food; and she was finally convinced that the windmill would at least be no extravagance.

When John Wise left after dinner, he carried in his wallet Henry's note for a hundred dollars, at eight per cent; and soon afterward a new wooden windmill wheel was whirling in the hot south wind.[2]

There was a little wheat the next summer, but it took all the wheat money to pay Doctor Poole, and corn was again a total failure. The dry weather in August and September cut the fall pastures short, and left the stock with little for the winter. The ground was too hard to plow, so Henry planted little wheat, and there was not much fall wheat pasture. In November it was clear that he would have to sell some of the cows or buy feed again. This time there was no difficulty in deciding which it must be. There was no possibility of raising more money to buy feed with. Some of the cows would have to be sold; and the sale turned out to be a domestic tragedy that would never be quite forgotten.

Among the milk cows was one named Lizzie that the girls, Laura and Alice, loved as one of the family. She was so friendly and gentle, and followed them about in the corral almost like a faithful dog. At milking time they would sometimes pull up fresh weeds and throw them over the fence for her, or try to filch some special contribution from the stable or hay stack.

The cattle buyer came out while the children were at school, and as Lizzie was a fat young heifer, she was one of those selected. Henry had a vague idea of her place in the family affections; but when the buyer picked her out and offered him eleven dollars for her, Henry thoughtlessly accepted, and Lizzie was driven to town with the rest of the cows. That evening, when the girls went out to do the milking, no Lizzie came up to the gate to meet them. They looked everywhere in the corral and in the stable, but could find no trace of her. Suddenly a cruel suspicion flashed across Laura's mind.

"Could Papa have sold her? I heard him talking about selling some cows yesterday."

Alice stood speechless at the thought. "He wouldn't do it!" she exclaimed. "He surely wouldn't sell Lizzie. She must be lost in the corn stalks."

"No, she isn't in the corn stalks. Look down there. Don't you see she's not there?" Certainly nothing as big as a cow could hide in the stunted corn stalks that grew in the field that year.

"She must be somewhere, because Papa wouldn't sell her without telling us; and he wouldn't sell her anyhow, when there are plenty of other cows to sell."

"I wonder whose cows those were that went by the schoolhouse this morning," Laura hinted, looking darkly at her younger sister. "You heard the man hollering and cracking his whip during our arithmetic class, didn't you?"

"Yes, but I couldn't see out. It couldn't have been Lizzie because—because you wouldn't need to whip Lizzie." Tears came to Alice's eyes at the thought that anyone might have whipped her pet. "Surely Papa wouldn't sell her without telling us."

"Well, we might as well milk the rest, anyhow," said Laura, as she started off with her bucket and milk stool. Alice could think of no words adequate to her feelings, and she picked her milk stool off the fence and started over to the nearest cow. She felt a fathomless grief and despair at the thought that she could not begin with Lizzie, but she dutifully milked her other cows.

With red eyes and tear-stained faces, the two girls came in to supper an hour later, afraid even to ask about Lizzie, for fear that their worst forebodings might prove justified. They tasted little of their supper, and flew out of the room when Rosie asked them why. Innocent of the cause for such strange behavior, Rosie took a lamp and followed them, and found them upstairs in their room. They looked at her as she entered, a bit shamefaced at their own grief, but hurt and rebellious and defiant.

"What in the world's the matter, girls?" she asked kindly.

For a moment the girls said nothing, but looked tearfully at each other and then at her. It was Alice who finally spoke:

"Why did you, why did Papa or anyone go and sell Lizzie? She isn't in the lot, or anywhere!" Her voice trembled, and she stopped and hid her face in her hands.

"Oh my dear girls, we had to sell something, don't you know?" Rosie felt keenly the weakness of her explanation, but she thought that she must say something.

"But you didn't have to sell Lizzie," cried Laura. "There were plenty of other cows; and she was our cow, that we always milked."

"Surely Papa didn't know you cared so much about her. He didn't think about it. It's too bad." Rosie placed the lamp on the box that served as a dresser, and sat down on the bed beside them.

"Can't Papa go and get her back?" There was a touch of hope in the grief with which Alice spoke, and her great dark eyes looked out at her mother.

"I'm afraid not."

"Why?" asked both girls in a breath.

"That man bought them to take them to Kansas City."

This brought a fresh outbreak of grief. Laura had a dark suspicion that Lizzie had been taken to Kansas City for no good purpose. She had heard men talk of taking cattle there, as if it were a place where cattle disappeared. Alice wept at the thought that there would be no one in Kansas City to milk the pet she cared so much for.

Rosie did her best to comfort them, but it was all of no avail. All her explanations brought only fresh outbreaks of grief, and she finally left them and went back to her work. She washed and wiped the dishes herself that night, for she had not the heart to call the girls back to their tasks.

With a keen appreciation of the grief his sale of cattle had caused, Henry had little zest for the job of selling other stock; but the next day he loaded his hogs into a wagon and took them to town. They brought three dollars a hundred—enough altogether to pay the interest on the mortgage, pay the note to John Wise, and buy some fodder for the cows and oats for the horses. Some of the blood money from the sale of the cows was used to buy an innovation for corn planting called a "lister,"[3] and forty dollars was spent to rid the pasture of prairie dogs again. This time a man killed them by throwing a ball of cotton saturated in carbon-disulphide down the holes.

With some of the rest of the money, Rosie bought several rolls of cloth from an itinerant pack peddler, she and Lizzie Graeber each taking half of the pack. It looked like a bargain, but Rosie soon regretted her purchase, for the cloth was mostly cheap shoddy, and she had to work much of the winter sewing the stuff into coats and trousers for Henry and the boys. Lizzie Graeber was even more helpless with her half of the pack, and, after making George a pair of trousers, she cut the rest into pieces to wrap around the children's heads.

In all the poverty and pessimism of these hard years, the spirit of adventure and enterprise in the community did not die. In the very depth of the depression of 'eighty-seven, Downs voted thirty thousand dollars in bonds to build a water works system, with a water tower nearly a hundred feet high—for years the "wonder" of the town. A company was organized to build an "opera house," to cost ten thousand dollars, and the Downs Mining Company, with twenty-seven thousand dollars "capital," leased two thousand acres of land and began a search for coal, oil and gas—or perhaps the real search was for the savings of innocent investors. The next year, at a meeting of the Downs Board of Trade, citizens were invited to join the Northern Kansas Immigration Association, for the purpose of advertising Northern Kansas and promoting immigration—as if the drouth were not advertising the state sufficiently.

Growing interest in the possibility of irrigation in Kansas seemed more to the point. Rain making was debated too, the favorite scheme being to explode large quantities of powder, perhaps from a balloon high up in the sky. Someone asserted that battles were usually followed by rain, and from this concluded that explosions of powder would bring the right atmospheric conditions for rainfall.

With a grant of ten thousand dollars, Stockton secured a Congregational Academy, where young people up and down the valley could broaden their culture.[4] President Mather and his wife roomed and boarded in the hall with the students, and as the Downs *Times* indicated, it was "truly a great advantage to the young people to mingle and associate with instructors who show such true culture." The next year Gould College at Harlan "gave up the ghost—that being about all it had to give up."

Although there was little freight for a railroad, and the Central Branch was reducing its schedule of trains into Downs, there was endless agitation for new railroads, and many meetings to consider the question of voting bonds for construction. Smith Center hoped for two railroads, Alton wanted one more, Delhi would have been satisfied with one, and Burr Oak wanted at least one. A road from Marvin to Phillipsburg was reported probable, and one running southwest from Gaylord into Colorado was almost a certainty. The most popular fairy story related to the Omaha, Dodge City and Southern Railroad, to run southwest from Omaha to Dodge City and Trinidad, passing through practically all the towns in Central Kansas. At any rate, most of the towns held meetings to consider the voting of bonds, and it was several times reported that construction was decided upon or under way. As the Downs *Times* stated: "If all the railroads for which charters have lately been granted were to be built, there isn't a quarter section in northwestern Kansas that would not be crossed by at least one road."

In the meantime, the population of Downs and Cawker City dwindled, the new townsite of Waconda Springs was sold at sheriff's sale, and the big hotel was abandoned to vandals, a favorite picnicing place for the people for many miles around. Devastating prairie fires added to the prevailing destitution. In April, eighteen eighty-seven, a fire started at Nicodemus in Graham County and, whipped by a forty-mile wind, swept northward along a seven

Elizabeth and George Yost. (Courtesy the Historical Society of the Downs Carnegie Library)

mile front, through Norton County and into Nebraska, killing live-stock, chickens, even birds and rabbits, and leaving hundreds of farmers destitute. On the same day another fire raced down the South Solomon, leaving a similar wake of black devastation. The fires never came within fifty miles of Downs, but the smoke hung in the air for days.

Chris and Mary Bartsch usually had the worst luck. One day, just when times seemed hardest, Mary fell from a load of hay and broke her collar bone and wrist, and dislocated her ankle. At first she thought her ankle was broken too, and when the doctor found that it was only dislocated, she lamented the fact that they had called him—just to set a wrist and collar bone.

"Oh, we could save as well the doctor bill," she moaned to Ro-sie, when Rosie went up to see her. "My foot feel so bad when I fall, I think it broke too. The other things get well soon all right, and no doctor to pay yet."

"Ach, liebe Mary,"[5] laughed Chris, who was sitting by the bed, the kindly wrinkles crowding about his eyes and mouth; "we must be thankful it is no worse, and the foot is not broke too."

In spite of drouth and depression, Henry gained a new neighbor on the quarter adjoining the Frank Hagel farm—a Switzer named Yost.[6] With his black hair and black mustache and his soldierly bearing, Yost was a striking figure. He had a booming bass voice, trained in the Swiss männerchor,[7] and at first sang rather better than he farmed, for he was several years forgetting his Swiss "hoe culture" and learning to use American farm implements. Unskilled in farming and burdened with a heavy mortgage, he had a hard time for several years, and he and his large family of children worked like beavers; but they pulled through. The Ises and the Yosts were destined to be very good friends during the years following.

One morning, soon after Yost moved onto his place, Henry appeared in the yard, driving a young heifer ahead of him. Yost came out to meet him with a booming "Hello," spoken in Switzer dialect, untainted with any trace of English accent.

"Hello, neighbor! I'm bringing your cow."

"My cow? I've lost no cow!" Yost looked perplexed.

"Yes, your cow. When Daniels[8] owned this place, I agreed to pay half the cost of that line fence over there, and I never got around to it. So I'll just pay you."

"But I knew nothing about it."

"Well, I owe it just the same; and I guess the cow will be about right, for my half."

Yost remonstrated, but Henry would agree to no other arrangement, and left the heifer there.

Chapter Twenty-eight

More Drouth and Anxiety
. . . and Hope

"When you have cattle and hogs you have to worry your head off about feed for them, or sell them for next to nothing; and as soon as you sell them you get good crops again, and have to worry about buying them back, at twice as much as you got. That's the way with farming out here. Whenever you raise anything, there's too much, and you have to give it away; and then when you don't raise anything, there isn't enough, and you have to buy feed, and pay three prices for it. You never can get anything for anything except when you haven't anything. It looks as if there was something wrong with the way the whole business is ordered."

It was Rosie speaking one day, in a mood of discouragement that threatened to become chronic. Rosie was changing fast. The back that had been so strong and straight was bending perceptibly, with too much carrying of babies and tubs and baskets. Each year her busy hands were rougher, more scarred and twisted, with finger nails always broken. She had never been able to walk with ease. Rosie had frozen her feet when a girl of eleven years, and they always bothered her afterward. It was very cold winter weather at the time, and she was working in a neighbor's kitchen, an unplastered lean-to. Disliking to ask special permission to go into the warmer rooms, she stuck to her task until her feet were so badly frozen that she never recovered free and easy use of them. Now her step, although as firm and resolute as ever, was more plodding and laborious. Her brown eyes were eager and friendly as ever; yet around them time and trouble had drawn wrinkles that deepened with every passing year.

Rosie was no longer the cheery, confident, hopeful girl who

216

had driven out with Henry in eighteen seventy-three. The wearing uncertainties of seasons and crops were telling on her; so were the strain of rapidly succeeding pregnancies—she was nursing her ninth baby;[1] the endless demands of the little children; and the long hours of work, with her poor, lame feet.

And there was Henry's poor management. In a single unfortunate deal he would sometimes lose more than she could save in six months, pinch and skimp as she would. It had been Rosie's lot since early childhood to have to look to a man for management who had nothing like her own practical sense, nor her own physical energy. Her father had been almost an invalid since he had typhoid fever, the very first week after he reached Kansas; and he was more of a student than farmer or manager.

He liked to write poetry—in German of course—and no family or neighborhood festival was quite complete without one of his poems. Rosie often thought other contributions would have been more useful than poetry, but her father was just that way, and there was no changing him.

Now, in her own home, it was somewhat the same. Henry was not really well, he always had to be very careful as to what he ate, and never could be quite careful enough. One shoulder always bothered him too, when he tried to do hard work—like his stomach trouble, a result of the hardships of the war. Marching through a swampy region of Tennessee, he was sleeping out in a cold rain one night on a bed of brush he had piled up to keep him out of the water. During the night the brush settled until one shoulder sank into the water, and then the sky cleared and the weather turned cold. He was so exhausted that he did not awaken until morning, to find his shoulder bound in a thin crust of ice. He was always bothered with rheumatism afterward.

Like Rosie's father, Henry liked to read better than to attend to the practical business of managing the farm. Although he always paid generous wages, he got less work out of hired hands than anyone else in the neighborhood; and this worried Rosie, who would rather have helped with the farm work herself than spend too much money for help. Henry was always too generous with everything that he had. At the table the children tried to get him rather than Rosie to put sugar in their coffee—when there was sugar—and they liked to go to town with him, because he bought them candy. In her strict economy, so essential to the real welfare of all, Rosie fell into the position of the stingy parent. She accepted this as part of her hard duty, and sometimes almost resentfully.

Discouraged and pessimistic she became, as the lean years followed each other, sometimes morose, and even harsh and impatient toward the children and toward Henry; although under it all there was a solid and unselfish affection that they trusted implicitly.

Rosie was never discouraged in the sense that she entertained any idea of retreating, or changing the course that her Spartan sense of duty mapped out for her. She never gave up. Tired and worn and sometimes sick, almost hopeless of the future during these hard years, troubled and perplexed, angry and rebellious at what seemed her unjustly heavy share of care and responsibility, she never paused or relaxed her tenacious grip. In the downward slanting lines of her mouth—each year more like that of her mother—was written the grim and invincible determination that would not admit defeat.

The next spring after Henry sold the cattle, there was plenty of rain and fine warm weather that brought the grass out green and lush. The cattle would not eat the last few shocks of the fodder that Henry had been doling out so carefully all winter. In March the ducks and geese and brants appeared in the southern sky, on their tireless flight northward, flocks of them every day; and covered wagons driven by incorrigible optimists again rolled past, on their way west or perhaps headed for the Cherokee Strip.[2]

The wheat that had been pronounced dead in January became a billowy sea of yellow and gold in early July, so tall that it was feared it might lodge. With harvest time came much complaint of the high price of twine, and widespread damning of the "Twine Trust"; but there was nothing to do but bind the cheap wheat with the expensive twine, and curse the monopolies. A week or two later the rattle of the binder gave way to the whistle of the threshing machine. Henry had one field that threshed out forty-two bushels per acre, sixty-pound wheat. More rains came, through July and August, and giant sunflowers grew in the stubbles. The corn grew big and green, and when hot, dry weather came in September it was largely out of the way of harm. That fall there was

corn to shuck, big ears that struck the bump boards with a heartening thump.

There was a poison in the corn stalks that fall, apparently in
the smut, and four of Henry's cows became sick when he turned
them into the field. At the suggestion of one of the neighbors, he
gave them a veterinary concoction of sweet spirits of nitre, asafet-
ida, Epsom salts, salt and vinegar. They all died, either of the corn
smut or of the medicine.

Kansas was a great country again. There were no movers
going east that fall. Bony cattle and horses grew fat, and disheartened people renewed their courage once more. Again there was
talk of more railroads; of an extension of the Central Branch westward to Denver; and of various and assorted roads running from
every flag station on the Central Branch to some other village in
Nebraska, Western Kansas or Colorado—the terminus seemed to
be a matter of no importance. Some of the farmers renewed their
efforts to find an economical process of making sugar from sorghum; and a meeting was called in Downs to whip up enthusiasm
and secure pledges for stock in a sugar company. There was even
talk of bonding the township or the city to secure funds for the
industry.

The county-seat row waxed in bitterness. The county treasurer
was reported short some eight or nine thousand dollars,[3] and the
county clerk was accused of padding population figures,[4] in order
that officials might get higher salaries. Apparently on the assump-
tion that the alleged crookedness was due to the moral miasma of
the town of Osborne, men canvassed the county with petitions to
have the county-seat moved to Bristow; while Osborne sent out a
man with a remonstrance list, and Osborne bankers threatened
with foreclosure mortgagors who signed the petition for removal.
Meetings were held in Downs to agitate the matter, whereas the
Osborne *Farmer* called Downs a "dirty little plague spot."

Of course everything was cheap. Henry kept his wheat, hoping for a better price later, but the next spring he had to fan it and
sell it for less than he could have got at harvest. The local elevator
was closed for a while, because neither wheat nor corn was worth
shipping. At twelve cents a bushel corn was a cheaper fuel than
coal, and some of the neighbors burned it in their stoves; but
Rosie could not stand the thought of burning corn.

"We'll manage somehow without that," she declared. "Next year there'll likely be a need for corn—poor horses and cattle and pigs and chickens running around without anything to eat!"

And manage they did, with the wood Henry was able to cut, with broken boards that the children gathered up around the premises, and with cow chips from the pasture, and cobs picked up in the hog pen. They burned no corn that winter. Fortunate it was too, that they did not, for eighteen ninety was about the driest and hottest summer since the grasshopper year. Early spring was pleasant, and in late January the meadow larks were singing in the pastures; but the weather turned so dry that the grass scarcely shed its winter brown. Almost every night the glare of a prairie fire could be seen somewhere in the sky.

One windy evening in April, a bright glow appeared in the north. By the time Henry had finished his supper, the glow was ominously bright, and the smell of smoke strong in the air. Good soldier that he was, Henry wet a couple of sacks and started up the creek to meet the enemy, leaving Rosie to fill the water barrel and guard the children and the premises. Two miles up he found the battlefront—sweating men fighting desperately with wet sacks, pitchforks, scoops, shovels, or anything they could find, shouting orders and warnings, retreating when too hard pressed, stopping occasionally to drink the water that the women and children carried to them. Scarcely noticed in the dark and in the excitement, Henry slipped into a detachment of men whipping out the advance line of a back-fire. An hour later the men succeeded in heading the red scourge into a bend in the creek where it died in a roaring blaze that reached out hungrily toward the other bank of the creek. Sparks and burning embers flew across, but the men watching there promptly smothered them out.

In a hot, dry May and June, wheat prospects faded, and in the ravaging hot winds of early July the corn began to curl. As George Graeber said, the corn was "almost as far along in July as it usually is in December." Henry had planted a small field of kaffir corn,[5] and this hung on a little longer, but before the end of July, it too shrivelled up and turned gray without forming a head. The tiring wind blew steadily from the south, weary day after weary day, cooking the garden plants and even the stunted weeds that grew in the fields and along the roadside.

The ruin of her own garden hurt Rosie almost less than the burning of the little garden the children had planted. Every year she gave them a little plot of ground in which to raise something for themselves, something to sell in town for spending money. This year they had planted onions, cabbage, tomatoes and sweet potatoes; and they spent much time estimating the amount of stuff they hoped to raise—bunches of onions, pounds of cabbage, and bushels of tomatoes and sweet potatoes. Their estimates were always generous, of course, and the hoped-for proceeds ran into high figures. When the hot winds came, and the cabbage and tomato plants began to wilt, Danny and Robert carried water to them, hopefully, for a while. Robert, fat, awkward little fellow, always walked with a slight stoop; and Rosie's heart ached for him especially, when she saw him trudging back and forth with a gallon bucket in each hand. Their efforts were fruitless, of course, for nothing grew in the searing heat.

The pastures, brown and bare as a carpet, afforded scanty sustenance for the hungry cattle that wandered restlessly about, trying in vain to find grass high enough to graze, nibbling for a while at the weeds growing in the buffalo wallows, wandering along the fence, reaching through here and there to get a mouthful of the weeds that grew at the end of the field, then trailing over to the last year's straw stack, where they stood chewing at the dry and unpalatable straw. Some of the neighbors had even less feed than Henry, and were forced to drive their cattle up into Nebraska to be sold or wintered there, or sell them to cattle buyers from Iowa for whatever pittance they were able to get.

Finally the children had to herd the cattle up and down the roads, along the railroad right-of-way, everywhere that a little forage could be found.

Herding cattle! How many long days the children spent driving them along the dusty roads, running off to the side to keep out of the clouds of dust, heading the leaders off at every opening in the fence, or running their little bare feet off trying to chase them out of the fields, always fearful of snakes, always on the lookout for hedge thorns and nettles and sand burs as they picked their way through the grass, and, worst of all, in constant fear of the herd bull, who was of a vicious disposition. With what shrewd and courageous resourcefulness did they watch him, keeping their eyes on trees or fences or other possible places of refuge whenever he was near, calculating how far from safety they dared venture! Occasionally he would chase them through the fence or up a tree, but with the luck which sometimes follows children they always escaped injury.

Jurisdictional disputes sometimes arose, for the neighbor's children were herding cattle too. It was a recognized principle of equity that each family should herd cattle only along a road bordering its own land, and one of the neighbors sometimes went beyond that—even herded his cattle right along the road between Henry's two farms, much to the children's anger and indignation. On the roads between different holdings, the two adjacent neighbors had equal rights, as between Henry's and Wilson Athey's farms. Here the two herds would meet occasionally; and then the rival bulls were certain to stage a fight, with such bellowing and pawing of the grass that the children were frightened half to death.

Generally, herding was a dreary business, and the children looked forward longingly to a day when they would not need to herd cattle. During the tedious hours when the cattle were grazing, they tried every expedient they could think of to help pass the time. They built play houses of corn stalks or sunflowers or slough grass joints, they dug little cellars for their houses, they told stories, guessed conundrums—the same ones over and over again—hunted bugs and flowers and birds' eggs, whittled when they could get a knife, caught gophers when they were able, and sometimes tried to catch prairie dogs, but invariably without success. The girls liked to pick flowers and spent many hours making larkspur wreaths and ropes—one day they found a patch of red larkspurs and made a long rope, which they took home to Rosie. And always, of course, they spent much time watching the sun, to see if it was not time to take the cows home.

One day Danny managed to catch a bumblebee, and tie a tiny scrap of red cloth to one of its legs. On being released, the bee flew away, Danny following at top speed. It made straight for its nest over in the prairie meadow; and Danny soon had plans for gathering honey. The next day, he and Billy got barrel staves and "whipped out" the bees, both getting stung several times in the battle, but they felt repaid with a taste of the honey they found in the nest.

Once Danny was playing with matches as he watched the cattle down in the prairie meadow, and set the grass afire. For a moment he was completely at his wit's end, for he had nothing to fight fire with; but suddenly an idea struck him—he pulled off his trousers, and in a few minutes had whipped the fire completely out with them. Henry came past on his way home from town just as Danny was putting out the last sparks; but he did not scold him, although playing with matches was strictly forbidden.

Danny and Robert were herding the cattle on the railroad right-of-way one day, when the section boss came along with his gang.

"Hello, sonny!" the boss called out to Danny, who was nearest. "Do you live in that house over there?" He pointed across the field.

"Yes," answered Danny, a bit fearful that he was to receive a scolding for something he had done.

"Would you like to earn a nickel?" the man asked.

Would he like to earn a nickel? Would he like to own the Missouri Pacific Railroad, or the Homestake Mine, or the Kohinoor diamond? A nickel indeed—enough to buy a whole sack of candy! That was a strange question.

"Sure!" he replied.

"Well, if you'll go home and get me a drink of butter milk, I'll give you a nickel. Would your mamma have any butter milk?"

"I think so—churned this morning. I'll go and see."

With the vision of a shining nickel dancing before his eyes, Danny started across the field. Through the weeds and nettles and sand burs he picked his way, gingerly stepping on a cool, green weed whenever he could; but when he reached the road, he broke into a trot that soon brought him to the house, sweating from every pore, for it was a very hot day. He must run no risk that the man get impatient and leave before he got back.

Yes, Rosie had butter milk, and she poured a quart into a syrup bucket for him, pressed the lid on tight, gave him a drink of fresh water; and back he went to the railroad, three-quarters of a mile away.

The section boss was waiting, and drank the butter milk to the last drop, then fumbled in his pockets for the money. He seemed to find none, and turned to Danny.

"I haven't got a nickel with me today, my boy; but I'll give it to you some time—some other time."

Deeply disappointed, Danny picked up the empty syrup bucket and went back to his cattle. The next day the section boss was there again, and Danny hopefully asked for his nickel, but again the man had no money. Several times in the next few days Danny asked for his pay, but he never got it. The man had never intended to pay.

Rosie's father died in June, and Henry went down to the funeral. Rosie had been there a few weeks before, so she stayed at home and took care of the children. One night, not long after Henry came home, he was awakened from a sound sleep by one of the Graeber boys, who came to report that George Graeber was dead, of sudden heart failure.[6] The Graebers had never been genuinely friendly neighbors; but in their extremity, Lizzie and the children thought first of Henry. Although he was himself suffering from one of his attacks of stomach trouble and had not been able to do his own work, he went over to help wash and lay out the body, and get ice to keep it in until the funeral. From that time Lizzie Graeber became one of the kindest of friends, ready to do any good turn for Henry and Rosie—"Aunt Lizzie" to the children, who liked to go to see her and eat the good cookies she always had for them.[7]

Through July and August the drouth lay heavy on the land. The yellow sun glared through a dusty haze, pitiless, implacable, while the voiceless prayer for water rose from the hot earth, from the dead fields and pastures and gardens, and from trees that began to shed their yellow leaves in mid-summer. Day after day the sun rose out of the cool morning and burned its fiery path across the cloudless sky; day by day the stunted little stalks of corn bent lower before the scorching wind. Early in August Henry began to cut fodder, using a new type of cutter that had just appeared—a sled with knives on the sides, an invention that more than doubled the amount of corn he could cut, by a most dangerous device, as he was destined to learn.

There was no comfort for any living being in the heat of those weary days. The dog cooled himself in the dust on the north side of the house, and the chickens sought the shelter of the rose bushes by the bay window, their mouths open and their wings hanging loosely away from their bodies. In the afternoons, when there were no tasks to do outside, Rosie and the girls retreated into the house, and closed the windows and shutters to keep out the hot winds; but Rosie herself found little satisfaction in such avoidance of discomfort, for she always worried about Henry and the boys, working out in the dust and heat.

The horses in the field raised clouds of dust that almost hid them from view; and in the evenings, Henry and the boys came home sore-eyed and dusty as coal miners. Then came a time when they could not work in the field. It was too dry to plow, so they sat around in the house or barn, sad and sour, or pottered with odd jobs, oiled the harnesses, fixed fences, stopped up the holes in the grain bins with cobs or bits of tin—and dreamed of rain. Henry soaked rattling wagon wheels in the tank, and lengthened the rope at the house well with bits of wire, that the bucket might dip in the lowering water. Rosie drove the hoops down tighter on the rain barrel, but the bottom finally fell out, and the staves crumpled into a pile.

At evening the cattle came home in a cloud of dust, which lifted occasionally to reveal Robert and Danny trailing along behind. The thirsty animals hurried past the house and into the corral, fought for places around the water tank, and then crowded miserably together in a compact mass, stamping, swinging their heads and switching their tails, in a vain effort to keep off the swarms of tormenting flies. Rosie and the older children did the milking, while the little children brushed the flies away with leafy branches cut from the cottonwood trees. Not until dark, when the flies had settled down, did peace and quiet come to the restless cattle.

Occasionally clouds appeared in the west at evening, then thinned out against the red glare of the sun, while Henry and Rosie and the children watched anxiously, then sadly, from the west porch.

One evening a white-fringed bank of clouds loomed up in the west, a bank much like others that had appeared. No one dared believe that it might bring rain. For months, every time Henry and Rosie had permitted themselves to hope for that infinite blessing, the clouds had faded out, with the hopes that they had called into life. After every such disappointment they were always more dour and disheartened than before, and they refused to allow themselves to hope. Even the children had caught the contagion of pessimism. "It never rains! It never will rain!" was a thought often expressed when the weather was up for discussion.

So they went about their various tasks that evening, hardly venturing to look into the west, lest they see again the red sun shining through the vanishing clouds.

This time the clouds did not thin out and scatter, and when the sun sank below the white fringe it was seen no more. By the time the chores were done, the great blue bank had turned to gray, and the rain curtain had emerged in the gray expanse, lighted up with incessant and vivid flashes of lightning. The curtain rose higher and higher, and the thunder that had muttered and grumbled in the distance now boomed and crashed and echoed along the hills across the river. A cool and gusty wind blew over from the advancing clouds, a wind that smelled of rain.

Surely it was going to rain! Surely it could not fail this time! The cynical pessimism of past weeks was forgotten. Henry stood with arms folded, a smile on his face, silently watching the clouds approach. Too busy with her bread kneading to stand watching, Rosie came to the door every few minutes to look, with shreds of dough sticking to her fingers. The children ran and danced about in the yard, yelling at the top of their voices, except Danny and Robert, who climbed the windmill that they might better mark the progress of the coming rain.

"It's raining across the river!" shouted Danny, from his high vantage point.

"It's raining on this side of the river!" cried Robert, a few moments later. "You can't even see the trees!"

Never shifting his position, Henry watched the clouds in silence, but his smile broadened; and the children danced and shouted more excitedly as the rain came nearer.

"It's raining at Graebers!" shouted Danny. "It's raining at the cross roads! It's raining everywhere!"

On it came! No thinning out this time, no veering to the north or to the south, no dissipation into gusty winds and streak lightning! A few big drops came hurrying down, raising tiny whiffs of dust as they struck the arid ground; then came a downpour that sent the chickens scurrying for shelter. Henry retreated into the house, but the children continued their wild dance in the rain, shouting a bit of doggerel that they had learned somewhere:

Rain, rain, come from Spain;
And never go back again.

After a while they came in, drenched to the skin. All had to have a change of clothes, but Rosie did not scold. It was a happy family that sat around the table that evening, and ate their supper of dumpling soup and fresh bread and milk.

Chapter Twenty-nine

Good Crops and the New Barn

Wheat rose to a dollar a bushel before the end of the summer of eighteen ninety—after Henry had sold the little that he had—and in September some of the successful business men in town, who had filled great cribs with corn at ten cents a bushel the year before, sold it back to the farmers at forty cents. Henry sold enough of his hogs and cattle, and of the corn he had kept, to pay off the mortgage, and to buy shoes and school books for the children. With a dollar and a half that he had left, he bought Rosie one of the new fascinators which were so fashionable at the time. Rosie was more than pleased, although she could not help wishing that she might have used the money to buy a few extra pairs of stockings for the children.

What a blessed relief to be rid of the mortgage! It had hung like a pall over the spirits of all, even the children. All the uncertainties of the weather, crops and prices had borne with heavier weight, because no matter how crops or prices were, no matter what income there was from the farm, the inexorable interest had to be paid. As long as the mortgage stood against the farm, Henry and Rosie had never been free to indulge a single whim or extravagance, had felt that every possible penny must be saved, lest some unforeseen misfortune prevent them from meeting the payments when they came due. Around the dinner table, where pleasant and cheerful talk should have been heard, the mortgage had often been the recurring and absorbing topic of conversation—the mortgage, and the interest payments, and the hoped-for final release. Weather, rain and drouth, crops and prices, family needs and expenses, had been critically important matters largely because of their bearing on the one overshadowing problem of the mortgage; and the family conversation, no matter where it started, usually led finally back to that engrossing and disturbing theme.

On the day when Henry made the last payment, and came home with the release in his pocket, there was more happiness and festivity in the home than there had been for many a day. Even the smaller children felt the spirit of the hour. Rosie had baked a big cake especially for the occasion, and when the children were seated around the supper table, the conversation turned to the mortgage once more; but this time it was not the relentless master of the family destinies. It was now the beaten and vanquished enemy.

In October grandmother came out to visit, and stayed a month. Rosie had to dress and undress her, and carry her meals to her, for she was helpless with asthma. Soon after she left, another little baby was born—a sweet-natured little girl with big blue eyes, but none too robust in health.[1]

It was a hard winter. In January, there was zero weather and snow, and later rain; and at the end of March, with the fodder almost gone and the cattle hungry and thin, a terrible blizzard blew in from the northwest for two days and nights, covering what stock feed there was in the fields with drifts of snow, and blocking the roads in every direction. For several days it remained cold; and when the snow melted, the roads were impassable with mud. Unable to get into the fields with a wagon to haul out the few shocks of fodder that were left, Henry turned the cattle into the fields, where they roamed about in search of gleanings of feed, trampling in the mud much of what they found. When the fodder was gone, they clustered around the straw stacks, eating grotesque tunnels far into the stacks, where they stood almost hidden from view on chilly, misty days. Straw was poor feed, but it was all there was, and Henry's cattle lived.

The cold damp weather and the bottomless mud everywhere made it necessary to take special care of the young livestock. Several little pigs died, but Rosie converted the kitchen into a hospital where the weakest of the survivors were kept warm. Almost every morning, Henry or Billy brought in one or two shivering, almost lifeless little porkers to be warmed back to life and vitality in the oven. And when there were no little pigs in the oven, there were usually boxes of little chickens that Alice and Laura brought in for resuscitation. For the little children these were great days, with the kitchen full of squealing and peeping pets, but for Rosie they were days of unending work and worry. One day, not noticing a box of little chickens in the open oven, she closed the oven door and built a fire in the stove. For years afterward she never closed that door without recalling the tragedy.

In March, Rosie went down to Holton, taking Alice and little Rosina with her. At Holton, the weather was even worse than at home, and the roads were impassable everywhere. Rosie became sick on the first day there, and for weeks lay in bed, looking out of the window much of the time at the rain and mud. How she longed for her own home again—her home, where the children were—largely forgetting the years of discouragement she had been through there! Never in all her life was she happier than the evening her train rolled in at Downs, past the railroad water tank and up to the station, and she saw Henry standing there on the platform. He helped her and the children down, and with little Rosina in one arm and an assortment of boxes and packages in the other, led the way to the wagon. Sunset glow still lingered in the west as they rattled out of town, and it was dark before they reached home. Both of the children were asleep in Rosie's arms when the wagon stopped at the kitchen door. The dog leaped about and barked a whole-souled welcome to everyone.

"Well, Watch! You're glad to see us again, aren't you?" said Rosie; and his answer left no room for doubt on that point.

Rosie brought home a dozen cups and saucers that Uncle Chris had given her, big cups beautifully decorated with a variety of designs—one for each of the children, as well as for Henry and Rosie, and one to spare. Knowing how easily such things are broken, Rosie kept them in the bedroom closet; but the children persisted in going in to admire and handle the wonderful new cups, and broke one of them the very first day after she got home.

There was no discouragement at home about wet weather. There could be no discouragement about rain, or mud, after the long drouth of the year before. Rain was always good in this country, and mud always a harbinger of good crops. The subsoil was thoroughly soaked, and everyone hopeful of another wheat crop.

That spring Henry planted several acres of alfalfa—a new crop that some of the neighbors were experimenting with.

When a few warm sunny days came in April, the wheat seemed almost to jump out of the wet ground, covering the fields with a rich green that the buffalo grass tried in vain to match. The hungry cattle left the straw stack and grazed contentedly about in the pasture. A new generation of bandy-legged calves was presently capering about, and bleating answers to the bawling mothers, from the calf pen where they were being weaned. Soon there was an abundance of milk to drink, and some butter to sell. Hungry for greens, the children went down into the pasture and gathered "wild lettuce," or dandelion leaves, lambs-quarters, and sheep sorrel. Rosie served the wild lettuce and lambs-quarters with vinegar, and the sheep sorrel made very good pies—but it took too much sugar.

There were many days of anxiety concerning the wheat. Early in May, it developed a yellow discoloration, which some said was due to Hessian fly, and others thought was a kind of scald or bleaching from the hot sun soon after the snow melted away. At service on Sundays, and at every casual meeting of neighbors, the condition of the wheat was argued pro and con, some holding that the crop was irreparably injured and might as well be plowed under, others believing that it would come out well enough.

The weather turned very dry, and the ground that had been so wet began to bake and open up in great cracks. Chinch bugs appeared in the wheat, and as the dry, windy days followed each other, the bugs penetrated farther into the fields. It looked like the wind-up of so many years of early promise.

But the rain finally came; and in June, a great crop was harvested, in spite of later rains that threatened to keep the binders out of the fields. An opportune crop failure in Europe drove the price of wheat to seventy-five cents a bushel, a price that meant new comforts and conveniences—not only clothes and shoes, but a new cultivator and a cart.

It was a wet year. Rains came regularly, almost all summer. In October, a fair corn crop stood in the fields, and the price was better—twenty-five cents a bushel. Billy stayed out of school until Thanksgiving to help husk. Before the winter was over, hogs had almost doubled in price; and Henry sold a load for enough to buy a two-seated surrey, and pay for music lessons for Laura. The older girls urged Rosie to buy a washing machine, even insisted that she could not afford to be without one, but she would not be persuaded. "I've always noticed," she argued, "that the people who buy all the things they can't afford to be without, never have anything."

Rosie really needed a washing machine too, for with all the long, pleated underskirts and fluffy, ruffled dresses that modest women wore—seven yards around at the bottom was not unusual for underskirts, and proper women wore three—Monday was a day to be dreaded—a day when the fire roared steadily under boilers of water, when tubs and buckets of soapy water stood on every chair, and the floor was littered with piles of soiled clothing, assorted according to color. On Monday mornings Rosie was up early and worked with driving energy, more than pleased if she could get her washing on the line before Lizzie Graeber did. If she saw Lizzie's washing out first, her day was not a complete success. Rosie really enjoyed washing and was happy when she could see a long line of clean clothes flapping in the wind—happy with a sense of solid achievement; but, true to her careful ways, she did not buy a washing machine until several years later.

That was like Rosie. Anything in the way of farm equipment she always favored—any productive investment, likely to bring better returns from the farm. And, with wisdom born of many nights of worrying and fretting about the future of her children, she was always anxious to do whatever she could to make the home a good place for the children. She would save and skimp on herself, wear rags and work beyond her strength, to be able to furnish the home as attractively as possible so that they could entertain their friends without embarrassment, to be able to clothe them well when they went out, and buy the books and other things that they needed. In conveniences for lightening her own tasks, however, she took no interest whatever. What difference whether her work was a little easier or not? She was used to doing it in a certain way, and she did not mind working—even felt a bit contemptuous of the whole idea of trying to make work easy.

In March of the next year another little boy was born—a mischievous, helter-skelter, rough-and-tumble little fellow.[2] His mother named him Herman, but the children usually called him

Tom, or Happy, or Buckskin—much to Rosie's disgust, for she disliked nicknames for the children. While she was in bed with Herman, Henry bought some bananas for her, a delicacy she had tasted only once or twice before.

They harvested another wheat crop that year, and another fair corn crop, and Henry now had money to build a fine big barn, with a cupola large enough for a covey of pterodactyls, but, much to the disappointment of the children, without a gilded weather vane. When the new house was built, the old log house had been torn down and rebuilt into a stable near the corral. It seemed a landmark, an essential detail in the sky line, an indispensable part of the farmstead; but more room was needed, so it was torn down, and the logs were used to make an ice house. Ice cream was becoming a fashionable luxury, and on Sundays Rosie often let the children make it. It was a good way to keep them at home.

The country was prospering again, in spite of low prices. There was renewed talk of railroad building. Even the failure of the bank could not stop the growth of Downs. With trainloads of grain and livestock rolling out of town, some of the railroad men were able to "knock down" handsome incomes in addition to their wages, some of which they spent on fast horses—and fast women, of whom the town now had several, despite sizzling editorials in the Downs *Times* and crusades by the town's morality squad. "Cat wagons" came through the country occasionally too, building up a surprisingly brisk business before the sheriff intervened, and bringing the physicians custom from a few of the boys of the community. While the preachers fulminated against the theater, the young people of the town organized a dramatic club which played "The Octoroon" before an admiring audience of relatives and friends. Some of the young men organized a flambeau club and soon learned to strut around with their torches, making a grand spectacle on the night of the Twenty-seventh celebration. A few of the town plutocrats were buying croquet and crokinole sets for less spectacular entertainment, and a very few of the ultra-rich bought bicycles, which sometimes frightened the horses on the roads. John Wise bought bicycles for several of his oldest children, at a hundred dollars each; and Danny invested his savings, amounting to a dollar, in a second-hand cycle with solid tires and a front wheel as high as he was—so high, indeed, that he rode it at a

Children of Henry and Rosa Ise in 1893. Back row, left to right: Danny, Laura, Billy, Robert, and Alice. Front row: Joe, Rosina, Louise, Mary, and Hap. (Courtesy the Historical Society of the Downs Carnegie Library)

considerable risk to life and limb. Treading was a job only for a strong heart; but for a few weeks he managed to convince himself that he was having great fun with it, riding it to school and even to the corral at milking time—with a milk bucket hung on the handle bars.

Fred Wetzel used the money from his wheat crop for no worldly purpose. For the glory of the Lord in general, and for the upbuilding of the Congregational Church of Downs in particular, he bought a parsonage for the church, at a cost of seven hundred and fifty dollars. Not long afterward, one of his sons came home from a Methodist revival announcing that he been converted and had joined the Methodist Church, whereat the old man ordered him out of the house—it was eleven o'clock at night. The young man left and never came home again. Needing help in his farm work, Fred adopted an orphan, ten or twelve years old; but his merciless whipping of the poor boy became a neighborhood scandal and the asylum authorities had to take him away.

Singing schools were being organized, and Laura and Alice joined the Mistletoe Club, conducted by a man named Magaw.[3] Alice had a sweet soprano voice, and Laura sang alto, and at the club meetings, which were held at the homes of the members, they learned to read music and had rare good times.

Magaw was a leader, not only in singing, but in every movement for the betterment of the community. For years he fought valiantly for enforcement of the prohibition law, against forces that would have disheartened a less courageous man. One night his house was burned—by members of the booze faction in town, many believed; but he did not abate his zeal in the least, and finally saw the joints closed and the druggists reduced to selling drugs. When the county attorney announced a policy of law enforcement, both the druggists of Downs hastily sold their liquor stocks and left town.

That summer the horse company, which had proved so disastrous an enterprise, was wound up at a loss of all that had been invested.[4] When the last assessment was to be paid, the stockholders gathered at Henry's house in their patched overalls and leaky boots, and piled up the greenbacks and silver dollars on the table—more than a thousand dollars in a heap. The next investment that Henry made proved somewhat better than the horse company—

MISTLETOE CLUB CONCERT PROGRAM.

Osborne Kan., Saturday Evening, March 3d, 1894.

FIRST PART.

"Welcome"—Quartette	Messrs. George, Nelson, Huff and Johnson.
"Softly Roam"—Ladies Trio	Misses Tagader, Jones and Mrs. Magaw.
"A Merry Heart goes all the Day"—Quartette	Messrs. Barry, Magaw, Garner and Lodwick.
"Wouldn't you Like to know"—Quartette	Messrs. Nevil, Magaw and Garner.
"Loves Sweet Broken Dream"—Quartette	Messrs. Nevil, Magaw and Slothower.
"Song of the Ducks"—Part Song	Misses Tagader, Ise, Messrs. Magaw, Barry and Garner.
"Village in the Valley"—Duet and Chorus	Miss Ise and Messrs. Garner and Picken.
"When I was a Tiny Boy"—Quartette	Messrs. Nevil, Garner and Picken.
"Voices from the Farther Shore"—Duet and Chorus	Misses Jones & Tagader, Messrs Jones & Magaw.
"The Girl who Sassed her Mother"—Solo	E. D. Jones.
"My Home is on the Sea"—Quartette	Messrs. Nevil, Lodwick and Picken.
"Leander and Jennie Dix"—Duet	Rose Tagader, and Samuel Magaw.
"Dearest Heart Good-bye"—Quartette	Messrs. Garner, Slothower and Lodwick.
"Tommy Went A-gunning"—Quartette	Messrs. Nevil, Slothower and Garner.
"Our Boys are in danger"—Solo and Chorus	Blanche Jones.

SECOND PART.

Song	Performers
"What Yer Gwine ter do?"—Quartette	Messrs. Garner, Slothower and Lodwick.
"Friends of Long Ago"—Duet	J. W. Lodwick. Blanche Jones.
"Riding on a Rail"—Quartette	Messrs. Barry, Jones, Picken and Garner.
"Cottage on the Hill"—Quartette	Misses Delay and Ise, Messrs. Barry and Lodwick
"Charming Fellow"—Ladies Quartette	Misses Jones, Tagader and Ise.
"Brook Miller's Song"—Quartette	Messrs. Nevil, Slothower and Picken.
"Life's Fair Morning"—Solo and Chorus	Mabel Picken.
"The Wise Man"—Quartette	Messrs. Nevil, Lodwick and Garner.
"On the Silvery Sea"—Quartette	Misses Tagader and Ise, Messrs. Magaw, Garner.
"Reverie"—Quartette	Messrs. George, Jones, Slothower & Garner.
"Who'll Buy"—Quartette	Messrs. George, Nelson, Huff and Johnson.
"Hie Thee, Shallop"—Part Song	Rose Tagader, Messrs. Nevil, Magaw,Garner.
"Be Kind to Old Grannie"—Solo and Chorus	Hermon Picken.
"Aunt Dinah's Hymn"—Solo and Chorus.	
"Good Night"—Chorus.	

Mistletoe Club concert program. (Courtesy University of Kansas Archives)

several lots in the new town of Downs. Downs was booming, and it seemed likely that lots would rise in value.

Grandmother died in July, and Henry and Rosie went down to the funeral, taking the baby and Joe along. When the estate was settled, Rosie's share was enough to buy another farm.[6] It never occurred to her to invest the money otherwise. Rosie liked land, and she always thought it the best of investments, never dreaming that not one of her children would ever want to farm any of the land she was buying for them.

Henry and Billy worked on the farm that fall, and Danny and Robert had to stay out of school to husk the corn on the new place. Youngsters of twelve and ten years, they spent quite much of their time in fighting, wrestling, throwing ears of corn at each other, talking and building air castles, in computing just how much they had husked and how much they had yet to husk, and in trying to devise some easy and expeditious way of completing the job. Winter came, and one cold day Danny froze his toes, in spite of the old socks he had put on over his shoes. That slowed down operations still further, with the result that as Christmas time approached, the husking was still far from done.

Finally Laura agreed to stay out of school and help them for a week, if they would work hard. The agreement was easy to secure, for the job had become a terrible bore, and the boys wanted to get to school with the other children. The schoolhouse was only a quarter of a mile across the pasture, and as they tussled with the big ears of corn, they could hear and see the school children at noon and recess, playing darebase and pullaway. They were glad enough to get help and worked hard for a week to finish the field.

When the corn was all out, Danny wanted to do something for Laura, to show his appreciation of her help. After talking the matter over with Robert, he decided to buy her an autograph album; and when he went to town to buy school books he looked at albums too.[7] There were several at various prices, but the one he particularly wanted—a blue plush album with silver lettering—was priced at fifty cents. Danny had only thirty-five cents. He stood comparing the various albums before him, trying to reconcile himself to one that would fit his purse; but every time that he was on the point of doing so, a glance at the rich blue cover and silver letters unsettled him again. Scott Carney's was the only store in town that carried such things,[8] so it was useless to think of going elsewhere to buy; but finally Danny decided he would go home and talk it over with Robert anyhow. Perhaps Robert would know some way to raise fifteen cents more. He was on the point of leaving when the storekeeper noticed the troubled look on his face.

"Wait a minute, sonny," he called out. "What can I do for you?"

Danny turned at the door. "Nothing, I guess. I was just looking at some albums."

"Well, couldn't you find one to suit you?"

"Yes, but it cost fifty cents—and I got only thirty-five cents."

"Come on over here, and we'll see what we can do." The

storekeeper went over to the counter and picked up the blue album.

"Is this the one?" he asked kindly.

"Yes, that's it. I think she'd like that—my sister—I want it for her—but I haven't got that much." Danny looked longingly at the album that the man held up before him.

"Well, if you've got only thirty-five cents, I'll have to let you have it for thirty-five cents, I guess." The storekeeper handed the gleaming treasure over across the counter, Danny handed back the money. Too happy even to thank the storekeeper for his kindness, the boy turned and was gone. On the way home, he took the precious album out of its wrapping a dozen times, to admire its wonderful color and texture; and when he presented it to Laura that evening at the supper table, he was prouder and happier than he had been in years.

Chapter Thirty

Trouble in School and Church

"They're not so much trouble when they're little. Washing a few diapers won't hurt you. It's when they get big that they make real trouble—the kind that keeps you awake at night. When they're little, they're little troubles; and when they're big, they're big troubles."

Rosie was talking about the children. Billy was no longer in school, and Laura and Alice had graduated from the country school; but the rest of the children went to the little schoolhouse across the pasture, and occasionally the girls would tattle on the boys, who were in open conflict with the teacher much of the time.

School troubles were not usually very serious. One day Joe and some of his playmates painted mustaches and beards on their faces with yellow crayon that they found on the teacher's desk. On noting the adornment, the teacher promptly ordered the boys to come to the desk and let her wipe the chalk off. The other boys marched up to the desk, and docilely permitted her to wipe their faces with her handkerchief—a most humiliating spectacle, it seemed to Joe; and he refused to submit to any such degradation. Since he was lame, Joe was humored at home, and not accustomed to accept dictation from others. The teacher promptly accepted the challenge and soon had Joe on the floor, with her knee on his chest.

Here came the tragedy. Joe had a shingle dart in his inside pocket, a treasured possession, one of the best darts in school, and as the teacher's knee bore down on this, it broke with a snap. This was too much! Humiliating enough indeed to have her wiping his face with her handkerchief, or even actually with her apron, but to have her break his prize dart was adding injury to insult!

"There you broke my dart, so you did! Doggone you!" he shouted, and began striking wildly at her with his clenched fists.

The teacher was frightened at the violence of the revolt and got up with what promptness and grace she could command. Joe carried his chalk mustache the rest of the day, but this moral victory was small consolation for the loss of his dart.

School troubles were far more common and more serious for Danny, who was six years older. Danny was the leader of a gang of young rebels who carried on a guerrilla war with some of the teachers. School discipline was always a serious problem anyhow, when the pupils had to sit three in a seat, when a few of them had no books, or even slates or paper or pencils, with which to keep themselves occupied, and when the cult of the boys was a hoodlum heroics that flourished under the harsh discipline that some of the teachers tried to impose. "Lickin' and larnin'" were supposed to be the reciprocal functions of teacher and pupils; and some of the teachers did their part religiously, if not with any great cultural results. Like so many people of the time, they thought they must have strict discipline, not as a means or condition to the education of the pupils, but as an end in itself.

Some of them, for instance, had systems of signs the students were required to use—one raised finger to leave the room, two fingers to whisper to a seat mate, three to borrow a pencil, and so forth; and the most expert disciplinarians had elaborate schedules of pains and penalties that would have made the penal code of medieval France look rather simple. The fact that a few of the teachers showed great partiality in administering their penal codes did not contribute to their success or popularity.

One of the teachers, a tall, angular, lantern-jawed tyrant affectionately nick-named "Slats" by the boys, was more than commonly rigorous in her discipline, and more than commonly hated for it.[1] So rebellious the boys became that she feared to whip them without help, so she chalked their offenses up against them for an entire week, then did the whipping wholesale on Friday afternoon, when her big brother Jim came to school with her. For rather trivial offenses, Danny was beaten until his legs swelled quite beyond their natural size and he could walk only with difficulty. He of course never complained at home, for it was Henry's unvarying rule not to interfere with the discipline of the teacher. Although a kindly man generally, Henry had the prevailing attitude toward discipline.

One Friday afternoon, the teacher had an unusually heavy grist of beatings to administer, and sent Joe out to get her a supply of switches from the neighboring hedge fence. Joe's heart did not warm to his task, and he cut the switches quite too small to do any serious hurt, for which misfeasance the teacher promptly wore out two of them on him. She next sent two of the older boys, who cut cudgels large enough to kill a small boy, but as if through awkwardness, cut them half through at several points so that with the first stroke they broke in pieces. This so angered the teacher that she proceeded to pound the boys with the heavy stubs until she was tired. Danny was so sore that night and for days afterward that he had to call on Robert to help him get his coat on and off.

The next Friday Danny again had a long list of offenses chalked up against him, whispering and giggling, mainly; and after school he was dragged into the outside hall to be beaten into another week of physical misery. This time the teacher had provided her own hedge switches, of serviceable size and quality, and she wore out three of these on him. As she reached for the fourth, the boy stepped back and pulled his knife from his pocket.

"If you hit me again—I'll cut you to pieces," he shouted, opening the long blade and squaring himself for a finish fight.

For an instant the teacher stood dumbfounded. She raised her whip and took a step forward, but insanely angry as she was, she saw something in the boy's eyes that fortunately arrested her step. Brother Jim was not with her this time, and after a moment's hesitation, she backed into the school room and closed the door. Danny closed and pocketed his knife, grabbed his coat and cap from the hook, and was soon trotting across the pasture, trying as he went to get his tight little coat on with the minimum hurt to his battered arms and shoulders. He was not quite sure he had done the best thing, for likely Henry would whip him if he learned what had happened; but he had been beaten about enough—just for whispering a few times. He did his chores with extra care that evening, and carried in two extra armfuls of wood, but the teacher never reported the occurrence to anyone.

Danny sometimes dressed for the occasion, when he knew that a hard day was coming—wore several shirts and pairs of trousers, and once he even wore board splints along the back of his legs; but the teacher detected the armor, and shifted the point of attack.

The next year, there was another teacher, a really estimable young woman, and thoroughly trained; but she had a merciless disciplinarian philosophy, and an ungovernable temper.[2] As soon as she was elected to the place, her mother announced to one of the neighbors that for once there would be order and discipline among the young savages of District 37. In a day or two the news of the declaration had reached every boy in the district; and long before school opened, the rebels were united in a firm resolution that order and discipline there should not be.

The new teacher decided to strike hard at the very first sign of insubordination or disorder, strike terror into the hearts of the boys before their rebellion had time to get under way; and her opening came before the term was a week old. Cramer Graeber was the victim.[3] He popped a hackberry seed one day, as he was sitting in his seat. At the resounding crack of the little seed, the teacher turned from her class, seized the piece of rubber hose that she kept on her desk, and marched back to his seat.

"Did you do that?"

He quailed before the vicious light of her eyes.

"Yes ma'am," he replied, and there was no rebellion in his voice.

The rubber hose descended upon his shoulders, once, twice, thrice, a dozen times. As she plied it, her temper rose, until she was no longer content to beat him on the shoulders. She began striking him across the back of his neck. He held his hands up to protect his neck, but then she struck him on the head, the supple rubber snapping around and into his ear and face and eyes. Again and again and again the stinging rubber fell on his neck and hands and head, leaving each time a welt or a bruise; again and again and again—would she never stop?

Finally she did stop. Exhausted and panting, her face red and swollen with anger, her hair dishevelled and in disarray, she ceased to beat the sobbing boy.

"Now will you be good?" she demanded.

Between sobs he managed to say, "Yes, ma'am."

Quiet there was, for the rest of the day, the quiet of terror and pity, indignation and smouldering anger, perhaps of fear; but the rebels soon regained their confidence. Danny and a few of the bolder ones declared among themselves that they would not be good and would not promise to be good, let her beat them as hard as she could. A few modest wagers were laid—wagers of marbles and pencils—as to who would be the next hero to be whipped. Danny always commanded considerable odds in such bets.

At the first rumble of growing revolt the teacher made preparation to suppress it summarily. She bought a new rawhide whip, which she laid on her desk in plain view of the pupils. Her psychology was bad, for the new rawhide immediately became the object of endless jokes and jibes among the boys. Without the grace to recede from her position and hide the whip in her desk, she nursed her growing wrath and bided her time.

Her time came soon enough. One day one of the boys handed Danny a slate, with a picture of the teacher on it; and he was giggling gleefully over the grotesque cartoon when the teacher came past his seat.

"Where did you get that?" she demanded.

No answer.

"Where did you get that slate?" Her voice rose sharply.

No answer from Danny, but just as the teacher started after her whip the other boy spoke up: "I gave it to him."

"What did you do it for?" She transferred her attention to the other culprit.

"I don't really know. Just for fun, I guess."

"Will you promise not to do it again?"

The other boy was not a fighting rebel, and he promptly promised not to repeat the offense. The teacher stepped back to Danny's desk.

"Will you promise to be good?"

No answer.

"Very well. You may stay after school."

Danny knew what that meant. The teacher had taken to whipping the boys after school, as there were fewer witnesses then who might make trouble.

There was an unusual batch of whippings to administer that

evening, and as Danny was the worst offender, he was left until last. One by one the boys were taken out into the hall and thrashed with a severity proportioned to their respective iniquities. The strokes of the rawhide and the occasional cries of the miscreants were not heartening music to the waiting boy; and when the last of his comrades had been dragged out into the hall, Danny opened a window, and at one bound was out and on his way across the pasture.

He shrewdly guessed that the teacher would follow him straight home, and he had no stomach for a conference with her and his father, so he headed for the cornfield and hid in a shock of corn. From here he soon saw the teacher striding along the path toward his home. It was a cold day, and his tight little coat was inadequate protection against the biting wind. He wondered about his chores, too, for it was milking time; but he stuck to his fortress until he felt sure his persecutor had gone on home.

When he finally emerged from his dusty hiding place, it was almost dark; and with many misgivings he sneaked up along the fence and through the corral to the barn. All well there, for Robert had milked his cows, and was just straining the milk.

"Is she gone?" he asked, cautiously poking his head in through the door.

Robert looked up in surprise. "Yeah. Long while ago."

"What did pa say?" The children no longer called their parents "papa" and "mamma."

"Nothing much, I guess. When I went after a milk bucket I heard him say it was her problem—she'd have to tend to it the best she could."

"What did she say? Madder'n hell, I bet!"

"Said you was the worse boy in school, and she'd have to whack it out of you somehow. Ma said you wasn't so bad at home."

Danny watched the milk sink along the sides of the strainer.

"Got the calves fed?"

"Alice fed 'em while I did the milking. Louise picked up the cobs. Got to carry the wood in yet, and that's all."

Robert carried the milk to the house, and Danny picked up a big armful of wood and carried it into the kitchen. Not a word was said, even at the supper table; and he began to breathe freely, even to hope that he might get off without a serious mauling. At any rate it was clear that Henry was not going to help the teacher out.

His relief was of short duration. The next morning, when the school bell had rung and the pupils had taken their seats, the teacher called Danny up before the school.

"Stand there!" She reached for the whip lying across her desk and bending it in her hands to test its suppleness, stepped to his side.

"So you jump out of the window when I tell you to stay after school! I'll teach you to disobey me!" And without waiting for answer or apologies, she proceeded to beat him over the arms and shoulders with the rawhide—one stroke, two, three, four, five, ten, a dozen, fifteen, twenty!

"Now will you promise to be good!" she panted, stopping for a minute to rest.

No answer. The boy's face was white and drawn, and the blood was trickling from gashes on the back of his hand where the end of the whip had snapped around and broken the skin; but there was no surrender.

Again she raised the whip, but she happened to glance around the room, and saw faces that caused her to stop—faces of the older girls, some of whom were crying, wide-eyed in horror and anger at this exhibition of brutality. She hesitated a moment, poised the whip for another stroke, but those eyes were upon her. She laid the whip back on her desk, and ordered Danny to his seat.

Danny was black and blue for a week, but the very next day was rolling up his sleeves before a ring of admiring boys and girls, and boasting of the flag of the "red, white, and blue" that he carried on his arms. The teacher stood by but said not a word, defeated, not altogether by the stubborn will of this fearless boy, but by the rising standards of humanity that had rendered her principles of school management obsolete. The frontier was becoming civilized.

While Danny was getting the fundamentals of a disciplinary education in school, Billy was the cause of much anxiety to his parents for his wildness outside of school. Like most of the older boys in the neighborhood, Billy often had to stay out of school for a month or more in the fall, to husk corn or do various fall jobs; and he fell into the habit of staying out the rest of the school year, choring around with the horses and cattle, hunting rabbits, and even occasionally entertaining himself less innocently. With some of the neighbors' boys he often went over to the home of an old bachelor,[4] where the boys learned to smoke and chew tobacco, tell smutty stories, play cards, and even drink beer occasionally. The old bachelor had hair clippers, and the boys offered the excuse that they went there to get their hair cut; but when everyone's hair had been cut, the party seldom ended.[5] Billy often got home late at night, much to Rosie's distress and Henry's anger and disgust.

These rowdies served as the nucleus of a band that officiated at charivaris[6] whenever there was a marriage in the neighborhood; and these charivaris sometimes wound up in trouble. The boys loved to torment old man Duckett,[7] an irascible old widower who lived a mile or two across the creek; and when the old man, at the ripe age of sixty-five, married his second wife, they organized a charivari party in his honor.

On the night of the charivari, most of the big boys in the neighborhood were there, with rolling cutters, cowbells, guns and powder. For a while they contented themselves with hammering the rolling cutters, ringing the cow bells, and firing their guns into the air; but all this brought no results. The old man never appeared or gave any sign that he was at home. Determined that they would be treated, the boys hung a heavy rock to the door knob, tied a long rope to the rock, and from their hiding places in the yard, pulled at the rope, banging the rock against the closed door. The lock gave way almost at the first impact, and a few more blows would have shivered the door completely, but the knot loosened and the stone fell to the ground.

Billy, always one of the most reckless in any crowd, rammed a formidable load of powder into his shotgun, and stepped up near the house to shoot.

"Don't try that! You'll blow your shoulder off!" shouted Nate Winters.[8]

Luckily too, that he said it, for when Billy reached around the corner, braced the stock against the house and fired, the butt of the gun tore through the siding, through the plastering inside, and knocked a pile of dishes off the old man's cupboard. If he had shot from his shoulder the kick would have maimed him for life.

Long after midnight they ran out of powder; and two of the younger boys were detailed to one of the neighbors to get another keg, while the rest employed themselves catching the chickens that were roosting in the trees, and throwing them into the house through a broken window.

When the boys came back with more powder, the guns were soon booming again, and stones crashed against the house and through the windows.

Finally the old man appeared at the door with his gun, and pointed it defiantly out into the crowd. In an instant one of the boys grabbed the barrel of the gun and, swinging it over his shoulder, started toward the road, dragging the poor stumbling old man out of his own house before it occurred to him to release his gun and retreat inside again.

"I'll get him out!" shouted one of the boys, Bartley Yost,[9] just coming up from the stable with several grain sacks in his hand. With a lift from one of the others, he clambered up on the roof, and stuffed the grain sacks in the chimney. In a few minutes the smoke was pouring out of the windows, and not long afterward the door creaked open and the old man appeared dimly in the dark.

"Treat! Treat!" shouted the boys, from their various stations and hiding places in the yard.

"I will not be imposed upon, and in the name of the law——"

"Treat! Treat! We want a treat!" they shouted.

"In the name of the law——"

"Treat! Treat!" The chorus drowned his voice completely; and one from around the corner added, "Damn the law!"

"In the name of the law I command——"

"Treat! Treat! Let's see the bride. The bride! The bride!"

"I will not be insulted, and I will not be imposed upon. I——"

"The bride! Trot 'er out! The bride!"

But the old man did not need to trot her out, for she needed fresh air as badly as he did, and jostled him to one side as she appeared in the door, coughing and wheezing. It was too dark to make out any features, but the boys gave her a round cheer.

"Treat! Treat!" they began shouting again.

"I'll treat you all right!" shouted the old man. "I'll treat you to the law, for the destruction of my property."

In the Dist., Court of the 15th Judicial Dist.,

OF THE STATE OF KANSAS.

SITTING IN AND FOR THE COUNTY OF OSBORNE.

February Term, A. D. 1892

BE IT REMEMBERED. That on this the _23d day of February_ 189_2_ personally appeared in open Court, _Henry Ise_ a native of _Germany_ _having been a soldier during the war of_ and applied to be admitted a citizen of the United States, and produced a certificate of his declaration of his intention to become a citizen of the United States, issued by the Clerk of _the Rebellion in the union army_, dated _September 14, 1864_ and proved to the satisfaction of the Court here, that he has resided in the United States for more than the period of five years next preceding this application, and for one year last past within the State of Kansas: and that during the whole of that period, he has conducted himself as a man of good moral character, attached to the principles of this Government, and well disposed to the good order and happiness of the same.

Thereupon, the Court being fully satisfied that said applicant has fulfilled all the requirements of the laws of the United States respecting the naturalization of Foreigners, and the said _Henry Ise_ having declared on oath that he will support the Constitution of the United States, and renounce and abjure forever all allegiance and fidelity to every Foreign Power, Prince, Potentate, State or Sovereignty whatever, and particularly to the _William_ _second Emperor of Germany_ of whom he was he was heretofore a subject, it is ordered by the Court, he, the said _Henry Ise_ be, and he is hereby declared a citizen of the United States of North America, with all the rights and privileges thereto.

JoJHilton Clerk.

_____Deputy

Henry Ise's naturalization certificate (1892). The usual requirements to become an American citizen were waived because of Henry's Civil War service. (Osborne County Courthouse, Osborne, Kansas)

At first there was uproarious laughter and jeering, but the hilarity subsided rather quickly, for some of the boys began to see that their spree had been highly destructive. It was past two o'clock, and they had been making merry at high pressure for several hours. They were getting tired and sleepy anyhow, and cold. With a few parting shots into the air, they began to disperse, afoot, on horseback, and in wagons that lumbered noisily off through the still night. The old man was left to get the chickens out of his house, clear out his chimney, and patch up his windows the best he could.

The boys had trusted to the old man's blindness as a shield from recognition; but their trust was not well placed, and the very next day he drove into Henry's yard with his little pony and told Henry of the night's celebration. Henry disliked every form of rowdyism, and he promptly called Billy in for a serious conference. The upshot of it all was that, to avoid a lawsuit, Billy, and most of the other participants in the charivari, dug deeply into their small

savings to pay the cost of repairing the old man's house and salving his ruffled dignity.

Not all charivaris turned out so badly. One night ten of the
neighbor boys assembled at Henry's house to go to a charivari
across the creek. A prairie fire lighted up the sky to the northwest,
and Henry was watching it with some anxiety; so he asked them to
wait awhile and see if the fire should come down near enough to
be dangerous. They sat around on the porch for a while, joking
and telling stories; and when some of them began to get sleepy,
Billy suggested that they go to bed and sleep while they waited.
Without undressing, eleven of them got into two beds, lying crosswise, and were soon sound asleep—so sound asleep that not one
of them awakened until the killdeers were calling from the south
field the next morning.

Disturbance of church services was one of the favorite amuse-
ments of some of the young men; and Billy's participation in this
indoor sport was the cause of much anxiety to his parents. There
were perhaps a dozen of the larger boys in the gang that took their
places in the rear of the schoolhouse that served as a church, at every evening service and at quarterly meetings. They laughed and
snickered and rattled the desks, shot paper wads, scattered pop
matches on the floor, even sometimes did worse, until the preacher
was at his wit's end. The presiding elder, a pompous and important churchman, often referred to the corner where the boys gathered as the "devil's corner," which of course afforded them huge
amusement. At the quarterly meetings, he always spent considerable time consigning the boys to the correcting and refining influence of everlasting fire, but they enjoyed this too.

A new preacher came—an energetic, egotistical little fellow
named Froeliger[10]—whose boast was that he would tame the rowdies in short order. He earned Billy's deep dislike very soon after
he came, by his cruel treatment of his horses. In getting from one
appointment to another, he drove two horses to death; and once,
right in front of the church, he would have worn out a buggy whip
on one of his horses, had not one of his parishioners intervened
and stopped him.

The church disturbances turned worse, and Froeliger threatened the boys with divers pains and punishments, but to no avail.
After all, how could you arrest boys for laughing at something

funny—and the boys seemed to find much that was funny in every sermon. Several times the preacher accosted them after church, demanding that they stay away or be quiet during the services; and once or twice his threats nearly led to a fight.

One Monday morning, after a particularly serious church disturbance, the preacher drove into Henry's yard and reined his foaming horses. Henry was hammering a plow lay and did not hear him until he came up close behind him.

"Good morning, Brother Ise."

At the greeting, Henry dropped his hammer and turned to his visitor.

"Good morning. I didn't hear you drive in. How are you? Won't you unhitch and come in?"

"Oh no, thanks. I must be getting on to Kill Creek. I just wanted to see you a moment about your son Billy."

"Is he making trouble again?" Henry seldom went to the evening service, and did not know all that had been happening.

"Every evening that we have meetings. And it will have to stop, Brother Ise. We can't have our divine services broken into that way. I have tried to get the boys to behave or stay away, but they refuse to do either; and if you don't see any better way, I will have to invoke the power of the law and have them arrested."

Henry put the plow lay down on the bench, with a confused and troubled expression on his face.

"Well, if you have to do that to keep order, I'll not interfere. Billy is old enough to know how to behave. He's too big to be whipped."

"Right enough! I will get a warrant in Osborne today, on my way over; and I hope we will have no more difficulty." The preacher's cheerfulness grated on Henry; in fact, the preacher usually grated on Henry more or less; but he made no reply and even, as the man turned to go, urged him to unhitch and stay for dinner.

"Well, I don't mind if I do," he replied, and turned to unhitch his horses. Henry helped him and could not help noticing how the poor brutes trembled and pulled away, whenever he got close enough to touch them. He wondered just how a man who was preaching the religion of the kind and gentle man of Galilee could be so inhuman in his treatment of helpless animals.

At dinner, Rosie learned of the preacher's mission, and she immediately objected to Billy's arrest.

"No, we don't need to do that," she said decisively. "We can see to it that there is no more trouble. If he is arrested that means a mark on him that will never help him, or any of us."

Brother Froeliger was eating a piece of fried chicken as she said it, and was hardly in a position, or even in the humor, to insist on having the son of his hostess arrested; so the matter was dropped.

The next Sunday evening, when the boy came down from his room with his Sunday clothes on, Henry stopped him.

"Billy, you're not going up to church tonight," he said with decision. "We can't have any more disturbing of church services."

One of the neighbor boys, who was sitting there waiting for him, blushed and presently slunk out of the room and went home. Billy put his hat back on the hook, sat down by the table, and began reading the Kansas City *Star.* That was the end of it. There was no more disturbing of the church services; and the young hoodlums soon grew into staid and dignified manhood. The manners of the frontier were improving.

Billy was not the only one of the children whose attitude toward the church disturbed his parents. Indeed Billy was not so much critical of the church and religion as he was disrespectful of everything, like most boys at the age of rowdyism. Some of the younger children early evinced a disposition to question religious doctrines that Henry and Rosie held sacred, and this disturbed them not a little. Henry and Rosie were both reasonably liberal in their own views, indeed they were far less serene in their own faith than they ever admitted, even to themselves; but they believed that it was impossible to have a good community without a church, and that it was good for the children to go and preserve at least an outward attitude of conformity. Rosie saw that church services brought people out washed and combed and dressed in their Sunday clothes; and she tacitly assumed that this outward decency was associated with desirable spiritual graces. She always made the children wash and comb and dress up on Sunday morning, and then she and Henry took them to "Sunday school"—as the service was commonly called—in the lumber wagon, Henry and Rosie and the baby riding in the spring seat, and the children sitting on board behind.

The older girls, Laura and Alice, fell into this scheme of things with reasonable docility, but the younger children showed a distinctly skeptical attitude. They could not see any particular virtue in going to church—where they had to listen to long sermons, some of them in German, which they could not even understand. Sermons preached in English they cared little more for, and promptly picked to pieces on the way home from church. They had no great reverence for most of the preachers, even thought most of them were preaching merely because they were too lazy to do anything else and because they liked the yellow-legged chicken that was served wherever they went. The Reverend Mr. Froeliger they disliked particularly because he was so cruel to his horses and to his wife and children—from Rosie the children had learned to think of cruelty as the worst of vices, especially cruelty to animals. Rosie seldom resorted to spanking the children, but when the boys tied a tin can to the dog's tail, she adopted corrective measures that they had no difficulty understanding, and remembering.

The children resented the pompous arrogance of the presiding elder—but Henry had to sympathize with them in this, because he resented the man's ways too. Once when Rosie was sick, Henry had bought her a bottle of beer, and when the elder heard of this he made some strongly vituperative remarks about church members who "befoul themselves with the devil's brew." Henry did not get angry about it. He always welcomed the elder hospitably when he came to visit and went to hear him when he preached; but he did not rate the prelate's manners very high.

The children noticed too that several of the most devout churchmen were cruel to their animals, that they drove their horses to church on cold winter days and stood them out in the cold without blankets, while they went in to pray for themselves, and for each other, and for the kingdom of God generally. The children thought there was something wrong about this—just as indeed did Henry and Rosie. And, like Rosie, they wondered how the good Lord could send drouths so that cattle would have to go hungry. This indeed was one question that Rosie was never able to answer to her satisfaction. She could not reconcile her religion with the suffering that drouth always brought, especially to the animals.

She once argued the question with the preacher and his wife, when they came to stay all night. They had been discussing the usual questions—the weather, and the condition of the crops—Rosie darning socks all the while—when she suddenly burst out:

"Why, Mr. Mattill,[11] should we have such weather, to burn up the feed for the cattle? Why couldn't we have rain, so there would be something for them to eat?" It had been a very dry season.

The minister looked up, too much surprised at the question to answer promptly, but he finally admitted that it was rather hard to understand.

"I can't see why it should be," she declared. "Surely we've done our part. We've planted the crops, and cared for them, as well as we know how; and if we could just have a rain or two, there wouldn't be any need for cattle to go hungry. I can't understand, anyhow, why cattle should ever have been created to stand around and bawl and bawl for something to eat, the way so many have to do when feed is scarce."

The minister made a somewhat halting reply to the effect that the Lord's ways are not our ways, that his wisdom is above our wisdom, and that we should not question his plans for us.

Rosie came back with vigor: "But it surely isn't right. Anybody can see that much. These hot winds won't leave anything for the cattle to eat, or the poor horses that have to work so hard all summer."

"We can only trust in God," replied the minister, with somewhat more assurance. "And if we see to our own stock, and to our own responsibilities, God will care for His own creatures."

"But He doesn't do it," argued Rosie, so much in earnest that she dropped the sock she was mending and straightened up in her chair. "I don't see that He does it at all. And with weather like this we can't do it ourselves either."

Henry was visibly embarrassed by the turn the conversation had taken. He was not greatly in awe of preachers, generally, and was much of Rosie's mind on this question, but he was more timid than Rosie in pushing his own side of an argument. He disliked arguments anyhow, and feared that this might become uncomfortably heated, so he stepped in to turn the conversation into pleasanter channels.

"Oh, we had several good years," he asserted, rather weakly, "and have much to be thankful for. We can't be held responsible for anybody else's cattle, surely."

"Nobody's responsible. That's what I mean. I don't understand how a good Lord, who watches over His people the way He is supposed to, can pay so little attention to hungry cattle and horses. They have to eat, or ought to."

"But we are not supposed to understand all things," said the preacher. "God's ways are mysterious and inscrutable. God's ways are not our ways. We must have faith in Him. Have you no faith? Can't you put your trust in God?"

For a moment Rosie was taken aback, and could make no answer; but she recovered quickly. "How can we have faith that God will provide, when we see the corn burning in the fields right now? How can we have faith that people's cattle will be cared for when we know they probably won't? Much of the corn is gone now."

"There are many things that are hard to understand," admitted the preacher, apparently willing to drop the subject.

"It isn't only the cattle and horses, either," declared Rosie. "There are Gesner's children, with no shoes all last winter; and yet Glenn and Clarence had to herd cattle far into November—nearly to Thanksgiving.[12] Poor little boys, hiding from the wind in a corn shock one day when we drove by, covering their feet with husks. They won't have any shoes this winter either, the way things look now. And Duffy's children are just as bad."[13]

"Yes, but Rosie, we can't be held responsible for other people's children," argued Henry. "We have enough to do to buy shoes for our own."

"More than enough to do, I think, the way things are going now. It surely seems hard to have to see everything burn up that you've worked so hard to get started."

"Yet, Sister Ise, we might get too proud and stiff-necked if we had everything we wanted. The Lord has a purpose in visiting trouble upon his children, and it is not for us to question His purpose." The preacher delivered this polemic with far more assurance than he had yet displayed.

"Oh, I guess those children wouldn't get so stiff-necked with just shoes and stockings on, or even with decent coats when they're herding cattle. I can't see how they are so responsible, anyhow. They have nothing to say about coming into the world, and not much about anything they find here—as much perhaps as some of those poor cattle have." Rosie dug into the basket for another sock.

"We have failed somewhere." It was the preacher's wife who spoke this time. "We have failed in something and God has sent the drouth to chasten us. We should not rebel against His will, but should rather try to seek out the ways in which we have failed to do His will." She radiated humility and complacency as she said it.

"Amen," echoed her spouse.

"Oh, shucks!" replied Rosie. "I'll admit we may have been wicked and sinful, in some ways. Perhaps we forgot to read our Bible a night or two." Rosie bit the thread off and threw the sock back in the basket. "And we could have given more to the church—by making the children go without shoes, and by starving the cattle. That's the way old man Metz does,[14] and Wetzel, and some more of the good men of our church."

"Judge not," protested the minister. "We must not condemn those who put the Lord's service first, even before shoes and feed for cattle."

"Not before their own shoes. Just before the children's shoes." Rosie snipped a ragged edge with her scissors.

"You wouldn't have us without a church," the preacher's voice rose in injured protest, "without a place to worship God, without a place to teach our children the message of Christ and His redemption from sin and death everlasting, without an altar for——"

"Yes, I think I would—if it has to be paid for by making the children go without shoes, and the cattle without enough to eat. I shouldn't think the Lord would want that. Do you think He would, really?"

Rosie's question seemed to smack of irreverence, and the minister could hardly find an appropriate answer, before Rosie was attacking on another front.

"If the Lord had just sent us a rain a couple of weeks ago, we could have fed the cattle, and dressed the children, and built a church to take the place of the school house; but we can't do it now." Rosie threw the last sock back into the basket, and looked up at the clock. "But I guess it is about time to go to bed. We can't do much about it, anyhow."

After family Bible reading and prayers and singing, the preacher and his wife were shown their bed. Before getting into bed Rosie prayed for rain, as she had done every night, and very likely the preacher prayed for Rosie.

Chapter Thirty-one

A Dust Storm

Two years passed—'ninety-three and 'ninety-four—grim, desperate years, two years without even a fair crop, two years of bare pastures and short fodder, of hungry cattle breaching the fences, herded here and there by the little children but always wandering restlessly in search of better feed. For Rosie they were years of patching and cutting down old clothes for the younger children, of churning and working butter late into the night after the children were in bed, of planning and scheming to make every dollar do the work of two.

Despite hard times, Henry and Rosie managed to get enough money—twenty dollars—to buy Laura a watch and chain for her eighteenth birthday, and gave a big party for her. The young people played "Buffalo Girls," "Old Brass Wagon," "Miller Boy," "Old Dan Tucker," "We'll All Go Down to Rousers," and "Skip to M'Lou, My Darling," prancing up and down the big dining room and singing their doggerel with lusty good-will, with accompaniment by the harmonica. Then they played "Tin Tin" and "Clap In and Clap Out" for a while and afterward went out in the yard and played "Drop the Handkerchief." It was near midnight when they came in for a supper of sandwiches, cake and ice cream. Even the smaller children had a great time, sitting around in the corners, watching the older ones dancing, and eating cake and ice cream in the kitchen afterward.

For the younger children Henry subscribed to the *Youth's Companion*, which the youngsters fought over every week and read from cover to cover. Henry usually brought it home from town on

Saturday evening, and on that evening the children were all anxiety, listening for the rattle of his wagon down the road.

In August, eighteen ninety-three, Henry and Laura went to the World's Fair at Chicago.[1] It seemed an extravagance, but Rosie wanted Henry to see his brother, who was to be there from Pennsylvania—he had not seen him since they came to America. Rosie had no clothes for such a trip, and the baby was too small to be taken, so she herself did not consider going. Someone had to stay at home anyhow and attend to the farm business. Laura had a position for the next winter, teaching school a few miles from home, and she was to pay back the cost of her trip.

It was a wonderful trip for Henry and Laura. Brother John was there, and many other friends and relatives. They all stayed with hospitable relatives in Chicago, and had great times marveling at the buildings and exhibits of the fair, and at the wonders of the city itself. When they got together at night, they had good visits that sometimes lasted until midnight; but it was hard work. After two weeks of it, all of the relatives had a group picture taken, and Henry and Laura returned home, with presents for all the rest of the family—souvenirs which cost much more than they were worth, but seemed very fine indeed.

When they got home from Chicago, the hot winds were burning the corn; and Henry and the boys and the hired man had to begin cutting fodder immediately, using two of the new corn sleds, with a knife on each side. The first day out, when Henry happened to be standing for a moment in front of the knife, the horse moved forward a step, almost severing his tendon of Achilles. Wild with pain, he rolled on the ground for a few minutes,. but finally managed to crawl back onto the sled; and Joe, who was riding the horse, took him to the house. Rosie helped him into bed, where he stayed for weeks. That fall, out in the field one day, he left the team standing a moment, and they started to run away. He jumped to reach the lines and tore the partly healed tendon loose again. The pain this time was excruciating, and he was unable to get around to do anything until early in the spring.

The next year, Henry and Rosie managed to get enough money—one hundred and twenty-five dollars—to build a picket fence around the yard,[2] a fence of fine white pine, inclosing enough land for a small farm almost, as was the custom of the

Left to right: Henry Ise, Kate Riemenschneider, and John Eisenmanger in 1893. Photograph taken at the Columbian Exposition in Chicago, Illinois. (Courtesy of the Historical Society of the Downs Carnegie Library)

time. It took two weeks to paint it. It never kept the chickens out of the yard, as Rosie had hoped; but it was effective against the pigs and cattle and added greatly to the attractiveness of the yard. Rosie always did her best to make the home attractive for the children.

"When they're at home, they're not in anybody's way, and they're not in any mischief," she once said; "and they won't stay at home unless there's something there that they like."[3]

In February of the next year came a terrible blizzard and dust storm. The morning of that memorable day dawned mild and bright, and the children went to school without mittens or heavy wraps. Not long afterward the clear sky began to turn a murky brown, out of which the sun shone dimly, like a full moon through a yellow fog. The wind shifted quickly to the north, and in a few minutes a hurricane was roaring through the cottonwood grove, carrying dense clouds of dust and dirty, dry snow that hid the barn and granary and other outbuildings completely from view. The house became so dark that Rosie lighted the lamp, but when she felt the house shake with the wind, she blew it out. It was no time to risk a fire. In a few hours the temperature reached zero, while the wind shrieked around the corners of the house, rattling the windows and shutters, and piling little drifts of dust on the window sills.

Henry put on his overcoat and mittens, and went out to drive the chickens into the coop, and see that the pigs and cattle and horses were under shelter. In the clear sweep of the wind, he was at times almost blown from his feet, and in the driving dust and snow he dared not face the wind; but he made the rounds, found chickens scattered about on the south side of various buildings, pictures of abject misery, and managed to get them under shelter. The cattle were clustered under the projecting shelter of the straw stack, contentedly chewing their way farther under the stack. Returning to the house, he had to feel his way, since he could not see into the face of the wind.

"Oh, Henry, isn't this terrible!" exclaimed Rosie, as he opened the door and kicked the snow from his shoes.

"The worst I ever saw," he answered, shaking the dust and snow from his cap and unbuttoning his coat; "the worst I ever saw, except the blizzard of 'seventy-one. That was worse in some ways, but not so dirty—the time we stretched a rope from the house to the stable to keep from getting lost."

He poured some hot water from the tea kettle into the wash basin, bathed his eyes, and then sat down to dinner.

Henry and Rosie were anxious about the children at school, but concluded that they would not start home until the usual time, four o'clock; and at three-thirty Henry started across the pasture with an armful of caps, coats, mufflers, mittens, and old socks to put over the children's shoes.

With the wind at his back and pushing him along, he made his way rapidly in the general direction of the schoolhouse. The clouds of dust shut off the distant view entirely, and even sometimes obscured the very ground on which he was walking; but he knew that if he let the wind drive him forward he would strike the fence somewhere near the schoolhouse, and could follow the fence until he came to the stile.

As he hurried along, hanging tightly to the wraps that the wind tried to wrest from him, and peering ahead in a vain attempt to discover the outline of the schoolhouse, he heard the sound of children's voices—yes, it was the children, one of them crying. They had started home!

His ears were so bundled up with cap and muffler that he could not tell clearly where the voices came from, but he stopped and listened. Yes, there was the cry again, but farther away. It seemed to come from the west. He shouted, but he could scarcely hear his own voice, it was so lost in the commotion of the wind. He turned and hurried in the direction from which that cry had come, now with the wind and dust cutting the side of his face like a sand blast. He knew that the smaller children could never find their way home in the face of that wind.

He shouted as he hurried along, then stopped to listen.

There was no sound but the roar of the wind, and the rattle of dust and sand on his cap. He shouted again and then stopped with his back to the wind to listen, but there was no reply. He pulled his muffler back from his ears and shouted once more. He thought he heard voices . . . just an instant . . . then the din of the wind drowned everything. He ran frantically back and forth, shouting and peering in every direction through half closed eyes; but he heard no answering call, and he saw nothing but clouds of dust and snow driven by the raging hurricane. Somewhere behind that wall of flying dust the children were struggling along—and he knew not even what direction to go to help them!

He stopped a moment to deliberate—it was no time for a false step. The children would drift westward—yes, the wind would push them that way. If they drifted far enough they would strike the west fence . . . no, they could never reach it in that wind, not the little children! He turned and ran—to the right—shouting, pausing an instant to listen, running again, shouting, keeping the wind on his right. He pulled his muffler off, that he might hear better, and shouted, and listened, and hurried on.

Could he have passed them? Could they have drifted the other way—to the east? Or had they drifted south before the storm—oh, surely not that! Danny and Robert would know better than to retreat before that wind. Danny and Robert would know what to do—until they got tired and confused, and began wandering in a circle, perhaps never to reach the fence—grown men had been lost on the prairie in storms less savage.

The children lost, wandering helplessly about in a circle that could only end beneath one of the drifts that were piling up so fast! At the thought, he ran on, halting, stumbling in the drifts of snow, shouting frantically, hoarsely, but going on—to the right, to the west. Undoubtedly he was going west! To the right, that was west—no mistake about that. Surely he was not confused himself! He was tired, breathless—getting older, he thought to himself dumbly, as he paused to get his breath—but not lost, not confused. He knew where he was, and where he was going—to the right, to the west. The ceaseless cudgeling of that pitiless wind had dulled his senses, but he would find the children yet. They would be over at the fence—the west fence, to the right.

He shouted once more—a wild cry of desperation, of entreaty, that the wind snatched from his lips and carried away into the depths of the hurrying, bellowing storm. He turned his back to the wind and listened. An intense and unreal silence seemed to fall around him for a moment . . . and in that moment he heard a cry— behind him. He turned and dashed toward that voice, shouting, shouting, and then pausing to listen. An answering call pierced the blanket of eddying dust and snow—closer, clearer—Danny's voice—Robert's voice—one of the little children crying! Dimly he saw the figures of the children lined up hand in hand, with little May at the end of the line. They were battling the wind heroically, but making little headway, for May could scarcely plough through the drifts of snow and was crying bitterly as the other children dragged her along. The Graeber children were there too, lined up with his own, all struggling along together.

"There's Pa!" shouted Danny, catching the first glimpse of his father.

How happy they were to see him, and to get more wraps, although they were already so cold they could scarcely feel when he put them on! They stopped a few moments with their backs to the wind to pull on their coats and caps and socks, and Henry wrapped their mufflers tightly about them. Then they started on.

They drifted over to the fence and followed it home, up through the corral, past the garden and to the house. Rosie was waiting anxiously, with a roaring fire and a kettle of hot water on the stove. The dirty, snow-covered wraps were soon piled in the corner, chairs were set about the stove; and nearly a dozen boys and girls thawed out their ears and faces and fingers, while Rosie went about washing the dust from their faces and ears. Henry then wrapped up the Graeber children in extra coats and mittens and took them home.

Other days and weeks of wind and dust followed. Early in April, another little boy was born, the twelfth child, and the first one to be helped into the world by a doctor.[4] Rosie had been sick for some time. The wind blew a hurricane from the south that day, sending tumbleweeds, dry corn leaves, and even corn stalks flying through the air, with clouds of dust and sand that rattled against the windows and drifted on the sills and floors. At times the bedroom was so dark that Rosie could scarcely recognize faces across the room; and in the din of roaring winds, swaying cottonwood trees, flying sand, rattling shutters, and creaking doors and screens, the voice of the tiny baby was nearly lost. It was an unpropitious day to start an unsuspecting baby on the way of life, and Rosie found little happiness in bringing him to share the discouragements that rained so fast upon her—especially since several of the children were not disposed to welcome him.

Danny and Robert had declared that there were enough kids in the family, and had made an agreement that they would not even go near the new baby. This hurt Rosie deeply, for she always thought of her many babies as a sort of visitation of the Lord's displeasure anyhow; but the older children were kind and friendly toward the new baby. Danny and Robert kept their agreement for several days; but one morning, when the girls were giving little Harold his bath, the boys condescended to look on from a safe distance in the adjoining room, much more interested than they were willing to appear. The next day, they ventured into the sick room, and were soon great friends of the baby, who was a happy, good-natured little boy, with a broad grin which soon earned for him the nickname "Dutch."

Chapter Thirty-two

The Darkness Before Dawn

There was more to worry about than the weather and the crops and the baby. There was the elevator, on which Henry had lent Steve Linge's money.

Steve had always been one of Henry's best friends, since the years when they bached together in Henry's cabin. He had come to the new country without a team or wealth of any kind, except his honesty and his powerful physique. Some pathetic tales were told of his early poverty. One cold day in the fall, he rode down to Cawker City with a neighbor, to see if he could buy a pair of shoes, for it was getting too cold to go barefooted. At Parker's store he finally found a pair large enough, and asked Parker if he might take them and pay for them a little later.

"Hell no! I came to this country to make money, and not to loan money," was the harsh reply of the merchant, who did not know how good was the word of this rough German. The neighbor with whom he had come had no money either, so Steve went home without shoes, and had to go without for several weeks of the early part of the winter, until he could earn the price of a new pair.

Having no team, he had to carry the windows and door for his dugout on his back from Cawker City—a distance of twelve miles. Each fall, like many of the settlers, he walked back to Eastern Kansas to get work for the winter—a two hundred mile walk—and in the spring he returned, with whatever he had been able to save. Soon after Rosie came, he married a girl whose father had been killed by the Indians while out buffalo hunting; and the charivari that followed his marriage came very near being a tragedy. Some of the boys invaded his premises with the usual equipment of tin boilers, horns, cowbells, rolling cutters, revolvers, and shotguns, and proceeded to make the night hideous. Steve came out and told the boys that he had no money, and had nothing in the house to feed them. This was not satisfactory, and they not only continued their clamor and noise, but one of them stamped on the roof of the dugout until the clods began to roll down through the straw.

This was too much. Steve promptly sallied out with an axe in his hand, and in a fit of rage threw the axe at one of the boys, knocking him senseless. The rest of the noise makers thought the boy dead, and began to mutter threats of lynching; but the injured member of the party revived, and Steve was saved.

A year or two afterward, a prairie fire burned almost everything he had—dugout, stable, hogs, and corn. The neighbors wanted to help him get another start, but he refused all assistance.

By hard work and unbelievable economy, he was able to accumulate livestock and build improvements again, and even finally to develop one of the best-improved farms in the community. After many years, however, he decided to go back to his former home in Wisconsin; so he sold his livestock and other goods, and on leaving, asked Henry to collect some of his sale notes and invest the money for him. Henry collected the money for his old friend and invested it in a mortgage on a cooperative elevator in town; but in the hard times that followed, the elevator declined in value until it was no longer worth the mortgage. Before foreclosing, he consulted a lawyer, who advised him he could hold the cooperators—it was a cooperative elevator, and not all the stock subscribed had been paid. Henry told him to go ahead; but the only proceeds of the action was a bill of fifty dollars for the lawyer's fee, and court costs of nearly as much. Then he foreclosed and took over the elevator, but there was so little grain in the country that there was not much business for an elevator. Henry had to hire a carpenter to make a few repairs, and the bill for this work took all Rosie could make in six months with butter and eggs. The elevator was a continual expense, and there seemed little hope that it would ever be worth much. Henry had to drive to town every day or two to attend to business connected with it; and he got so tired of the whole business that he would gladly have torn up his deed and forgotten all about it, but he dared not. It was Steve Linge's money he had invested, and he would have to pay it back. Henry was not one to take such an obligation lightly. He must stick to his task, plan and bargain and manage, much as he disliked it.

This was hard enough; but it was even worse to have to listen to Rosie and the children scold and admonish him for his bad judgment. Sometimes they spent the supper hour in this unhappy fashion—the children had yet to learn how easy it is to make such mistakes. There had been a time when he would not have tolerated criticism from the children; but he saw his fault clearly enough, and he was losing self-confidence as he grew older. Still worse it was when they did not complain, when he saw Rosie working so hard and saving pennies to make up for the dollars he had lost, and noted how many things everyone had to do without because of his mistake. The less they complained, the more keenly he felt the hardships of the situation.

He worried almost incessantly, day and night. Sometimes he would sit for a long time lost in thought, utterly unmindful of the boisterous noise of the younger children playing about him. He fell into the habit of talking much to himself, whenever alone; and on his way to and from town, he was often observed arguing to himself, gesticulating earnestly to emphasize his points, so engrossed as to be almost oblivious of his surroundings, and scarcely noticing the people he met on the road.

And well he might feel beaten and dispirited. Sometimes, as he listened to the knocking and moaning of the wind, his memory went back over the years of his life in America. Thirty-eight years it was since he had left his childhood home in Sindringen—thirty-eight years since the stage pulled out, and he waved goodbye to his mother. How she had clung to him as he climbed up into his seat, ran stumblingly after the stage as it rolled out of the yard—bearing the last one of all her six children away from her! In memory he could see her still, as she stopped and stood by the little stone bridge, his mother, so gray, and so stooped and thin, yet trying to smile bravely through her tears as she waved goodbye. And despite the homesickness that clutched at his heart as the stage rounded the green hill, and the bridge and his mother disappeared, he had felt full of hope. He would work and save, and build a good home in America, and then he would send for her. He had pictured her coming in on the train—somewhere in America—

and how she would marvel at his fine home and his horses and cattle and barns and granaries!

How unlike these dreams had been the drab reality of the years; the war, the death of his mother alone in the old home in Sindringen—he heard of it months afterward as he lay sick in camp near Atlanta—and then the lonely drag of breaking prairie in Iowa, the theft of his savings, the move to Kansas, and the years of hope and despair since then! And now, almost an old man, at the end of his strength and his faith and his courage, too late to start again, he found himself in debt to Steve for more than he could possibly scrape together in ready cash, and his only possessions three farms in a country where it was impossible to live decently, with all the work he and Rosie and the children could do. It was the end of dreams. It looked like the final failure of a life.

Although not much given to retrospection—there was little time for it—Henry sometimes felt homesick for his childhood home in Sindringen. It was now several years since he had come home from town one day, with a smile and a strange, faraway look in his eye. He had seemed almost oblivious of the rest of the family as he ate his dinner, but presently he spoke up:

"I heard something today that I haven't heard for many years—not since I left the Old Country."

"What was that?" asked two of the children at once.

"Sparrows. There were several sparrows down in the cornice of Washburn's blacksmith shop today,[1] chirping away so cheerfully. It seemed like the old home in Sindringen to hear them. We always had so many there, in every stone building; and I thought I would never hear one again." There was a trace of tear in his eye as he spoke.

In his despondency Henry even entertained a wild notion of moving away from the country where he had fared so ill. His first thought was to go back to Iowa, but a little reflection told him that was impossible, for Iowa had had no drouth, and Iowa land was too expensive for him to buy. He remembered some of the land he had seen in Alabama while he was marching through there during the war, but a family conference around the supper table one evening left not a shred of his scheme for moving to Alabama, once the necessary details of such a move were outlined: the sale of the home, endeared as it was by adversity, and of so many treasured possessions, and the loading of the rest, with eleven children, into covered wagons for a long trek into an unknown country, away from all friends. It was clearly a fantastic dream. No, there was nothing to do but stay and "manage somehow," as Rosie always expressed it.

April passed, and the days of May followed, yet no rain came. Prayer meetings were held in some of the churches where the people went to pray for rain, and Henry went several times; but the prayers did not raise a cloud. With pastures bare, it was clear that most of the cattle would have to be sold or shipped out of the country to be fed. Henry finally decided to take them to Iowa—to Iowa, where there was always corn and feed for cattle. The last day of May was set to drive them to town and load them on to the cars.

On the day before that, Rosie baked fresh bread and a cake, and fried a chicken, so that Henry might have a good lunch to take along. The cake seemed an extravagance, but it would be a hard trip for him. Since Henry could take only part of the cake with him, the little children watched the baking with interest and antici-pation, and two of them staged a spirited fight to see who should "lick out" the cake pans. For them the day took on a definitely fes-tive air, in spite of the wind that blew clouds of dust up from the barn yard, and in spite of the air of discouragement that Henry and Rosie wore as they laid out Henry's clothes and packed his valise for the trip. There were many things to attend to that day and eve-ning, and it was late at night before Henry dragged the tub out into the kitchen, took a "wash off," and then lay down to sleep, tired and thoroughly discouraged.

Hours later, he was awakened from a sound sleep by the pat-ter of a few great rain drops on the shutters at the head of his bed— just a few big drops, then a peal of thunder, and an answering downpour that splashed through the window onto the pillow.

"What's that?" exclaimed Rosie, starting from her bed. "Rain?"

"Rain!" Henry echoed, as he reached for his shoes.

"The barn doors! You shut the barn! I'll attend to the cellar windows and the rain barrel!"—and Rosie disappeared as she said it. She was still struggling with the spout leading to the rain barrel when Henry joined her.

"You shut the barn!" she cried. "I'll fix this!"

"The barn's all right!" He yanked the spout into place, and the water poured into the barrel.

They dashed back into the house, drenched to the skin, but happier than they had been in weeks, as the rain beat with a heartening roar on the shingle roof. With dry clothes, they were soon in bed again, luxuriating in the cool air that breathed in through the shutters.

Oh, the blessed rain! Oh, the peace and benediction of its steady downpour on the roof; the music of the washing rivulets that ran down from the eaves and gutters and splashed upon the thirsty ground; the cool rumble of thunder rolling from cloud to cloud, or crashing through the darkness; the flash of lightning far and near! Wild, heroic music it was, yet how soothing to the tired spirits of those who had waited, hoped and prayed, despairing, for the blessing of the rain!

"I guess I won't have to take the cattle to Iowa tomorrow," said Henry, as he pulled the quilt up over him.

"Not if this continues a while longer," said Rosie; and she sank into a restful sleep.

The rain did continue, all night and the next day; and the chicken and cake were eaten for dinner, to the accompaniment of a steady, cool drizzle.

"Do you remember how everything looked when we were baking this cake?" queried Rosie of the older girls, as she cut it deftly into twelve equal pieces.

"Yes," answered Laura; "I guess we should have baked it a few months sooner."

Toward evening the cloud canopy lifted in the west, to reveal a narrow strip of emerald sky through which the sun shone out, dazzlingly bright in the clear, fresh air, touching with a magic light the diamond rain-drops that hung on the cottonwood leaves and on the grass that was already turning green. Danny and Robert went down after the cattle, making numerous detours on the way to wade through the little pools that stood in the buffalo wallows; and afterward, all the children went over to Dry Creek to see how high the water had risen. It was a wonderful world, after the rain.

That day Charlie Ellison died, of "inflammation of the bowels"—appendicitis.[2] There were five of the Ellison boys, all powerful young men, able to out-run, out-box, and out-wrestle all chal-

Rosa and Henry Ise. (Photo courtesy Bill Haag)

lengers. Charlie became sick very suddenly one day, rolling on the floor in pain. A doctor was called, but he could do nothing. Several days of agony turned the good-natured young giant into a raving madman, who saw spirits and ghosts and devils in the room about him, and tore his bed to splinters in his hallucinations. Four men then attended him constantly, and it was all they could do to hold him when he became violent. After a week of cruel suffering, one evening he fell back on his bed, the blood spurted from his mouth and he was dead. At sight of this, his mother fell to the floor in a faint; in all the years following, Mrs. Ellison was seldom seen to smile. Charlie had been utterly uninterested in religion, and when the preacher came to see him in his illness, drove him from the room; and his mother, who was very religious, always worried about his soul. To his everlasting honor, the preacher preached a funeral sermon full of kindly charity, pointing only to Charlie's virtues—which were ample text for a sermon. Kindly, reckless Charlie Ellison was liked by every child in the community—which is "an excellent thing in men."

Poor Mrs. Ellison's life was a sad one.[3] A few years later her next son, a handsome young Apollo with black, wavy hair, just entering the ministry, was run over by a train; and later her next son died in the West. Her husband Dave was not unkind, but neighbors often smiled at some of the domestic arrangements of the Ellisons.[4] In the evening they were often seen walking out to the corral, arm in arm, Dave with his violin, his wife carrying a milk bucket. While his wife milked the cow, Dave sat on a milk stool and played the violin; then they went back to the house, Dave carrying his violin, and his wife the milk.

In June Uncle John and his family drove out from Holton for a visit. Henry and Rosie now had eleven children, and Uncle John had nine—a total of twenty children and four grown folk to cook and wash dishes for; but even with her baby, two months old, Rosie was equal to the occasion. Uncle John and his family were always generous. They never came home from town without a big sack of oranges or bananas or cookies or other delicacies for the children; and Aunt Minnie and the older girls helped faithfully with the work. Farm work presented some difficulty. Billy and Danny and Robert did not like to leave their guests to go out to the field, yet if they took them along they usually started talking or playing or went swimming and forgot all about their work. And these town boys brought with them certain kinds of wickedness which might have worried Rosie if she had known about them. They carried a deck of cards, and soon had Danny and Robert and Joe playing high-five and seven-up out behind the barn.

On the last day of the party Joe fell from the lumber wagon and broke his arm, and this caused some anxiety and extra work; but Joe was soon hobbling about, as cheerful as ever—and a few weeks later broke his arm again in the same place.[5] Everyone had a good time; and there was genuine regret when the party broke up.

Uncle George came out in August with his family. Again there was a round of cooking and dish washing for Rosie and the girls, but again a visit of two weeks seemed none too long. The main source of friction among the children was the question as to who must eat at the second table. Louise and Joe and May and Rosina had not yet developed their spirit of hospitality to a point where they could graciously allow their guests to eat at the first table all the time, for the second table fare sometimes lacked important items of the menu.

Soon afterward, Rosie went down to Holton to see her folks, taking Aunt Lisa Meirhoffer with her.[6] Tommy Meirhoffer and his wife had come from Switzerland in early days, and had built their little stone house and stable in a ravine up in the hills—the loneliest place in the world. Here good Aunt Lisa lived, patient and cheerful under the abuse of her brutal husband, seldom permitted to go with him when he went to town, yet working slavishly to provide the eggs and butter that he traded for liquor, opening the gate for him when he came home, and unhitching the horses while he went in to sleep off his debauches. On the rare occasions when she went visiting with him, she always managed to have a pocketfull of candy for the children, and at home the cookie jar was seldom empty.

While Laura was teaching at the Sandersville school, she stayed with Aunt Lisa part of the time, and in her sympathy for the poor old woman, conceived a plan to persuade Tommy to let her take a trip to Holton to visit her brother, whom she had not seen since they left Switzerland. Laura's tact and diplomacy were equal to the task; and Tommy finally bought his wife a new dress—the first she had had in years—and gave her money for the trip. Aunt Lisa had never ridden on a train and was quite unequal to the complicated problems of railway travel, so Rosie went along with her.

Arriving at Holton, they went to Uncle John's home; and that night one of the children put a Swiss yodel record on the phonograph. The effect was electric. Aunt Lisa started from her chair, looked intently at the horn and around the horn; then, as the high notes of the yodel came through clearly, she burst into tears and started back and forth across the room, waving her hands up and down, then clasping them ecstatically, crying: "Herr Je! Herr Je! Herr Je!"[7]

She dropped into a chair, sobbing as if her heart would break; then, as the falsetto notes of the yodel sounded again she started up and resumed her walk back and forth, waving her hands, alternately crying and laughing hysterically: "Herr Je! Herr Je! Herr Je! Herr Je!"

For a moment it all seemed very funny, and even Rosie could not help laughing; but her laughter faded quickly, and she reached for her handkerchief as she sensed the stark outlines of the picture before her—the picture of the broken old woman, after long, lonely years in her home up in the wind-swept hills of Kansas, hearing again a song of her native Switzerland. Even the young people in the room were fumbling for their handkerchiefs when the record ended.

In September Laura and Alice started to college.[8] Neither of them had gone to the high school, but a high school diploma was not necessary to enter the normal college. They had saved enough money teaching school to pay part of their expenses; Henry would be able to help them a little, and the rest of their expenses they hoped to make in some way. Daylight was breaking that morning when Henry lifted their telescopes and shiny new trunks and lunch box into the wagon, and they kissed Rosie goodbye. They rode two miles into the reddening east before the sun broke above the horizon. Looking back with misty eyes, at the red barn partly hidden by the grove of cottonwoods, they almost wished they might turn around and go home; but ahead were all the vaguely roseate dreams that education meant to them: great buildings and a splendid campus, literary societies, class and college yells, men friends, "comprehensive courses" that would give them a "thorough grasp" or "mastery" of any or all the important fields of knowledge, other courses that offered useless and ornamental erudition and accomplishments which most people did not have, and a job of teaching afterward. They swallowed their homesickness bravely as they rode into town.

The train was waiting, and when they had bought their tickets off the grumpy ticket agent and had checked their trunks, Henry helped them on and bade them goodbye. There were tears in his kind blue eyes as he left them, and bigger tears in their own, as the raucous "All aboard!" sounded and the train moved slowly out. An obtruding freight car shut off their view of the street just as Henry was untying the big gray team that stood in front of the hotel.

In the meantime, Henry discovered, when he got back to the wagon, that he still had Alice's purse, with her money and ticket. Knowing how frantic she would be, he hastened back to the depot and asked the agent to telegraph her that he had the purse. It all turned out well enough; but Alice got little enjoyment out of her first trip to college.

Early in December Rosie and the younger children began looking forward to the time when Laura and Alice would be home for the holidays. Every day or two, Happy and Rosina and May asked "how many nights they must sleep" before the girls would come home. Even Rosie and Henry began to count the days; and they tried to get the butchering and other disagreeable chores out of the way, so that everyone could enjoy the holidays. A day or two before the girls were due, there was a general air of expectancy about the house. Rosie was baking bread and pies and cookies and cinnamon rolls. Half a tubful of cinnamon rolls—the kind of cinnamon rolls Rosie baked—was only enough for a breakfast or two when all the children got together around the table. On the night when Henry went down to meet the train, even the little ones were allowed to stay up until he returned; and when the rattle of the wagon at last was heard, they all ran pellmell out into the yard and down the road to meet him. Of course Laura and Alice brought presents for the smaller children, inexpensive but very fine indeed. Altogether it was a happy occasion for everybody.

One day Laura told Rosie of a new food they had tasted at the boarding club—tapioca. Henry bought some the next time he went to town, and Rosie cooked a kettle of it—no, it was two kettles—full, before she was through. The children liked it so well that she often cooked it afterward, sometimes with dried peaches or apricots to give it more flavor. Not long afterward, during a hailstorm, Happy came running in from the porch, his eyes gleaming with excitement. "Ma! Ma!" he shouted. "It's raining tapioca!"

Chapter Thirty-three

Better Times

In 'ninety-six, prices reached the lowest point that anyone could remember. Henry sold wheat for thirty-five cents, corn for eleven cents, oats for ten cents, hogs for two and a half cents, eggs for a nickel; and the butter that Rosie worked over so carefully and pressed into decorative round molds brought seven cents at Portis, eight miles away. Before winter was over, however, corn was selling for seventeen cents—local Republicans said it was because of the election of McKinley.[1] The next summer the best wheat crop in years sold for seventy-five cents a bushel—enough to pay for some farms bought the year before; and soon the first surge of a land boom was in evidence. Henry found a buyer for the elevator,[2] at a price that repaid him all the money he had invested, but nothing for his years of anxiety. He also managed to sell his town lots for as much as he had paid.[3] If he had held the lots two years longer he might have doubled his money.

With all debts paid, there was money for improvements. Henry bought several thoroughbred shorthorn cattle, and started to build up a herd of registered cattle. He bought a riding pony for the older boys, and a wicked little Shetland pony for the younger children. Jingle-Brains, the driving horse he had raised on the farm, was now old enough to drive, and Henry got a single-seated buggy to take the place of the cart that had served so long. Jingle-Brains was fast and handsome, but he seemed to need a runaway every month or so to keep him in good spirits. At the suggestion of the boys, Henry had the blacksmith make him a barrel cart in which to haul water and swill to the hogs—a convenience far more important to him than the surrey[4] or the buggy, or the Sun Dial watch that he bought for five dollars at a jeweller's auction. He had always carried water and feed in buckets, which sometimes meant a score of trips from the well to the hog-pen—a task that was perceptibly rounding his shoulders.

He and Rosie enlarged and remodelled the house.[5] They built two new porches, with lattice-work below to keep the dog and chickens from getting under—the children had always complained about having to crawl under the old porch to get the eggs. They added a summer kitchen with a tin roof—probably called a summer kitchen because it was always tropically hot in summer—and a bath room. The bath room was used only as a pantry in the winter time, because there was no way of heating it; but in the summer, enough of the groceries were moved out to allow access to the tub. The rain barrel had never held enough soft water, so they dug a cistern and installed a pump and sink in the kitchen. They built new cement sidewalks from the kitchen door to the well, and to the picket-fence gate. They tore out the board ceiling and wainscoting of the big living room, and plastered the walls and ceiling. Plastering looked better, and was much more fashionable; but later they almost regretted this change, for Rosie could no longer awaken the children who slept in the room above by tapping on the ceiling with a broomstick. They bought new doors for the parlor, with colored glass lights that cast a rich, bilious glamour over the room; grained all the woodwork to imitate oak—or was it ash, or pine, or perhaps a topographical map of Saskatchewan? They bought a new golden-oak lounge, a secretary with a mirror above, book shelves, a little cabinet for the albums, and a writing leaf that always stuck at the sides when it was closed, and when open sagged at an uncomfortable angle. Then they bought a huge lamp for the parlor, and a fine set of silver-plated table-ware for Sunday use. Henry bought a stereoscope and some views from a travelling salesman one day, and Sunday visitors were always invited to look through the wonderful new instrument.

Occasionally Henry bought "store groceries" which seemed very delicious—cookies, crackers, cheese, dried herring and candy. Rosie had to keep the children out of the cellar, for fear they would eat everything at once; but on special occasions they were allowed crackers, or even cookies and candy—they seemed to find it easy to curb their desire to eat the herring. Once in a great while Rosie bought a loaf of baker's bread, which she regarded as a great delicacy, although it was by no means as good as her own.

In the spring one must always plant trees too; and Henry and Rosie set out several little cedar trees in the front yard. They had never been able to get evergreens to grow, but this time Rosie carried water to them every day, and they lived. Nearly all of the grape vines and fruit trees they had planted in earlier years had died, but one day Henry yielded to the persuasion of a tree agent and bought fifty cherry trees, which he set out beyond the garden.

Home was pleasanter now. For the first time in twenty-five years, there was no baby to care for. Dutch, the youngest—not baby, but just the youngest, as he once explained when a neighbor woman asked Rosie if he was her baby—was four now; and Rosie had more time for the amenities of home life. Released from the strain of bearing and caring for babies, and from the grinding necessity of worrying constantly about the pennies, Rosie was turning gentler and mellower. Henry was changing too. A kindly man generally, he had always been subject to occasional fits of temper, when he would perhaps strike one of the children cruelly; but this happened less and less frequently as he grew older. He and Rosie had never been given to punishing the children often or severely, but now they seldom resorted to such means of discipline, partly because there was less occasion for it as the children grew up, and partly because the spirit of the time was against it. The family was becoming more and more of a democracy. Each year the children had more to say about the management of affairs; and, as in many other homes of the time, the children were unconsciously leading their parents to a more humane philosophy. As always in human affairs, with the abandonment of the philosophy of force and discipline, there grew up a more genuine affection on the part of all. The children were growing older, quieter, more orderly and decorous, more appreciative of Henry and Rosie, and of each other. There was less "bossing" and slapping by the older children, and less occasion for resentment by the younger ones—less harshness everywhere.

Laura was a graduate of the normal school now, a teacher with a rare talent for making friends. Friendly herself, talkative and tactful, she was equally happy talking to one of the old German farmers up on the creek, or to the banker in town. She loved

Billy Ise on the farm. (Photo courtesy Frank Ise)

people, old people, young people, good people, bad people, smart people, dull people, the fair and the freckled, the washed and the unwashed, anybody, everybody; and they liked her too. Billy was a big, awkward, stoop-shouldered young farmer, with a rough exterior that only partly concealed his innate gentleness and timidity—the kind of man that little children like. He never could sit down five minutes where there were children about without having them clambering all over him.

Alice had grown to be a beautiful girl, with big brown eyes that looked kindly on everyone, and a sensitive nature that was hardly fitted for some of the rougher aspects of the life about her. Danny, boisterous, whole-hearted little rowdy as a boy, no longer wore coats that seemed too tight, but was developing a strong bent toward good clothes and girls, and a grand ambition for what the world calls "success." He was very different from Robert, whose shrewd, salty humor led him to think girls were too much trouble, fancy clothes too much expense, and great ambitions generally rather ridiculous. Some of the other children accused Robert of being lazy; but this was not quite just. He merely did his work without any proclamations or unnecessary noise, and in the easiest way possible. Louise, already in the high school, was developing literary and social interests alternately. She liked both books and boys, but was never able to lose herself wholeheartedly in either, or to apportion her time and energy satisfactorily or consistently between her studies and her social interests. Without any definite philosophy of life, she was never quite happy; and was destined never to be so.

Joe was growing into a hectic adolescence. Naturally stubborn, individualistic and restive under any sort of discipline or control, he had become even more of a maverick because he was humored—Rosie could never bring herself to punish him much, no matter what he did—and because he had never had the healthy discipline of play with other children. Sensitive, and keenly desirous of the approval of others, he had little knack for earning it, partly because, although he was full of humane sympathy for people in general, he had little of Laura's love for people in particular. Alone much, he spent a great deal of time at music, for which he had distinct talent. Often when Joe heard a pretty melody at a concert, he promptly made it his own and began playing it over as soon as he got home.

May, or "Bumptikee," as the boys called her, was an independent little tomboy with a mind of her own. She was equally at home on horseback or in a tilt of wits with the older children, who enjoyed the rather hazardous business of teasing her. Rosina was very different. She loved most everybody, but particularly Henry and Laura; and often when Henry sat down, Rosina would run for the comb, and comb his hair and beard as long as he sat there, patting his head affectionately from time to time. Still too young to go to school, Happy, or Buckskin, was something of a replica of Danny, perhaps less obstreperous but equally generous and whole-hearted. Once Mary Bartsch gave him a little duck, which he fed and cared for all summer. By Thanksgiving Day his duck was grown, and when someone suggested that it would make a fine Thanksgiving dinner, Happy was vastly pleased with the idea; yes, it would surely be great fun to eat the duck for dinner. With the greatest glee he helped Billy catch it, and ran over to the block with it, the happiest little boy in the world; but when the head fell from the block, and the blood began to flow, he suddenly realized that his duck was dead. He picked up the severed head and insisted that Billy put it back on; and when Billy failed to do so, his

Hap and Dutch Ise on the Ise farm. (Photo courtesy Frank Ise)

grief was uncontrollable. He had never realized that they could not eat the duck without killing it, and his Thanksgiving Day was ruined.

With his broad grin and his quaint philosophic questions and remarks, Dutch was always a bushel of fun. He wanted to know what water-snakes ate, whether giraffes' necks were made of rubber, whether God smoked, whether God knew as much as Billy, and whether God wore an invisible coat, like Jack the Giant Killer, so people could not see him. But he had a bad habit of swearing once in a while, which gave Rosie some concern. He also slighted his task of hunting the eggs occasionally; and one evening, after Rosie had found several nests of eggs in an advanced stage of development, she scolded him for his neglect. Rather crestfallen, he started out with his egg bucket that evening, and diligently explored coops and barn and granary and every promising patch of weeds, but with poor success. He stopped at the granary, where Joe was whittling out a little wooden gun.

"Joe, do you know where any eggs is?" he asked, sadly.

"No, Dutch, I don't believe I do."

Dutch sat down on a big rock and looked down at his little gallon bucket, only half full, a world of discouragement in his face. Presently he spoke, as if to himself:

"Damn it! That's a hell of a mess o' eggs!"

Several of the children were learning to play and sing. It was long years since Henry had played his accordion, but Laura played the organ; and to her accompaniment she and Alice often sang songs and duets—mostly very sad: "My Angel, Little Nell," "Sweet Visions of Childhood," "Sweet Evening Bells," "Fading, Yes Fading," "The Dying Cowboy," "The Little Rosewood Casket," "The Little Girl That Played upon My Knee," and various songs about the "Old Home by the Sea"—or perhaps it was the "Cottage by the Sea," in which a bereaved widow lamented her sad fate, and reminded her dead spouse that he had not done as well by her as he had promised. Most of the songs wound up with a death or two—violent deaths were not uncommon—and burial in the "cold, cold ground" was the most popular, all-round satisfactory denouement. It was sometimes thought better, though, to go a step further, and get the grass growing over the grave, perhaps have some surviving relative water it with salty tears.

There was the song about Charlotte, who lived on the mountain side and was unaccountably frozen to death on the way home from a dance; "The Gypsy's Warning," which wound up with: "So she perished, now she's sleeping, in the cold and quiet grave"—Rosie often sang it when she was working the butter—and another song, of about the same salt water content, which closed with the noble theme: "Oh Edward, I'll forgive you, if this be my last breath. I never did deceive you, so close my eyes in death." Perhaps a drouth-haunted country needed a few such songs.

Joe was apt at music, and when Danny traded a revolver for a fiddle, Joe was soon scraping the dance tunes on the new instrument: "Little Brown Jug," "Sweet Evelina," "Turkey in the Straw," "The Arkansas Traveller," and "The Drunkard's Hiccough"—"The Drunkard's Hiccough" had some pizzicato in it, which always sounded very fine and professional. Danny himself had a poor ear for music, and his tones often wandered far from orthodox pitch; but he had enthusiasm and a sense of rhythm, and played with reckless abandon, stamping out the time with his foot till it sounded like the march of the Prussian army. Alice and Joe bought guitars and learned to play duets. Sometimes they would sit out on the porch on quiet summer evenings and thrum on their guitars for hours at a time—or until the mosquitos drove them in. Henry enjoyed music, and would often sit down on the edge of the porch and listen quietly as long as they cared to play.

The G.A.R.[6] had meetings and parties that Henry and Rosie sometimes attended. The country had been settled largely by veterans of the northern army, and the G.A.R. had a large membership. Henry enjoyed telling and listening to stories of the war, and singing war songs. His favorite was a German song, "Morgen Rot,"[7] which always brought applause when he sang it. Of course, these meetings usually closed with a supper.

Neighborhood relationships were pleasanter now, generally. Most of the neighbors were comfortably situated, so that they could afford to be more generous. Even Wilson Athey was proving to be a first-class man and neighbor. He had a fine new house—much finer than Henry's—good horses and tools and implements of all kinds, so that he did not need to borrow; and the Athey children were growing up to be upstanding young men and women, several of them very talented musically.

The region had changed greatly since the first days, it is true, and Henry often missed some of his old friends. Frank Hagel, John Higginbotham, George Graeber and Jake Hunker were dead; Jesse Bender had moved to Wyoming, and Steve Linge had gone back to Wisconsin. Only recently Chris Bartsch had died, after weeks of cruel suffering in a hospital run by a medical charlatan in Kansas City.[8] Chris Bartsch, with the kindly wrinkles that always played about his eyes and mouth, too generous to accumulate wealth, had piled up for himself a mountain of love and respect; and when he died, even the children knew that one of their best friends was gone—knew how they would miss his friendly "Ach, das ist der Billy,"[9] or Danny, or whichever of the children he happened to meet. He knew them all, and he loved them all. For Henry, the neighborhood would never be quite the same with Chris Bartsch gone.

Chapter Thirty-four

The End of a Brave Fight

As the favorable years came and went, there was new cause for anxiety. For several years Henry had been losing strength, slowly and almost imperceptibly. One task after another he found himself obliged to turn over to the boys, or to the hired man. No one thought a great deal about it, for of course his stomach had always troubled him, and he was getting older. There had always been so much else to worry about that even Rosie had not thought of Henry's condition as immediately serious. She had fallen more and more into the habit of favoring him a little in various ways, cooking special delicacies for him, letting him sleep late in the morning, and in general lightening his share of the load wherever she could. It seemed quite natural that Henry should not be very strong.

Corn was poor on the uplands in the fall of 'ninety-nine; but there were a few nubbins on the upper place, and Rosie helped husk these out early, so that Henry could turn the cattle into the stalks. Henry had not been well enough to husk corn, and Billy could not help either. A few weeks before, he had dropped carbolic acid into his eye, mistaking a bottle of it for his eye medicine; and his eye was still so sore that he could not stand the dust of corn husking. He worked up in the hills instead, digging medicine roots. The younger boys might have done the husking, but Rosie disliked to keep them out of school. After the corn on the upper place had been husked, Henry and Rosie drove up to Hastings, Nebraska, to visit an old friend Henry had known in Illinois—Jeff Savery, the son of the man Henry had worked for when he first came to America. It was a pleasant drive of eighty miles, along a road which followed the Hastings Trail of the early seventies.[1] Henry had driven along the trail many times, with wheat or corn, before the railroad came. Here and there, as the horses trotted along, he recognized the landmarks that had guided him in his earlier tiresome journeys—hills and creeks and ravines—and at times he could trace the two-wheel tracks of the old trail as they led across the pasture, grown up in weeds where the soil was good, still white and barren where it ran up over the rocky hills.

One crisp morning, after they came back, Henry decided that he would go out and husk corn in the south field of the home place. He had contented himself with easy pottering jobs that fall; but from the neighboring corn fields came the resounding thump of the ears of corn as they struck the bump boards, and the familiar sounds called him irresistibly. He walked down the lane and into the field, where Dick the hired man was husking.

"Need another good man out here?" he inquired jovially, as he picked off an ear and threw it into the wagon.

"Sure!" said Dick. "There's a lot of corn out here yet."

Henry took the down row and the one next to it, and started down the field. It was fine to be husking corn on such a day. Corn always seemed to him something rich and kind and beautiful. Corn meant feed for cattle and horses and hogs and chickens. Corn meant contentment for everything about him, and he loved the fragrance of its leaves, even the brittle leaves of November. It was seldom enough that he had seen even a fair crop in the field, and it seemed a blessed privilege to be able to shuck it out.

His first enthusiastic strength and energy did not last long. Before he had been down the row and back again, he began to feel tired; and it hurt him to stoop for the ears on the ground. Dick then took the down row, and that relieved him of most of the pain of stooping; but the work was beyond his strength. He stuck to the job tenaciously, until the yellow ears were heaped high against the bump boards; but he felt tired and sick when he climbed up on the front of the load, and rode in to the house. Rosie was busy cutting dumplings into the soup when he entered, singing a song she often sang:[2]

> There we laid our loved one,
> Our loved one, our loved one,

There we laid our loved one,
In her mossy bed.

Where the dewy lilies,
The lilies, the lilies,
Where the dewy lilies,
Crown her peaceful head.

She did not look at him closely as he came in.

"Dinner will be ready in a little while," she explained. "Just wash and go in and read the paper."

Henry washed with his usual deliberate care, combed his thinning hair and beard, pulled the loose hair from the comb, dropped it into the waste pail, and walked into the living room. He sat down with the paper but felt too sick to read; and presently he laid the paper aside and went into the bedroom, pulled off his shoes and clothes, and slipped into bed.

Rosie soon had the dinner smoking on the table, and when Dick came in she called to Henry. She heard no response.

"Oh, he always gets so interested in that paper!" she exclaimed. "Harold"—addressing her youngest, who was already in his high chair—"go in and tell your pa to come to dinner right away."

Delighted with his errand, Harold—or Dutch—ran into the living room, but came back in a minute. "Pa's not there," he reported, disappointment in his eyes.

"Oh, I guess he surely is," said Rosie, and laying down the loaf of bread she was cutting, she hurried into the living room.

He was not there. She opened the door into the parlor. There was no fire there, and it was cold.

"Henry!"

No answer; and she turned to the bed room. She opened the door. There he was in bed, his face pale, even against the white pillow, his jaw set with a rigidity she had seen once or twice, years before. Something in the picture made her stop at the threshold.

"Henry! Don't you feel well?"

He did not turn his head to answer. "Not so very well." His voice was weak and strained.

"Is it your stomach? Can't I bring you something?" She was at his side, stroking the hair away from his forehead. "A little soup, or tea, or coffee, or hot lemonade?"

"Not now. Not for a while."

"Is it your stomach trouble again?"

"Yes." He paused a moment; then he reached out to grasp her hand and held her palm over his stomach.

"Doesn't that feel like a kind of a lump there? I've noticed it since last summer; and it hurts today, from stooping."

"It feels like something of that kind. You'll have to go to see the doctor. He may be able to give you some medicine for it."

"Medicine won't help much, probably—"

Rosie evaded the pessimism of his reply. "You must not try to do such hard work again. Someone else can husk the corn."

"Somebody else will have to." Henry lay silent for a moment, and then added, "I shouldn't have tried it, I guess."

Rosie remembered her dinner and hurried out to attend to it. When she came back she had hot bran sacks to pile about him, and a hot flat iron to put at his feet. She also brought a bowl of hot broth, but Henry could eat nothing.

In a few days, he was well enough to be around again, almost as well as ever; but the rest of the winter he did little but potter around with easy chores, feeding the hogs, chopping wood occasionally, and caring for the horses after Dick left.

He had to eat more and more sparingly as the weeks passed, and grew steadily weaker, although so slowly that he scarcely noticed it himself. Spring came, with its green pastures and meadow larks and daisies. He sometimes took short walks out into the pasture and around the home place, to see the cattle and calves and pigs, and the little chickens that followed or led their clucking mothers about the yard. In April, the plum thicket became a bank of fragrant white blossoms. In May, the lilacs, yellow roses and Bouncing Betties burst into bloom; and he loved to wander about the yard, smelling of the flowers like a little child. Like Rosie, he had always loved flowers, and they had planted them in every corner of the big yard. Rosie was never too busy to attend to flowers. It seemed a beautiful world, and this year there was no worry about notes or mortgages or bad investments to cloud his enjoyment of it.[3]

In June, Henry insisted on running the binder in the wheat

harvest. When the boys tried to dissuade him he replied, "I want to help cut one more crop. It has always been my job."

Perched upon the high seat, he drove the binder bravely around the field, contentedly watching the yellow grain fall thick upon the canvas, studying the bundles that fell into the carrier to see if the knots were properly tied, listening, in the steady hum of the machine, for any hint of loose bearings or need of oil. Occasionally, when he saw a pretty flower fall onto the canvas with the wheat, he was almost tempted to stop the machine, and pick it out to take to Rosie, as he had often done; but the horses pulled him steadily on. Scarcely a breeze stirred. The sun beat down hot from above and glared back from the white stubble, while the line of the horizon across the valley flowed and danced with the waves of heat.

In the middle of the forenoon, as he drew near the home corner of the field, there stood Rosie, with a jar of water for him—no, it was cold lemonade! He braced up the binder tongue to ease the burden on the horses' necks, and then drank deeply.

"Isn't it pretty hard for you?" Rosie asked, as she picked up a ball of twine and handed it to him.

"Oh, it seems good so far," he replied; "but I'm afraid I'll wear out before that wheat's all in the shock."

He leaned against the seat of the binder for support, his exaltation gone, and a crushing sense of weakness and insufficiency bearing down upon him. But he would not give up yet, and after oiling the binder carefully, he pulled himself up into the seat and started off again, while Rosie walked slowly back to the house.

That night, the boys unhitched his horses, and he had scarcely strength to walk back to the house. The next morning he let the boys take the binder, while he lay in bed all day.

On Sunday Henry did not go to church—or Sunday school, as it was called—and in the afternoon several of the neighbors drove in to see him, one of them a widow whose husband had died not long before. The conversation turned naturally to the subject of Henry's illness, and as Rosie described his symptoms, the woman's face turned very grave.

"It sounds like Charlie's trouble; and it turned out to be cancer," she said.

The dread word fell like a heavy clod.

"But the doctor has never said a word about—about that," Rosie remonstrated. "It surely can't be that!"

"I hope not," the woman replied, and the matter was not mentioned again.

The next morning Rosie was up at five o'clock, after a sleepless night.

"We will take pa to the doctor this morning," she announced to the children at the breakfast table. "Danny, you hitch up the buggy as soon as you get the milking done—the single buggy—and I'll take him down. You better hitch up Nance, so there won't be any trouble."

"But we need Nance on the plow," Danny interposed.

"The plow can wait till noon."

Danny sensed that there need be no argument about it. After the milking was done, he hitched Nance to the buggy and Rosie took Henry to town to the doctor.

Although Henry had gone to see him a number of times, the doctor had never hinted a possibility of cancer; but when Rosie called him aside and asked him if that might not be the trouble, he admitted the possibility, and made a careful examination. His face grew serious as he proceeded, and when he was through and had ushered his patient into the outer room, he called Rosie back.

"We can never be quite certain, Mrs. Ise; but I fear it may be what you have suspected," he said. "It looks much like it in many ways—that growth, and other symptoms. We can only watch him closely for a while, and time will tell."

"If it isn't too late then," she answered. "Is there nothing that can be done for him now—nothing at all?" She was pleading with tears in her eyes.

The doctor could not say the words that she dreaded to hear.

"Perhaps it might be worth while to call someone else into consultation." He did not speak hopefully, but Rosie seized upon his words.

"Oh yes, get anyone you think might help."

"Doctor Dailey at Beloit is one of the best men I know. I might bring him out as soon as I can get him."[4]

"Any time, and as soon as you can." Rosie hurried out to join Henry, who had sunk into a chair in the waiting room.

The very next day the doctor drove out to the farm with Doctor

Dailey; and the two bent over their patient, pressing here and there, asking questions—"And does that hurt you?" and "How long has that bothered you?" and "When did you first notice that?" They asked Rosie many questions, too, and she answered them, hoping, desperately hoping, that her answers might somehow have a favorable significance.

When they had finished, she followed them out to the porch. The consulting doctor turned to her and said:

"If it is cancer—and I fear there is little doubt that it is—you can only make it as easy for him as possible."

"An operation would not help, would it? Is there any chance it would help—any hope at all?"

"I'm afraid it would do no good," he replied; then as he saw the tears start, he added, "Of course, it might be something else; it is never quite hopeless."

But Rosie now knew that it was.

The next day a letter was sent to Billy, who was working in Emporia, telling him to come home, and one to Henry's sister Kate in Iowa. He had seen her only once since he came to Kansas to take his homestead. She was a young woman then—nearly twenty years before. He had always intended to go to see her again just as soon as he could, as soon as he could spare the money and the time; but something always forced him to postpone his trip—just *postpone* it of course, until a more favorable time. Now she must come to see him; and in a few days she was there. How glad he was to see her again! She was changed in appearance, so fat and stocky, she who had been such a fragile little girl a half century before. But her voice was the same, with the same nervous break whenever it rose above a certain pitch; and when he heard her speak, he could see again the light-haired little girl who, so long ago, played hide-and-seek with him about the lime kiln at Sindringen.

For Henry the siege was on—the siege of a tenacious vitality by slow, relentless starvation. Day by day he surrendered an imperceptible portion of his already pitiful allowance of food; day by day his once rugged frame became more emaciated, his cheeks hollower, his eyes more sunken and despairing.

It was hard to find food that he could eat safely even in small amounts. He liked asparagus, and it "agreed with him" fairly well;

A picnic in the Ise front yard in 1900. Hap and Dutch are under the tree, with May and Rosina on the far right. Henry is sitting in the chair at the back, with his sister Kate on his right and Rosa on his left. (Photo courtesy Marcy Wright)

so day after day, Rosie carried buckets of water out to the asparagus bed to keep it green and succulent. When the fresh asparagus was gone, she bought it in cans, but for some reason he was not able to eat much of that.

He never complained. Through a hot, dry July and August he sat patiently in his big rocker, listening to the hot winds moaning through the shutters, moaning in cadences that rose to a weird whistle as the wind whirled the loose slats around, and then sank again to a tired sigh that breathed all the weariness and discouragement of the years since he first came there—years that would soon be only a memory for others. He sat in his rocker, watching Rosie and the girls at their sewing, or patching, or preparation of meals, reading the newspaper, or perhaps talking briefly with neighbors who called to see him. Hours and hours were beguiled by a blessed little brown mocking bird which sang from the top of the maple tree—sang as if it knew how its songs were needed and appreciated. Hours each day, he watched the little wrens that were rearing their young in the cornice of the old stone house.

One day he heard a great commotion among the wrens, and forgetting his weakness, hastened out to see what was the matter. There was a big bull snake, climbing along the rafters toward the nests! The mother birds—there were several of them—flew to meet him as he stepped out into the yard, and buzzed frantically about his head, so obviously trying to tell him of their danger, while he got a stick and killed the snake.

The summer wore on into a dusty September and October— the fall time, with its mellow, sunny days and cool, crisp nights, when the fodder stood in the shocks, and the morning glories bloomed in the corn rows between; when the blackbirds flocked in the cottonwood grove in the evenings and chattered their noisy conventions; when the cane heads turned black, and the new wheat thrust its blades up through the soil in well ordered rows of green; when the children started to school again, the smaller ones to the schoolhouse across the pasture, the older ones to the high school in town. Laura resigned her position teaching and stayed at home to help take care of Henry. She and Henry had always been close comrades, and this year she must be with him—there would be many years yet when she could teach and earn money for herself. She had a knack at nursing, a quiet and sympathetic way with sick people, and Henry was very glad she could be with him.

He was getting so weak that he had to leave his chair and rest much of the time in bed; and when the cool days came, his was moved into the big dining room, where the stove was kept burning. Rosie then had to set the table in the kitchen, so that Henry would not see the family at meals.

One sunny day in early November, he asked to be taken on a ride around the farm. Danny hitched up the surrey, and after piling the back seat high with comforts and cushions, he and Laura and Rosie helped Henry into the seat. Rosie got in beside him, and Danny drove slowly about the place, over to the west eighty, where the wheat was coming up in closely crowded rows of fresh green, then up to the new place where another expanse of green greeted them.

"There will be plenty of good fall pasture for the cattle, anyhow," Henry remarked, as they drove by the field.

It was a hazy Indian summer day, the last gentle reminder of the summer that was past. The oak trees along the creek clung tenaciously to their leaves of russet and brown, but the elms and cottonwoods and hedges were bare, except for a straggling yellow leaf here and there, fluttering in every breath of wind. The hedge apples that lay scattered under the hedge rows were still green, but the dead leaves lay thick on the ground, and an occasional frightened rabbit darted out as they drove along. Down along the river and creek the crows cawed garrulously to each other, as if constantly remonstrating about something; but the day breathed peace and serenity.

After a while, Henry began to feel tired, and they turned homeward. As they crossed the little creek at the corner of the home place, he turned to Rosie and said: "It doesn't seem so long since we crossed here the first time, does it, Rosie?"

"Only a little while, when it is past; yet so much has happened."

"So much good, and so much that seemed hard. If we could have seen it all ahead of us . . ." Henry sat silent for a time, looking across the valley at the familiar outline of Terry's Bluff, while the horses walked lazily along, kicking up clouds of dust that rose behind and hung motionless along the road. It was getting cooler as the sun sank lower in the southwest.

"We could hardly have gone ahead with so much courage," answered Rosie, after he had almost forgotten the trend of his remarks.

"And if we had known that all our hopes and plans, and all our work and worry, would lead only to this; and so soon—I'm only sixty now—" He paused a moment in his weakness, losing the thread of his thought, but presently continued: "Perhaps we could have found more good in the years as they passed. We might have done better with our time—such a short time, it seems now."

"Oh, yes, dear Henry, we could have done better; but we couldn't know. We always look too far ahead; and then when we come to the end, and it's too late, we look back and wish we could live it all over again." Rosie reached over and pulled the comforts more snugly about him, and then continued: "If we could just start out again, with dear old Frank and Sam, and drive across the prairie to our new home, to our little cabin, as we did that time, wouldn't it be wonderful . . . with everything before us?"

"It seemed good then," replied Henry.

"Oh, yes. It did seem good. We were so hopeful—we lived in the future then."

"We always live too much in the future . . . and too much in the past."

"And now it's all past."

"Oh, no. The children are still with you and will need you. There will be so much to live for, even when I'm gone. I wish . . ." Henry paused a moment, as if searching for the right words, and then resumed haltingly: "I would have liked to see the little boys grow up yet."

"If it could only have been so! They will scarcely remember you at all."

"Only as a name," he replied. "And Joe . . . Joe will never be able to farm; perhaps you can give him an education, as we've always planned. That would be the right thing. He seems to take to books."

"Oh, surely we can manage that somehow."

Nothing more was said until they turned into the lane.

"It was the third of June—that day, wasn't it?" he asked.

"The third of June. And what a fresh, bright green everything was, the prairie and the little field of wheat—not like today!"

"Not like today," he answered.

They were home again; but before he moved to get out of the surrey, his mind returned again to that earlier day.

"Frank Hagel isn't here to welcome us, this time."

"Poor Frank! He's been gone so long," replied Rosie, and she began to undo the comforts that covered him.

Danny lifted him out and set him on his feet; but his poor legs would no longer bear him, and his son had to carry him into the house and help him to bed.

In dreams that night, Henry found himself back in Iowa again, breaking prairie. The prairie stretched interminably ahead of him; but he followed on, the endless ribbon of grassy sod turning over smoothly before him. He felt tired, so tired that he could scarcely drag his feet; but he hung onto the plow handles and pulled himself along. At the end of the field he would eat his dinner—he was so hungry—and drink from the water jug, and rest in the shade of the wagon.

At last he saw the wagon, on the land-side far ahead. The horses walked faster, the harnesses strained and creaked, and he hung onto the plow handles with all his might. When he reached the end of the field, he walked over to the wagon, lifted out the grub box, and opened it. There before him was such a dinner— great dishes of delicately browned chicken and potatoes and gravy, and at the end of the box a piece of apple pie that covered the plate and dripped lusciously over the edge! He picked up a piece of the chicken; but as he tried to raise it to his mouth a paralytic weakness stayed his hand, and he awakened, to find himself lying in bed, looking up into the cool darkness of the room, the usual dull hunger gnawing at his vitals.

Rosie heard him stir and was soon at his bedside.

"What's the matter, Henry?" she inquired. "Can I get anything for you?"

"Oh, no," he replied faintly. "I'm all right. I've just been dreaming."

A few days later, the preacher[5] and the presiding elder came. Henry was now so weak that few visitors were allowed to see him; but Rosie ushered the two men in and, thinking that he might wish to talk to them alone, left them and went back to her work.

Not long afterward, she heard someone in Henry's room talking in a loud voice. She stepped to the door and listened.

"It is the last chance you will have, Brother Ise, to do something for the Lord, who has done so much for you. He has surely blessed you abundantly in this world's riches, and you should not neglect his cause." It was the authoritative voice of the presiding elder.

She could not hear the answer.

"Even renters who own no farms are giving more than that," the portly elder was remonstrating, as she opened the door and entered.

"We can only live up to the light that we have. I can pledge nothing for others to pay." Henry was speaking in a weak and faltering voice, not noticing at first that Rosie had come.

"He will have to rest now," said Rosie to the two churchmen. She ushered them out of the room, then came back to Henry.

"What did they want?"

"They wanted money for the preacher's home—wanted me to make a pledge each year for three years."

"Oh, were they scolding about that?"

"Yes." He hesitated a moment, and then resumed: "Because I gave only ten dollars, and because I would not pledge anything."

"I would rather you had done it than to have them worry you so."

"You can do whatever you want to, later. You'll have enough expense yet this winter."

Rosie stroked the hair back from his forehead. She could say nothing. In a short time he was asleep.

"For once, poor pa was able to say no," she said to Laura, as she came back into the kitchen.

Another week passed. Henry grew steadily weaker, until he could talk only indistinctly and with the greatest difficulty. Someone had to sit up with him at night, Rosie and Laura taking turns.

It was Tuesday night,[6] and Rosie was sitting by his bedside stroking his hair, as he loved to have her do. Near midnight he raised his hand and whispered that he wished to sleep. She shifted his pillows a little, put another hot bran sack at his feet, and sat down at the table to mend stockings while he slept.

An hour later, she stepped over to his bed. He seemed to be sleeping well. She felt his feet, which were sometimes so cold, but they were warm. His eyes opened as she stood there. "I'm all right," he said. He spoke more distinctly than he had spoken for days, and then he went to sleep again.

The fire died down, and she put more wood into the stove. The lamp began to smoke and sputter, so she got another from the kitchen and turned it out. Then she sat down to mend again, glancing at him from time to time.

An hour passed, and he still slept. She got up to put more wood into the stove, and felt his pulse and his hands and feet. His pulse was strong, and his hands and feet were warm. She sat down by the table and began patching again—a pair of Henry's socks this time. He had had them a long time, but he was always careful with his clothes.

Another hour passed, and yet another. The clock ticked out its regular beat—sometimes it seemed louder to her, and sometimes less strident—measuring out inexorably the remaining hours and minutes of the life that was ebbing away. No other sound broke the stillness, save the faint moaning of the draft through the stove and in the chimney, the occasional fall of a bit of wood on the grates as the fire burned lower, the creaking of the rocker, the snip of the scissors, as she trimmed frazzled edges and cut the patches to fit.

Through the chilly stillness of the November night came the distant crowing of a cock from the neighbors west, and answering calls from those perched in the trees outside. Soon a chorus of cheery greetings from all the neighboring premises proclaimed the coming morning. A tinge of gray slowly lighted the darkness outside, and sifted in through the drawn blinds.

"He's sleeping better than usual," thought Rosie, as she pushed aside the sewing basket and rose stiffly from her chair. She opened the stove door. The fire had died down to a few dimly glowing embers, and she stepped out on the porch to get more wood. Seeing her, the dog shook off the blanket with which he had been covered and came to lick her hand, wagging his tail in that sincerity of joy and affection which only a dog can know or express. She stroked his head gently, picked up an armful of wood, and came back into the house. When the fire was replenished, she stepped over to the bed and laid her hand on the sick man's forehead. There was no vital warmth there. She lifted his hand, and felt for a pulse in the limp and fleshless wrist; but the heartbeat of sixty years was over.

"Henry!" she cried. "Dear Henry! Can you speak to me just once more—only once more?"

There was no reply. Henry was asleep; and the lips that had always answered her kindly were set in the meaningless smile of death. Rosie buried her face in his breast, and wept aloud.

The morning brought with it all the heart-wringing tasks of arranging for a funeral—that crowning indignity demanded by convention of those already stricken with trouble and sorrow. Henry had attended to some matters weeks before, and kind neighbors offered their friendly services; but many things had to be decided upon and arranged. Many of the tasks fell to Laura and the older children; and for the first time in her life, almost, Rosie was content to let others take all responsibility from her shoulders.

When the wreaths were placed on the coffin, little Rosina insisted that she must put something there too, and she hunted diligently in every corner of the garden, until she found enough pansy leaves to make a little green wreath, which she laid beside the others. For weeks Rosie and the children had kept flowers in

Henry Ise's handwritten last will and testament, which he wrote in summer 1900. His wife Rosa was to receive everything. A special clause ensured that his son John (Joe) would receive a small inheritance in the event that Rosa died without leaving a will. (Courtesy University of Kansas Archives)

Henry's room, ordering them from a greenhouse in Concordia when their own flowers were gone; and they placed no flowers on the casket. "It seemed better," Rosie explained, "to give him flowers while he was alive and could enjoy them."

It was a long procession that followed him to the grave. Neighbors who remembered his friendly greeting and openhanded generosity came from far and near to pay their last tribute. They buried him in a little cemetery fenced out from a pasture near the town, beside little Albert, who had been moved from his grass-covered mound under the elm tree. Henry's grave was in a far corner, near the fence, where the meadow larks would sit and sing in the summer mornings, and the winds would bear the fragrance of the buffalo grass and the wild flowers he had loved so well.

It was nearly sundown when they returned home that evening. Aunt Kate Winters had stayed there while they were gone, and she had a good fire burning. The chairs had been set stiffly against the wall, and the bed had been moved out—everything was at rights—but how empty seemed the room from which only one had gone! When the children had changed clothes, they stood about the stove for a few minutes, warming their hands, and then they went out to do the chores—except Laura, who stayed in the house with Rosie.

The next day, Henry's army canteen and knapsack, the G.A.R. badge that he always wore in the procession on Decoration Day, and all the keepsakes accumulated in the war and in the years following, were packed carefully in his valise and stored away in the bedroom closet.

Soon afterward, Rosie bought another farm with the money received from his life insurance. She wrote the check with tears in her eyes, as she recalled how hard it had often been to pay the premiums—how Henry had sometimes gone without decent overshoes and mittens and woolen socks, had always shaved with a nicked razor, had carried a broken-handled jackknife for many years, had never had a watch until the year before he died—in order that they might have more land in the good years that were to come, and more comforts and luxuries than he himself had ever known.

Chapter Thirty-five

Rosie and the Children Manage

For a while life seemed utterly empty, flat and profitless to Rosie. Not to be able to greet the one who had long lain there in the narrow bed, so patient and uncomplaining, and so appreciative of every kind word and attention, not to be able to shift a pillow or pat down a sheet or comforter, or hand a glass of water, or fetch another bran sack! Life seemed suddenly to have lost its chief aim and purpose.

For years Rosie had been too busy to think about anything but the practical problems immediately ahead: shoes and stockings for the children, mortgages and interest and taxes; too busy for rest and relaxation, for enjoyment of the time that was sweeping so relentlessly by. In the back of her mind was always a vague hope that some day, when the children were a little older, she and Henry would be able to take a little more time for living and enjoy an old age of reasonable freedom and leisure together. And now, when for the first time the family fortunes would have made such a life possible, Henry was no longer there to enjoy it with her. She had never realized how dependent she was on him, for companionship and even for advice and help on many problems. In her grief and loneliness she reproached herself for having taken so little time for their common enjoyments while he was living, even bitterly questioned the use of all she had ever done. The material world she had worked so hard to build—the world of land and cattle and barns and granaries, the world which had once seemed all-important—now seemed to have crumbled to uselessness.

The days stretched into weeks and months, and the broken current of family life slowly found new channels. With the companion of so many years no longer at her side, Rosie became more and more engrossed in her children. For them she worked early and late; for them she saved and skimped, ate chicken neck, sewed and patched and darned, hoped and planned and schemed and fretted. Remembering her own half-day in school, she wanted them all to have an education; and no sacrifice was too great that promised to help toward that end. Rosie and Henry had always had a Germanic faith in education; and nearly all of the children grew up in the faith that a college education would open the door to success, although they had scarcely even a vague idea as to how it was to help them. Not until many years later would they realize that Rosie, with only a half-day in school, in her long struggle with the hardships and disappointments of the treacherous climate, in her years of buffeting the perplexing problems that arose in the rearing of her children, had secured a better education in the essentials of a good life than they could get from any college curriculum.

There was enough income to keep some of the children in college most of the time. Although crops varied from year to year, as they had always done, prices were better. Wheat sold at sixty-five cents a bushel, or often even more; corn and hogs and cattle brought prices that were hardly dreamed of in the hard years when Henry had managed the farm. Added to all this were the salaries of the children who were teaching—salaries that seemed generous at the time—and Rosie's pension.

Although Henry had never been well after the Civil War, and died while yet young, probably as a result of the hardships and privations of the war, he had never drawn a pension until a few years before he died. Like so many of the soldiers in the war, he had disliked and distrusted the hospitals—so many men died when exposed to the unsanitary conditions prevailing in them—and, no matter how ill, had always refused to be taken there. Without any hospital record of illness or injury, he had not been eligible to a pension, even for years after he was unable to do heavy work. Soon after he died, a law was passed granting an allowance to all widows of war veterans. So Rosie got the pension that Henry should have had years before.[1]

Year by year, new improvements, conveniences, and luxuries were added. The boys got a horse-power stacker[2] and rakes to han-

Rosa Ise shortly after Henry's death in 1900. (Photo courtesy Marcy Wright)

dle the alfalfa hay, a feed rack for the cattle, a new six-shovel culti-vator, and a riding plow.³ A new chicken coop was built beside the old one, a new well curb, and a milk house, with the water for the stock running through it to keep the milk cool. A new invention—the cream separator—was coming into use, and Rosie put one in the new milk house. The old surrey, which had seemed so fine a few years before, was beginning to look shabby and to rattle in an undignified way; and Rosie bought the children a new one, with rubber tires.

There were refinements for the inside of the house, too. The girls urged Rosie to have the parlor carpet torn up, the floor planed and polished, and a rug put down—town people were treating their floors in that way. Of course Rosie acquiesced. They sug-gested that the old organ was not an up-to-date musical instru-ment, so Rosie bought a piano and, with a heavy heart, moved the organ up-stairs. At the suggestion of the girls, she bought a new dining room table—a large, round table in golden-oak, and moved the old one into the kitchen. She bought a set of Haviland china, to take the place of the old Alfred Meakin ware, for Sunday use; a kitchen cabinet and a flour chest; and from time to time added various new cooking contrivances—egg beaters, toasters, apple parers, paring knives, pancake griddles, and new shapes and designs of baking pans.

Rosie found little happiness herself in buying such things. In her long years of self-denial she had lost the faculty of selfish, personal enjoyment. After almost a lifetime devoted to thinking of others, she scarcely knew how to give any thought to her own needs or wishes. When the children asked if she would like this or that, she invariably replied, "Oh, whatever you children want—I guess it will suit me well enough." She would have worn her old clothes until they fell apart, but the girls took her to town once in a while and bought what they thought she should have. This she accepted resignedly, as long as they did not try to get anything too expensive. She never could get away from the idea that it was hardly fair to spend money for luxuries, since Henry was gone.

"Poor pa!" she so often said. "If he could only have been here now, when we don't have to skimp so!" But she was always glad to be able to make the home attractive for the children, and within the limits of her income, was willing to buy anything they wanted.

It was not an easy matter to treat all of the children with absolute fairness. Rosie knew how much ill will could be stirred up by any partiality, real or fancied. There were plenty of examples of this in the neighborhood; and she resolved that there should be nothing of the kind in her own home. So she studied every expenditure critically to see that it would be of use to all; she always tried to dress the children equally well; and if she had only an apple or a pawpaw to divide among the children, she cut it with the most meticulous care into the right number of equal parts. When the children started to college, she lent them money, but they gave her notes for it, at current rates of interest.

"It seems a kind of a hard way to do," she once said, "but I don't know any other way that would be fair. Father and mother always did that way, and we certainly never had any trouble or hard feelings."

Henry had not been quite so careful in this respect. When he brought candy from town in earlier years, he would often hand it to the first youngster who came, with instructions to divide it with the rest of the children—instructions which were not always car-

ried out with entire fairness. Rosie scolded him about it and sometimes insisted on dividing the candy herself, so that all should
share equally.

Henry and Rosie had always followed a policy of giving each
of the children a colt at the age of fifteen, and a gold watch at eighteen, if he had not learned to smoke or chew. The colt proved a gift
of uncertain value, as the price of horses varied from year to year.
Some of the children sold their colts, when grown, for as much as
a hundred dollars, others for as little as thirty. Rosie worried about
this, and finally decided that the only fair thing would be to give
each of the children enough to make up a hundred dollars.

Each summer the girls brought home new ideas and notions
about the way the household should be run. They wanted not only
different furniture and rugs, but new window curtains, wall-paper
of different design. Alice was taking home economics at college,
and she was constantly trying out new foods and new methods of
cooking. Rosie had usually boiled the meat, often in making some
kind of soup; Alice hinted that broiling and roasting were better
ways of cooking meat. Rosie never made any but white bread,
sometimes serving it hot from the oven; Alice thought white bread
constipating and, eaten fresh, utterly unhealthful.

The girls were not unkind or inconsiderate—Alice would not
have known how to be unkind. They tried to be tactful and diplo-
matic. Yet every suggestion seemed to Rosie almost a slap at her
own way of doing things. She did not get angry or stubborn. With
modesty and generous wisdom, she saw that times and methods
were changing and must change, and that better ways were bound
to come. So she worked and saved to send the girls back to college,
to get more of the notions that were upsetting her regime.

The children could enjoy many advantages that seemed fine at
the time. A Chautauqua was started in the park a few miles on the
other side of town, where programs of lectures and music were
presented;[4] and Rosie and the children sometimes drove down to
hear them. Danny bought a cornet and Joe got a piccolo, and both
of them were soon playing with the town band. Away from home,
at college and in their teaching, the children learned to dress and
deport themselves like town folk; and when they came home,
some of them were admitted to select social cliques in town—social

circles that had once seemed almost as far away and as unattainable as the European orders of nobility.

They had good times together, playing pranks on each other, and occasionally on others; as they did one Thanksgiving vacation when several of the Holton cousins came out to visit. The children were having rare sport together, but it was about time for the quarterly meetings up at the church, meetings that lasted several days; and quarterly meetings usually brought an invasion of devout brethren from Kill Creek, twenty miles away, where there was another Evangelical church.[5] Rosie always assumed that the Kill Creekers came in a true Christian desire to absorb more spiritual uplift than was available at home; and she fed and bedded them without any uncharitable misgiving. The children were less generous, and hinted that two or three of the unctuous brethren who attended the quarterly meetings so regularly were hungering less for the bread of life than for Rosie's chicken and pie and cake. At this time, particularly, with the house already full of guests, the Kill Creekers would fill no long-felt want; yet the children knew that if they came, Rosie would invite them in and make a place for them somehow. And then everyone would have to be quiet and sanctimonious, likely as not go to church every evening, and certainly would have to listen to long prayers and singing at home every night, which always made them sad and rheumatic.

The outlook was depressing, and on the day before the meetings were to begin, several of the children held a secret conference to devise ways and means of keeping the Kill Creekers away. They succeeded too. The Kill Creekers came over, of course, but they drove by without stopping. Rosie wondered a little at this, and almost began to feel a bit hurt, for it had never happened so before; but she had no idea why the Kill Creekers evaded her. A day or two later the neighbors began to call up and ask who was sick and how everyone was getting along. She was still puzzled, and declared that no one was sick. When the Downs *Times* came out with the statement that the Ises were having a siege of the smallpox, she was even more mystified. Finally one of the children confessed to her that they had nailed a big, red smallpox sign on the front gate.

Rosie took a trip to California and came back with marvelous accounts of that fairyland of flowers and peaches and oranges, of year-long summer and snow-capped mountains. She spoke often too, of homesteaders' cabins she had seen in the West on her way out and back. "Cute little homes!" she exclaimed, whenever she mentioned them, her eyes shining with enthusiasm. "I just wished I could get off the train and move into one of them, and start out again—plant trees and flowers and a little garden, and build up another home." Rosie would always be a pioneer at heart.

The next year she went to Europe with Louise, visiting Henry's old home at Sindringen, and the early homes of her own parents at Kleinbottwar. Laura spent a year travelling in Europe and studying in Zurich, Switzerland. Robert got a position teaching in the Philippines, where he had some harrowing adventures with the wild mountain men; but he escaped with his life, and later came home by way of Europe—with interesting stories to tell.[6]

The management of the farm was always a vexing problem. There was no real head or master. Will—they no longer called him Billy—the oldest of the boys, assumed control; but the other boys quarrelled with him and among themselves about the details of management, and Rosie often had to settle their disagreements.

The boys managed as well as Henry had done—better indeed, in many respects. They were quicker to see the value of new kinds of crops, new methods and new implements; and they had better implements than Henry had ever used. They had more horses, better horses; and they were more skillful in handling them. With more generous and more up-to-date equipment of all kinds, they were able to eliminate much of the farm drudgery, especially the hoeing of corn. There was no lack of man power, either, for three of the boys were grown now, and they were stronger than Henry had been in his later years.

So the boys were able to handle the farm reasonably well, but Rosie worried about it a great deal. In her long years of constant struggle with the problem of finance, she had developed shrewd business judgment, far sounder than Henry had ever had and sounder than any of her children ever were destined to have; yet she had been shut up in the house with her babies so long that she lacked an intimate knowledge of the details of farm management, and she distrusted her own judgment as much as she distrusted that of the children. With her restless ambition and energy, she could not turn over any of the problems of the farm entirely to anyone else; so she fretted and worried about everything.

The Ise family on the farm about 1907. Back row, left to right: Robert, Louise, Hap, Billy, Joe, Alice, and Danny. Middle row: Rosa, Laura, and Dutch. Front row: Rosina and May. (Photo courtesy Frank Ise)

All the work of keeping house was hard for her too—the cooking and baking and washing and ironing and churning, the patching and darning, the sweeping and dusting and scrubbing and hoeing, the countless trips down to the cellar and up-stairs, out to the well, to the milk house and back again to answer the telephone—the telephone was a new-fangled device, still a novelty, and the neighbors kept it ringing much of the time. In the summer, the older girls were usually at home to help; but when school was in session, most of the older ones were away at school or teaching, and the younger children were busy with their books. So most of the housework was left for Rosie to do. Although the family was dwindling as more of the children grew up and started off to college or began teaching, there was usually a hired man to cook and wash for, and there seemed to be no diminution in the amount of work to be done.

As the children proceeded further in their studies, and as more of them reached the age where they were interested in school, the family conversation around the table turned more and more to school matters; and Rosie found herself isolated and lonely in the midst of her family. She decided to do some studying herself, and managed to find an arithmetic that the children had discarded. In the evenings, after the dishes were washed, the floor scrubbed and the bread set to rise, she sometimes sat down at the table with the children, studying her arithmetic, furtively holding the book in her lap below the edge of the table lest the children see what she was doing. When she had learned the multiplication tables she found that she could solve many problems, especially problems in interest, which had always been hard for her to work out "in her head."

How fast the children were growing up! Almost with apprehension Rosie saw them pass, one by one, out of the schoolhouse across the pasture, into the high school, and on into the normal school or university—all except Will, who did not care for school. When Dutch finished his last year in the little schoolhouse, and came home with his books and slate tied in a bundle with twine, she sat down and had a good cry, to think that she would never again look out beyond the corral and across the pasture to see the children come trudging home.

One evening in June, soon after the older children came home from college for the summer, the conversation at the supper table took a turn that was to upset Rosie's peace of mind for a year and, after long discussion, completely change the family destinies.

"Say, Ma," Joe piped up, from his place second to Rosie's right at the long dining table, "Danny and I have an idea."

"One apiece, or one between you?" asked Robert, who had come home from the Philippines a few weeks before.

"You're sure it's an idea? You're sure it's not a streptococcus?" Rosina was taking physiology in the high school.

"Why don't you wait till you get over your other idea, before you risk a new one?" Will wanted to know. "Ideas are dangerous things, if you get them mixed."

"Yes, you know what a fever your last idea gave you!" May warned. "You don't want to risk too much."

"Is it another scheme for trapping flies in the milk house?" asked Louise.

"Or shutting off the hot winds with a cottonwood windbreak?" It was Robert who spoke again.

"Or making a million dollars raising turkeys?" queried Happy, passing his glass to Rosie for more milk.

"Well now, I think you kids might at least let him finish what he has to say, before you get so smart," interposed Alice, always sympathetic with anyone who was being badgered.

"I'm afraid it will cost me some money, anyhow," said Rosie, smiling. "Joe's ideas usually do."

Joe was visibly less enthusiastic about his idea, but Danny came to his rescue:

"Yes, sir, it's a good idea, anyhow, a cracking good idea."

"Well, trot her out and drive her on the scales. Don't keep us waiting so long."

"And so expectantly!"

"Let's have the idea—the new idea—the new, unfinished idea."

"Lead it out, so we can appraise it."

"From every angle—fore and aft—let's have it now—quick!"

"Quickly! Quickly, my boy!" Alice always said "quickly," and Happy sometimes got facetious about it.

The barrage of banter and raillery dampened even Danny's confidence, but he cleared his throat and proceeded:

"Well, Joe and I have been thinking that mother ought to move to Lawrence, so the kids could go to school, and be at home."

They were upon him before he had finished:

"Oh, yes. Will could drive out to his work. It's only a hundred miles."

"Mother could take in washings, and cook for a frat—in bad years."

"And in good years we could all join a frat ourselves, and get poise and polish."

"And keep the cows in the basement, and sell milk to the—"

"And if they object, we can start a frat of our own—there are enough of us."

"Yes, and charge initiation dues to pay expenses. All frats are started that way."

"Exactly, and keep the farm for a summer home for the cows."

"Lawrence is the place! Quantrell raided it once,[7] and they won't mind us."

In all this youthful levity, Dutch preserved a serious face, and in a lull in the conversation, he turned to his mother:

"And would we have to leave all the horses here, and the calves and pigs, and Roozer, and the cat?"

"Oh, no, my boy; we won't need to worry about that now."

So lightly and so easily the matter was disposed of, the idea so utterly impossible. Rosie hardly gave it a moment's consideration in the weeks following. To leave her home—the home to which she had come as a girl of seventeen, where she had borne her twelve children and reared all but one of them—the youngest would be grown in a few years—the home that was almost a prison sometimes, yet so full of precious memories, where every stick and stone, every tree and shrub and flower was partly her own planning and her own work—the home that *was her life!* No, the idea was so clearly impossible that it scarcely got across the threshold of her consciousness.

Yet, like many another unfamiliar and impossible proposal, this one gradually assumed familiarity and plausibility. In September, the older children went back to school and to teaching, and Rosie found herself again at home alone with Will, who was usually busy outdoors with the farm work. Dutch was going to the high school, Rosina, May and Joe were teaching in neighboring schools. They left early in the morning and did not get home until evening. After so many years with the children about, Rosie was much alone.

Sometimes it seemed pleasant to be alone, to sit quietly by the stove, sewing or darning, or paring potatoes. There was something restful in the drowsy hum of the tea-kettle and the monotonous "tick tock, tick tock" of the clock on the shelf. Sometimes she got the dinner dishes out of the way in time to rest in the rocker a while in the afternoon, sewing or even reading; and on rare occasions she fell asleep, perhaps to be awakened by the ring of the telephone, or by the noisy shouts and laughter of the neighbors' children as they passed the house on their way home from school.

Such a quiet life it was, and pleasant in a way, for the children presently came home from their schools, and Will came in from his
work—always something to look forward to. At the supper table
there was conversation enough. Rosina and May were full of stories of the cute little children they had in their schools, or of the
hopeless dunderheads who take up so much of every teacher's
time and energy. After supper, the girls took turns practicing on
the piano, Dutch struggled weakly with his algebra and geometry,
while Will buried himself in the Kansas City *Star*. When the girls
had done their practicing, they joined the rest of the family around
the big dining table, and read or studied until bedtime. Joe applied
himself diligently to the reading of his ten-volume collection of the
"Literature of All Nations"—an all-round scholar Joe was going to
be, if diligence and leather-bound tomes would do the miracle—or
played on his guitar or violin or piccolo, or sang a while, to May's
or Rosina's accompaniment. The evenings were cozy, and usually
pleasant.

Looking ahead a few years, Rosie saw a time coming when all
of the children but Will would be gone. Will would stay and manage the farm, but Will was only one, and she had always had so
many about. Henry had been gone nearly ten years now. Rosie had
lived for her children; and when they were gone, what was there
left that was worth while? If she could keep them about her a few
years longer by moving—but no, she wouldn't face that yet. So she
worried and fretted about the proposal which in June had seemed
so utterly absurd. Like a mother hen with a brood of ducks, she
saw that she could not keep her brood about her, and began to
think of following them where they would lead her. At Lawrence,
she might be with several of them for some years longer. What
might happen after that—well, she could think of that later.

The children all came for the Christmas holidays, and there
was more discussion of the question of moving; and this time it
was at last decided to have a sale in March and move to Lawrence.
Rosie finally said helplessly: "You children will just have to do
whatever you think is best. I'll try to manage somehow, wherever
we are."

That was like Rosie—always ready to "manage somehow."

A hundred times in the next three months, she was minded to

cancel all arrangements and stay on the farm. One Sunday she came home from church with her mind fully made up.

"We'll just forget about this moving business, for the present," she announced at the dinner table. There was a decisiveness in her manner that she showed less frequently as she grew older. It was evident that she had been thinking long and seriously before she came to this decision.

"Everybody is so nice and so kind, inquiring about us wherever I go, and always wanting to help us in every way. There are so many good neighbors here that we have known so long. We would never find another neighborhood where there are so many good friends—the kind of friends that you have tried out for forty years and know are your friends." Rosie slapped her spoon down into the empty dish with a clatter of finality.

"Oh, you would find a lot of friendly people anywhere— probably in Lawrence," interposed one of the girls.

"Not my kind, I'm afraid—with professors and educated people around. That's no place for anyone with only half a day's schooling."

"All the professors I ever saw in Emporia," May remonstrated, "were just as nice as anyone—not the least bit snobbish or stuck up.[8] A lot of them have education, but not much else. Some even keep roomers."

"Anyhow, there are not so many professors altogether." Rosina was joining in the argument. "Most of the people in Emporia—and I guess Lawrence is about the same—are just ordinary people, about like us."

Rosie knew little about Lawrence; but her mind was unchanged, and as she reached for the butter, she turned the conversation into another channel, hoping to put an end to the matter.

"Well, perhaps that's so; but new friends are not so easy to make, when you're my age—new friends that will take the place of some of our old neighbors."

"Oh, I don't know about that," Rosina replied, laughingly, "I believe you are better at that than most of your children ever will be, and enjoy it more too."

"You can't sit down by anybody on the train for an hour," added May, "without having another friend that you have to write to for the next ten years."

Rosie had to go to the kitchen for more bread, and when she returned, May resumed the argument: "You don't really need to worry about friends, ma. You'll have all you want, and the kind you want, most anywhere."

Rosie hardly knew how to get around this; and before she could collect her wits, May was at her from another angle.

"It's the work and worry that I wish you didn't have always, mother"—the children were beginning to call her "mother" occasionally. "It's not so bad now, in the winter time; but in the summer, when the hot winds and dry weather come, and flies and dust——"

"Oh, shucks! After all I've seen of hot winds and dust, I guess they won't hurt me—as long as I have something to do that needs doing."

"You'll find something to do most anywhere, I guess. But it is surely hard to have to worry about rain from March to September, as you do out here. Even in good years, when you have plenty of rain, if you look back at the end of the year you can always remember that you have been worrying about it most of the time. When it gets dry, you know it will probably get worse; and even when it is raining, you have to be afraid to see it clear. It seems to me I have spent most of my twenty years sitting on the west porch looking for rain."

"Oh, yes, my dear girl. It's no wonder you have that in your makeup. I surely never wished for rain as I did the summer before you came." Rosie buttered a piece of breadcrust and started to eat it meditatively.

"If there was any reason why you should stay, it wouldn't be so bad," May resumed; "but your work is about done; and you ought to be able to take it easier—now that the children are nearly all grown."

"Yes, the children don't really need me any longer. There isn't much that I can do for them now. I've seen that coming these last few years"—Rosie's firm lips trembled—"and don't think it's anything to be happy about—to know that you're . . . that you're no longer needed." Her head fell to her breast, and, covering her gray hair with her twisted fingers, she burst into sobs that shook her body.

"Oh, but you *are* needed, mother!" Rosina bent over her and stroked her head in an awkward effort to comfort her—awkward, because in all her life she had never had occasion to play this role. Rosie in need of comforting and reassurance! Rosie, who had always stood foursquare to every wind that blew, strong and ready to help and protect and comfort her children in every crisis, but so seldom calling for anything from them—now sobbing helplessly in fear that her usefulness was ended.

"You *are* needed, as much as ever, mother!" Rosina continued. "You could make a home for us in Lawrence as well as here."

"And leave Will?" Rosie raised her head and straightened up in her chair.

"Will may not stay here long anyhow; and if he does, he'll want to be married someday, likely."

"Yes, he really ought to. And I'd only be in the way."

"You could get a house in Lawrence; and some of us would be there for several years at least—we don't seem to learn very fast. Dutch and Happy aren't through high school yet, and May and I want to go to the university next fall. Joe and Robert are talking about the law school, and Louise wants to do some graduate work as soon as she can. You'd have enough to do, with all of us there; and we could save a lot, staying at home."

"Yes, I suppose you could. But those little town houses, where you just turn on a faucet for water, and turn a little button for light, and have a man drag ice in at the back door, and another one brings in your milk, and another the meat, and another the groceries—somebody else always doing everything for you—without any garden or flowers or chickens! What would I do with all my time? A person can't cook and dust furniture all the time. And likely as not you children would want somebody to come in and do the washing yet—some stranger always messing around in the basement! Alice has been fussing about that already, the last couple of years. A person has to have something to do."

Rosie was weakening, and Rosina seized the moment to press her argument:

"We'll agree, mother, to let you do your washing as long as you want to, and we'll get a house where you can have a garden, and all the flowers you want. You could have lots of flowers, if you didn't have so much else to do."

"Yes, I could have flowers. I used to think it would be so fine to have lots of time for flowers; but when it comes right down to it, flowers don't seem so important. Caring for the children, planting the trees, and building up our home here, so it would be a good home for us—that always seemed to be something substantial and worth-while. But I suppose I can go and try to build up another home, if that seems best for you."

Rosie gathered up a precariously balanced pile of dishes and started to the kitchen. The girls picked up a handful of each and followed her, but she promptly objected to this:

"You girls get to your work, or your practicing, or whatever you have to do. I can wash up these dishes in a little while. When I'm done, I will have time enough to worry about moving, if that's what we ought to do."

Chapter Thirty-six

The Sale, and the End of Pioneering

The long-dreaded day broke clear but chilly, upon red eyes that had known little sleep. It was the day of the sale, the day when cheap but prized possessions, accumulated through many years of saving, were to be held up before neighbors and strangers, puffed and praised by a blatant and haranguing auctioneer, and sold to the highest bidder. It was a day when all hands must be activity and bustle, all minds be alert, while hearts hung heavy as lead.

Breakfast of coffee and rolls was eaten in the twilight of early dawn, and soon all were busy with the thousand tasks of the day. Will curried and brushed the horses, and tied up their tails in odd little knots. Happy rolled the implements out into the yard, and threw some of the garden tools together in a pile, with the scythe, pipe tongs, scoops and pitchforks and the heavy tools that were to be sold. Rosie washed the dishes and put some of them away in a barrel for shipment, then helped move the furniture out onto the porch. She would have liked to take it all along, but the children said that it would not be good enough in town, and, as usual, she had acquiesced. Chairs and tables and beds and lounges and bureaus and rugs were soon brought out onto the porch, or into the yard, and stacked in discomfiting confusion.

At nine o'clock, there was still much to be done, but the sale was started. The auctioneer picked up a picture—the big Rhine picture that Rosie had bought the year of the Chicago Fair, with five dollars that grandmother sent.

"Here we are, gentlemen! How much am I offered? A hand-

316

some picture, an elegant picture—grace any home! What shall we say?"

"Twenty-five cents."

"Twenty-five cents! Who says fifty? Fifty cents! Fifty cents! Do I hear the dollar? Sixty cents! Sixty cents! It's a shame to sell such a picture for sixty cents. The frame alone, gentlemen, would cost five dollars. Sixty cents once! Sixty cents twice! Do I hear the seventy-five?"

Rosie choked down a lump that was rising in her throat. How fine that picture had seemed when they bought it, and how everyone had admired it!

"Sixty cents—third and last call—sixty cents—and—sold!"

The other pictures followed, except the river scene—or was it a prairie scene?—that Laura had painted years before, and the clock that had stood for so many years on the little shelf, ticking out the steady seconds, day and night—how many long nights!

"How much for the clock, this nice clock? Runs fine, doesn't it, Mrs. Ise?"

"Oh yes, it runs well enough." Rosie hardly knew how she managed to frame the words.

"How much? Twenty-five cents? Oh, pshaw now, gentlemen! I must have a better offer. Who says a dollar? A dollar! That's better. Only a dollar for this fine clock? Who says a dollar and a half? A dollar and a quarter did I hear?" He held the clock up and gave the pendulum a swing. "Only a dollar and a quarter? Dollar and a quarter once . . . twice—did I hear the half?—a dollar and a quarter three times—and—sold."

Then followed the stoves, the churn and the butter mold, the soap settle, the sausage grinder and the lard press, the lounge, the beds, the bureaus, the clothes wringer Henry had bought at Bender's sale, the cupboard Chris had given them when he moved back to Holton, the organ the children would no longer play, the plum sieve Henry had made the year Alice was born, the kraut cutter he had made the year grandmother died, the chairs he had bought with a load of oats, before the grasshoppers came.

By noon, the household goods had been sold. After dinner the auctioneer moved to the barnyard to sell the farm equipment. It took only an hour or two to dispose of the machinery: the fanning mill—Henry had taken it out with him before he came to

PUBLIC SALE

2 1-4 miles west and 1 mile north of Downs

Wednesday, March 17

Commencing at 9:00 a. m.,   the following property:

100 HEAD OF CATTLE

ALL WELL BRED—6 registered Shorthorns (3 cows, 2 heifers, 1 bull). 61 milch cows, heifers and calves. 23 steers, 2 years old, fine. 10 bulls, one year old, good color.

8   HEAD OF HORSES   8

Span grays, perfectly mated, wt. 2850; span bays, well mated, wt. 2600; mare with foal, wt. 1490; fine single driver wt. 1150; coming three-year-old horse, wt. 1250; two-year-old mare, wt. 1100.

4 Thoroughbred Poland China Sows

Will farrow in April.   200 Chickens.

FARM IMPLEMENTS

McCormick corn binder (new), McCormick wheat binder, 3 riding cultivators, 3 wagons, 2 mowers, hay stacker with sweep rakes, surrey and buggy, 2 listers (riding and walking), harrow, stalk cutter, sulky plow, walking plow, disc weeder, disc harrow, 2 saddles, milk separator, 3 sets double harness, driving harness, single harness, cane seeder, ETC., ETC. PRAIRIE and ALFALFA HAY.

HOUSEHOLD GOODS, including steel range, stoves, etc.

Lunch Stand on Ground.   **Free Hay.**

TERMS: All sums of $10 and under, cash. On sums above that amount 7 months time will be given, purchaser giving bankable note bearing 8 per cent interest from date of sale. Discount of 2 per cent for cash on sums over $10.

Col. J. M. CLARK, Auct.
D. H. Harrison, Clerk

MRS. ISE.

The sale bill advertising the upcoming Ise farm auction in 1909. (Courtesy University of Kansas Archives)

Holton for Rosie—the corn sheller—seldom or never used in later years—the stalk cutter, the binder and other farm implements, the harnesses, fly nets and saddles.

Rosie did not go down to the barn, but from the kitchen door she saw much that was going on. She saw the buggy sold for thirty-seven dollars, the surrey for fifty. The Peter Schuttler wagon that had served so many years brought only eleven dollars. As the auctioneer hawked and shouted its doubtful merits, she could not help recalling how often she had seen Henry come home, sitting there in the spring seat, so absorbed and preoccupied, and the children running to meet him.

Over the heads of the crowd, she saw the two big grays led out, Joe and Dick—no longer gray, really, not these many years, but white, white from the sun and wind and sweat and rain of fifteen years. A bit stiff and stodgy they were, with age and with their years of dragging the plow, the wagon and the lister; but there was always a solid reliability and a serene dignity about the big grays. They seemed a part of the family, almost; yet here they were, sold as soon as they were no long needed, sold like so many bushels of wheat, like so many senseless machines. Rosie and May and Louise stood together at the kitchen door, listening intently to catch the words of the auctioneer, now growing hoarse from the strain of his task.

"Hundred five! Hundred five! Do I hear the ten? Do I hear the ten? Do I hear the ten?" the auctioneer shouted.

"Oh, dear old Joe and Dick!" cried Rosie, wiping away the tears. "That it would ever come to this!"

"Ten, do I hear the fifteen? Come on, my friend, let's have the fifteen! Fifteen do you say? Fifteen? Fifteen for this fine animal, kind and gentle, and sound as a dollar?"

"Ma, he's selling Joe alone, he's parting them!" cried May. "Why does he have to do that? They were never parted before!" Even in the pasture, Joe and Dick always grazed near each other.

"Fifteen, do I hear the twenty? Thank you, thank you, my friend! Twenty! Make it twenty-five—even twenty-five. Come, gentlemen, this horse will be sold before you know it! Twenty, do we hear the five? Twenty once, twenty twice, twenty—three times, an—d sold! Sold for a hundred twenty, to this man over here at my right—John Kaser."[1]

"I wonder who it was that bought him. Oh, I hope he will be good to him!" Rosie could stand it no longer. When she heard the auctioneer's voice again, she walked quickly into her bedroom, where Rosina later found her sitting on the bare springs of the bed, with her head bent down over her breast, and her ears covered with her scarred and knotted hands to shut out the sounds that hurt her.

That evening, when the sale was over, the horses were taken away by their various purchasers, the cattle were driven away singly and in small herds, and most of the household goods were loaded onto wagons that soon rattled away down the road. Rosie and the children stood watching the horses as they were being led away, past the house and down the road by the cottonwood grove, followed them with damp eyes as they turned at the cross-roads and disappeared beyond the railroad intersection.

Rosie could not leave her house—not tonight. She had kept her stove and a few bed clothes. She and Will and Joe would sleep there that night, while the rest of the children stayed with friends in the neighborhood; but they could all have supper in the old home once more, sitting on boxes and eating from the tops of other boxes and barrels.

"Well, this time we won't have to do the milking after supper," suggested Joe, as he slid a fried egg onto his plate. He was trying hard to be cheerful.

"Oh, if we only *could* do the milking! And feed the calves and the pigs and the chickens, and dear old Joe and Dick and Nance, and all the rest! If we only had never started this awful business!" Rosie was crying as she moved restlessly from the stove to her seat and back again, forgetting to eat. "Who would have realized what it means to leave everything you've worked and saved for—everything you've cared for!"

The children sensed the inadequacy of words, and the rest of the supper was eaten in silence. When it was over, they went out and sat on the west porch, and listened to the cry of the killdeers darting about in the pasture, while the evening shaded slowly into night. The great white moon rose over the cottonwoods, and bright Venus appeared in the west, before the last red tints died out in the evening sky. Across the field at Graebers, a light appeared—they had probably finished their chores and were eating supper.

After a while one of the neighbors drove in to get the girls. When they were gone, Rosie and the boys felt their way among the boxes and barrels, and through the empty halls and rooms to their beds—but not soon to sleep.

Rosie sat down on the edge of her bed and looked out of the window. How still and lonely the old home seemed, with the roofs of the barn and sheds shining white in the moonlight, and the shadows pressing close! There was no peaceful rustling of the corn stalks down in the corral, no half-audible call of the cow to her calf, no contented grunting of the hogs ranging about the lot seeking a few more tid-bits for late supper, no sleepy remonstrance of chickens jostling each other on the roosts, no complacent quacking of the ducks wandering about in the plum thicket—not one note of the soft nocturne of a contented farmstead. Yet from the distance across the river came the faint tinkle of a cow bell, the sound of a dog barking, the far away staccato of a horse trotting along the town road. From a lower corner of the pasture came the weird "ku ku" of the prairie dog owl,[2] and from the still leafless cottonwood grove, the eery tremolo of his cousin in the trees. Faintly on the air came the honking of wild geese on their way northward.

Across the valley, someone was burning rows of corn stalks. Farther up the slope of Terry's Bluff, a straw stack burned brightly. Yes, it was the time to burn stalks and straw. Rosie almost imagined she could smell the faint odor of smoke on the damp spring air that breathed in at her window.

The air grew chilly, and she got into bed and drew the covers up over her. Aching in every joint and muscle, and with a thousand kaleidoscopic recollections of the day dancing feverishly in her mind, she finally fell into a troubled sleep, from which she did not awaken until the sun was up.

After breakfast the children went off to their various tasks; and she spent the day wandering about the place, through rooms that were cluttered up with packing boxes and cases and barrels, carrying smaller articles from place to place—sometimes with little definite idea as to why she did it—packing away keepsakes that she found here and there, dusting off the things buyers had not taken with them the day before. She found a melancholy satisfac-

Joe Ise, Coalie, and the dog cart. (Photo courtesy Marcy Wright)

tion in being there, where she had been so many years, in walking about where she had walked so often, up the steep stairway to the rooms where she used to tuck away the children on cold winter nights, out to the well for water—"we always had such good water, anyhow," she thought to herself—out to the garden, where last summer's tomato and cabbage stalks were rotting in the warm, mellow earth. She dug up a root of the yellow rose bush she had planted on the grave of Joe's black dog—the dog he had driven to school when he was a little boy.[3] "I'll surely find some place to plant it," she said to herself, as she wrapped it carefully in moist earth and wound an old dish cloth about it. In the bushes behind the plum thicket, she found a nest of eggs, but there were no noisy biddies to remonstrate as she gathered them up in her apron. Everything was so quiet, except the bees that hummed in the blooming maples, and the sparrows that twittered and chattered and quarreled in their nests under the eaves of the house—the sparrows Henry had always loved to hear.

That evening she must go. The train left at eight o'clock. The girls came home for supper again, but they went away soon afterward. The tenant who was to take over the farm drove in,[4] and Will borrowed his team and buggy to take Rosie to the train.

When Rosie had closed the door and started out to the buggy, she saw that her hardest trial was yet before her. There was Roozer, the little lame dog, following close behind her! She and the children had planned to leave him with the tenant. They had not thought of it as a hard problem to decide; but here he was, hobbling along on his three sound legs, wagging his tail so vigorously as to shake his entire body, and looking up with a dog's expression of absolute loyalty. Yet in his eyes there was written clearly his fear that she intended to leave him behind. He seemed to know that she would not come back. As she got into the buggy, he leaped up and, resting his paws on the step, looked at her entreatingly.

"Oh, you poor little Roozer!" she said. "And I have to leave you too! What can I do?" She turned to Will helplessly. "What can I do with him? I have no way to take him now."

Will looked down at the little dog, as helpless as Rosie herself. The tenant, who had been sitting on the porch, came out, and taking the dog in his arms, pulled him away from the buggy.

"If he doesn't get reconciled to us, we will send him to you when you get settled," the man said.

"Oh yes, and please be good to him! He has always been so faithful."

The little dog did not struggle to get away from his new master, but in his eyes there was a look of pathetic disappointment and reproach, as he watched the buggy roll out of the yard.

They drove along the old familiar road, across the creek and on up the hill beyond. They reached the top of the little knoll as the sun was sinking, round and yellow-red, into a field of green wheat studded with scattered broken corn stalks that had resisted the disintegration of winter.

"Could you stop here a minute?" asked Rosie. "I'd like to look just once more."

Will reined in the horses, and she turned in her seat to look back upon the home she had built and was now leaving. How friendly it seemed in the last slant rays of the setting sun: the white, gabled house with its great brick chimneys, the red barn and sheds and cribs, almost hidden among the great cottonwoods—the cottonwoods she had helped to plant! From this very knoll, seated in the wagon with Henry, she had first seen the little log cabin and the straw stable, so many years before. The picture floated before her—the log cabin and the stable, standing out on a treeless and fenceless expanse of waving grass—bare and lonely. Yet how full of hope she had been, that green June day, how full of plans and dreams! There beyond the pasture was the field where she and Henry had cut fodder, while the grasshoppers swarmed about them, the field where she had husked corn that wonderful year following, with Laura in the feed box behind. In the gathering dusk, she could still trace the path across the pasture, the path along which Henry had driven out of sight that day when little Albert lay dying in her arms, the path along which Laura had started to school, and Billy, and Alice, and Danny, and Robert, and Louise, and the little children. Oh, if she could only be back there and see them coming home again, see them coming home along that well-worn path, shouting and laughing in their boisterous, childlike play!

The last segment of the sun's red disk sank into the field of wheat, throwing up a burst of rays that fringed the low-lying clouds with yellow and gold, slowly turning to red and maroon and gray. The flute-like call of a meadow lark floated across the pasture through the deepening twilight, sweet and full and clear, with its finale of gurgling melody. The last clear call before the night should close, it seemed to say: "Good night, dear Rosie! You've been here with us so long. Good night! Good night! And goodbye!"

"Oh, those dear little birds! Henry always said they sang their best out here." Rosie turned in her seat and faced forward again. At a slap of the lines the horses started on; and they drove down the other side of the hill.

Chapter Thirty-seven

Afterword: Sale Auction Book (1909)

The sale held on the Ise homestead in March of 1909 was conducted by Col. J. M. Clark of Osborne. His clerk, D. H. Harrison, was responsible for the writing down of winning bids and bidders. The ledger Harrison kept during the course of the sale, found among the John Ise papers at the University of Kansas Archives in Lawrence, is reprinted here. Some spelling mistakes are evident, such as *hefer* for *heifer, trought* for *trough, by* for *bay,* and the names *Youst* and *Kazer* instead of *Yost* and *Kaser.* Abbreviations consist of *Pd* (paid); *sund* (sundry); *sunds* (sundries); and *bbls* (barrels). The meaning of *c* is unknown. The proceeds from the sale came to over five thousand dollars.

SALE
MARCH 17, 1909
NO. 7

Other:	*Bidder:*	*Items Bought:*	*Amount:*
Pd	J. B. Reddick	oil can	25¢
Pd	Ira Headly	sund	70¢
Pd	Bert Danehy	2 cans	30¢
	C. H. Wright	cans	30¢
	C. Denker	milk cans	50¢
	Robt. Kimble	wire cot	5¢
	Robt. Kimble	2 cans,	
		35¢ each	70¢
	H. Miller	bbls	10¢

Other:	Bidder:	Items Bought:	Amount:
	C. E. Hammond	trought	10¢
	J. G. Ruby	trought	15¢
	H. Smith	lounge	10¢
	Frank Smith	vaccinating outfit	$1.25
	H. Miller	boules	50¢
	Bert Rouse	sausage grinder	$1.00
	C. A. Sellers	tub & ringer	50¢
	Dave Coop	churn & mold	85¢
	Harry Sanders	sunds	15¢
	C. A. Sellers	jugs	25¢
	S. T. Kindley	jugs	30¢
	Will Fink	jugs	25¢
	H. Miller	sunds	$2.10
	Hopkins	stove	$5.50
	Coop	bed	$1.75
	Coop	bed	25¢
	W. E. Kaup	bed & springs	$2.50
	S. T. Kindley	rocker	75¢
	H. Miller	bed lounge	$1.75
	Harry Ray	lounge	$3.00
	J. E. Young	picture frame	40¢
	Mrs. Hofer	shelf corner	50¢
	Harry Saunders	table	75¢
	A. M. Schoen	dresser	$1.25
	C. E. Hammond	dresser	$1.60
	Sealy	kitchen sofa	$4.50
	Robt. Kimble	carpet rags	75¢
	Dave Kimble	kitchen cabinet	$10.00
	Robt. Kimble	carpet	$4.50
	H. Smith	hose	$1.00
	J. J. Reddick	wagon box	25¢
	F. D. Kimble	oil can	$2.40
	B. D. Courter	cable stacker	$3.50
	J. B. Reddick	drag	$6.00
	Hall McCormic	corn crib	$1.00
	H. Miller	fork	50¢
	H. Miller	bbls	10¢

Fred Baertsch	buggy tongue	$2.25
Yergeson	double tree	80¢
George Schoen	seeder	$3.50
H. Miller	junk	10¢
Dave Kimble	box iron,	
	$0.20 each	$1.10
Robt. Hull	shingle & c	$1.38
George Schoen	bbl salt	$1.10
J. J. Reddick	pipe	$2.10
Ira Headly	sideboards	60¢
Ed Hull	scoops	35¢
William Asper	wire stretcher	35¢
H. Muck	scythe & c	20¢
H. Miller	sunds	50¢
F. C. Coveson	sunds	$2.10
John Youst	chain	$1.50
W. Anderson	double tree	25¢
H. M. Schoen	2 shovels	$1.00
S. T. Kindley	rope & c	80¢
Robt. Hull	fork & sund	60¢
Tom Ray	rope	$1.40
George Hefly	saw	90¢
Robt. Hull	scythe	40¢
M. H. McConnell	fork	60¢
Ed Getty	fork	35¢
George Youst	fork	35¢
A. M. Schoen	scythe	25¢
Bert Donehey	sund	$1.00
Robt. Kimble	blankets	$2.25
(deducted) J. M. Clark	rope	25¢
B. D. Courter	post digger	40¢
Spolinger	wagon	25¢
Dave Coop	ladder	50¢
J. E. Dodd	tent	$1.25
Ira Headly	sunds	80¢
	grindstone	25¢
Woddel	wheelborough	50¢
S. T. Kindley	sunds	45¢
George Schoen	well outfit	$2.75

Other:	Bidder:	Items Bought:	Amount:
	G. K. Baker	mower	$27.50
	John Huiting	disc	$14.75
	Spolinger	stalk cutter	$7.00
	Foster	cultivator	$20.00
	Hopkins	lister	$20.00
	H. W. Holesburg	corn binder	$55.00
	W. E. Kaup	mower	$15.00
	George Hunker	cultivator	$12.50
	Will. Hoover	cultivator	$9.00
	C. E. Hammond	sulky plow	$12.00
	T. P. Ray	rake	$10.00
	Ed Ruth	disc weeder	$7.50
	Ed Worley	trough	$4.50
	Ira Headly	plow	$5.00
	Edenfield	tester	$2.75
	L. L. Peters	corn sheller	$3.25
	George Hunker	wagon	$31.50
	Isac Diol	wagon	$13.50
	H. Fink	separator	$19.00
	H. E. Smith	wagon & rack	$12.00
	M. Londsmon	binder	$35.00
	A. M. Schoen	hog trough	75¢
	Ben. Gellson	surry	$52.00
	John J. Goheen	top buggy	$37.50
	P. M. Shafer	saw	$28.00
	W. H. Guy	2 saws,	
		$27.00 each	$54.00
	C. E. Hammond	saw	$24.00
	Foster	hog trough	$1.50
	A. J. Platt	buggy	$5.00
	Woddel	5 doz. chickens,	
		$4.50 a dozen	$22.50
	Ed Getty	14 doz. chickens,	
		$4.25 a dozen	$59.90
	Isac Diol	by mare	$179.00
	Roy Gibson	mare colt	$157.00
	John Kazer	white horses	$250.00
	M. H. McConnell	harness	$27.50

Irl Cross	bay horses	$232.00
Jess. Clark	harness	$10.50
W. J. Frost	light harness	$17.50
M. Schoen	single harness	$8.00
C. E. Hammond	bay colt—3 year	$148.00
T. T. Reddick	bay mare	$170.00
L. L. Pormell	harness	$3.50
R. W. Coop	harness	$3.25
W. H. Goheen	britchen	$3.00
T. W. James	saddle	$11.75
Sollinger	sunds	50¢
Yergeson	sunds	50¢
Pommell	sunds	50¢
Earl Coop	sunds	40¢
W. W. Goheen	lot harness	60¢
Woddel	saddle	$10.00
Will Getty	fly net	$1.50
J. E. Gibson	red cow	$46.00
Joseph Kazer	cow	$56.00
C. H. Wright	cow	$48.00
Sam Beck	cow	$46.50
Bert Underwood	2 cows	$86.00
S. Miller	bull	$32.00
Tom Carnes	bull	$29.00
Ira Bickell	bull	$25.00
H. E. DeBay	bull	$25.50
H. E. DeBay	6 bulls,	
	$22.50 each	$135.00
George Lee	2 hefers	$76.00
Joseph Kazer	13 hefers,	
	$21.25 each	$276.25
S. T. Kindley	2 cows	$102.00
W. C. Cody	1 cow	$50.00
C. H. Lattin	bull	$74.00
W. C. Cody	cow	$44.00
C. H. Lattin	cow	$39.00
B. Miller	6 cows,	
	$38.50 each	$231.00

Other:	Bidder:	Items Bought:	Amount:
	B. Miller	7 hefers, $26.75 each	$187.25
	Breon	6 hefers, $32.50 each	$195.00
	C. H. Lattin	2 cows, $39.50 each	$79.00
	Breon	2 cows, $28.75 each	$57.50
	H. M. Schoen	5 cows, $38.00 each	$190.00
	Bayne Sutter	15 steers, $48.70 each	$730.50
	Joseph Jackson	8 steers, $34.00 each	$272.00
	S. J. Van T. Lowick	3 tons hay, $5.60 a ton	$16.80
	Sam Welch	2 tons hay, $5.50 a ton	$11.15
	Nate Winters	2 tons hay, $5.50 a ton	$11.00
	J. E. Young	1 ton hay	$5.50
Paid to Ed	Ed Hill	stack hay	$30.00
	M. F. Smith	stacker	$41.00
	M. F. Smith	2 bucks	$43.00
	T. P. Ray	stove	$10.50
	S. J. Van Choick	more hay	$6.30
	Tom Ray	hay	$12.25

Part Two

Sod and Stubble—The Ise Family Before and After

Chapter Thirty-eight

The Haag Family and the Early Years in Kansas

The road traveled by Rosa's family, the Haags, during the twenty-one years following their departure from Germany was every bit as difficult and demanding as the one Rosa herself would later travel with Henry Ise. Rosa's grandfather, George Adam Haag, was a peasant and small vineyard keeper in the village of Kleinbottwar, located near the town of Marbach in the Republic of Württemberg, in what is now southern Germany.[1] He died there in August 1843. He and his wife, Johanna Klump, who passed away some fifteen years later, had a family of eight children—John Christopher, George Adam, Johanna, Friedricka, John William, John Frederick, Eberhard, and Katherine.

The eldest, John Christopher Haag, was born 13 November 1817 in Kleinbottwar. After serving a six-year compulsory term in the Württemberg army, he inherited his father's estate and continued working in the vineyard. On 20 October 1846 he married Rosena Christina Friehoffer of the village of Mundelsheim, who was born 25 October 1825. Her father was a shepherd and also a vineyard keeper. The text said at their wedding was Philemon 2:15. For six years John and Rosena continued to live at Kleinbottwar. Their first two children were born there—Christopher Gottlieb Haag, on 19 November 1847,[2] and John William Haag, on 6 July 1851. Shortly after John William's birth, it was decided that the family should emigrate to America, as Rosena's three sisters had already done so. Two of the Haag brothers decided to come also.

In 1886, Henry and Rosa's eldest child, Alma, spent the winter in Jackson County with Rosa's parents. Years later she wrote a description of them for the rest of the family:

Reunion of the John Christopher Haag family at Holton, Kansas, in 1889. Henry Ise is seated second from left; Rosa is standing behind him. (Courtesy the Historical Society of the Downs Carnegie Library)

Grandfather was tall, around six feet, I believe, slender, angular, but very stooped through the shoulders, and his hair and burnsides were white, yet, when he was serving his guests with wine and cookies, there was something gracious and stately about him, almost courtly. I can see him yet, after more than 75 years! Grandmother was only about medium height and, after I knew her, always overweight and tortured by asthma. She had soft brown hair, only slightly streaked with gray, and pretty hazel eyes and, even in her advanced years, somewhat rosy cheeks. If grandfather's judgement could be considered unbiased, she was a very beautiful girl. When I was in their old home village long years later, many there spoke of her kindly ways and beautiful face. . . .

Grandfather's frail health he attributed to his army service . . . he was often so late that he had to gulp his soup quite too hot, and that ruined his stomach. His favorite dish was browned or toasted white bread with hot water, a little salt and butter or cream.

Once when grandmother was telling me so rather longingly of the beautiful country of Germany, I asked her if she was sorry they had left their homeland. She thought a while, then said seriously that she and grandfather would doubtless have suffered less had they stayed where they knew the language and customs and how to get along among the more favored group in their community. Then she added sadly she hoped I would never have to know how hard it was to come to this country, strangers in a strange land, finding yourself part of the poorest class and feel you had to work out of it against such great odds. "In Germany, our children would have had a good education, while here some, like your mother, got almost none, but this country has given them a better chance, as they all own their own homes. That could not have been so in Germany."[3]

The following, fairly lengthy account was compiled by John Ise from the many stories and notes his mother told of her family's life in America after their arrival in 1852.[4] Completed in 1952 or 1953,[5] with additional notes added in 1961 by Robert Charles Haag, the narrative serves to further understand Rosa's constant concern over money and position in *Sod and Stubble*.

Mother's Recollections of Her Early Life
It has seemed to me that some of Mother's recollections of her early life, before she was married, might be interesting to some of the folks, so I have written it up here. No doubt there are mistakes in it, for Mother's memory was hazy on some points; but it is about fifty years too late to do much about that. I haven't tried to be "literary," but have told most of the story in Mother's own words, somewhat as I took them down when I was getting the material for *Sod & Stubble*. I will let Mother tell the story.

Mother's Story
Father (John Christopher Haag), peasant and vineyard keeper, and Mother (Rosena Christina Friehoffer) were married in Mundelsheim, Württemberg, on October 20, 1846, and came to the United States six years later, in July, 1852 with Christ, aged five, and Willie, aged one.

In New York a very sad thing happened. Father and Mother

and a couple of friends who had come over with them were walking up the street from the ship landing when a hack came up; three men jumped out, grabbed the daughter of one of the immigrants, a young woman, forced her into the hack and drove off. The parents never saw her again.

Father and Mother settled near Racine, Wisconsin,[6] where they bought thirty acres of land—a good-sized farm as they had thought of farms in Germany.

I remember only one thing about our life there, for I was only five when we left—wagon loads of fish going by. Mother was very unhappy there, perhaps partly because she had two of Father's brothers living with them, and they "made her feel so unhappy and homesick," partly because she broke her arm there, never had it set, and it bothered her for a long time, but mostly because of the death there of her second child, Willie. Willie, a little over a year old, was sick, and one night Father insisted that he should sleep in a separate bed. Mother didn't want to do that but finally let Father have his way, and the next morning the baby was dead, whether from the cold or from his illness she never knew.[7] At any rate, Mother was heart-broken, and "used to go out and cry at his grave." She used to say later that she often thought she could never live through those years in Wisconsin. Perhaps that is the reason why Ike and I, who were born there,[8] were so pessimistic and despondent.[9] She felt so sad about Willie's death that forty years later, in 1892, although she was sixty-six years old, and fat, and helpless with asthma, she insisted on going back to Wisconsin to see his grave again. She died there that same day.[10]

With one arm disabled, Mother wasn't able to cook well, and made corn mush so often that Ike was hardly able to eat mush afterward, and I never liked it, or corn bread. I never quite understood how my children could like corn bread so well.

Father's two brothers, by the way, went west but were never heard from. They may have been killed in some way, perhaps even murdered for whatever money they had.

Father didn't manage the Wisconsin farm well, for he knew nothing about American ways of farming, and was not a practical man anyhow; and of course the winters were hard and long there. So, in the spring of 1859, he sold the farm for $300 (or was it $600?), and came down with Christ, who was twelve years old, to Jackson

County, Kansas, near Holton, where he stayed with Pete Riederer about a year.[11] He bought the home farm, six miles north of Holton, in 1860, from an Indian, for $200;[12] and with the rest of his money brought the rest of the family down—Mother, Ike, myself, and George, who was the baby.[13] George was a pretty baby, and on the train a man offered to buy him for $200. Of course Mother refused, but it made her feel sad to think that anyone would try to buy her baby. Perhaps she was sad, too, because she had to refuse such a large sum of money that was so much needed.

Father had expected to work and earn some more money, build a house on his farm, and get everything ready for the family before they came; but soon after he got to Holton he came down with typhoid—the dreaded disease in those days—and nearly died, perhaps he would have died if Pete Riederer had not cared for him. So he built no house, and had nothing ready when we came. He never recovered entirely. I don't believe I ever saw him sit down with the rest of us and eat a real dinner. Naturally he couldn't do much heavy work. It may be that he didn't care too much for hard work anyhow or at any rate that he liked to read or write poetry better. Typhoid wasn't Father's only trouble that year. The winter of 1859 was very dry, with practically no snow, and the next summer there was practically no rain all summer, and no crops of any kind. So we reached Holton in the spring of 1860 with no money, found no house and no crops growing. We were really hungry that winter, for a while not far from starving. We came as far as Leavenworth on the train, and Father brought us on to Holton in a wagon. I believe he had to borrow the wagon and team.

The country around Holton had been surveyed only a few years before and was only partly settled. To the north of our home, lived the Farrs, who were well-to-do, and had a big house (which we copied in some respects twenty-four years later when we built our new house in Downs). The Farrs lost both their children on the same day from scarlet fever, and Mrs. Farr was always sad and lonely afterward. In her later years she gave her house to the church and lived on a church allowance until she died.

North of the Farrs lived the Footes, Porterfields, and Littles. The Footes were from Vermont and had many nice things; a surrey (the first I ever saw), hair-cloth furniture, beds and white sheets.

When Mrs. Foote died, he married again and his second wife got the property over into the hands of her other children. He had nothing then, and his children were so angry about his marriage that they wouldn't keep him, and he went to the poor house, where he died. I worked for the Footes a great deal. Only about twelve years after we came though, we were able to buy one of the Foote farms. When the boys grew old enough to do the work and manage the farm we got along pretty well. Ike and George were at home for about eight years after I left, and they worked hard and managed better than Father ever could. John and Willie were younger and of course Willie went to California fairly early.[14]

To the northwest of us were the two families of Lutz, John and Godfrey. They were extremely poor. Mrs. John Lutz used to leave her baby with the other children while working in the field, and it would cry until its navel protruded like an orange. Her husband was not kind, he would ride a horse to town and she would walk behind carrying the baby. I think I saw her once shocking wheat the same day her baby was born. Godfrey Lutz was there before Father came. He had two children, but the wife soon died of fever and was buried on the place—and her grave is still there. He took his children back to Wisconsin, married again, and returned to Holton. He was honest but a poor manager, and his wife was not very efficient and couldn't do much. At meals he and his wife would sit at the table and the children would eat at benches here and there.

West of Lutz's was mostly unsettled prairie, with high grass, especially along the creeks, which made terrible prairie fires sometimes.

About my first recollection of Holton was of the funeral of the little daughter of Mr. and Mrs. Bossly, one of our neighbors. Mr. Bossly had put out poisoned meat for the wolves that were taking his chickens, and the little girl had found and eaten some of it. I remember that when they brought the coffin out, I thought they would have a present in it for each of us. The girl was buried in the yard, and later they moved the house so that the grave was right under the front step.

Father was a studious and an impractical man, better at writing poetry, in his beautiful script, than at farming. He used to read to us children, and I think he was the best reader I ever heard. He wrote poems for Christmas, Children's Day, birthdays, and various occasions, but was no business man, always being fooled by someone. Once a pack peddler sold him a big pack of cloth, which proved of little use, and Mother and the children were very unhappy about it. John Davis once told me that, at a somewhat later time, he had seen Father on his way to town, driving his team of little mules, the mules grazing along the trail and Father sitting in his spring wagon reading the *Bottschafter*, not noticing anything around him. John said that once when Father got home from town the little mules went straight into the stable and Father couldn't get around them to back them out. He pulled at the lines a while and scolded, then gave it up as a hopeless job, went to the house and began reading his *Bottschafter*, leaving the mules stuck in the stable door. Yet in some ways he was unusually progressive. Later, in his will he divided the property equally among the boys *and girls*, not just among the boys as so many Germans did. So too, before he died he told Mother to pay for her board and keep whenever she went to visit children, which seems sensible. There were never any serious quarrels among our folks.

As a result of his typhoid sickness, he was never able to eat what we ate, couldn't eat corn bread, or meat in the later years when we had meat to eat, but only rye bread and milk, or later wine. He hoed in the garden and cared for the fruit trees and vineyard, and pottered around with odd jobs.

At first he followed the farming methods that he had used in Germany, and they often cost a lot of unprofitable work. In planting fruit trees, for instance, he dug the holes deep and then filled them partly with loose dirt before planting. Some of the neighbors dug the holes only deep enough for the roots, and their trees thrived just as well. Father trimmed the fruit trees high, but in the Kansas winds these trees didn't yield as soon as Godfrey Lutz's trees that weren't trimmed. So at first, too poor to afford a fence, he tried to dig a trench around his field, throwing the dirt inward to make a sort of fortress; but he and Christ got only a small part of the field inclosed, with a lot of hard work, and the cattle jumped over the ditch anyhow.

Livestock and the lack of fences caused a great deal of trouble. The first team of oxen Father had got into Foote's corn field one day and Foote shot and killed one of them. There was a "fence law" (farmers were required to fence in their livestock) but our folks were afraid of "the law" and got nothing from Foote. The other ox fell into a well and was not found for eleven days. Father and the boys finally got him out but he died soon afterward. So Father had no oxen, but still owed Wise, the blacksmith, the $100 he had borrowed to buy them. A few of the farmers like Stauss had big herds of cattle that wandered everywhere and were an awful nuisance. One summer Mother slept out in the corn field to guard the corn from cattle. Later Father got enough money to build a rail fence.

Father had enough trouble with cattle to dishearten an iron man. He lost his first team of oxen, as I have said. Several years later he borrowed $200 from Wise to buy eight cows, but by the next spring all of them had died of hollow horn or in the sloughs. Along the creeks were "slough holes" where the cattle went to drink and got bogged down in the mud, particularly in the spring, when they were weak after a hard winter. I remember many times when Father and Mother had tried to pull cows out of the sloughs or pry them out with poles. Another time Father borrowed $200 from Wise and bought a bunch of calves, but the next summer they all died of blackleg. We thought they got the disease because they were so fat, but this of course wasn't the reason. By about 1865, though, the folks had enough money to buy a team of horses.

Mother and the children worked so hard and often had to walk long distances. The children usually planted the corn with a hoe, using a "cross marker," and cultivated it with a hoe, although a few years after we came they got a single shovel cultivator. Mother often took eggs and butter to town, five or six miles, carrying one bucket on her head and one or two in her hands. She knew how to twist a towel and lay it around on the top of her head so she could carry even a bucket of eggs on her head. At home she carried three buckets of water up from the creek in this way, a distance of nearly a quarter of a mile. The folks never were able to get a well near the house. Sometimes when Mother carried her eggs and butter to town she would visit Mrs. Wise, who gave her tea and cookies, which she was glad to get because the tea stimulated the flow of milk and helped her to nurse the baby when she got home. It took a long time to walk to Holton and back, and the baby—there always was one—was usually crying with hunger when she got home.

Once when Mother took the eggs and butter to Holton, Father asked her to get a grain sack, but she didn't have enough produce to buy everything else and the grain sack too; but the storekeeper wouldn't let her have the grain sack "on time," so she had to go home without it. She cried so when she got home because the sack was needed and she was deeply hurt because the storekeeper wouldn't trust her for so little.

Usually we walked wherever we wanted to go, because the oxen were likely to be working, and we could walk farther than they could anyhow. So Mother often walked to Holton with her produce. Once she even tried to walk to Atchison, forty miles away, in the winter of 1860–1861, to try to get something for us to eat. 1860 was the year of the great drouth. This story is told in *Sod & Stubble*. George thought she reached Atchison, but I don't think she did. The man who rescued her and later brought her home was "Colonel" Rust, and he brought her home on horseback, not on a wagon. Later Colonel Rust, who was an agent for distributing relief, gave us some corn meal and beans, and perhaps a little clothing—I'm not certain about that. Three or four months after Mother's trip to Atchison John was born.

Speaking of Colonel Rust reminds me of the rebel who was hung, up by the school house. There was a lot of trouble between the Free Staters and the slavery people, and quite a few people were killed, houses burned, and cattle driven off by one side or the other. In one fracas a rebel stabbed a Free Stater, in self defense and not fatally; but the neighbors caught him and held him in the school house all night threatening to hang him. People told how he begged for life, for the sake of his children, but they hanged him in the morning, after Colonel Rust prayed for him.

When I was about fourteen years old, a girl once stopped at the house for the night. During the night it turned cold and when she left the next morning, Father loaned her a coat, which she promised to bring back. Soon afterward her folks moved about twelve miles away, and they never returned the coat; so one Sunday Minnie and I were told to go and see her and get the coat back, or if we couldn't do that try to get three dollars for it. The girl was working for a family there, but had cut the coat up to make wraps for her illegitimate baby; but she finally borrowed two dollars from the family and gave it to us, and we started back home. Minnie, who was not entirely recovered from typhoid, got so tired that she had to rest frequently and we did not get home until evening. We had a little lunch along, but of course not water, and although we stopped a few times at the creek and at wells along the way, we were terribly thirsty and hungry when we reached home. We were so tired for two or three days that we could hardly walk.

One Sunday morning, when I was working in Holton, I decided to go out to prayer meeting, which I thought was to be held at our home. When I got there, after a six-mile walk, I found that my folks were not at home, so I went on to Godfrey Lutz's, a mile or two northwest, where there was no prayer meeting, so I went on to John Lutz's, three miles farther. There I was told that the meeting was being held at Knoll's, seven miles east, so I went on to Knoll's, where I found Mrs. Knoll browning real coffee for the church dinner—Mrs. Knoll thought coffee had to be browned just before being used. After the dinner and prayer meeting I walked back to Holton, seven miles—a twenty-four mile walk to attend prayer meeting, in my bare feet, carrying my shoes to put on when I finally reached the meeting place.

Once when the boys were mowing, they broke a casting on the mower and Christ had to carry the casting, a fairly heavy piece, to Leavenworth for repair—forty miles each way.

With so little money and so much bad luck, and with Father unable to work much, some of the children worked for neighbors and for people in town a great deal. I started working for the Footes when I was about eight years old. I got no regular wages, but once they gave me a dress. I washed dishes and carried water and helped with the washing and milking. I ate at the table with them except when they had company, and they were fairly kind to me. Later I worked for the Moores, who were well-to-do, and had a son who was paralyzed and unable to walk, and for Mrs. Peck, sister of the photographer, when her first baby was born, and for some other folks whose son was in a terrible condition with what I think may have been some venereal disease, but I can't be sure. If so it must have been a dangerous place for a little girl with no knowledge of such things. I remember the bloody sheets that I had to wash. I worked for the Tabors a great deal. Mr. Tabor was from Illinois, a fine man, educated, a banker, and something of a musician. The Tabors had an organ and many fine things. Minnie the oldest child, taught me to write. I was working here when I was married, and I worked for an extra week to get the two dollars with which to buy a little photograph album.[15] Later Mr. Tabor committed suicide when his bank failed. I also worked for the Doctor Adamsons for a while.

It was at one of these places—I don't know which—that I once froze my feet.[16] It was bitterly cold and I was working in an unplastered lean-to. My shoes were poor, and when I had to go out to get water I got snow in them. I didn't have the courage to ask permission to go into the other rooms where it was warmer and almost before I knew it, my feet were badly frost-bitten. For some time I treated my feet by wrapping them in greased cloths, but they were always stiff and awkward in walking. I was eleven years old at the time and was getting 75¢ a week.

Christ worked out quite a bit too. One summer when he was still just a boy, he went back to work for a man in Wisconsin. He worked several months; but when he finished his term the man paid him only half of his wages. Father and Christ apparently started a suit for the unpaid wages, but when Mother found that the man was going to swear to lie in court she insisted that the suit be dropped. So Christ lost half his summer's wages.[17]

Christ once worked several weeks for the Fredericks, when they were sick with small pox. He had had the small pox in Germany, so was immune. It was very hard work, caring for the parents, five or six boys and a girl, day and night; and it was most unpleasant work, for the bed sheets on which the sick people lay became so stiff with the pox discharge that he could almost stand them up against the house. With little sleep at night, he almost ruined his eyes, and could not see well for a long time. The mother and daughter died, and one of the boys was blinded in one eye. While he was working here, he would come home to the windward side of the house, and call for his change of clothes. The Fredericks had got the disease from a blanket they bought at the store, perhaps a Civil War blanket. Christ got nothing for all his hard work, although he was needed at home; but when some time later Mr. Frederick helped Father he charged him for it. I've forgotten just what.[18]

Toward the end of the Civil War, Christ decided to enlist in the army as a substitute for Mr. Foote; but when he got to Leavenworth he found that the war was over. A little later, in 1865, the year after Jennie was born,[19] he wanted to go to California. Father raked up eighty dollars for his expenses, and he went to Leavenworth, and down the Missouri and Mississippi into the South somewhere; but someone stole his money and he had to hire out to work for a man whose slaves had been freed. The man drove him like a slave and fed him very poor food from which he got a bad case of dysentery, and had to quit before the end of his term, so got no wages. He fell in with a company of soldiers, fortunately, and managed to get back to Leavenworth free, dressed as a soldier. He walked on home to Holton, sick, dirty, infested with lice. When he came into the house he just fell down over the table—he was so weak—and said he would never leave home again.[20]

In the fall of 1871, Ike, aged eighteen, went to Leavenworth, hoping to find a job, and a man there said he wanted a man. The man wanted to buy some stuff to take with him, but pretended that he had forgotten his money and asked Ike to lend him some. Ike lent him what he had and soon afterward he disappeared. With no money, Ike started home but at night could find no place to stay and finally crawled into a straw stack to sleep. In the morning his feet were badly frozen. Working around Holton, then, he was able to earn enough to buy a horse. While he was gone Christ got married in Ike's suit, because he himself had no Sunday clothes.[21]

Ike had his share of bad luck. Some years later he traded a bunch of cattle for a stallion, but got only three colts the first season. Then he traded the stallion for the patent right for a machine for plowing cornstalks under without cutting them; but he never got anything out of it and so lost all he had—about $600.

One fall, when I was twelve, Ike and I husked corn for the Moores. We of course went early and the Moores always invited us in for breakfast—a wonderful breakfast, with the best biscuits I had ever tasted. One morning we got there a little late though, after the Moores had finished breakfast. We went ahead with the husking, but by about ten o'clock we felt so weak that we could hardly work and let it out somehow that we had had no breakfast, and Mr. Moore took us in and gave us something to eat. Ike and I felt terribly embarrassed to have to eat alone.

Once when I was eight, Mother was asked by some people

over on Elk Creek, three or four miles away, to come over and do their washing. She couldn't leave her baby, Mary, so Father took Mother and me over the night before, driving the ox team. We slept on the floor that night, got up early the next morning and Mother washed all day while I cared for the baby. For breakfast that morning we had pancakes and syrup, which seemed very delicious, but we didn't really eat all we would have liked, and after we were through the woman poured the remainder of the batter into the stove. How that hurt Mother, and me too! That evening Father came to get us. It seems to me Mother got only fifty cents for her day's work, but that hardly seems possible.

George and Minnie used to pick wild strawberries and gooseberries on the way to town, and sell them for about sixty cents a bucketful—although George hated to peddle things. Once they kept out a nickel, but Father found it out and they had to give it up. When Albert died, in June, 1870, we had to borrow money from Wise for the funeral and paid it back by picking and selling gooseberries. Father and Mother had a sort of religious notion that Albert would not rest quiet in his grave until we paid the debt, so Mother and some of us children picked gooseberries for quite a while wherever we could find them and made enough to pay Wise. I think we got three cents a quart for them. The chiggers just nearly ate us up.

Our first shanty was about ten feet by twelve, of logs, the cracks filled with mud, with a dirt floor, a couple of little windows and a warped door that wouldn't close tight. The walls of the cabin were not tight, either, for on snowy, windy mornings we sometimes found snow drifted on the beds. There was a kind of attic above, with a ladder leading up to it.[22] We had a cook stove and Christ and I used to gather sticks and small logs down on the creek which Father cut into short lengths for the stove. We didn't have any chairs at first. For a table we had a big long plank, made soon after we got to Holton, and we ate from plates and pie pans. Our straw beds were raised above the floor by boards nailed on the sides and we had sheets over the straw and for cover used feather ticks that the folks had brought from Germany. These were nice and warm in the winter time, but too hot for spring and fall and summer.

Food for our growing family was a problem, but we usually

had corn bread and corn mush, Irish potatoes—never sweet potatoes—and in summer cabbage and lettuce and in later years some
fruit. We raised corn and rye and had it ground at the grist mill in
Holton. A few years later we began raising wheat and could eat
wheat bread, which tasted very good to us. We almost never had
meat, although in later years we would occasionally kill an old cow
about Christmas time, and boil the meat in making soup, dumpling and vegetable. At first we never ate eggs or butter, because we
had to trade them for the essentials; and sugar was a rare luxury.
We didn't can anything, and didn't smoke our meat, but kept it in
salt brine—a nasty, tough, mess when we took it out in the spring.
Father's fruit trees didn't begin to bear until several years after we
came. Once in a while we could get wild fruits and berries, but
most of these had to be sold in Holton to get cloth for our clothes.

Clothing was scarce. Mother used to get wool from Lutz's
sheep and a spinning wheel from Mrs. Lutz and spin yarn "on the
halves." With this yarn she made all the stockings and mittens that
we ever had. Father and Mother made the boys' overalls and
coats—for those that had coats—Father cutting the cloth and
Mother sewing. We never had knit underwear, but Mother made
us "shimmies" of muslin, which she sometimes colored with dyes
made from walnut shells. These shimmies and dresses were all we
girls had to wear, even in the winter. One suit each, that was all we
had, and on Saturday nights Mother put us to bed early and
washed our clothes and hung them up around the stove. We
smaller children never had shoes, even in winter. We just sat
around the stove in winter, and when we wanted to go out would
put on some old shoes that the older children could no longer
wear; or if it wasn't too cold we could go out barefooted, perhaps
play for a little while and then come in and warm our feet. Here
was the main reason we couldn't go to school—we never had warm
enough clothes to go in the winter term. I started to school once, a
summer term, but at noon I was called home to go and help Mrs.
Foote, who needed me badly. It was several years before even the
older boys got any Sunday clothes.

In the early years we really didn't have any kind of entertainment. There were no books in the house, except a few of Father's
religious books; and the only paper was the *Bottschafter*, a religious
newspaper which I wouldn't have cared about even if I had been

able to read. In the first years there was little to go to, and we had no clothes fit to wear anyhow. Occasionally a circuit rider would preach somewhere and we would go to hear him. Only a year or so after we came to Holton, when John was the baby, Father and Mother drove the oxen to Circleville to such a "preaching" and were converted there. Around Circleville there were quite a few pretty noisy and hilarious church people. The children stayed at home.

The Evangelical Association was organized two years after we got here, in 1862, with about fifty members. I must have been six or seven years old when we got our first preacher, Mr. Pfeiffer, and was about eleven when I was converted at a camp meeting and joined the church, along with some other children. George used to walk seven miles to the Fankopf church. In 1870 the Evangelicals built a church that cost about $5000, and Father gave $100 toward it—the price of a yoke of oxen.

After the first few hard years other kinds of entertainment than church meetings came in—spelling schools, literary societies and singing schools. I went to a couple of spelling schools, and one winter to singing school. Mr. Foote taught singing, and while I was working there I was able to go. Mrs. Ware and I often went together.

With such a poor house and poor clothes and poor food, there was quite a bit of sickness. Albert, just a baby, died of black measles in 1870.[23] The boys were breaking two oxen one day, and one of the oxen broke his neck. Father called for the butcher knife, hoping to bleed the ox and save the meat, and when Mother ran out with the knife, forgetting to close the door after her, Albert ran out into the yard. He had been recovering but immediately he got much worse. We got a doctor, and he wrapped the boy in hot corn mush, but it did no good and he died soon afterward. I can still remember seeing Mother standing there with her hands uplifted, shouting with joy when he died. She said she could just see him "going over," but it always seemed strange to me anyhow.

Typhoid fever struck the whole family, except Father and myself, in 1868. One of the Bateman boys got it a little earlier, then in July Minnie got it, just before camp meeting time. We had threshers at the time, but Father and Mother went to camp meeting, with the baby Mary,[24] leaving me and the rest of the children with the threshers. The threshers worked until dark and finished their job, and then one of them went to get Father and Mother. Minnie was very sick for two months. In August Jennie came down with it, and the boys got it in October, and didn't get over it until spring. Ike felt it coming on while he was plowing, and I have heard him say that he felt so tired that he just wished he could lie down in the furrow and be covered up. Ike was more or less delirious for twenty weeks and George for sixteen weeks. I remember one day when Ike was at his worst; he stretched out on the bed several times, and Father said: "There, he's gone!" But he finally recovered. George was sick in the same bed with Ike and Mother in another bed, very sick, and expecting her next baby. I was thirteen then, and it was my job to care for the family in the day time, do the cooking, baking and washing, and keep the fire burning. Godfrey Lutz came over in the evening and stayed until midnight, and Father watched from midnight until morning. It was a hard job to take care of the sick ones, for they were always so hungry and thirsty and sometimes delirious. One of the neighbors, Hermann Vogler, was being given a sip of water with his medicine one day, and he grabbed the cup and drank it all. He died the next day. His mother was sick, too, and gave birth to a child on the day her son died. Her people didn't tell her of this, and found it hard to keep the news from her during the funeral. I was warned to be careful, but couldn't be careful enough. Once while I was out of the house for a few minutes, Ike got up and found a loaf of bread, ate some of it and gave some to George, then hid what was left in his bed. He had been recovering but turned much worse. I couldn't imagine what was the matter, but finally he told me. I guess the doctors know that typhoid patients should have water, but in those days they had a different notion, and it caused terrible suffering. Perhaps the doctors did know something though. We didn't have a doctor for Minnie. Father thought such things were rather natural and just gave her medicine to "cleanse her system," and she got very, very sick; but later when Christ got the fever Father called the doctor; and the doctor seemed to head off the disease somewhat. Christ never got so sick.

If we hadn't lived so poorly, it wouldn't have been quite so bad; but we had no well and I had to carry all the water up from the creek, nearly a quarter of a mile away, rather dirty creek water. I had to have quite a lot of water. We of course had no bed pans, and for all the sick ones I just had to put rags under them and then wash the rags out. But some of the rich people didn't fare even as well as we did. The Littles had money, and a doctor, and both of their children died of typhoid. Most of our family were sick practically all winter; a cold winter, and it was almost impossible to keep the house warm. I finally had to burn some fence posts, but they were too long and stuck out a couple of feet at the end of the stove so I couldn't close it and the room was filled with smoke much of the time. Finally Christ said, "Ach, what in the world are we doing?" and went out and cut some wood to proper-length, although he was still weak. Later one day Pete Riederer, the one who had cared for Father when he was sick with typhoid in 1859, sent a wagon load of wood down to us and that carried us over a three-day blizzard that struck the next day. Father said he believed we would have frozen to death if it hadn't been for that load of wood, and long afterward one of the Riederers said his father thought so too. Pete Riederer was surely a good man.

We never had any small pox or diphtheria, but some of us were sick with malaria for a while. I got it when I was twelve years old, and for several months I was so miserable, freezing one minute and burning up the next. Helping Father build a board fence that summer, I was so weak and miserable and shivered so that I could hardly hold the boards up. I don't think we used any quinine.

Rattlesnakes were always a serious danger in those early years. George was bitten when he was about seven, right near the house. He went out to the cane patch, barefooted of course, to get a stick of cane to chew, and a small rattler bit him on the foot. He was delirious for a couple of days. Ike was bitten a few years later, through a hole in his shoe; but Father threw him down and sucked the poison out and he didn't get very sick. Down by the creek, where we went to get water, there was a rattlesnake one summer which had a hole in the bank and probably young ones in it. When we children went down to get water we would tease it with a stick. When Father found out about it, he went down and killed it.

Prairie fires were very common, because not much of the land had been plowed. The grass grew high, especially along the creeks, and prairie fires were terrible, much worse than they were later out at Downs where there was mainly buffalo grass. During one very dry spring season I remember that we used to see one or more prairie fires somewhere in the distance almost every night.

I suppose people would laugh at some of the remedies we used for sickness. Father once had a carbuncle on his back, right over the kidneys, which caused terrible painful cramps; and after trying various poultices he finally put a cow manure poultice on, clear across his back. It brought the carbuncle to a head so that he could lance it. When Mary had bone cancer, he used the same kind of poultice, but of course it did no good.

Poor Mother! She surely had a hard life, and her funeral was unpleasant to remember. She died in Wisconsin on Sunday, and her body didn't get to Holton for burial until Thursday and in the summer heat it was terribly decomposed and swelled so badly that it pushed the coffin lid up. They couldn't have the funeral in the church.

Well, I was married in 1873 and went out to Downs with Pa. I met him in the winter of 1872–1873. Out on his claim near Downs—or what is now Downs—he had needed money for more implements, and in the fall of 1872 he turned his log cabin over to a man, with the agreement that the man would care for the live-stock, and went down to Holton with Mr. Hunker to find work.[25] He worked for Hunker's son-in-law, old man Arnold, much of the winter. Pa had been engaged to Madie Laughlin, the daughter of a man who had come part of the way from Iowa with Pa. In crossing the Missouri at Peru, Nebraska, one of Pa's cows had got lost and after hunting a while he asked Laughlin to try to find her and bring her along. Whether Laughlin found her or not, he never knew. Pa had given Madie twenty-five dollars to buy some wedding clothes, but she suddenly married another man. Many years later she was living near Kirwin, and not living well.

Well, I was working at Tabors that winter, and one night when I went to church I met him. He had come to church with some of my folks. He borrowed a team from old man Hill, and took me out to my home. He came to see me at Tabors a few times, and we vis-ited in the kitchen because the parlor was cold. Mrs. Tabor put live coals under the floor, so it was fairly warm. Pa would come and stay a few hours, and I would knit. He wasn't there more than two or three times before he proposed, and I accepted him. I had heard good things of him, from Christ and from Boomers and others;

and my folks liked him. He had once worked for Mr. Hill, and Hill said that if that man Ise wanted to marry one of his daughters he would "throw her at him." He had a farm and a better team of horses than I was used to, so it didn't seem too bad to marry him. I don't remember that he ever gave me anything except a brown silk veil. I have a little piece of it yet.

When we decided to be married, he went out to his claim to put his crops in and put a floor in his cabin, then came back in May to get me. Our wedding was a rather simple affair. Pa took me to town with a load of corn, left me with some friends while he drove over to the mill, and then came back for me and took me to the preacher's home where we were married, in the presence of the preacher's wife and a friend of mine—none of my own folks were there. I wore a new calico dress, green with orange and white stripes. I still have a little piece of it.[26] Also a green straw hat. After the wedding, Pa helped me into the wagon, and we drove out home for dinner.

While Mother was getting dinner ready Pa and I changed our clothes and then loaded the wagon. The big "scuttle-box" which Pa had brought all the way from Iowa was filled with some of the more valuable things; a few dishes, knives, forks and spoons, a table cloth, a sheet and two comforters, two picture albums, extra dresses, a pair of Sunday shoes and a shawl for me. Pa's valise, with his Sunday suit and shirt, was wedged in at one end of the box. The scuttle-box served not only for our valuable things but as a seat for Pa and me. In the rest of the wagon we had some other things and supplies; several sacks of flour and corn meal, a jar of lard and one of butter, a wooden churn filled with molasses, a skillet, coffee pot, bucket and cup, some bread, butter, bacon, lard, eggs, salt, coffee, and sugar. Pa hung his army canteen, full of water, from a wagon bow. A sack of home-made soap was put on one corner of the wagon, to be given to the Joe Boomers, and a few gifts from Mother to Christ, who lived a mile west of Pa's. Enough straw was spread on top of everything to make a bed.

When we had about everything ready, I asked Pa if we couldn't take some flowers and he and I dug up some slips of the yellow rose bush, some marigolds, bachelor buttons and asparagus roots, which we put in a box with fresh dirt.[27]

After dinner—and it was surely a good dinner—Pa hitched up

the horses and the boys drove the cattle out into the yard, four of Pa's and three of mine, and we started, Pa walking behind to drive the cows; but we had scarcely reached the main road when Mother called to us to stop. She ran into the house and soon came out with a sheet that she had taken from her bed, and hurried out to the wagon.

"You will need two sheets out there," she said handing it up to me, "and I can get another one easier than you can. Leb' wohl, meine Kinder, leb' wohl! Und schreibt mir wenn ihr könnt."[28]

With everyone waving goodbye's at us we started on again, but had gone only a mile or so when it became clear that one person couldn't keep the cows together; and Pa had to go back to get a couple of the boys to help drive them for a while. After a few miles the cows tamed down a little and the boys went back home; but the next morning when we awakened we found that my heifers were gone. While I cooked breakfast, Pa went back after them but when he returned with them it was late morning. I was much relieved, because I was afraid they might have been stolen.

That was about the only trouble we had on the trip. At the crossing of the Republican River, the river was up, but there was a ferry and for a dollar we were ferried across without any trouble. On the last night, near Glen Elder—"Havensville" at that time[29]—a hard rain struck us, with wind, thunder and lightning, which scattered the cows; but we got them together the next morning and moved on. *Sod & Stubble* takes on from here.

A note on the post office business at New Arcadia—the name of the post office that we kept in our cabin. Someone on the stage line was opening registered letters and taking out money, so neatly that Pa never noticed it and passed the letters on; but Mr. Lindley, postmaster at Portis—called "Bethany" at that time—noticed the fraud and notified the mail inspector. It looked a bit serious for Pa, but he wasn't really suspected; and they found the thief in the Cawker City office.

John's Postscript

This is the disjointed story, as well as I could get it and write it—a story, it seems to me, of almost unbelievable hardships and bad luck, yet of amazing endurance, courage and perseverance. To some of you older children, Alma and Doll, much of it is already known, but perhaps not all. Reading it, I believe we Ises will understand better why Mother was always so extremely frugal, why she counted the pennies so carefully, why she never could bring herself to spend more than the barest minimum on herself; why she was often gloomy and pessimistic; and also why, in some later years, she faced piled-up discouragements with such tenacious determination. Starting in such grimly meager surroundings, isn't it rather amazing that she should have grown until she could meet the Governor or the Chancellor or William Allen and Sally White without much self-consciousness?

The Haags were not weaklings. They had what it took; and it took a lot. By the time Mother left Holton in 1873, or perhaps a little later, they had bought two more farms and were living fairly comfortably. I don't quite understand how they could have done this, but certainly the hard work and saving of the children and of Grandmother were largely responsible. All the boys finally achieved considerable fortunes.[30]

People who are extremely poor sometimes quarrel among themselves about small things; but there was little of this in the Haag home. There was rather a strong family affection and loyalty. Reading the story I can see how Mother, in one of the last letters to her children, should have written: "Should any great misfortune befall any one of you, stick together and help wherever you can. God will bless you for it." We Ises, who used to get barrels of apples and other good things from the Holton folks in the drouth years at Downs know that there was generosity too. Mother's last letter to us points this up: "Thank my Holton people for the many good things they did for me and all of us in years gone by. We hardly knew what to do at times if it had not been for their goodness. May God bless them all for it." To that we would surely all say "Amen."

This is the story, the best I can do with it. To my own people I will quote again from Mother's letter: "Some of you children will rewrite it if you care to have it better."

Thanks are due to Will Haag and to Theodore and Percy for helping me in checking some of the information.

John

Chapter Thirty-nine

Henry Ise and the Eisenmanger Family

It is a curious irony that only twenty miles to the northeast of the Haag family home at Kleinbottwar in Württemberg lay the small village of Sindringen, the home of the Eisenmanger family and the birthplace of Henry Ise. The Eisenmangers were tile makers and lived in the *Ziegelhütte,* or little tile factory, where they made the red tiles for the roofs of the village.[1] As artisans they were considered higher in class than the ordinary peasant. Henry's father, Georg Christoph Eisenmanger, was born in 1801 in Sindringen.[2] The oldest of five children, he inherited the family trade. In 1828 he married Johanna Klumpf (born 1807).[3] Six children were born in the tile factory: Georg Christoph, Johann Georg, Ludwig Friedrich, Luise Katherina, Christoph Heinrich, and Friedrich Karl.[4] The Anglicized names they were later known by were Chris, John, Fred, Katherine, Henry, and Carl. The children attended the German schools and helped their father in the factory, and so the family enjoyed status and a comfortable living.

At this time in Württemberg, military training was compulsory for a period of three years. A mass migration from all the German states to escape this requisite training was in progress, and after the eldest son Chris had served his time in the military, the Eisenmangers felt that the rest of their sons should leave before they also reached eighteen, the legal age of induction. The two best destinations were America and Australia, so by 1850, John had left for America, while Chris and Fred headed to Australia.[5] The parents would then use their letters to help determine to which country the rest of the family would emigrate. At this time letters from America took a month to reach Germany; from Australia, three months.

The Ziegelhütte, or tile factory, in Sindringen, Germany, where Henry Ise was born in 1841. (Photo courtesy Marcy Wright)

John sailed to New York City, eventually moving on to Utica, New York. He later moved to Canada and lived in Hanover, Ontario, where he met and married Magdalena Richard. They had eight children, Magdalena dying in childbirth with the last.[6] When John later moved to Erie and Williamsport, Pennsylvania, he married Sophia Waltz, and they had two more children.[7] He entered into the ministry of the German Baptist Church and long served in that occupation. In 1909 he made his only trip to Kansas, performing the marriage service for Fred Lindley and Alma Ise, Henry and Rosa's eldest child. He passed away in 1915 in Williamsport.

Chris and Fred landed in Australia at Brisbane, in the state of Queensland. They quickly got jobs near the village of Esk as sheep herdsmen. A week later the two were far into the outback, each alone with their respective flocks, when tragedy struck. A violent storm came up on Chris, who took refuge under a large tree. The tree was struck by lightning, and Chris was killed. Fred was later led to the body by Chris' dog. Swollen streams prevented him from returning to camp with his brother's body, and Fred was forced to dig a grave under the tree, wrapping the body in two sheets of bark. He decided to stay on in Queensland, eventually settling near Merlwood. There he met and married Margaretha Klupfel (born 1846) in 1863, and together they raised a family of eight children.[8] Two daughters died of German measles within two weeks of their father's passing away in 1883.

Before it could be determined where the rest of the family would go, the father, Christoph, died tragically. During the winter months there was little work to be done in the tile factory, and Christoph would undertake trips for goods and supplies for the merchants in the village. Often he would go for salt to Austria with his team of oxen, a three-day trip. In February 1855, however, one such trip proved disastrous. Years later Alma Ise Lindley wrote down the story as Henry had related it to her.

The next word came . . . that his body had been found on the bank of a small creek or river with legs and arms outstretched and frozen completely stiff. He had turned his oxen loose and they were not far away from him. The schoolchildren found the body on the way to school . . . the doctors felt there were some signs of life, so his body was placed in a box or tank and covered with snow and ice so that it might thaw out gradually . . . I cannot remember whether it was two or three or even more days before there was any real indication of life, but after the first signs of life, he recuperated rather rapidly and by the end of the week was back sitting in his rocking chair and talking with the family. . . . he had been home several days when the doctors came to see him, and on Saturday decided that his toes and fingers would not revive as they had been frozen too badly and were turning dark. They feared gangrene and said they would return Monday to take off his fingers and toes. He apparently felt reasonably well and ate. Like all Germans, he was a pipe smoker, but with his numb fingers he could not manage his pipe, so Grandmother had been filling his pipe and lighting it and doing the honors. Around four o'clock Sunday, he felt his jaw stiffening and he could not even hold his pipe in his mouth. They worked with him for some time, but during the night he died, and the Monday morning amputations were not needed.[9]

In 1857 it was decided that Katherine, or "Kate," and Henry would leave their home.[10] On 8 March they sailed for America and joined their brother John at Utica. The two stayed there for ten days before they went on to Perry, Ohio, where Kate worked briefly with the Underground Railroad, helping escaped slaves flee into the North. By September of the next year Kate and Henry had moved to Somonauk, Illinois, where Henry lived and worked on a farm owned by Mr. and Mrs. J. M. Severy. It was about this time that their brother John decided to become a minister.[11]

The youngest Eisenmanger child, Carl, was determined to join his siblings abroad and in 1862 he was set to go. The Civil War was raging in the United States, so he went to Australia to join his brother Fred. A former neighbor of the Eisenmangers told Alma Ise Lindley in 1904 of the tearful goodbye.[12] "She said they all went down to the stage, or post wagon as they called it, to see him off. Then she said Grandmother walked after the stage to the beautiful little stone bridge across the Kocher, and she leaned against the abutment weeping and watched the stage pull out of sight, then turned and still weeping, went back to her lonely home." It was always the children's intention that their mother should come and live with one of them, but this was not to be. Johanna Eisenmanger died in Sindringen in 1868 and was buried with her husband.

Carl, or "Charles" as he was called in Australia, arrived in Brisbane on 2 August 1862 and joined Fred in shepherding. When Fred died in February 1883, the family in America wrote and offered to do what they could to help the widow.[13] Carl told them not to worry, as he would see that Fred's family would be taken care of. He moved in with Margaretha and married her the next year. The couple had five more children.[14] Margaretha passed on in 1926; Carl in 1931.

Back in America, Henry was breaking sod for neighbors of the Severys when the governor of Illinois called for six regiments of volunteers in April of 1861. He was one of the first to join Company H, which was made up of local boys from around Somonauk and Sandwich and was one of the four companies to report at Springfield, Illinois, on 20 April 1861. There they formed the 10th

Illinois Volunteer Infantry, which was mustered out to Cairo, Illinois, and sworn into service by Captain John Pope for an enlistment that was not to exceed three months.[15]

Henry's enlistment and his changing of his last name from *Eisenmanger* to *Ise* signaled his break with the past and his belief in the future of his new country. The description given of Private Ise listed him as being twenty-one years of age, a sturdy five feet six inches tall, having gray eyes, and with light complexion and hair.[16] The occupation he gave was "a farmer." His three-month tour of duty ended back at Cairo, where he signed up again, this time for a three-year stint. He survived the war without major injury, though his company encountered heavy fighting many times, particularly at New Madrid, Missouri, where Henry's commanding officer, Captain Carr, was killed; Four Mile Swamp, Mississippi; and during the battle of Chickamauga. Henry and Company H were then with General Sherman's army on the march to Atlanta, encountering more fighting at Buzzard's Roost and Resaca, Georgia, before entering Atlanta when it fell.[17]

Henry rarely talked about the war in years afterward. Once he was asked by one of his sons whether he had killed anybody. He looked rather perplexed and said, "I am not sure that I ever killed anybody, but I did shoot at one man, as we all did, but we never did know just what happened."[18] But during his final sickness he felt the need to share some of his life experiences with his children, and he spent many hours dictating what he remembered to his daughter Alma, who kept careful notes. One day he offered to give her "the story of the War," as he put it. Alma later organized his reminiscences into the following narrative.

Trip of Henry C. Ise Through the Civil War

Enlisted August 28, 1861, at Sandwich, Illinois in 10th Illinois Infantry Co. H. Left for Cairo where we arrived next morning hungry and almost without money. Were soon sworn in and remained in Cairo about a month, then moved to Mound City, Illinois, where we guarded the building of some gunboats till about June 1, 1862. From there we took an expedition across the Ohio River over into Kentucky down to the rear of Columbus to keep the rebels from drawing off troops supposed to be leaving Columbus.

After 11 days march through the country we returned to Mound City and we always considered those 11 days the worst service we did in the three years. It was said the sun never shone in those 11 days—either rain or snow and we were with our tents most of the time. We stayed at Mound City about another month then moved to Bird's Point, Mo. across the river from Cairo. Laid there about a month then took part in the expedition under Gen. [John] Pope against New Madrid and Island No. 10—being the 10th island in the river below Cairo. In that expedition the 10th and the 16th Illinois comprising about 1,100 able men captured about 5,000 rebels at Tiptonville who had escaped from Island No. 10. Then we lay near New Madrid until about the middle of April, then went with the expedition down the river against Fort Pillow, but never got to see the fort. While we were lying at Osceola, Ark. making preparations for moving against Fort Pillow, but never moving against Fort Pillow, the battle of Shiloh was fought. Then the expedition turned about and all of Pope's army moved up the river. We went up to Paducah, Ky. at the mouth of the Tenn. where we got our new uniforms. Our first uniforms resembled those of the rebels. Then we went on up the river to Pittsburg Landing and went with the main army against Corinth. I think Gen. [Henry] Halleck was in command. The rebels left Corinth 'long about the fore part of May and we followed as far as Booneville. Lay at Booneville about three weeks then returned to Camp Big Springs about 10 miles S. E. of Corinth and lay there until about the 1st of August '62. The weather was hot but we were in the timber most of the time.

Then we marched to Tuscumbia, Ala. via Iuka. We lay at Tuscumbia until about the 1st of September. Then we left via Florence, Ala. where we waded the Tenn. River. Took a back track for Nashville via Pulaski and Franklin where we found the first turnpike road. We got to Nashville about Sept. 12 where we lay without communication with the outside world until Christmas—except what we received from rebel sources. We were watched by Gen. Joe Wheeler. Gen. [William S.]

Rosecrans then came through with his army and raised the siege but we stayed at Nashville until about May 1st, 1863. Then moved to Murfreesboro, or rather Fosterville about 10 miles south. There we lay about a month when we moved to Athens, Ala. via Columbia, Tenn. We lay at Athens about a month then moved to Bridgeport, Ala. and lay there about six weeks from where we used to guard trains up Siquachta Valley to Anderson's Cross Roads. There I received my only injury—unjointing my wrist—while shoeing an ugly mule. For a couple of months I could do nothing.

We were still lying at Bridgeport when the battle of Chickamauga was fought and witnessed the explosion of about 300 loads of ammunition. The accident occurred while loading to haul it to the front. From there we moved to Igos Ferry on the Tenn. about 10 miles above Chattanooga. There we built huts for winter quarters but left about the 1st of December for Rossville, Ga. which in the Cuban War was known as Camp Thomas. There we again built ourselves log huts for winter quarters and stayed there until about the 1st of May. During that time—I think 'long about in February—we started in the expedition with [Gen. William Tecumseh] Sherman against Atlanta. We went with the main army as far as Resaca then we branched off to Rome, Ga. The main army went via Kingston and met again at Dallas just in front of Marietta where a battle was fought and [Gen. James] McPherson was killed. Then we moved to the Chattahoocha River eight miles N. W. of Atlanta and lay there on one side or the other of the river about a month or so. When Sherman pulled up to make his expedition to the rear of Atlanta our Co. was left with the 20th Corps to guard the baggage train. When the rebels evacuated Atlanta to fight Sherman who had gone around to the rear we entered Atlanta from the front. Then we moved down to East Point, Ga. where we lay until the 14th of September when our enlistments had expired over two weeks and we were discharged.

We went home via Atlanta, Chattanooga, and Nashville. I rode all except about one hour on top of a box car. We got our final discharge papers and pay at Louisville and went on to Chicago via Evansville and Lafayette. From Chicago fourteen

of the 56 who left soon found our way back to Sandwich and I
returned to Mr. Severy's where I was staying when I enlisted.

Names of the Sandwich boys who returned in '64: Henry
Bircham, Ike Hamlin, Chas. Hamlin, Geo. Kinsle, Sam
Hinken, O. Conner, Henry Ise, Geo. Shriner, Will Cannon,
Geo. Gletty, Thos. Jeff. Latham, Ed Easterbrook, John
Baldwin.

Dictated to Alma Ise, August 27, 1900

After Company H had been mustered into service, the men
were paired off, two to a tent. These bunkmates were partnered for
the duration of their respective services and were often devoted
friends long after the war was over. During Henry's long terminal
illness, his Catholic bunkmate from Marshalltown, Iowa, regularly
sent him letters and small gifts and kept in touch with the family
even after Henry's death.[19]

The soldiers in Henry's company at first suffered from all
kinds of foot problems during the forced marches, as no one had
brought adequate footwear able to withstand such abuse. Many
soldiers tried to doctor themselves, since hospital stays often left
them worse off than when they went in. Henry did his best to prevent problems and ailments, which meant that after the war he
had no hospital records on which to base his claim for a military
pension. Men who had a hospital stay on their records could claim
a pension even for the most minor ailment.[20]

War forced Henry to quickly master English, and contact with
soldiers and civilians of different ethnic backgrounds and locales
helped to educate him about his new country's customs and diver-
sity. Later, when his father-in-law threatened to cut the Ises out of
his will for speaking English instead of German in their home,
Henry ignored the threat.[21] Although he had no objections to his
children learning German, his own experiences from the war had
brought him to the conclusion that it was easier to live in a new
country if one readily embraced its ways instead of clinging to old
ones.

One custom he did adhere to. He received thirteen dollars a
month in pay, but as he neither drank nor gambled, he had little
use for the money during his army service. He therefore sent
nearly all or even the entire amount to his mother back in Ger-

many. It served as the basis for her estate when she died in 1868. However, since his last name was now Ise, affidavits from all the other heirs had to be sent out and returned, affirming that he was indeed one of the family. The length of time this process involved meant that Henry did not receive his share of the inheritance until the turn of the century.[22]

For two years Henry stayed in Illinois. His sister Kate had meanwhile married and was living on a farm a mile west and a half mile south of State Center, Iowa. In 1866 Henry went west also, living with Kate and her husband, Chris.[23] He worked for area farmers at breaking sod, a job he had come to excel in over the years, earning $1.25 an acre. The team of horses he acquired for pulling his breaking plow, Sam and Frank, was considered the best there was at the task. He set about raising enough money to buy a farm of his own. Before many years had passed, he felt that he had enough and made an offer on a tract of land. Henry went into town, and withdrew his savings, stuck the five hundred dollars in his pocket, and returned home, only to discover the money was missing. Frantically he retraced his steps, with the help of a neighbor's wife, but the money was never found. He hunted throughout the day and the next morning, but to no avail.

Some time passed and Henry began making plans anew,[24] this time to take advantage of the Homestead Act. Several area men were of like mind, and with them he set out in April of 1871 to search for suitable homestead land in Kansas. When they came to the North Fork Solomon River valley, Henry initiated a fruitless search for available land along the river that would offer a copious wood and water supply. Failing in this, he decided to go with some land in the secondary river bottom, entirely level and above the floodplain. He then returned east to Cawker City and filed a claim on the 160 acres comprising the northeast quarter of Section 19, Township 6, Range 11, in Ross Township of Osborne County. He went back to Iowa and on 18 September left there for his new home with a "span of horses and wagons, some farming machinery, five head of cattle and about $500 in money and began to improve my homestead."[25]

Henry sank a well on the land and built a log cabin, which area bachelor homesteaders such as Frank Hagel and Stephen Young often frequented. Another of these homesteaders was

Christopher Haag, who felt that this particular German bachelor would be a good match for his sister Rosa back in Jackson County. In October of 1872, after much discussion with Chris and his wife and his neighbors, Mrs. Hunker and Mrs. Boomer, who had lived in Jackson County before coming west and knew the Haag family, Henry was persuaded to sit down and write Rosa a letter of introduction.[26] He opened by begging Rosa's "parton" for his imprudence in writing her and ended by signing it "from an unknown Friend, Henry C. Ise, New Arcadia, Osborne Co., Kansas." In the envelope he included a poem clipped from a newspaper. The letter must have worked, for over the next year and a half he was encouraged to write her seven more before their marriage on 19 May 1873. At this point *Sod and Stubble* begins.

With his kind heart and generosity, Henry earned the respect and gratitude of his neighbors. He served in many locally important capacities—on the school board, as secretary to the local Grange, as postmaster and justice of the peace. Time after time, he went to great lengths to help those in trouble, frequently over Rosa's opposition. But these neighbors assisted him and his family in return, for helping each other to survive was the cornerstone of existence on the prairie. When a Mr. Ernst was dying, he asked Henry to be the executor of his estate and to help the widow and her seven children get the best price possible for the farm. Henry did so, and the family was well taken care of. In the early 1900s when Rosa and Alma were on a trip to California and Washington, the Ernsts, who had moved to Seattle, repaid Henry's kindness by taking in the Ises during their stay there.

Henry was also unusual in treating his daughters with much more equality than most men of his age did. When each Ise child turned eighteen, he or she received a gold watch and $100 to invest. For example, Alma's investment turned out to be a town lot in Downs that Henry kept for her in his name. His enlightenment did not go so far as to let him consider letting his daughter own the land herself.

Chapter Forty

The Writing of *Sod and Stubble*

By 1924, John Ise was an established professor at the University of Kansas in Lawrence. He lived just down the street from his mother, and when they got together, the talk at some point would turn to his father, Henry. As one of the younger children, John had not known Henry very well before he passed away, and Rosa sought to fill this void by talking about the Haags, the Eisenmangers, and the first days on Henry's homestead. John was of course very interested, and his passion for economics drove him to wonder how the struggling farmers in Rosa's stories managed to survive, when they had so many years of meager, and occasionally no, crops without outside help of some kind.[1] What were the relations of the farmer to his land? How did he market his product? How did he get credit, and, if not, how did he survive without it? How did farming transportation of the time compare with now? His interest in the idea grew, and he soon convinced Rosa to write down her memories. Using a pencil and yellow tablet paper, she spent many hours at this task. John also sat long evenings with her, taking additional notes of his own. Yet another method of note-taking came in Rosa's use of small slips of paper that seldom carried more than a single sentence on each subject.

By 1928, he had decided that there might be an economic essay in his parents' story, perhaps even a book. That summer he went back to the Downs area and began researching in earnest, reading old newspaper accounts and courthouse records and interviewing former neighbors and friends of his family. John stayed at the old homestead, where the current tenants, Sabert and Mertie Hampton, eagerly assisted him with his work. Their son Dwight,

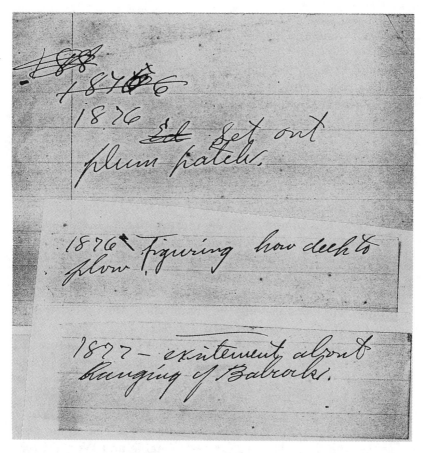

Examples of notes given by Rosa to John, which helped John establish a chronology for the events of Rosa's life. (Courtesy University of Kansas Archives)

then sixteen and the proud owner of a new driver's license, was designated by his father to drive John wherever he needed to go. Each day after breakfast John would inform the young man what the day's itinerary was.[2] "Let's go see Boomer over by Portis," or "Jeff Durfey lives down south of Osborne. Do you know the way?" It was a summer that Dwight was never to forget, the two of them putting in many miles over the rutted back roads of the county. And each night the Hamptons would find John sitting either in the parlor or at the kitchen table, jotting down notes on the information he had gleaned that day. Afterward they confessed that they had often wondered just what he was writing down.

Aug. 5, 1928—Sitting here in the parlor. It seems strange, with only a rug on the floor where we long ago had a rag carpet stuffed with straw until we could hardly walk on it . . . the woodwork still has the grain that Cox put in over twenty years ago, and the little colored frames of glass in the northwest door are all there. The frame with Albert's hair used to be on the east wall, but I can't place the other wall decorations. . . . How many memories crowd and jostle each other. Of Thanksgiving long ago, when I looked at the snow falling through that same bay window, and then turned to read *Columbus and Columbia?* Of the Christmas tree that I once set afire, in that bay window; of the days when I used to have to play "Sweet Evalina" and "Drunkard's Hiccough" for the company. . . . Here was held Father's funeral, while we stayed in the bed room. Here I was playing the organ when Alma scolded me because Pa was sick.

The kitchen. Big Huff talking about Barber County and some man said, "So & so came thru & said 'there wasn't a peach.'" I recall Pa picking up a live coal and carrying it across the room and putting it in the stove. When had a wooden ceiling would rap on it with broom stick to waken the girls. What was the order around the table? Pa on north side at center, Ma across from him. Hulda next east? Charlie and Walt, Ed on N.E., etc., etc.? Stella, Mary next to Pa. I was on S.W. mostly. Ma had "a milk" at her side and passed it out to us, & we put a little sugar in it. Remember the last dinner we all had together with Pa. Cinnamon rolls & coffee. 28 years ago.

See Mrs. Young; Arthur Hefley; Lon Stroup & Tom; Will Fink; Ruth Ruede; Charlie Ray; Joe Rathbun; Mr. & Mrs. Ed Getty; see Jeff Durfey on Covert Creek (12 miles).

John continuously wrote during this period, consulting often with his brothers and sisters about stories and incidents they remembered. Alma described Henry's last illness and death. Charles told of herding cattle and incidents at school. Walt remembered husking corn—a lot of husking corn. These new stories would of-

The first page of John Ise's "Prairie Pioneers" manuscript. (Courtesy University of Kansas Archives) ten remind Rosa of the same events, and she would give an adult point of view to incidents the others had considered only from a child's standpoint.

The wealth of material he was gathering convinced John that there was enough for a substantial book, and within the next five years he completed his first workable manuscript. "Prairie Pioneers" was essentially an extended economic essay, giving a detached look at the life of the homesteaders with his parents' lives serving as a running theme only. Wanting an informed opinion on the manuscript, he sent it to his friend William Allen White, noted editor of the *Emporia Gazette*. Although White enjoyed the story very much, he thought that it lacked the "dramatic background" and character development needed to make a good book.[3] John took this in stride, and after a little tinkering he submitted the manuscript to a publisher in New York. The reply was not encouraging.[4] The publisher agreed that the story seemed to be "lacking in sustained narrative interest" and turned the manuscript down.

Accepting these two critical views, John abandoned the economic essay idea and wrote a narrative, changing the names of the various people mentioned. He also tried to avoid what he would later term "the Mari Sandoz error," after the writer whose own book about her parents' homesteading life in Nebraska drew fire for its graphic representation of the homesteaders in both deed and language.[5] John's book would be noticeably cleaner in content. He called this new version "Breaking Sod: The Story of Pioneer Life in Kansas," and over the next two years he submitted it for publication fifteen times to such organizations as Charles Scribner's Sons, the Macmillan Company (twice), and the Oklahoma Historical Society. The critiques ranged from "an unusual piece of work"[6] to "interesting and authentic."[7] The most common concern expressed was the question of audience—a problem all too clear when considering the probable amount of sales for a book based on the trials and hardships of everyday homesteader life that would be published at the height of the Great Depression. Doggedly he kept submitting the work, and the pile of rejection notices grew to nearly fifty.

Convinced that he needed help in giving the story a more dramatic look, in July of 1935 he submitted his manuscript to a writer's workshop in New York City conducted by a Miss Mathilde Weil. In her long reply she stated that while "Breaking Sod" was original and interesting, for $250 she would be glad to edit it into a more publishable work.[8] John declined the offer and spent the next two months requesting that she return the manuscript, which she had kept, explaining that "I don't think that anyone would buy it."[9] Her price for editing had come down to $150. John again declined her offer, and she at last returned his manuscript.

He continued to hold out hope of selling "Breaking Sod," while simultaneously compiling *Sod-House Days*,[10] a book based on the letters and writings of Howard Ruede, a homesteader who went to Osborne County in 1877. While John was still submitting "Breaking Sod," *Sod-House Days* was accepted by Columbia University Press for publication in the spring of 1936.[11] John's luck appeared to have at last turned, for at the same time the New York firm of Rufus Rockwell Wilson, Inc. (soon to become Wilson-Erickson, Inc.), expressed interest in "Breaking Sod," provided that John would cut the manuscript by nearly a third and that he would underwrite the first 300 copies at two dollars each.[12] Ironically, Rufus Wilson had been a cub reporter in Topeka during the time John's parents "were making such a brave fight in western Kansas," which prompted his interest in the manuscript.

With the advice of his sister Mary and his brother Charles, John dropped the first chapter, virtually all of the second, and two other chapters. With a little reediting, the manuscript was ready for print. In May he reached an agreement to publish the book in October 1936. William Allen White, an "old friend" of Wilson's, would be asked to write an introduction for the book "that will have its effect with the Eastern reviewers."[13] Eight years had passed since Rosa Ise had written down those first notes.

John had sent along a list of alternate titles with his manuscript, among them, "The Soldier's Homestead," "Hot Winds," "Sod & Stubble," and "Mother Manages Somehow." With the first week of November came the first shipment of the book under its new title.[14] Fifteen hundred copies of *Sod and Stubble* were printed, and the very first one was sent to Rosa Ise. Due to other commitments, White was unable to find time to write an introduction, and the book was published without one.

There were some criticisms: "Too sentimental." "Hostility toward preachers!" "Too heroic of father and mother." But the overwhelming response from all regions of the United States marked the book a critical success, and by December discussions began concerning a second printing.[15] But then the agent the company had retained for printing its books refused to "remit us our agreed portion of the receipts" until he was paid, and Wilson-Erickson, Inc., was forced out of business.[16] In November 1938, Rufus Wilson expressed his apologies to John and told him that *Sod and Stubble* had not sold very well after all and that the printers demanded $1,138 for the remaining copies and plates.

With help from his sister Alma, John paid the printers and received the unsold books. They were given away to libraries, friends, and relatives, with John or Alma personally signing many copies. Although the book had been a commercial failure, John had gotten his wish to see it published before his mother passed away, and with the publication of *Sod-House Days*, John's life began once more to revolve around economics and teaching.

It was quite a surprise, therefore, when in 1968 *Sod and Stubble* reappeared in print. Word of mouth over the past thirty years had generated renewed interest in the Ise family saga, and the questions asked concerning the book grew so numerous that John's brother Frank[17] decided a new printing was justified and approached the University of Nebraska Press with the idea. The press agreed, and *Sod and Stubble* was again released in both hardcover and paperback. The reprint was an instant and enduring success. *Sod and Stubble* was rediscovered by the public and scholars alike, and was recognized as one of the classic tales of Kansas frontier settlement. John Ise passed away the next year, but not before having the satisfaction of seeing his long-enduring faith in the book justified at last.

Chapter Forty-one

After *Sod and Stubble:* Of Rosa and the Children

Perhaps the question most often asked since *Sod and Stubble*'s initial publication in 1936 has been, What became of Rosa and her children after they moved to Lawrence? In 1968, when Alma Ise Lindley and her husband, Fred, found out that *Sod and Stubble* was to be reprinted, they wrote the publishers to let them know that John Ise was still living and if they cared for a final chapter describing what had become "of all those little children," he could write one.[1] But the publishers said that they were not interested. Ironically, with the book's subsequent popularity, the question persisted. The following summaries attempt to provide some answers. The children's names as given in *Sod and Stubble* are in parentheses.

Alma Laura Ise (Laura) served well and faithfully in the duties of the eldest child and set an admirable example for her younger siblings. She was adept both at domestic work and at husking corn in the field. In 1894 she received her first teaching certificate and taught for several years in local rural schools. In 1899 she graduated from the State Normal School at Emporia, Kansas. Alma went on to attend the Polytechnic Institute in Zurich, Switzerland, where Albert Einstein and Vladimir Ilyich Lenin were fellow students. She served as principal at Frankfort and at Dickinson County high schools, both in Kansas.[2] In 1909 she was married to Fred Lindley (born 1876) in Lawrence by her uncle, the Reverend John Eisenmanger. Fred had been born and raised at Portis, seven miles from Alma's birthplace. The couple first lived in Chicago before moving to San Diego, California, in 1912. Fred was a lawyer and was in practice for fifty years. He was a member of the California state legislature from 1919 to 1921. Alma was a member of numerous organizations and societies, including the Zoological Society of San Diego and the San Diego Bar Association Auxiliary, and chaired the American Association of University Women's Scholarship Loan Fund.[3] They had four children—Laura, Edward, Mary, and Ruth. Fred Lindley died in San Diego in 1971, and Alma passed away 11 December 1974 at the age of ninety-nine.

As a boy, Edward William Ise (Billy) worried his mother with his unruly ways. But he was intelligent and inquisitive, often engaging his father in discussions on military strategy, the battles being drawn out on paper and sometimes on the tablecloth itself.[4] He also had a fascination for railroads and followed avidly the wheelings and dealings of the railroad barons during the latter half of the eighteenth century. But Ed was quite content to be a farmer and never attended college, choosing instead to take over many of his father's chores in farming the family homestead. Standing over six feet tall, he was idolized by his younger brothers. When the family left the farm and moved to Lawrence, Ed decided to head west, settling on a farm near Delta, Utah. He passed away there 18 April 1920 and was buried in the Downs Cemetery next to his father.

Minnie Alice Ise (Alice), who was also known as "Doll," attended the Kansas State Normal School in Emporia with Alma but had to drop out due to ill health. She later graduated from Kansas State Agricultural College in Manhattan and became a teacher. Her siblings provided the music for her wedding to Joseph Chitty, which was held 30 December 1906 in the Ise home on the farm. Joseph (born 1879) was a farmer and stockman from Frankfort, Kansas. After a time running his parents' ranch they moved to Altadena, California, where Doll died 23 September 1961 at the age of eighty-three. Her husband passed away the next year.[5]

Charles David Ise (Danny) always preferred to use "Daniel" as his middle name. Outgoing and athletic, he made use of both qualities in becoming a teacher and lawyer. He taught at Downs and at the high schools in Holton and Coffeyville, where he served as principal and head football coach. Ise Field there was later named after him.[6] In 1908 he graduated from the University of Kansas and its law school. He married Belle Stagg in 1910 at Topeka, and they had two children, Elizabeth (Betty) and Thomas. Charley served as Montgomery County, Kansas, attorney from 1912 to 1917 and with the army during World War I. He was killed at the age of fifty-seven in a car accident 13 August 1938 near Carthage, Missouri. His son Tom, who was running for the state legislature, was also killed.

Ever the serious one, Walter John Ise (Robert) was gangly and awkward as a boy. He got into many scuffles with Charley and usually lost. Their father tended to let them have it out to settle the matter, but Rosa could never stand any of her children fighting. Walt followed Charley to the University of Kansas, where they starred together on the football team. He then graduated from the Yale University School of Law. From 1904 to 1908 he served as the district supervisor of schools on Negros Island in the Philippines, where during some guerrilla fighting he and another American were declared missing for a time and feared dead.[7] After his return he practiced law with Charley for a while. In 1917 he married Jeanette Spalding (born 1885) at Kansas City, Missouri. They had three children—Marjorie, George, and Henry. In 1921, they moved to Denver, Walt working first with the U.S. Forest Service and then as an assistant regional attorney for the U.S. Department of Agriculture. He died 29 June 1945 at the age of sixty-three.

Hulda Louise Ise (Louise) graduated from the University of Kansas in 1912. She held teaching positions in both New York and Idaho, where she served as the dean of women for the State Technological School at Pocatello. Hulda was a rising young writer, having won several competitions. She had nearly completed her Ph.D. at Stanford University and had just started teaching English and journalism at Long Beach Polytechnic High School in California when she died of a heart attack on 22 September 1923 at the age of forty.[8] Hulda was buried in the family plot in the Downs Cemetery.

Earmarked by his parents to be a scholar, John Christopher Ise (Joe) had both the intelligence and tenacity to become a successful teacher and author. His crippled leg was removed in 1903, and after it was replaced with an artificial one he could walk almost normally.[9] He mastered a number of musical instruments, particularly the violin, and taught school in the Downs area before graduating from the University of Kansas with a degree in music. In 1914 he received his Ph.D. in economics from Harvard University, and two years later he began teaching at the University of Kansas, finally re-

A gathering at the Rosa Ise home in Lawrence, Kansas. Back row, left to right: Charles, Walter, Herman, Frank, and John. Front row: Estelle and Mary are on the left; Rosa and Alma are on the right. The identities of the man and child are not known. (Courtesy the Historical Society of the Downs Carnegie Library)

tiring in 1955. He then taught at Amherst College. John married Lillie Bernhard (born 1886) in 1921 at Lawrence. They had two sons, John, Jr., and Charles. He was the author of many works on economics and conservation, but he is perhaps best known for the book *Sod and Stubble*. John passed away in Lawrence in 1969 at the age of eighty-four and is buried there.

Estelle May Ise (May) graduated from the Kansas State Agricultural College in Manhattan. She was married in 1911 at Lawrence to Felix Gygax (born 1884), who was raised ten miles south of the Ise homestead in the Twin Creek community. Felix graduated from the United States Naval Academy in 1906 and rose through the ranks, serving as rear admiral during World War II.[10] The couple had two sons, Felix, Jr., and Rex. After Felix retired in 1946 the family moved to Rancho Santa Fe, California. Estelle passed away there in 1965, at age seventy-eight.

Mary Rose Ise (Rosina) taught in elementary and high schools in Kansas and Idaho before graduating from the University of Kan-

Aerial view of the Ise farm taken in the 1950s. The buildings look as they did when the Ises lived there four decades earlier. (Photo courtesy Martha Hampton)

sas in 1912. In 1914 she married Merle Holmes (born 1887), a civil engineer, at Lawrence. They had two children, John and Rosemary. Merle served in both world wars and worked for the Santa Fe Railroad for nearly fifty years.[11] After his death Mary moved to Berkeley, California, where she died in May of 1981 at the age of ninety-two.

The nickname of "Happy" was bestowed on Herman Thomas Ise (Happy) by fellow doughboys in the Rainbow Division during World War I. He had an infectious smile and was eternally of remarkable good cheer. He was devoted to his mother, to whom he sent a special delivery letter every Sunday for as long as she lived.[12] He was the second of the Ise children not to go to college. He moved to Greeley, Colorado, in 1911 and first worked as a registered pharmacist. He then joined the Hibbs Clothing Store, which he later managed and then owned. In 1925 he married Edith Stephens (born 1896), with whom he had two children, Mary and Frank. Hap was sixty-nine years old when he died of cancer at Greeley on 1 August 1961.

The youngest of the Ise children, Frank Harold Ise (Dutch) graduated from the University of Kansas in 1917 with a degree in economics, and in 1920 he graduated from the Needles Institute of

The Ise schoolhouse in spring 1995. The trees around the Ise farm buildings can be seen in the background on the right. (Photo courtesy Von Rothenberger)

Optometry. He practiced first in Lawrence before relocating to Wichita in 1925. In 1930 he married Dorothy Davis (born 1904). They had two children, Rosemary and Frank, Jr. Frank continued his practice until his retirement in 1960. He passed away in Wichita in 1974 at the age of seventy-nine.

Rosa Ise (Rosie) settled into her Lawrence home with her family just in time for her daughter Alma's wedding there. She helped her children through school and served as a substitute mother for many of their friends also. At times the house at 1125 Mississippi Street seemed the center of activity for the entire university. John's school chum Alfred Landon came so often that he was considered practically one of the family. Her later years she spent traveling a great deal, and Lawrence's proximity to Holton allowed her to see her relations there often. To her surprise and pleasure, the publication of *Sod and Stubble* made her a celebrity, and she thoroughly enjoyed the number of people who stopped by wishing to pay their respects. Rosa died 2 August 1947 in Lawrence at the age of ninety-one. She was buried in the Downs Cemetery, reunited at last with her beloved Henry.

The Ise homestead stayed in the family for nearly one hundred years. Wilton Edgar (Bill) Bowers was the first tenant, living there with his family from 1909 to 1920, the same year that Frank Ise bought the farm from his mother. A new tenant came, and Sabert and Mertie Hampton and their two children, Irene and Harold Dwight ("Red"), lived on the homestead even longer than the Ises had. In 1947, the Ise school was closed, and the building fell into disuse. In 1965 Frank approached his remaining siblings about selling the farm. It was finally sold to Viola Weeks, on the condition that the Ise children would be allowed to come back and picnic on the farm at least once a year. By 1974 the Weeks family had moved to Downs but retained ownership in the farm.

The farmhouse and school are still standing on their original sites northwest of Downs. Efforts to preserve the school have met with little success but continue to the present day. So for now, the pages of *Sod and Stubble* serve as the only lasting legacy to the Ise family and the homesteading way of life on the Great Plains.

Notes

Editor's Preface

1. John Ise to the Macmillan Company, 21 July 1933, John Ise papers, University Archives, University of Kansas, Lawrence.

Chapter One. A Simple Wedding

1. Henry's homestead was located in the northeast quarter of Section 19, Ross Township, in Osborne County.

2. Henry and Rosie were married by the Reverend B. Hoffman, Evangelical minister of the Unitarian Church in Holton, Kansas. Her friend in attendance was Sophia Maier. In the original 1924 story that Rosie wrote down for John Ise, the load of corn they rode into town with belonged to Rosie's father. After the service, Henry gave the minister a dollar. Later on the trip west to Osborne County, Rosie's brother Chris accompanied them, sleeping beneath the wagon.

3. A mountainous and hilly region of southern Germany, today part of Baden-Württemberg. Henry was born in the town of Sindringen.

4. This was Captain Lindsay H. Carr of Sandwich, Illinois, who enrolled Henry and forty-six others into Company H, 10th Illinois Infantry, on 28 August 1861. Carr was killed during the siege of New Madrid, Missouri, the next year. Taken from Brigadier General J. N. Reece, *Report of the Adjutant General of the State of Illinois, Volume 1* (Springfield, Ill.: Phillips Bros., State Printers, 1900), pp. 509–11.

5. "Dutch" is the English corruption of the German word *deutsche*. German-speaking people in America at this time were thus commonly referred to as "Dutchmen."

6. For more on Henry's war experiences see Chapter 39.

7. In 1866 Henry moved from Illinois to State Center, Iowa, where his sister Kate lived (Mary Lindley Wright, *Prairie Legacy* [N.p.,1981], p. 19). See also Chapter 39.

8. The Neckar River lies in southwestern Germany, rising in the Black Forest and flowing north and west into the Rhine; it is 246 miles long.

9. John and Rosena Haag sailed from Germany to America in July 1852, five years before Henry. They settled near the town of Theresa, Wisconsin, where Rosena Christina Haag, or Rosie, was born 7 October 1855 (Charles Robert Haag, *A Record of the Descendants of John Christopher Haag [1817–1890]* [El Segundo, Calif., 1962], p. 29).

10. Black leg is another name for the black measles, a highly contagious disease.

11. "Children's friend."

12. The soap was for the Joseph Boomer family, who once lived in Holton. See also Chapter 38.

13. Five years Rosie's senior, Christopher Haag, or "Christ," as Rosie usually called him, homesteaded in Western Kansas only a few months before Henry.

Chapter Two. The Hopeful Journey

1. *Grüssen* means "greetings." The German phrase translates as "Farewell, my children, farewell. And write to me when you can."

2. This was probably the Vermillion River; their camp was near the town of Havensville in Pottawatomie County, Kansas.

3. *Corn planter:*—implement that allowed farmers to plant their corn in even rows. *Cultivator:*—horse-drawn plow designed to loosen the soil and kill the weeds between the planted rows in a field. *Fanning mill:*—implement used to clean the grain after harvesting. *Corn sheller:*—device used to separate, or "shell," the corn from the cob.

4. Prairie schooner refers to the famous Conestoga wagon, a broad-wheeled wagon covered with canvas that was used to travel on soft soil and over the prairie. These wagons were built in Conestoga, Pennsylvania.

5. This "creek" was the Big Blue River, which was at very low levels when Henry and Rosie crossed it a mile below where the Little Blue and Black Vermillion Rivers converge to form the Big Blue.

6. This road, a major exodus route for settlers and other travelers, extended west from Atchison for some two hundred and fifty miles. It was so named because it roughly "paralleled" the 40th Parallel, which forms the boundary between Kansas and Nebraska, thirty miles to the north.

7. The ferry mentioned in the text was near the town of Clyde in eastern Cloud County, Kansas.

8. The north and south forks of the Solomon River both rise in extreme Western Kansas and flow east, converging near the town of Glen Elder in Mitchell County. From there the river turns to the southeast and empties into the Smoky Hill River in Dickinson County. Henry and Rosie seem to have come upon the river valley a few miles below the joining of the two forks.

9. The Blue Hills of Osborne and Mitchell Counties at this point rise some three hundred feet above the river valley, eventually reaching a height of eighteen hundred feet above sea level. The principal limestone in the region, of the Greenhorn formation, was widely used by the settlers for building.

10. According to Rosa's notes about the journey, they "camped for the night on Limestone Creek on the west side of the town of Glen Elder."

11. 19 June 1873.

12. Buffalo wallows were crater-shaped holes, being almost perfectly round, fifteen or twenty feet in diameter, with no depth at the outer edge but perhaps two feet deep at the center. They were made by buffalo bulls pawing the sod until it loosened; then they would roll in this loose earth, taking a dust bath in the dry weather or a mud bath after a rain. They did this to protect themselves from tormenting insects and to take off dead hair in the springtime. The same wallows were used over and over again until they became quite deep. As the buffalo became scarce, these depressions became grassed over and can still be found today (see Gladys Buck Enoch, *Osborne County Revisited* [N.p., 1971], p. 21).

13. This saltwater spring was held sacred by many Indian tribes. It was situated on a mound rising twenty-two feet above the valley of the Solomon River. The spring was forty feet across and round at the surface, with natural perpendicular walls. It had been sounded to a depth of four hundred feet with no bottom having ever been found. Trappers and traders used to call it "the Devil's Wash Bowl" (*Cawker City Sentinel,* 15 March 1872). During the 1870s the town of Waconda was founded alongside, and for some time the spring was popular as a tourist attraction and a health spa. In the 1960s the site was inundated by the waters of Waconda Lake.

14. Founded in February 1870, Cawker City was named for Emanuel Harrison Cawker. The Government Land Office, where prospective homesteaders went to file on their claims, was located here from 1872 to 1874. Taken from A. A. Andreas, *History of Kansas,* 2 vols. (Chicago, 1883), pp. 1026–27.

15. Alexander Parker was born in 1829 in New York. He came to Mitchell County, Kansas, in 1870 and started a mercantile business in the town of Cawker City in that year. He was hugely successful, and the store became the largest of its kind in Northern Kansas. In 1878 he also started the first bank in

town. He married his wife, Melissa, in 1847, and they had one son and three daughters—George, Flora, Effie, and Ettie.

Chapter Three. A New Homestead

1. First called Booth's Hill after the man who homesteaded the land around it, this knoll was given its present name of Deck's Hill after the second family to live there (see Chapter 9 n.1).

2. The Homestead Act of 1862 allowed any head of a family, or anyone over twenty-one years of age, to claim 160 acres of government land for their own as long as they lived there and made improvements on it for five years. After the Civil War, special compensation was given to army veterans, whereby their number of years in service would be deducted from the standard five years. Hence Henry, having served three years, was in fact eligible for a patent on his land only three months after his marriage to Rosa.

3. Henry's claim lay in the secondary river bottom, a terrace located between the immediate river bottom and the ascending hills. This nearly level terrace is well suited for grass-related crops such as wheat and corn. The surface soil is a very dark grayish-brown, fifteen inches thick and rich with calcareous particles that give it a very high natural fertility. The subsoil is an additional seventeen inches thick, allowing for a moderate permeability and a high available water capacity. Wells sunk in this terrace average anywhere from ten to fifty feet in depth, allowing for easy access to the water table compared to other areas (U.S. Department of Agriculture, Soil Conservation Service, *Soil Survey of Osborne County, Kansas* [Washington, D.C., 1977], p. 19). Not only did the proximity of Dry and Twelve Mile Creeks to Henry's claim give the Ise family yet another source of water, but the sparse woodlands along the creeks also gave the family access to a wood supply desperately desired by other settlers. Other families that came later were forced to earn a living from poorer land above the hill line, so often they did not prosper as much as Henry and Rosie.

When Henry had his well dug, the "water was found in considerable quantity at twenty feet, but it was more than a year later before the well was walled with stone."—Alma Ise Lindley, in Wright, *Prairie Legacy,* p. 45.

4. Aptly named, Dry Creek cuts southward for ten miles across the western half of Ross Township, emptying into the North Fork Solomon River. Its four-foot-high banks shade a three-foot-wide streambed that a moderate rain can fill very quickly.

5. Frank Hagel was born 17 March 1845 in Bavaria, Germany. He came to America with his parents and four siblings—Frederick, Conrad, Filomina, and Teresia. The Hagels were of the Catholic faith and settled in Sheyboygan

County, Wisconsin. In 1870 Frank and his brother Fred went west to Kansas seeking land; Fred settled near the town of Everest in Brown County, Kansas, and Frank located a claim in the northwest quarter of Section 19 in Ross Township, Osborne County, Kansas.

6. A stout, closely woven cover or pillow filled with straw, husk, or some other material and used in place of a mattress.

7. The plains cottonwood tree (*Populus sargentii*) absorbs large amounts of water to sustain it during times of drought. The amount of water held in the wood of freshly cut, or "green," cottonwood lumber makes it warp much more than other kinds of wood.

Chapter Four. The Neighbors

1. The country within a six-mile radius of Henry's claim offered a diverse and informative assortment of the people and cultures then settling in Western Kansas. A mile to the west of the Ises was a colony of "town- and city-bred Yankees" from New England. Grouped around Henry's and Frank Hagel's claims were many German or German-speaking farmers whom Henry, and particularly Rosie, already had acquaintance with, as many of them had either passed through or had lived for a time in the Holton, Kansas, area. To the northeast was the Dutch colony of Rotterdam, with its own unique language and culture, while just two miles to the north was the Rose Valley community, which was founded by German-speaking Swiss. The city of Osborne, twelve miles away and the county seat, was started by a colony of German-speaking Pennsylvanians from the Reading-Lancaster region. Even among the German-speaking settlers there was confusion, as many different dialects of German were represented. A variety of religious faiths abounded: Roman Catholics, Evangelical Lutherans, Dutch Reformed, Congregationalists, Baptists, Methodists, Moravians, and others. This caused unexpected problems, often with unique solutions. A case in point was the Rose Valley Church, which for many years offered separate services and Sunday schools conducted in both German and English.

2. Nickname for the Disciples of Christ, followers of Alexander Campbell (1788–1866). In 1832 Campbell helped form the Christian Church.

3. The majority of the people who settled in Ross Township were members of the Republican Party. Doctor A. B. Collins, mentioned here, was indeed the only member of the Democratic Party in the region at this time.

"Doctor Collins was a middle-aged man, rumored to have killed someone in Kentucky; had a nice young wife. Was killed by sawed log in October 1872. Mrs. Collins had ten children; she gave the older ones money to buy farms, but they gambled it away within three months. A sheriff came from

Kentucky, but he [Collins] was dead by then."—F. M. Wells recollections to John Ise.

4. The New Haven and Hartford Colony was formed in January 1871 for the purpose of establishing a colony in Western Kansas. Sixty-five members were recruited from various cities in Connecticut and Rhode Island. Pamphlets passed out among the recruited families told of the ample stores and provisions available, and of the houses and lumberyards already built and waiting on the colony lands, which ran along either side of Twelve Mile Creek in Osborne County. When the settlers arrived, they found one crude cabin of cottonwood logs "and were laughed at when they asked where the colony lands were" (*Smith County Pioneer*, 9 April 1908). The colony was an illusion. Few of these colonists were farmers, and within five years most had left.

5. As long as its name, Twelve Mile Creek rises in southeastern Smith County, Kansas, and flows south to empty into the North Fork Solomon River in eastern Bethany Township, Osborne County, Kansas. For a time it straddles the boundary of the townships of Bethany and Ross.

6. Wilson and Frances Athey's real names were Wiley and Elizabeth Jones. Wiley Wilson Jones was born 3 November 1846 in Cedar County, Missouri, the youngest child of ten. His father and his brother John went to California in 1849 in search of gold. Thomas Jones was killed there in 1853, and John died at age fifteen of yellow fever. The mother kept the family together, moving them to Iowa. There, on 8 March 1866, Wiley married Elizabeth Walker. The couple moved to Jackson County, Missouri, then headed west. Wiley located a homestead in the southwest quarter of Section 17 in Ross Township, Osborne County, in 1871.

The first house was a dugout with two rooms, in which six people lived. In 1883 Wiley had constructed the Big House, as it came to be called. The Big House cost $2,500 and was two stories high with fifteen rooms, an attic, a finished basement, and no closets. The sixteenth room was an immense kitchen measuring twenty-four feet square.

The Joneses needed the space to feed their fourteen children—Cordelia, Frances, John, Harvey, Nathan and Marion (twins), Sarah, Laura, Clara, Martha, Maude, Alice, Anna (Arlie), and Arthur (Zeke). In order to care for such a large family, Wiley engaged in many activities. In addition to farming, he drove freight wagons to Russell, Waterville, and Red Cloud, Nebraska. He was a mechanic of rare ability and had an early threshing machine of his own design. In 1879 he entered into a partnership with H. D. Washburn, opening an implement business in the new town of Downs. Wiley Jones was a highly moral man, never "tippling" or smoking. After his wife died during a visit to California, he leased the Big House and bought a farm south of Downs along the South Fork Solomon River, where he ran a forty-acre orchard and truck farm. He remarried but quickly divorced. He died in 1931, and his six-page, handwritten will urged his children to "join in a unity in spirit and friendship."

7. George and Lizzie Graeber were really Joseph and Rosa Boomer. Joseph Boomer was born 25 December 1845 at Pfortsheim, Baden, Germany. In 1852 he moved with his parents, Barnard and Mary, and his brother John to America, settling in Greensburg, Pennsylvania, where the two brothers worked in a carriage factory, painting buggies. Here his father remarried and a half-brother, Frank, was born in 1854. He married Rosa Sollner (born 1845) in 1868, and they moved to the town of Holton, in Jackson County, Kansas. In 1872 the Boomers moved onto a homestead located in the southwestern quarter of Section 18 in Ross Township, Osborne County, across the road to the north from the claims of Frank Hagel and Henry Ise. They had two children—Sarah and Frank.

Pennsylvania Dutch are descendants of immigrants to Pennsylvania in the seventeenth and eighteenth centuries from southwestern Germany and Switzerland. Lancaster County, Pennsylvania, is the center of the largest and most famous Pennsylvania Dutch region.

8. Christopher Gottlieb Haag was born 19 November 1847 at Kleinbottwar, Württemberg, Germany. He came with his parents to America—first to Wisconsin, then to near Holton in Jackson County, Kansas. In 1872 he ventured out to Osborne County, where he took a homestead in the south half of Section 24 of Bethany Township. He struck up an acquaintance with Henry Ise, who had staked a claim a mile to the east, and brought him back with him to the Holton area during the winter of 1872, where Henry soon became intrigued with Christopher's sister Rosena. Christopher married Louisa Agnes Wehmeier on 4 May 1872 at Holton. Louisa had been born 19 February 1853 at Deilingen, Westphalia, Germany. She came to the United States with her parents in 1869, also settling near Holton. The Haags were members of the Evangelical Lutheran Church and had five sons—Albert, Theodore, Frederick, Henry, and Otto.

9. Jacob Hunker was born in Württemberg, Germany, 12 October 1837. He came to America in 1869, staying for a year at Holton, Kansas. In 1868 he married Maria Maier. In 1870 they homesteaded a farm located in the northeast quarter of Section 24 in Bethany Township, Osborne County. There were five children—John George, Jacob, Mary, Katie, and Ida. After the death of their daughter Katie in 1878, the Hunkers moved to Falls City, Nebraska, where Jacob died on 14 February 1915.

"Hunker was the man Pa went down to Holton with the year before Mother married him. Hunker worked for Arnold—Mrs. Arnold a Hunker. Pa worked for Hunker, too."—John Ise notes.

10. Katie was the daughter of Jacob and Maria (Mary) Hunker. She was born in 1873 on the family homestead along Twelve Mile Creek near Downs.

Her tragic death occurred in 1878, not shortly after Rosie's arrival in the neighborhood in 1873 as is implied.

"It was about this time that Jake Hunker's little daughter—half a mile west of my father's—fell over the creek bank and broke her neck. Wiley Jones happened to pass by a short time afterward and they brought her out to him, and he worked with her for a while, but of course could do nothing. The nearest doctor was more than ten miles away, so none was called. Jones made a little coffin for her, and the girl was buried on a knoll near the creek, where her grave was later forgotten, as were the graves of a great many of the people buried out there the first years."—John Ise notes.

11. A machine used for cutting grain and binding it into bundles, once widely used on grain such as wheat.

12. As can be seen in many places in the text, there was an innate distrust in the Ise neighborhood of all preachers—and perhaps none more than those of the Baptist persuasion. The Reverend Apollos Phelps Viets, born in Granby, Connecticut, on 20 September 1819, is a striking example. Contrary to the portrayal of him in the text, he was an intelligent and respected man, self-taught in geography, botany, trigonometry, Latin, and Greek. He was ordained in Canton, Connecticut, and served at churches in Milford and at Hancock, Massachusetts. In 1848 he married Henrietta Louisa Webster, who was born 11 June 1830 at Bethlehem, Connecticut. They had six children—Ellsworth, Wordsworth, John, Mary, Beulah, and Henrietta.

"In 1870 a plan was conceived for the settlement of a community in Kansas, called the New Haven Colony. By request and inclination I went out to avail myself of the government offer of a homestead to those who would accept one. The opportunity seemed good for one to till the ground, do gospel work among the pioneers, and secure a good home and refuge for old age. The colony scheme was failure, but the country good. I enjoyed four years of pioneer life on the prairie, and organized a Baptist Church. For family reasons, and much to my regret, I was compelled to return East."—The Reverend Apollos Phelps Viets in his autobiographical sketch, in Dorothy Dean Viets Schell, *A Viets Genealogy: Dr. John Viets and His Descendants* (Baltimore: Gateway Press, 1990), pp. 111–14.

13. Jessie Bender and his wife were in reality E. F. and Lucy Booth. E. F. (born 1835) and his wife Lucy (born 1834) homesteaded in the southwest quarter of Section 17 in Ross Township, Osborne County, in the early 1870s and later bought the homestead of the Reverend Viets. The Booths had three children—Homer, Elisha, and William.

"Booth a lawless man, alright if he liked you, but dangerous otherwise. Never dependable or frank and sincere. He was rude to us."—Rosa Ise notes to John Ise.

14. His real name was Stephen Young. He was born 4 December 1848 in

Aappeledinging, Luxembourg. He was christened in the Catholic Church and came to America with his parents in 1856, settling at Fort Washington, Wisconsin, where he grew up working in the Lake Superior copper mines. In 1871 he went to Marysville, Kansas, and later that year moved to Ross Township, Osborne County, taking out a homestead in the northwest quarter of Section 32. For two years he labored without a horse and made several trips to Marysville, where he worked for Henry Hudson, a miller. He married Phoebe Hewitt on 13 November 1877. They had six children—Elizabeth, Joseph, Jennie, Mabel, Thomas, and Mary. In 1891 the family leased the farm and moved back to Wisconsin, but returned three years later. Stephen passed away on his farm 9 December 1915 and was buried in the Downs Cemetery.

"Pa and Hagel and Steve Young, Philip Fink, and another man who had Yost's place [John Owen] bached together during the winter of 1871 and 1872. Once several fellows wanted to camp at night—and these boys were trying to hang Philip Fink—but those fellows got out very quickly."—Rosa Ise notes to John Ise.

15. During this storm the men baching together on the Ise claim "stretched a wire from Hagel's log cabin to our stable, so that the men wouldn't get lost."—Rosa Ise notes to John Ise.

16. James W. Terry came to the town of Waconda in Mitchell County, Kansas, in the fall of 1871. He formed a partnership with Colonel W. C. Whitney in a sawmill and lumbering business. After leaving Waconda, Terry and his wife homesteaded land in the northwest quarter of Section 6 in Corinth Township, Osborne County. "Terry has enclosed his large stone house and about one acre of land with a solid stone fence, which makes it like a castle. It is situated one hundred and fifty feet above the valley," reported the *Osborne County Farmer* in its 13 May 1880 issue. Shortly after the completion of this imposing house the Terrys abandoned it and moved to Lyons, Kansas.

"Jim Terry, who had started the little town of Waconda, a mile south of Cawker City, was forced to leave on account of the town being broken up by Colonel E. H. Cawker, John J. Huckle, R. G. F. Kshinka, and Captain A. A. Thomas. They spent $60,000, mostly furnished by Colonel Cawker's father's estate. Then Terry built a house on a big bluff southwest of where Downs now stands. He calculated to drill an artesian well, so drilled but got no water. He left the bluff, but stayed long enough to give it the permanent name of Terry's Bluff."—F. M. Wells recollections to John Ise.

Chapter Five. The First Months in the Log Cabin

1. The 1876 presidential campaign was between the Republican Party candidate Rutherford B. Hayes and his Democratic opponent Samuel A.

Tilden. Tilden garnered the popular vote in the subsequent election, but Hayes won the electoral vote, and thus the presidency.

2. "May 16th, 1873—Mrs. Beal and two children drowned. River higher than ever before known." "May 23, 1873—Ella Beal found this morning on the school land in a drift pile. Ella found at two p.m." "July 15, 1873—One of the Beal children finally found. Funeral was that afternoon."—Rosa Ise notes to John Ise.

The father, John Beal, made it across the river and ran for help, but it was too late. He later married the widow of Doctor Collins, who had died at about the same time as John Beal's wife and the children.

3. The lone Democrat was the Doctor Collins mentioned in note 2. "We voted in 1872 in Cole Young's dugout, about a dozen of us. Eleven of us voted for Grant, one Democrat voted for Greeley. Two weeks later, the Democrat accidently rolled a sawed log over himself and killed him. We did not have another Democrat until 1874, when one Isaac Cross came."—F. M. Wells recollections to John Ise.

4. Tipp's real name was Sidney Pitt, Sr. He was born in England in 1830. In the fall of 1870 he went from Peoria, Illinois, to Ross Township, locating a claim in the southeast quarter of Section 13. His wife, Sarah, was also born in England, in 1837. They were married in 1855 and were the parents of seven children—William, Elizabeth, Mary, Lucy, John, Bell, and Sidney, Jr. After Sidney's death in 1873 the family remained on the homestead, William (then sixteen) taking over supervision of the farm. Sarah Pitt died in 1923 and was buried beside her husband in the Oak Dale Cemetery in rural eastern Ross Township.

"On July 29, 1873, Sidney Pitt was accidently shot through the heart in his blacksmith shop. He had his rifle lying on the bellows and when he moved the bellows the rifle fell off, the shot killing him instantly. His widow was left with six small children. When he was buried, the preacher said, he 'didn't love his Lord.' Sid Chapin objected—said Pitt was a Universalist. Said Pitt was a good man. Nearly had a fight about it!"—F. M. Wells recollections to John Ise.

5. Sidney Pitt, Jr., was born only a few months after the death of his father. He married Sarah Hill, who was born in 1878. Sidney died in 1935, and Sarah passed away six years later. They were both buried in the Oak Dale Cemetery in eastern Ross Township.

6. "Strangely indeed it may seem, there were very few deaths in child birth, only one that I learned of, in my father's neighborhood, that of Mrs. Cox. This happened in July of 1873. It is said that she was buried in the forenoon and her husband John called a dance that night."—John Ise notes.

7. Nathan and Marion Jones were born in 1873.

8. The McConkeys were in reality the Huff family, one of the more colorful families in the region. William C. (born 20 February 1815) and Mary Francis (born 22 May 1818) Huff came from Indiana in 1872 to a homestead in the southwest quarter of Section 20, Ross Township, in Osborne County, Kansas, that was filed on for them by their son Allen. There were ten sons altogether and four daughters, one of whom passed away when only an infant. The boys were big and rough, as described in this list of their names by Rosa Ise: "There was Kittie; Mrs. Daniels next—killed by a sand burr; Wellman— went to the pen, stole some cattle down south; Jim; Andy—got shot in a card game, was overbearing and foul-mouthed fellow; Allen—demented, got killed stealing a train ride; Clint—died a natural death; the twins, Little Lon— went to the pen for stealing mules—and Big; and sweet Pell."

William Huff was the area blacksmith, opening a shop in Downs when the town was founded in 1879. He ran this shop for many years until he sold it to H. D. Washburn and retired. William died in 1899, his wife passing away two years later. They were both interred in the Downs Cemetery.

The oldest children were the twins Leonidas and Alonzo, called Big and Little Lon. They were born in Indiana on 16 September 1847 and after coming to Kansas selected homesteads in the northern half of Section 5 of Corinth Township in Osborne County. They farmed their land until their deaths, Big in 1907 and Lon in 1915. They were buried with their parents in the Downs Cemetery.

Big Huff was "a likeable enough fellow," commented one person to Hulda Ise. "He's always wearin' khaki clothes and rides around here like a calvary officer. Big's swearin' ain't really meant to be offensive; it just takes the place of the periods and commas you teach the kids, and brightens up his collection of words" (Bartley F. Yost, *The Yost Family* [N.p., 1928], pp. 24–25).

Next among the children was Allen W. Huff. He died in 1884 at the age of thirty-one while working at the trainyard in Gaylord, Kansas. He was also buried in the Downs Cemetery. After Allen came Josephus (born 1856) and Wellman. Wellman K. Huff was born near Wabash, Indiana, on 9 April 1860. After living in Downs for most of his life, he moved to New Mexico in 1914. He died in Ventura, California, in 1940. Next in line were James W., Andy, and Clinton B. Huff (born 1863). Clint married Julia Monhague and moved to Blackwell, Oklahoma, where he died in 1933. There were also three daughters—Lavina, Kittie, and Marcella, known as Pell. Lavina married the Huff's neighbor Ezra Daniels. Marcella was born in 1857 and passed away in 1936. She was buried in the family plot in the Downs Cemetery.

9. The words to the song "My Western Home," now known as "Home on the Range," were written by Dr. Brewster Higly in the early 1870s. About

1873 Dan Kelly and Cal Harlan collaborated on the music, and they began performing the song locally. In 1947 it became the state song of Kansas.

"My parents were invited down to the Huffs for a musicale by the Harlan Bros. Orchestra, Harlan being a settlement about twenty miles up the river and named for the Harlan family. As nearly as we can figure dates, it was the fall of the 'grasshopper year,' 1874. To my mother it was a remarkable experience. She'd been so music hungry and the Harlans played, she thought, beautifully. But the things that carried in her mind were the two new songs, 'Oh give me home where the buffalo roam, And the deer and the antelope play,' and 'Silver Threads Among the Gold.' "—Alma Ise Lindley, in Wright, *Prairie Legacy,* p. 29.

10. A kind of custard.

11. The much-loved and respected Christian Baertsch was born in Seewis, Switzerland, on 20 January 1835. There, on 5 March 1857, he met and married Ursula Sutter. Three children were born to the German-speaking couple while there—Leonard, Christena, and Anna. A fourth child, Fred, was born during a brief stay in Germany. In 1868 the family emigrated to America, settling near Sauk City, Wisconsin, where two more children were born—George and Louisa. By 1872 the Baertsches were ready to move again, this time to Jackson County, Kansas. There they were converted and joined the Evangelical Church and met many of the families that were soon settling farther west—the Boomers, Sollners, Lutzes, and Rosie's family, the Haags. Soon the Baertsches also headed west, claiming a homestead in the southwest quarter of Section 6 in Ross Township, Osborne County, where three more children were born—Rosetta, Minnie, and Rosena. They were charter members in the Rose Valley Church and instrumental in forming the Rose Valley School District.

"Ma homesick at first. Coopers were there, great people to let everything run. One Sunday morning Pa was chasing Cooper's mules away and one kicked him—knocked him insensible. Cooper's hogs and everything ran loose."—Annie (Baertsch) Sellers' note to John Ise, John Ise papers, University Archives, University of Kansas. The Coopers were Edwin and Jane Cooper, who lived next to the Baertsches on the west in Section 1 of Bethany Township.

12. The Reverend John J. Bauer was born on 9 May 1833 at Swinford, Pennsylvania. He had changed his last name to Bowers by the time he married Christiana Sechler on 15 May 1855. Christiana had been born in 1836 in Mifflinburg, Pennsylvania. They had eleven children altogether—Mary (Kate), Margaret, John, Orpheus, Martha, Susannah, Wilton, Lydia, Lemuel, Bessie, and Florence. The Bowers moved from Pennsylvania to Illinois to Iowa before finally moving to Kansas in 1872.

"Bowers place first owned by Pickett—Bowers bought Pickett's rights about 1874. Pickett a cattleman; had nicer things than the rest of us. From back east."—Rosa Ise's notes to John Ise.

Bowers also homesteaded more land in Sections 7 and 8 of Ross Township in Osborne County. He was a licensed preacher in the United Brethren Church, and the first meeting of the Rose Valley Church was held in his dugout on the Bowers farm. Reverend Bowers is found elsewhere in the text under the name of Higginbotham. His actual last name was probably included in the text by mistake.

13. The incident mentioned here happened, not to Henry and Rosie, but to their neighbors George and Eliza Sollner.

"Sollners had dinner one day. Indians hunting something to eat. Aunt Louisa was helping Mrs. Sollner get dinner. Preacher to be there; Sollner getting him. Indians came in—asked for something to eat. Sollner saw them coming and turned back. Gave them a loaf of bread with butter on it—wouldn't eat it. Got a gun out of the closet. Wouldn't shoot, but Indians went out when Sollner pointed gun at them. Didn't want butter. A fifth Indian came in and said others were bad Indians, and he took half loaf."—John Ise notes of George Sollner tale.

14. Butter made from the rind of the citron fruit.

15. The post office originally established for the New Haven and Hartford Colony was named LeGrand after the colony's president, LeGrand Stone. LeGrand was established 2 June 1871 in John Burns' log cabin on Twelve Mile Creek in Bethany Township. On 5 August 1872 the post office was moved to Leander Bell's cabin and the name was changed to New Arcadia. On 30 September 1872 the Reverend Apollos P. Viets became the postmaster, and New Arcadia was located in his dugout on the east bank of Twelve Mile Creek in Ross Township (U.S. Postal Department, *Record of United States Postmasters, Volume 40* [Washington, D.C.: U.S. Postal Department, 1879], pp. 722 and 1122).

16. "Old Viets had his post office over by the creek west of Bloomers, but he got into trouble with Booth, who threatened to kill him, and he presently left. Pa had been his assistant postmaster, and he brought his stuff, boxes, etc., up and told Pa to take care of it, then disappeared. Pa kept it for some time. Booth then got the Viets place somehow."—Rosa Ise notes to John Ise.

The Reverend Apollos Phelps Viets may or may not have been chased off his claim by E. F. Booth. After leaving Kansas, Viets returned to Connecticut and rented his land in Kansas to Booth. In 1877 Viets received his patent on the homestead property and the next year sold it to Booth. Viets became a correspondent for the *New England Weekly Review* and contributed numerous articles to other publications, including the *Christian Advocate*. His best-known works include "Voice of the Departed," "The Cloud-Veiled Throne," and "He

Giveth His Beloved Sleep," a poem written after his eightieth year and widely reprinted (Dorothy Dean Viets Schell, *A Viets Genealogy* [Baltimore, Md.: Gateway Press, 1990] p. 113). Viets passed away 19 January 1908 in Waterbury, Connecticut, and was buried there. His wife Henrietta died in 1923.

17. Henry was confirmed postmaster by the United States Postal Department on 8 July 1874 (U.S. Postal Department, *Record of the United States Postmasters*, p. 722). This position provided him and Rosie with a small but steady source of income that other settlers did not have.

18. Henry's primary duties were to hold judgment on minor disagreements and to grant marriage licenses.

19. This plow, designed in the 1840s, weighed around 125 pounds and had a much longer cutting surface than earlier plows. It was made specifically to turn the tough prairie sod completely over, thus exposing the roots and thoroughly killing the grass.

20. "Oh, the devil!"

Chapter Six. The Mad Wolf

1. Mart Starling's real name was Martin Stirewalt. Martin was born in 1844 and with his wife, Martha (born 1849), homesteaded the northwest quarter of Section 17 in Ross Township, Osborne County, by 1873. They had three children—Walter, Verzile, and Ethel Maude. By 1895 the Stirewalts had sold their claim and moved to California. There they located a homestead near Kingsbury and then later moved to the town of Pixley.

Oak Creek rises in eastern Smith County and flows southeast for twenty-three miles before emptying into the North Fork Solomon River just to the west of where the town of Cawker City, Kansas, now stands.

2. The episode of the mad wolf took place a year before Henry married Rosie. Nebraska was the son of William and Elizabeth Stevens. He was the eldest child, being born in February 1856 in the state he was named after. His father and mother were both born in 1835 in Ohio. In the 1850s the family moved first to Nebraska and then to Kansas in 1871, claiming a homestead in Mitchell County along Oak Creek two miles above its confluence with the South Fork Solomon River. In May 1872 a mad wolf appeared along the creek and bit two boys, Nebraska and a boy with the last name of Wolters.

"The other young man who was bitten by the wolf, had 'taken up' a claim, but he left for Ohio at once. He never returned and his fate to this day is unknown. Within a short time symptoms of hydrophobia were noticeable in a number of horses, cattle, hogs, and dogs, all of which were killed. It was the unerring aim of John King Belk that made the beast bite dirt."—*Downs Times*, 3 September 1908.

Nebraska's parents took him to St. Joseph, Missouri, for treatment, but the physician said that the bite was not severe enough and that he would be alright. Soon after they returned, however, he contracted rabies and was seized by violent spasms. Except for his oldest brother, the rest of the family was sent away for safety as men in the area tried to take care of him. After hours of constant agony he passed away and was buried on the homestead.

His parents moved the family to a homestead in Section 12 of Cawker Township in Mitchell County, where the father engaged in farming and stock raising. They had nine other children—Lotetia, W. H., Albert, John, Alonzo, Isaac, William, Olin, and Rosa. William Stevens died 21 July 1892, and his wife passed away the following October. They were buried in the Prairie Grove Cemetery north of Cawker City, and Nebraska was reburied next to them.

See also John C. Stephenson, *Downs Did It* (Osborne, Kans.: Osborne County Farmer, 1978), p. 38.

3. A concretion of matted hair and hardened mucus taken from the stomach of an animal that was used, often successfully, in the treatment of rabies. The stone was placed on the wound and "drew out" the disease. It had to be able to cover the whole wound to be effective; in Nebraska Stevens' case, the bite was too large and no stone of that size could be obtained.

4. John's real name was John Schoen. He was born 28 August 1841 in Ferril, Germany. He worked on the family farm until the age of sixteen, when he and a sister set sail for America to join a brother and other relatives in Illinois. He enlisted in Company F, Third Illinois Cavalry, during the Civil War, serving two years and nine months. Upon his discharge he was made a citizen of the United States. He then freighted supplies from Omaha to Denver, later helping lay track for the Union Pacific Railroad in Utah. His earnings from this enabled him to buy a farm in Nemaha County, Nebraska, near the town of Johnson. There he met and married Emma Yelkin on 30 December 1868. In 1872 the family moved to a homestead located four miles above the mouth of Oak Creek in Cawker Township, Mitchell County, Kansas. John and Emma raised eight children—Harm, John Jr., Albert, Will, Henry, Mary, Lydia, and Edward. The farm was prosperous and the family happy for many years. John was known for his generosity in helping his fellow settlers cope with life on the prairie. He passed away on 6 May 1919. Emma died 10 September 1941.

Chapter Seven. Horse Thieves

1. A relinquishment was a way that one could renounce the claim on one's homestead early, thereby allowing it to be sold and freeing the home-

steader of his obligations under the Homestead Act of 1862. These relinquishments were then made available to prospective buyers.

2. This well-traveled trail took the settlers from Russell north across the Saline River and over hills to the town of Waldo, then east to Luray. Then they would follow the courses of Paradise and Wolf Creeks north and west into Osborne County; after crossing over a short divide at the head of Wolf Creek, they would pick the course of Covert Creek as it flowed to the northeast and then cross the South Fork Solomon River at Osborne. Following the crests of divides northeast of Osborne, they would come to the North Fork Solomon River, which they could cross at the State Ford and so come into the Ise neighborhood.

3. It was customary to tie a rope or rawhide hobble to the front legs of a horse at night, limiting its mobility to a walk.

4. Green Oldacre was "very bad—lived on John Hicks place, used to let horse thieves stay with him. Posse organized in 1874 or 1875. Sheriff didn't handcuff horse thief that got shot, and lost him at the Little Blue River near Waterville. He managed to arrest Oldacre. William Belk bailed him out; he tried to run Blankenship out of country for his services."—John Ise notes on F. M. Wells recollections.

5. Martin Rychel was the son of John Rychel, who came to Osborne County in 1871. They settled in the Dutch community of Rotterdam, selecting a homestead in the south half of Section 2 of Ross Township.

"John Rychel traveled to Abilene in a covered wagon with the Sneller family; took a week to make it to Cawker City. Made Peter Kramer's home Rotterdam, where the Indians saw our campfire. They came to the house by two's, each couple talking English, saying 'me good Indian, Pawnee something to eat'; took our dead dogs and chickens and ate them, the braves taking the hams and the squaws and papooses the entrails."—Mrs. James Deters in the *Beloit Daily Call*, 23 January 1951.

6. "In the early days, white men stole our horses as well as Indians. We formed a vigilance committee and would capture them sometimes and use them pretty rough. We shot one at Green Oldacre's place. He in turn shot Martin Rychel through the body. Rychel very nearly died from the wound. The horse thief got away from the sheriff; Rychel slow in recovering, and other man spit blood a lot for a long time, too. Remember, we had no railroads and no way of communicating with the outside world nearer than Waterville or Solomon City. We had to take the law in our own hands for a time at least, but in '79 the railroad came and telegraph lines were established and since that time we could always catch the horse thief, which is not many now. There are very few horses to steal and the thieves want autos now anyhow."—F. M. Wells recollections to John Ise.

Chapter Eight. The Bright-Eyed Baby

1. Mary Bartsch's real name was Ursula Baertsch, and she was the wife of Christian Baertsch. Born Ursula Sutter in the village of Shriers, Switzerland, on 25 April 1834, she married Christian in 1857 in Switzerland. The mother of ten children, Ursula came with her husband to America in 1868, living in Wisconsin and Jackson County, Kansas, before settling in Osborne County in 1872. Despite the hardships of pioneer life and of raising a large family, she lived a long life; she passed away in Downs on 16 March 1917 and was buried next to her husband in the Rose Valley Cemetery in rural Ross Township.

2. Daughters of Christian and Ursula Baertsch.

3. The text uses the middle names whenever mentioning Henry and Rosie's children. Their first child, Henry Albert Ise, was born on the homestead on 15 March 1874. He was named after Rosie's youngest brother, Henry Albert Haag, who also died young (see Chapter 38).

"Mrs. Henry Wehmeier helped deliver Albert, Alma, Ed, and Doll. For Charles, Walt, and Hulda, didn't have anyone. Later, Mrs. Deck helped when I was low with John and Mrs. Hunker and Mrs. Baertsch helped with Estelle. No one also for Mary or Tom; and for Frank, had Dr. Dildine, because I was sick so long."—Rosa Ise notes to John Ise.

4. Site of the 1874 Fourth of July celebration, Stone's Grove later became known as Baertsch Grove.

5. Henry Albert Ise died 24 July 1874. When his father passed away in 1900, the baby was reburied in the family plot in the Downs Cemetery.

"Mr. Bowers preached a little sermon at the house, and some of the neighbors were there. He wasn't dead a half hour before he turned black behind the ears, and the next morning was dark all over, where anything touched him. So we buried him that forenoon over in a corner of the yard and the next spring planted a little ash at the head of his grave. Mr. Jones made a cute little coffin, of cottonwood; scraped it with glass, so it was right neat, and shaped like a coffin. Pa later allowed him $1.00 for making the coffin. Neighbors dug the grave for us.

Sollners, Mr. and Mrs., sat up the night before he was buried. Pa and I were so tired from several nights up with him that we slept, right there in the same room with them and him, until morning.

Buried him at 11 o'clock and we ate a little dinner and cut corn (Pa and I) until evening, ate supper and milked, etc., and then went out and cut until midnight or later. . . . Awfully lonesome after Albert died, for a while, but one gets used to anything."—Rosa Ise notes to John Ise.

Chapter Nine. Grasshoppers

1. Wetzel's real name was Frederick H. Deck. Deck was born 5 February 1832 in Chambersburg, Pennsylvania, to Christian and Catherine Deck. He married Charlotte Brake (born 1833) on 14 February 1856. Charlotte gave birth to four children—Sarah, Anna, Hanna, and William—in Pennsylvania before the family moved west, settling in Sterling, Illinois, in 1865. Here the last two children were born—David and Eva. They moved yet again in the fall of 1873, this time to a farm located in the southeast quarter of Section 17 in Ross Township of Osborne County, Kansas. Fred farmed and worked as a freighter for merchants in Cawker City, traveling long distances to such places as Russell and Waterville, both in Kansas, and Hastings, Nebraska. Once he even went to Colorado and worked for the Denver & Rio Grande Railroad while the family took care of the homestead (*Downs News*, 8 February 1906). The Decks were deeply religious people and were charter members of the Rose Valley Church (in 1874) and the Downs Congregational Church. Fred was also a stockholder in a variety of enterprises: a grist mill, a cooperative elevator, the First National Bank in Downs, and Downs Business College. Fred died in 1912, four years after his wife, and they were buried in the Oak Dale Cemetery east of Downs.

Chapter Ten. Two Letters

1. These families left Iowa for Jackson County, Kansas, around the same time that Henry filed for his homestead. Their descendants still live in the Holton area.

2. "You won't forget that."

3. George and Kate were Christian and Catherine Riemenschneider. Christian was born in 1833 in Brunswick, Germany. He emigrated to America in 1855, settling in Illinois. In 1860 he married Catherine Eisenmanger, the sister of Henry Ise, who was born 10 May 1838 in Sindringen, Württemberg, Germany. The Riemenschneiders moved to Marshall County, Iowa, during the Civil War, homesteading 260 acres near the town of State Center (*Marshalltown Times-Republican*, October 1921). They had eleven children—Alfred, Clara, Henry, George, Clara, Emma, Anna, Wilbur, Charles, John, and Laura. Christian died 13 June 1885 on the farm. Catherine passed away 11 October 1921. Both were buried in the Hillside Cemetery north of State Center.

4. John Eisenmanger was Henry Ise's brother. He was born 8 February 1833 in Sindringen, Germany, and emigrated to America around 1850, settling first in Utica, New York. For more on John, see Chapter 39.

5. Minnie was Wilhelmina Christina Haag, Rosie's sister. She was born 12 September 1857 at Theresa, Wisconsin. In 1878 she married John George Hinnen, who was in the harness and saddlery trade in Holton. She died 23 October 1904 at Holton; her husband died in 1930. They were buried in the Holton Cemetery. (Charles Robert Haag, *A Record of the Descendants of John Christopher Haag, 1812–1890* [El Segundo, Calif., 1962], p. 43).

6. Sedley (Sid) E. Chapin was born 1853 to Samuel and Lydia Chapin. The family went to Osborne County in 1873, homesteading the northwest quarter of Section 13 in Ross Township. In 1878 Sid married Elizabeth Jan Farher, taking a homestead in southeast Jewell County. They had six children—Lydia, Gladys, Florence, Pearl, Blanche, and Brad. Sid farmed and wrote many articles for area newspapers. He died in 1947.

7. Alice Jones was the daughter of Wiley and Elizabeth Jones. She was born 15 October 1884 at the family homestead in Ross Township and passed away 28 August 1885. She was buried in the Downs Cemetery.

8. His name was Carl David Eugene Haag, a brother of Rosie, also known as "Ike." He was born 19 November 1853 near Theresa, Wisconsin. He spent his life farming in the Holton area. He married Christina Knoll in 1881. They had ten children—Carl, Cora, Harmon, Lorena, Elsie, Nelle, Mary, Hannah, Minnie, and Joseph.

Chapter Eleven. Grasshopper Relief

1. The party was held at the home of John and Mary Russell, who had homesteaded the southwest quarter of Section 24 in Bethany Township.

2. George Sizer's real name was George Sollner. George's father was born in Byron, Germany, his mother in Wittenberg, Germany. They went to Greensburg, Pennsylvania, where George was born 6 July 1847. The family moved to Holton, Kansas, in 1866, and George worked as a boot and shoe cobbler. He married Eliza Haas on 15 August 1872 in Holton, and they settled on a homestead in Sections 13 and 24 of Bethany Township, Osborne County. They had two sons, Jacob (born 1878) and Clyde (born 1888). In 1902 the Sollners moved into Downs, where George continued his occupation as a shoe cobbler. He died 13 December 1928 and was buried in the Downs Cemetery.

3. John Frederick Fink was born 27 December 1844 in Württemberg, Germany. He came to America in 1865, stopping in New York before moving on to Letts, Iowa, where he met and married Katherine Blankenhorn (born 1851) on 5 March 1868. Their first two children, Rosa and Lizzie, were born here. In 1871 they moved to Bethany Township in Osborne County, on a homestead in Section 21.

"John Fink and family came here in time to celebrate Christmas in 1871. They lived in a dugout fifteen feet square on the old homestead. Their Christmas dinner consisted of buffalo meat and corn bread, and the corn bread was a pretty expensive thing, too. Corn meal brought $4.00 a hundred weight, and flour sold at $7.00. All of it was hauled by teams from Marysville."—*Osborne County Farmer*, 29 December 1910.

In 1880 the Finks moved to a new homestead located in the northwest quarter of Section 23 in Bethany Township. Here nine more children were raised—Henry, Lillie, William, Charles, David, Frank, Albert, Clarence, and Floyd. John Fink died 6 January 1914 at Houston, Texas. He and his wife were buried in the Downs Cemetery.

4. Forester was the Reverend Richard Baxter Foster. Foster helped found what is now Lincoln University in Jefferson City, Missouri, before arriving in Osborne, Kansas, on 16 May 1872. He had walked the forty-five miles from Russell carrying two heavy suitcases. His wife was Lucy Reed, with whom he raised ten children—Walter, Festus, Richard, Frank, Luard, Charles, Guy, Edwin, Alice, and Grace. Pastor of the Congregational Church, Foster was an extremely respected minister. Rumors concerning his alleged misuse of relief funds stemmed from his building a three-story stone house atop the divide two miles north of Osborne, overlooking both the North and South Fork Solomon River valleys. An investigation into the matter revealed no misconduct on Foster's part, but the suspicions continued. He died 30 March 1901 in Okarche, Oklahoma.

"In 1874 the Reverend Foster wrote a letter to *The Congregationalist*, published in Boston, appealing for, and receiving, $1700 in cash and sixty boxes of clothing valued at $5000."—*Osborne County Farmer*, 5 March 1935.

5. Lydia Sizer's real name was Eliza E. Haas, born 17 September 1854 in Iowa and died 9 February 1936 in Downs. She was the wife of George Sollner (see note 2 above).

6. Colonel Altman's real name was Colonel William L. Bear, and he cofounded the colony of Pennsylvanians that started the town of Osborne, Kansas, in May 1871. He reached the rank of lieutenant colonel during the Civil War and, after coming to Kansas, farmed a homestead in Penn Township. Bear served in many civic functions, including county school superintendent, county attorney, and state representative. He organized the first Sunday school in the county and the Moravian Church. He passed away on 26 November 1880 in Osborne and was buried in the Osborne Cemetery.

"Colonel W. L. Bear was secretary of the Osborne County Relief Committee during the grasshopper year of 1874. Other members were the Reverend R. B. Foster, the Reverend J. C. Ayres, Dr. D. E. Tilden, and John Alexander. Bear was also the receiving and distributing agent for the State Relief Committee, in charge of a five-county area. He worked without pay, and his family perhaps suffered worse than any other."—*Osborne County Farmer*, 5 March 1935.

7. The Reverend George Balcom (not Bascom) was a Baptist evangelist who preached the first sermon in Osborne County, on 6 September 1870, in the Walrond stockade in Bethany Township. He later died at his home near Cawker City.

"Just here we wish to pay a tribute to the life of Elder Balcom: in 1869 he was in Abilene and going down the street and with two preachers was passing a saloon. Spying a violin on the bar, Balcom walked right in, picked up the instrument, and began playing and singing, "Nearer My God To Thee," and followed with other sacred selections. Reverend Balcom was a musician of rare ability and soon the noisy crowd was silent. The card tables were vacant, the guzzler had quit guzzling and there was a tear in the eye of the bartender. Elder Balcom led in a sermon of prayer, followed by other ministers. The Lord heard their supplications to the saving of several of the company, notably the saloon keeper, who vowed never again to sell the damning beverage."—Del Cox in the *Osborne County Farmer*, 7 March 1912.

8. McConkey's real name was James W. Huff. The son of William C. and Mary Francis Huff, James was born near Wabash, Indiana, 20 October 1845. He served in the Civil War, and in 1867 he married Mary Clark (1848–1925). They went to Osborne County in 1872, homesteading the southeast quarter of Section 29 in Ross Township. James studied law and began a real estate business when Downs was established. He became a prominent businessman in Downs and helped organize the State Bank of Downs. In 1887 he was also elected mayor. He died 3 March 1926 and was buried in the Downs Cemetery. The Huffs had three boys—Arthur, John, Renald—and a daughter.

9. This rural one-room schoolhouse was located in the northeast corner of Section 14 in Bethany Township, Osborne County, Kansas.

"On Wednesday our city was greatly excited over the report of a shooting scrape that occurred on Tuesday night at a schoolhouse a few miles northwest of this city, while a literary was going on, wherein a young lady school teacher named Miss Dedman drew a revolver on a young man named Morton, the revolver going off in some manner, hitting an innocent fellow, but doing no damages. Miss Dedman was arrested and brought before B. M. Remy, justice of the peace of this township on Wednesday. The trial was put off till the next Monday, Miss Dedman being placed under $100 bond for her appearance."—*Downs Chief*, 3 March 1887.

On the following Monday, Miss Dedman was found guilty of assault and fined $2.50 and court costs.

10. His real name was Fate Morton.

11. Her real name was Harriet Olive Dedman. She was born 9 February 1856 at Monmouth, Illinois; her husband, Walter Farnsworth, was born in

1858 at Fremont, Illinois. Walter went to Kansas with his parents in 1871 and worked on the family farm in Section 10 of Bethany Township in Osborne County. He married Harriet on 5 March 1887, a week after the incident at the Green Ridge school. Harriet died in 1922 at Portis, Kansas, and Walter passed away in 1950. They are buried in the Farnsworth Family Cemetery, which is located on the banks of Plum Creek in Bethany Township.

Chapter Twelve. The Great Menace Again

1. "Messenger," a religious newspaper printed in German.

Chapter Thirteen. The Prairie Smiles Once More

1. Alma Laura Ise was born 1 June 1875 on the Ise homestead.

2. *Hard corn planter:* a revolutionary device that appeared in the 1850s. It consisted of two wooden slats with handles and a seed canister attached. A slide joined the slats in the middle, and two sharp pieces of metal joined the bottom end. The slide passed under the seed canister, and a small hole in it filled with seeds as the slats were pulled apart. The end was placed in the ground and the handles closed, causing the seeds to drop to the end and fall into the ground. The farmer then used his foot to cover the hole.

"At first would plow land and then plant corn with a planter; couldn't plant and care for more than fifteen or twenty acres of corn at the very first."—Rosa Ise notes to John Ise.

Cultivator: Horse-drawn plow designed to loosen the soil and kill the weeds between the planted rows in a field.

"Had no cultivator to start with, except the wooden frame and wooden wheel, what was called a 'double shovel'; had to go a 'round' to cultivate a row of corn. Later this doubled in the 'cultivator,' which did twice the work."—Rosa Ise notes to John Ise.

Drill: A planting device that allowed farmers to sow seed in larger quantities. It had adjustable holes to allow the desired amount of seed to fall and disks that opened and covered the furrow around the falling seed. The grain drill did much to allow for larger fields to be planted on the Great Plains.

Rake: A hay rake, or sweep rake, was a popular farming implement during this period for gathering hay.

3. Christopher and Louisa Haag left their Osborne County homestead and moved back to Jackson County, Kansas, in 1876. They settled on a farm north of Holton and lived comfortably for many years, until Christopher suffered a stroke. He died four days later, on 7 February 1907, and was buried in

the Holton Cemetery. Louisa passed away 8 October 1938 and was also buried in the Holton Cemetery.

4. "Mother" refers to Rosena Christina Freihoffer, mother of Rosie (see Chapter 38). Brother George was George Adam Haag, who was born 3 January 1859 in Theresa, Wisconsin. Although he was not able to attend school until he was nineteen years old, he became an avid reader and was an able student of the Bible. George possessed great strength and was known for his skill in tightening screws with his bare hands. He married Frances Ann Gruver on 17 January 1882 at Holton, Kansas. Frances had been born in 1862 at De Kalb, Missouri. Her family moved to Wathena, Kansas, when she was a child, and went to Holton several years later. George and Frances had four children—Rose, Percival, Levi, and Stella. George, a farmer by trade, died 1 July 1945 at Holton. Frances had passed away 11 March 1939 in Holton, and they were both buried in the Holton Cemetery.

Sister Jennie was Johanna Christina Haag, born 18 March 1864 on the Haag family homestead five miles north of the town of Holton in Jackson County, Kansas. She was the youngest of the Haag children and lived her entire life (except for one year) in Jackson County. Johanna taught Sunday school at the Holton Evangelical Church for twenty-five years and was an active member of the Woman's Missionary Society. On 14 February 1888 she was married in her parents' home to John Davis (1858–1946). They had two children, Anna and John. Johanna died 4 May 1946 near Holton and was buried with her husband in the Holton Cemetery.

5. The baby, Billy, was Edward William Ise, born on the Ise homestead 10 November 1876.

6. A machine designed to mow hay and grass. Two horses were required to pull the mower; the machines were gradually improved until by 1900 the cutting of ten acres a day was a common expectation.

7. The coal found in Osborne and Mitchell Counties is of the variety called lignite, a brownish coal of lesser quality for burning. The coal is found in shallow veins running close to the surface. Coal discoveries have been made in the area at Alton (Bull City), Twin Creek, Potterville, Covert, Tipton, Cawker City, Glen Elder, and many other places.

Chapter Fourteen. The New House, and a Trip Back Home

1. The Central Branch of the Union Pacific Railroad began in Atchison and was slowly built to the west. Waterville in Marshall County was the western terminus for many years. After Colonel W. F. Downs became superinten-

dent of the branch an ambitious building era began, and the tracks at last reached Downs in 1879.

2. The last (1877–1878) of a long series of wars between an expanding Russia and the Ottoman Empire, ending with the independence of Serbia and Romania from the Ottoman Turks.

3. The actual name for this hill at the time was Booth's Hill (see Chapter 3 n.1). It is located in Section 17 of Ross Township in Osborne County, Kansas.

4. The patent stated that Henry had fulfilled all the requirements of the 1862 Homestead Act and was now officially the owner of his claim. He received the patent 1 March 1879, signed by Rutherford B. Hayes, nineteenth president of the United States (1877–1881).

5. A farming implement used to smooth newly tilled fields prior to seed planting.

6. "Mother got a sewing machine only two or three years after going out. Had a breachy cow, and couldn't keep her in, so traded her for a sewing machine—a White Sewing Machine."—John Ise notes.

7. Their last name was actually Babcock. The men making up the posse were D. C. Bryant, William Hobbs, Charles Hollister, Benjamin Greenman, Frank Cox, Oliver Miller, Thomas Bryant, Charles Bryant, William Stevens, Thomas Stevens, Benjamin Hilliker, Henry Lackey, Frank Wells, A. B. Hilbert, John Tetlow, and Fred Barr. Court records in the Osborne County courthouse show that charges were filed by the Babcocks in April 1877, and when the case came up in court in September, the vigilantes were found guilty of assault and battery. Two weeks later the charges were dismissed upon agreement of the defendants to pay a fine of a hundred dollars each and court costs.

Chapter Fifteen. Dangers of Pioneering

1. Wenzel Rohowitz (born 1836) and his wife, Elizabeth (born 1844), were Swiss homesteaders of the southwest quarter of Section 5 in Ross Township, Osborne County. Wenzel and Elizabeth (called Minnie in the text) had six children—Catherine, Mary, Louisa, Calvin, Elizabeth, and Anna. At various times the family's name has been spelled Rohoway, Rohowentz, Rochowatz, Rohowec, or Rohowatz, among others.

2. "There is a story told by [Elizabeth Rohowitz] that a bull belonging to her neighbor Bowers once broke into her pasture and got her cow with calf, and Bowers tried to collect two dollars for service, which she refused to pay on the grounds, as she later said to a neighbor, 'It was anyway no work for Bowers.'—John Ise notes.

Higginbotham is an alias for the Reverend John J. Bowers (see Chapter 5 n.12). Bowers was a large man, a college graduate, intelligent, and mechanically minded. He was at times a miller, a carpenter, a bricklayer, and an irrigation designer for the region around the Ises.

3. "1878—Ma's runaway with the team and molasses barrel."—John Ise notes.

4. Overton's real name was John W. Owens. Born in 1827, he was locally famous for the "Higgins Bluff" incident, which happened on Oak Creek some four miles above its confluence with the North Fork Solomon River. Owens and his wife, Nancy, homesteaded the northeast quarter of Section 30 in Ross Township, Osborne County.

"Higgin's Bluff was named after Mr. Higgins, who was killed there in 1870 by Indians. While Mr. Higgins was preparing supper, his partner, Owens, went down to the creek to get a bucket of water. While he was gone the Indians killed Higgins. As Owens was coming back, he met the Indians, shot the chief and then ran back to the creek and hid in the water under a large drift until night, when the Indians gave up finding him and he came out. They had cut the wagon up and burned it with the harness and went away with the horses. So the bluff was named for Higgins who was killed."— F. M. Wells recollections to John Ise.

5. By the time Rosie had come to the homestead, the threat of Indian attacks was largely over. Under the supervison of government agents, bands of Indians from Eastern Kansas—Otoe, Ottawa, Delaware, and Pottawatomie—still passed through the area as late as 1879 on their way to hunt buffalo, which were being pushed ever farther to the west.

6. His murder occurred at around two o'clock in the morning on 15 March 1881.

"Henry Kuchell, an unassuming bachelor of some 32 or 33 years old, landed in Mitchell County in 1873, settling some three miles south of Cawker City, then sold out and filed contest papers on the land illegally held by Mr. Knox. All contest claims in those days were anything but pleasant business, and culminated seriously quite frequently, as it did in this case.

The contest case came up for hearing in September 1880, before Receiver Landis of the U.S. Land Office in Kirwin. During the long wait which was characteristic of contest cases, the Knox family became impatient and fearing they would lose the decision at Washington, made overtures . . . to buy Kuchell off. The man of German descent had all the tenacity of a bulldog and stayed. Warning letters had been written him as well as his friends by anonymous authors, mailed at different places throughout the state during the two years of his occupancy of the land in dispute, telling him that trouble would come and blood flow freely if he did not quit the farm and give it up to the neighbor owner. All of them passed unheeded.

When the trial came up for hearing in the August term of the Mitchell County district court it was extremely difficult to get a jury. Two hundred men were drawn and the list was nearly exhausted before a number of them were accepted. The trial, however, was of short duration. The preponderance of evidence was against the prisoners both circumstantial and direct, and the culmination was a sentence of twenty-five years for R. W. Knox; fifteen for Charles and a three-year sentence to L. M. Soules."—Del Cox in the *Osborne County Farmer,* 13 March 1934.

7. "The Knox family arrived in Cawker City in the spring of 1871, and the senior member shortly afterward filed homestead papers on the river quarter section two and a half miles southwest of Cawker City in Mitchell County, and simultaneously bought two hundred acres of school land adjoining on the west in Osborne County. For advantageous reasons the home was established and extensive improvements were built on the school land, and a mere pretense of habitation by the family was enacted on the homestead; in fact it was occupied at the time of the murder by Theodore Kenyon and wife, employees of R. W. Knox.

Mr. and Mrs. Knox, and daughter Eva, were members of the Oak Dale class of the Methodist Church, and Mr. Knox was the very able superintendent of the Sunday school—an expert at conveying the lesson on the blackboard. He was the father of two sons, five and twenty-two years of age.

R. W. Knox and son Charles were long since paroled, but never came back to the Solomon Valley home. The ranch was sold to L. A. Reece, then later to the Irey brothers."—Del Cox in the *Osborne County Farmer,* 13 March 1934.

8. "Leander M. Soules was a young man from Wisconsin who had worked on and off for Mr. Knox for a year or more."—Del Cox in the *Osborne County Farmer,* 13 March 1934.

9. His real name was Theodore Kenyon. Kenyon and his wife worked for R. W. Knox, but he balked at the thought of killing Kuchell. He testified that he was a willing helper in trying to buy off Kuchell, and when that plan had failed he was told of the plan to blow up the intruder, if it came to that. However, he could not condone the taking of a human life, and Mrs. Kenyon testified that her husband was at home the night of Kuchell's murder. In return for turning state's evidence he was released from custody and resumed farming (*Osborne County Farmer,* 13 March 1934).

10. Twenty-two years of age at the time of the murder, he and Theodore Kenyon were to take over management of the homestead for their involvement in getting rid of Kuchell.

11. John A. Martin, from 1885 to 1889 the tenth governor of Kansas.

12. Alfaretta Nevill was the oldest daughter of Henry Nevill and Frances M. Lightfoot. She was born 9 November 1860 and died of typhoid fever in 1876. Henry Benjamin Nevill was born 3 September 1835 near Paris, Illinois. He and Frances were married 7 October 1858. Henry served in Company C,

79th Illinois Volunteer Infantry, during the Civil War. The couple moved to Osborne County, Kansas, in 1872, homesteading the southwest quarter of Section 9 in Ross Township. They had seven children—Alfaretta, Elora, Idell, William, Mary, Jessie, and Philop.

"The Nevills were there when we got there, having come from Iowa. Ma never knew them well. Were musical; he used to bind wheat for us. Mrs. Nevill never got over the girl's death—almost lost her mind. Girl suffered, so no wonder."—John Ise notes.

Chapter Sixteen. Henry Signs a Note

1. Jake's real name was James G. Goheen. James, the son of Frank Goheen, was born 26 August 1854 in Pine Grove, Pennsylvania. He first went to Kansas in 1871 with Isaac Kaup's family but soon returned to Pennsylvania. Five years later he headed west again, this time with Isaac Kaup and his brother John, and settled in the Rose Valley neighborhood. James married Mary Mollie Monigal (born 1858) in 1876, and they had four children—Frank, William, Addie, and Maude. Mary passed away on 1 January 1900, and in the next year James married Flora Mize. They had three children—Maude, Flossie, and Paul. James died in 1923 and was buried in the Downs Cemetery.

2. Willis Blair's real name was Willis DeLay, one of the original homesteaders of the future townsite of Downs, Kansas. DeLay was born in Wapello County, Iowa, 25 August 1842, and at the age of nineteen enlisted in the 3d Iowa Cavalry during the Civil War. After the war he returned home and on 30 December 1866 married Martha Cross, whose family had moved to Iowa from West Virginia. In 1871 DeLay went to Ross Township in Osborne County, Kansas, to stake a claim in Section 28 for himself and for his father, Joseph, who arrived from Nebraska astride a mule sometime later. Willis lived on the homestead for thirty-two years before moving into Downs in 1902. Willis died 24 September 1921 in Downs and was buried in the Downs Cemetery. His wife passed away in 1924 and was buried beside him. The DeLays had six children—Zenobia, Otis, Olive, Essie, Bertha, and Nellie.

3. Although Miller families could later be found in the area, at this point in time the only woman with her own homestead, and so in control of her own money, was Mrs. Sidney Pitt, whom Rosie may be referring to here. John Hege might have been either John Fink or John Schoen. The Stegimans were probably Adam and Ora (Parsons) Stegman.

4. "Good day, Rosie. What is wrong?"

5. "What is wrong, Rosie? You got a cold job, don't you? Where is Henry?"

6. "Go inside and warm yourself, Rosie."

7. "Bad."

8. In Rosa's own notes about the incident she states that it was Theobald Lutz, not Steve Young, who came by and helped her.

Chapter Seventeen. The Coming of the Railroad

1. The tracks of the Central Branch of the Union Pacific Railroad were completed to the townsite of what became the town of Downs on 19 June 1879. There was some confusion over the name, "Downs City," "Downs-ville," and "Downstown" all being used. The name was later settled as Downs, as that seemed a more appropriate signal of the town's willingness to grow into a metropolis.

2. 23 July 1879.

3. Henry had been postmaster of the New Arcadia post office for over five years when he was informed that it was being discontinued as of 28 September 1879.

4. Minnie Alice Ise (nicknamed "Doll") was born on the Ise homestead 24 October 1878.

5. "Once in the spring (May 1st), it was very dry and we were looking for rain when a bad looking cloud came up. Pa stood looking at the cloud and said, 'As bad as we need rain, I hope this doesn't hit me.' It was a terrible hail storm—cleaned out Baertsch's wheat and turned into a tornado on east. Baertsch was so disappointed, but neighbors got together and each gave him ten bushels. He wouldn't take them as a gift and paid everyone back the next year."—Rosa Ise notes to John Ise.

6. A town in southern Marshall County, Kansas, Irving was devastated by twin tornadoes on 30 May 1879.

7. Land records from the Osborne County Register of Deeds office in Osborne show that 690 acres of land in the northwest quarter of Section 19 in Ross Township were deeded over to Henry and Rosie on August 11, 1879. For a few more months, Frank lived on the remaining thirty-six acres south of where the railroad had cut through his homestead, finally deeding this also over to Henry and Rosie in April 1880. For this parcel they paid him $288.

8. One of the many patent medicines of the time, S. S. S. was "guaranteed to cure all aches, pains, and arthritic problems for all time," according to its manufacturer.

9. In late 1880 Frank left Osborne County and went to live with his brother, Frederick Hagel, near the town of Everest in Washington Township, Brown County, Kansas. He did not live there very long, dying on 6 May 1883. He was buried in the All Saints Cemetery in rural Washington Township. When Frank died, he still owned three town lots in Downs worth a total of

$425 (Brown County, Kansas, Letters of Administration, Case Number 574, Clerk of the District Court [Hiawatha, Kansas, 1883]).

Anna Wetzel's actual name was Anna Catherine Deck. The daughter of Frederick and Charlotte Deck, Anna was born 23 February 1859 in Franklin County, Pennsylvania. She married James Allen May on 2 August 1882 and passed away 4 December 1923 in Kansas City, Missouri.

10. "May 6, 1880—Pa fencing the lower pasture. Mother used to drive them down and then dig out their drinking place every morning."—John Ise notes.

11. Joseph Boomer, alias George Graeber, began building his new house on 10 April 1879.

12. Colonel William F. Downs was born in Seneca Falls, New York, in 1837. In 1865 he went west to Atchison, Kansas, to take charge as superintendent and land commissioner of the Central Branch of the Union Pacific Railroad and was largely responsible for the building of that road westward from Waterville, Kansas (*Atchison Daily Globe*, 16 July 1894). Colonel Downs died in California on 16 March 1883, leaving a wife and four children. He was twice mayor of Atchison and the man for whom the town of Downs is named.

Bloomington, a village in central Osborne County, Kansas, was begun in 1871 as the town of Tilden—after its founder, Daniel E. Tilden. An early contender in the county seat contest, the town's name was changed in 1872 to Bloomington. At its height it boasted some seventy inhabitants; today little remains of this once-promising community.

13. His real name was Isaac Smith. The Smiths homesteaded the southeast quarter of Section 8 in Ross Township, Osborne County in 1879; Isaac died 5 August 1879 in his home.

"His wife, a town woman, didn't want to come out there and she liked it less after she came. He died, apparently poisoned by his wife, and a later husband was also poisoned. Didn't think of Smith's death as poison until her second husband died. He had such a nice team, and was a fine man. She was a nice-looking lady."—Rosa Ise notes to John Ise.

14. The event occurred on Sunday morning, 11 October 1879, and the funeral was held the following Wednesday in a partially completed livery barn. Two thousand people gathered, the largest funeral ever held in Northwest Kansas. The three men were buried in the graveyard a mile north of the town. When the Sumner Cemetery was organized a couple of miles to the east, the men were reinterred there.

Bull City, sometimes called Bull's City, the first town in Osborne County, Kansas, was founded in November 1870 by General Hiram C. Bull and Lyman T. Earl. A coin toss determined whom the town would be named after, and Bull City soon became the major distribution and supply center for the settlers throughout much of Northwest Kansas. After the death of the famous

Bull, there were several attempts to change the town's name to "something more respectable." To this end a petition for new waterworks was circulated in 1885, and the signatures were then cut off and pasted onto a petition to have the town's name changed to Alton (after Alton, Illinois), which was sent to the U.S. Postal Department. The petition was accepted, and the post office name was officially changed to Alton.

Hiram C. Bull was born in Chautauqua County, New York, in 1820. He became an attorney at the age of seventeen and removed to Johnstown, Pennsylvania, where his first wife died in childbirth. He moved to Milwaukee, Wisconsin, and opened a chain of lumberyards. He married again, but she died shortly after. In 1850 he was elected to the Wisconsin state legislature, and in 1856 he lacked one vote of gaining the Republican nomination for governor. He married Sarah Fifield of Janesville, Wisconsin, who was a daughter of one of the most influential families in the state.

The Bulls moved to Arizona and New Mexico, where Bull served as adjutant general of the Army of the Southwest. At the outbreak of the Civil War, he enlisted at Dubuque, Iowa, and was eventually elevated to the rank of captain. He was wounded in the Battle of Pea Ridge and served out the war as Major Bull in the army paymasters office in Washington, D.C. In 1868 he moved to Kansas where he opened a lumberyard in Leavenworth. Discussions with railroad officials prompted a desire to found a town in the Solomon River valley, and in 1870 the Bulls moved west. At Bull City he was the town postmaster, operating a general store and freighting business, and he was the acknowledged leader in advocating the settlement of Northwest Kansas. Bull was the first probate judge of Osborne County and was elected to two terms in the state legislature; he was serving his second term when he was killed.

In January 1879 the Bulls adopted a seven-year-old girl, Nora. For her and the other children of the community, Hiram enclosed a park behind his house in which he kept various animals—elk, buffalo, antelope, and others—so that they could see how the land was before the white man came. The male elk he had raised by hand, so when he was told it was acting strangely that October morning, he ignored the warning. The news of his death made national headlines. In 1930 a monument was erected over Bull's grave in the Sumner Cemetery by the citizens of Alton.

Mrs. Bull ran the store for a few more years, but in 1883 she and her daughter moved back to Janesville, Wisconsin, where she died in 1912. She was brought back to Kansas and buried alongside her husband.

At first the elk was roped and tied between two trees while the wounded men were attended to. Afterward the elk was killed and its antlers saved. Nearly forty years later a former citizen of Alton saw the elk horns in a shop in Mankato, Kansas. He bought them and shipped them back to Alton. They were then displayed in the county courthouse in Osborne.

15. Robert Bricknell lingered for three days, dying on Tuesday, 13 October 1879.

George Nicholas was an Englishman and one of the first settlers in Osborne County, arriving in March 1870. He died shortly after the attack from his many wounds.

William Sherman was a carpenter employed at the time by the Bulls to do improvements on the house. He was saved from serious injury by an account book kept in the inside pocket of his coat, which the horns could not penetrate.

16. Griffith Lytle, Jr., came to Kansas on 9 May 1879, settling in Section 6 of Ross Township in Osborne County. He was born in Lamont, Pennsylvania, on 21 November 1843, and was a Civil War veteran. On 25 October 1871 he married Mary Ellen Storer (1852–1931). The Lytles had five children—John, Selsie, Olie, Mabel, and William Boyd. Griff was a farmer and a carpenter. In 1885, while building the Rose Valley schoolhouse, Griff caught some splinters in one arm but thought nothing about it. Blood poisoning set in, and the arm had to be amputated. Griff Lytle passed away on 19 April 1934 in Downs and was buried in the Downs Cemetery.

"One day a message came that there was a lunatic up on the Wash Bailey place, and women and children were in danger. Griff Lytle and Jim Goheen went up there and stayed with the family one night. The man had been bitten by a dog and thought perhaps he was mad. There was only one bed, and the people were very poor—had only a basket of cob corn to burn—so Lytle must be very careful of fuel, as it was very cold. The man raised up once during the night and went wild and Jim Goheen ran out the door, leaving Lytle and the children and the woman with the man. Lytle wrestled with him and finally told him that he would knock his head off if he didn't be still. The man, he did be still, and later went to the insane asylum."—John Ise notes.

Chapter Eighteen. A Prairie Fire

1. His real name was Tommy Maier, a native of Switzerland. "Tommy Maier came about 1879. Settled on the Fred Heiser place for a while, then went up in the hills—not so cruel to his wife at first. Fairly quite loving at first. Lost skin of face trying out beauty medicine. He used to go to town and drink and come home drunk. Got rougher and rougher as he got older, and she was less able to do a lot of work."—Rosa Ise notes to John Ise.

2. "In 1885 or 1886 Mother finally bought one, and wishing she had bought one earlier."—John Ise notes.

3. Charles David Ise (he used "Daniel" as his middle name) was born on the Ise homestead 7 March 1880.

Chapter Nineteen. The Road Fight

1. According to Osborne County court records, the first petition to the county commissioners to open a new road was filed 22 January 1876 and signed by the following: Henry C. Ise, Christian Baertsch, Henry Wehmeyer, Theobald Lutz, Joseph Boomer, David Oliver, Jacob Hunter, W. Rochowatz, Frank Cooper, S. B. Cooper, Ervin Cooper, Christian Linge, Frederick Kaup, and Frank Hagel. A petition was filed 2 April 1877 saying that the road proposed in the first petition was not valid. Isaac Kaup was the lone signee.

The county commissioners upheld the first petition. In 1878 this was remonstrated in a third petition urging the commissioners to change their vote. This petition was signed by Isaac Kaup and twenty-seven additional people, including some who had supported the original petition.

2. By 1881 the Osborne County court records show seven successive petitions had been filed in the matter. At this point the antiroad faction, headed by Isaac Kaup, filed a lawsuit against the Board of County Commissioners, Henry Ise, Christian Baertsch, Henry Wehmeyer, David Oliver, Joseph Boomer, and Theobald Lutz. The lawsuit sought to prevent the opening of the new road, which had already been graded and was now in place. The lawsuit was rejected, and an appeal was made. More than five years after the petition was filed, the district court decided in favor of Kaup and his faction and declared the original petition invalid. The real loser as a result of the whole affair was Christian Baertsch, who had financed his side's court costs. Henry Ise, whose name stood at the nominal head of the "new road" faction, received five dollars in damages for the loss of land he suffered when the new road was built through his homestead—even though the road had just been officially declared illegal. This "illegal" road is still in place and currently in use.

Chapter Twenty. The Retreat of the Defeated Legion

1. The Osborne County village of Bloomington for a while seemed to be at last living up to its name when, a mile northwest of town, two men sinking a well came upon what appeared to be solid gold nuggets. This set off a small rush by the neighboring farmers to check out rock outcroppings and the small creeks that flowed through the area. The craze lasted only two days, for by that time it was discovered that the nuggets were of pyrite, more commonly called "fool's gold," instead of the real thing.

Chapter Twenty-one. Unkind Seasons

1. Anna Baertsch was the daughter of Christian and Ursula Baertsch. Anna was born 7 October 1864 in Seewis, Switzerland. Her brother Fred (Ford) was born 2 February 1867 in Germany.

2. Rosie and the children left on 28 April 1881.

3. Thomas Robert Malthus (1766–1834), an English economist.

4. Her real name was Mary Katherine Bowers, eldest daughter of John J. and Christiana Bowers. Mary was born 11 November 1856 in Pennsylvania. Her beau was John A. Morton, who was then in business in Osborne, Kansas, with the Morton and Parsons Store. They were married 29 November 1883.

5. In 1881 the Osborne County tax assessment rolls show that the Ise farm had two hundred and thirty-seven acres under cultivation. Henry had tried various crops, such as castor beans, flax, peaches, silk worms, apples, rye, oats, and spring wheat, but he had settled on corn, and the readily available water supply from his well and from the nearby creek enabled him to do so. Many of his neighbors were turning almost exclusively to wheat, but Henry had a rather nostalgic inclination for corn; it reminded him of his past farming days in Illinois and Iowa. The farm also sported six horses, nine hogs, and fourteen head of cattle.

6. Walter John Ise was born 22 January 1882 on the Ise homestead.

7. "Dear."

Chapter Twenty-two. Good Years and the New House

1. This occurred in the summer of 1882. E. F. Booth, alias Jessie Bender, went to Wyoming, but Lucy and their three children, Homer, Elisha, and William, stayed in Kansas. Bender's well-known contempt for the law was inherited by at least one of his sons, as stated in the 3 March 1887 issue of the *Osborne County Farmer*: "A merry chase we did not have the privilege to witness occurred yesterday after charges of assault were filed against Elisha Booth of Ross Township. Sheriff Nate Watson cornered him in a henhouse and arrested him after getting a ducking from breaking through the ice on the river. Booth fined $1 and costs."

The land records in the Osborne County Register of Deeds office show that by 1889 Booth had passed away and his widow had set up a mortgage on the land with the Kansas Loan & Title Company for $800, to be paid back in five years. This arrangement did not work out, for the land was foreclosed on and sold in 1892 at a sheriff's sale of property to C. S. Dittman.

2. The town of Waconda Springs was organized to take advantage of the tourism the spring promised and the popularity of the waters as a healing elixir. The town was undermined by the businessmen in nearby Cawker City and never really got off the ground, quickly becoming a ghost town.

3. W. F. Cochran was the treasurer of Osborne County from 1881 through 1885.

4. J. M. Babcock was sheriff of Osborne County during 1882 and 1883.

5. George W. Glick, from 1882 to 1885, the ninth governor of Kansas; John J. Ingalls, United States senator from Kansas (1873–1891).

6. Freddie was the son of Theobald and Jane Lutz. Henry and Rosa had known the Lutzes earlier in Holton. Theobald Lutz was born in Germany in 1852. He met and married Jane (born 1852 in Wisconsin) at Holton. They had come out to Ross Township, filing on a claim in the northwest quarter of Section 18 along Twelve Mile Creek. There were four other sons—Henry, Walter, William, and Jacob. In July 1897 Theobald sold his farm to Henry Fink, and the family returned to Holton.

7. "He is really dead! Is black!"

8. Rather than a little girl, Carrie E. Howell was actually a young woman when she passed away at the age of twenty-two in 1883. She and George W. Howell moved to Downs in 1879. George (born 1857) started a lumberyard, quickly building this business to more than sixty yards throughout Kansas and Nebraska. After amassing and losing three separate fortunes, he died during a business trip to Downs in 1934 and was buried in the Downs Cemetery.

9. The new school was built in November 1883. Henry, Griffith Lytle, and Wiley Jones were the principal builders. The move onto the Ise homestead was a strategic one for the school district, for the new schoolhouse was in the center of the families with the most children in the district. The Decks and the Bowers sent six children each through this school; the Ises sent eleven children, and the Joneses, thirteen.

10. David Coop lived on the homestead located in the southeast quarter of Section 20 of Ross Township in Osborne County. He was the son of John Coop and Sarah (Sally) Martin. Dave was born 20 March 1839 and was well-known for the struggles his family lived through. One baby died on 28 September 1876, and Henry and Rosie's son Edward helped make the coffin.

11. The first school term was held in Dave Coop's dugout during the spring of 1873, with a Mrs. Morgan teaching. She soon had to leave, as she could not handle the Huff boys. In the summer a log schoolhouse was built on the southwest corner of the Huff farm, and that fall it was used for the first time.

"Jones had to finish school term in fall of 1873. Mrs. Daniels had been teaching, but couldn't handle the Warners and the Huffs—her relatives. Jones took over the school—only a three-month term altogether. Jones taught the rest while Wellman Huff got into mischief, and Jones called him up before the school. Wellman wouldn't budge. Jones called a second time, and Wellman grabbed a hatchet from the stove and came after Jones. Jones held him off, and had George Shipton—who was there—go after Mr. Huff, who came and beat Wellman with a switch. Lew Warner used to carry a knife and even a revolver to school.

"School board put an axe in the school house for Jones' use. Huffs were sixteen or seventeen; some of them almost young men."—John Ise notes on Wiley Jones story. Mrs. Daniels was the former Lavina Huff, sister to Wellman.

12. The organ was actually bought in 1886 by Rosie's father for Alma, on the condition that Alma learn to read and write in German during a visit she made to the Haags near Holton in the fall of 1886. Alma later wrote of her visit in Wright, *Prairie Legacy,* pp. 142–55.

13. "Also called the 'Kansas itch' or the 'seven-year itch,' it was characterized by a breaking out all over the body but particularly between the fingers. It did not affect all alike; some for only a few days, others would be affected all winter. A person who had not had a bath for three or four months would perhaps even have difficulty telling whether he had the itch or whether he was enjoying normalcy. People usually treated it with sulphur and lard, sometimes with gunpowder added."—John Ise notes.

Chapter Twenty-three. Trouble for the Little Children

1. Hulda Louise Ise was born 13 November 1883 on the Ise homestead.

Chapter Twenty-four. A Happy Day, and an Anxious Night

1. John Caspar Hinnen (Johnnie) was born 8 March 1879 near Holton, Kansas. He was the son of Wilhelmina (Minnie) and John Hinnen. He helped in his father's saddlery business and later moved to Fairbury, Nebraska, where he started a grocery business. He died 5 January 1946 at Fairbury and was buried in the Holton Cemetery.

His brother Fred Henry Hinnen (Freddie) was born 1 July 1880 near Holton. He graduated from law school but never practiced law. Instead, he was in partnership with another brother George for thirty-one years in the grocery business in Holton. He died 5 January 1936 at Holton and is buried in the Holton Cemetery.

Rosa Caroline Hinnen (Rosie) was born 9 December 1881 near Holton. She moved to Fairbury, Nebraska, with her brother John and helped him with his grocery business.

2. A term used to describe a number of stomach and bowel troubles, including acute indigestion.

3. Milk that is drunk just as it begins to curdle.

4. His real name was David Franklin Deck, the son of Frederick and

Charlotte Deck. Dave was born 8 March 1867 in Sterling, Illinois. He passed away 22 January 1948 in Haywood, California.

5. The Clydesdale and Percheron Horse Company was organized at a meeting on 29 September 1886 at Joseph Boomer's home. Boomer was elected president, Arthur William Hefley the secretary, and John Fink the treasurer. Forty-two stockholders were confirmed at a cost of $100 each, giving the company a total working capital of $4,200. The purpose of the company was to make available for stud service in the local area two stallions of the aforementioned horse breeds. An annual company meeting was held every March, though special meetings were held often throughout the year.

"*The Clydesdale and Percheron Horse Company,* of Downs, has been chartered. Capital stock is $4,200. Directors, F. H. Deck, David Oliver, G. Hofer, W. F. Henry, and H. C. Ise, all of Downs."—*Osborne County Farmer,* 12 May 1887.

6. Lucifer was the Percheron stallion, and Richmond the Clydesdale stallion, purchased from E. Bennett and Son of Topeka, Kansas, in December 1886. When the company was dissolved in 1892, Lucifer was bought by John Fink for $700, and Richmond was sold to Theobald Lutz for $200.

7. The nineteenth-century political organization of farmers' concerns that later grew into the Populist Party.

8. This orchard consisted of forty apple trees, three pear trees, twelve peach trees, and twenty cherry trees.

9. John William "Blind" Boone was a famous ragtime pianist and composer. He was born at Miami, Missouri, 17 May 1864, and died at Warrensburg, Missouri, on 4 October 1927. Blind since birth, Boone's talents developed until he was playing a regular ten-week season every year from 1885 to 1915. He published a number of compositions, including waltzes, coon songs and classical character pieces. (Coon songs were ragtime and usually sentimental popular songs of the nineteenth century derived from or related to the songs of the southern Negro—*Webster's Third New International Dictionary*). Boone was also the inspiration for the character of Blind d'Arnault in the Willa Cather novel *My Antonia.* His works were rediscovered during the ragtime revival of the 1970s. Boone appeared at the Downs Opera House on January 29, 1889.

10. The 1885 Kansas State Agricultural Census lists Henry Ise as owning a farm of 240 acres that was worth about $4,000. He had planted 38 acres of winter wheat, 40 acres of corn, 4 acres of oats, and 6 acres of millet. Eighty acres were being used for pastureland. A thousand bushels of corn, 200 bushels of wheat, and 30 tons of hay were being stored on the farm. There were 5 horses, 27 cattle, and 18 swine. The Ise family had churned out 100 pounds of butter and took care of an orchard consisting of 126 apple, 2 pear, 50 peach, 2 plum, and 12 cherry trees.

Henry and Rosie's neighbors were doing equally well. The Reverend

John J. Bowers' 400–acre farm was estimated to be worth $6,000. Wiley Jones also farmed 400 acres, valued at $4,000. Joseph Boomer had a 160–acre holding worth $3,000. In addition to wheat and corn, Boomer and Bowers had planted rye, and Bowers had made and sold a staggering 1,000 pounds of butter over the previous year.

Chapter Twenty-five. A Sick Baby

1. Joe was John Christopher Ise, born 5 June 1885 on the Ise homestead. He was named for Rosie's father, John Christopher Haag.

2. Clara Winters was the daughter of Robert and Catherine Winters. She was born in Indiana and went with her parents to Osborne County in 1883. She first married H. D. Washburn; she later married John Greenman.

3. Robert Huey Winters was born 16 May 1838 at Portland, Indiana. He later lived in Missouri and Eastern Kansas before returning to Indiana in 1870 to marry Catherine Knight (born in 1838 at Casstown, Ohio), a rural schoolteacher. In 1883 the Winters family moved to Ross Township, Osborne County, Kansas, onto the farm located in the southwest quarter of Section 19 directly south of the Ise homestead. Robert Winters was an eternally cheerful man, even after he began to lose his eyesight only six weeks after arriving in the area. He eventually became totally blind. The couple had four children—Kiturah, Nathaniel, Clara, and a baby who died in infancy. In 1905, they moved into Downs and spent their last years there. Robert died in 1915, and Catherine succumbed three years later. Both were buried in the Downs Cemetery.

Kiturah Winters was born near Portland, Indiana, in 1874. She never married but took care of her father and later her mother, who was stricken with paralysis just before her death. Kit's life was a sad and lonely one, for after she had borne a child out of wedlock she was shunned by the community.

"Kit Winters wore dresses with a button-up back and had her baby either sucking a sugar rag or a water bottle. Baby was thin and yellow and cadaverous; died of cholera infantum. Kit was completely ostracized for years afterward. Milt George used to go with her, but wouldn't take her out, and never married her. She got ready to be married several times, but he finally told her he wouldn't marry her. Couldn't face the world with her."—John Ise notes.

4. This refers to David Gottlieb Fink, son of John and Katherine Fink. David was born 19 December 1883 in Bethany Township, Osborne County. Unable to farm, he earned a law degree at Washburn University in Topeka, Kansas. He was probate judge of Osborne County from 1911 to 1921, afterward practicing law in Osborne until he retired. He married twice, first in 1911

to Hope Curtis and then in 1916 to Susie De Fries. David died 16 July 1944 at Osborne.

5. Doctor J. G. Poole (born 1852) was an early physician in the Downs area, having located there by 1880. He and his first wife, Ella (also born 1852), had three children—Maud, Myrtle, and William. In 1886 he married a second time, to Sadie Hollister. He was a partner in the drug firm of Harvey & Poole and served as mayor of Downs and on the Downs City Council.

6. According to the Osborne County tax assessment rolls of 1887, the Ise family had one hundred acres of land under cultivation (all corn) and another one hundred and seventy in pastureland or not in use. They had four horses, six hogs, and twenty-six head of cattle. Their farm was valued at $2,800, and their property taxes that year came to $270.

7. Inflammation of the inner lining of the chest; causes fever and difficult respiration.

8. Her real name was Ida Hunker, daughter of Jacob and Maria (Mary) Hunker. She was born on the family homestead along Twelve Mile Creek near Downs and passed away 2 October 1903.

9. Estelle May Ise was born on the Ise homestead 22 August 1887.

Chapter Twenty-six. More Hard Years and Hard Problems

1. Records in the Osborne County Register of Deeds office show that on 1 July 1887, Henry and Rosie mortgaged the eastern half of their original homestead for $363 to the Pennsylvania Investment Company. They paid this off quickly, and were released from it 23 August 1887.

2. Wenzil Rohowitz died in February 1885 and was buried in the Downs Cemetery. The Rachowitzes lost their land in June 1887 and by the middle of July had left the area completely, moving east to Atchison, Kansas.

3. Frankie Graeber's real name was Frank Boomer. The son of Joseph and Rosa Boomer, Frank was born in 1874 on the family homestead in Ross Township. He continued to work the farm after his father's death in 1890. Later he removed to Garden City, Kansas. Johnny Wise was actually John Schoen, Jr., the son of John and Emma Schoen. John Jr. was born 1 November 1871 near Johnson, Nebraska. On 2 February 1895 he married Augusta Sonnenberg.

4. Still known by that name today, the Baertsch Grove stands along the banks of Twelve Mile Creek in the extreme northwest corner of Section 7 in Ross Township in Osborne County. The grove is a particularly wide strip of woodland that was very popular as a campsite for settlers heading west and

was also used as a place for religious meetings, picnics, and other celebrations.

Chapter Twenty-seven. Henry Buys a Windmill, and Sells
Some Cattle

1. This may have been John Pottberg, who lived between the towns of Downs and Tipton.
2. The Ises put up their entire original homestead as collateral when they decided to take out a mortgage to pay for the windmill. County land records show that on 17 January 1888 they mortgaged the homestead to the Lombard Investment Company for $350. They were a little longer paying off this mortgage but were finally released from it 4 January 1893.
3. A corn planter developed in the mid-1870s that allowed Great Plains farmers to plant their seed in deep furrows. This was necessary to ensure germination, because there was less moisture content in the plains soil than in the East.
4. The opening day for the Congregational Academy was mentioned in the *Osborne County Farmer* as being on 10 April 1888.
5. "Oh, dear Mary."
"This happened July 17, 1888."—John Ise notes.
6. George Yost was born 27 February 1847 in Seewis, Switzerland. His wife, Elizabeth Fluetsch, was born 22 April 1845 in Seewis. They were married 1 May 1870 in Seewis and were the parents of nine children—George, Anna, Burga, Bartley, Rosa, Hans, Nina, John, and Nicholas. George worked as a logger and twice broke his left leg in accidents, causing it to be considerably shorter than his right. In 1886 an older brother who had already come to America returned and convinced George to join him there. In 1887 they left Switzerland and bought the farm in the southwest quarter of Section 19, Ross Township, Osborne County, Kansas, for $2,000 and a $1,000 note at 12 percent interest (Bartley F. Yost, *The Yost Family* [N.p., 1928], pp. 1–10). George Baertsch built their house, which took the remainder of the family's savings.
In 1905 Elizabeth died, and George visited Switzerland, marrying Anna Fausch, a relative of Elizabeth's. George died in 1928, and Anna in 1931. They were buried in the Downs Cemetery.
"Mrs. Yost got teeth of hogs when butchered, and put a stack of them in bed to keep away cramps."—John Ise notes.
7. A Swiss *Männerchor* ("male choir").
8. Ezra Daniels had homesteaded the land where the Yosts later settled. Ezra L. Daniels (born 1846) had married Lavina Jane Huff (born 1846) a daughter of his neighbors William and Francis Huff. The Daniels had four

children—Larkin, Clinton, Carrie, and another daughter. After selling their farm the Daniels moved to near Alva, Oklahoma. One day Lavina stepped on a sandbur and did not get it completely out of her heel. She contracted blood poisoning and died on 8 September 1900, being buried in Alva.

Chapter Twenty-eight. More Drouth and Anxiety . . . and Hope

1. See Chapter 25 n.9.

2. Lands formerly owned by the Cherokee Nation that were opened to white settlement in 1889.

3. In October 1889, it was discovered that there was a deficit of over $8,217 in the Osborne County treasury that the treasurer, Captain James A. Beeman, was unable to account for. Beeman was arrested and later convicted of embezzlement. He had been treasurer of Osborne County since 1885. A full account was given in the *Osborne County Farmer*, 15 October 1889.

4. Isaac Grecian was clerk of Osborne County from 1887 to 1889.

5. Any of certain grain sorghum cultivated for grain and forage in dry regions; also called erron.

6. Joseph Boomer had been in poor health and died 25 July 1890 of sudden heart failure, as his half-brother Frank had four years earlier. He was buried in the Downs Cemetery alongside Frank.

7. Rosa Boomer, alias Lizzie Graeber, was born in 1846 and was a daughter of Paul Sollner. The wife of Joseph Boomer, she stayed on their homestead only a few years after his death before moving back to Holton, Kansas. Her daughter, Sarah J. Boomer (1871–1928), moved back with her. Rosa died in Holton on 8 February 1926, and was buried in the Holton Cemetery.

Chapter Twenty-nine. Good Crops and the New Barn

1. Rosina was Mary Rose Ise, born 13 December 1889 on the Ise homestead.

2. Herman Thomas Ise (nicknamed "Hap" or "Happy") was born 10 March 1892 on the Ise homestead.

3. One of the Mistletoe Club's concerts was at Osborne on Saturday evening, 3 March 1894. The program shows that thirty songs were performed by various members, of which Alma and Doll sang on four: "Song of the Ducks," "Village in the Valley," "Cottage on the Hill," and "Charming Fellow."

Sam Magaw, Jr., was born near Columbus, Indiana, on 2 August 1867. He went with his parents in 1878 to Cloud County, Kansas; when he was twenty-two he moved to Downs, locating on a farm two miles west of town. Sam married Leah Clark of Downs on 17 February 1897. Leah had been born 9 October 1876 in Mitchell County, Kansas. They had three children—Lelah, Donald, and Edith. Sam was a rural mail carrier while at Downs, continuing to work in that occupation when the family later moved to Concordia. In September 1927, Sam dropped a package on his foot while at work in the post office, causing a small bruise. Blood poisoning set in, and the leg was amputated, but gangrene had already developed and Sam Magaw died 7 October 1927. Leah Magaw passed away 13 March 1947 in Omaha, Nebraska.

4. The Clydesdale and Percheron Horse Company, which had been established in October 1886, lasted nearly five and a half years. The second president of the company was S. D. Wagner, who stayed at that post for three years before giving way to John Fink, who was elected for one year. Wagner was reelected for the final few months. Henry Ise was elected secretary and was later the treasurer. At the end the directors were Henry Ise, John G. Hunker, Christian Baertsch, Godfrey Hofer, and William F. Henry. The company's last regular meeting was on 7 March 1892 at the livery barn in Downs, where it was decided to sell the two company horses. Soon after that came the meeting at Henry's house to dissolve the company and split the profits.

There had been a few unexpected problems over the years. First, the insurance company engaged to cover potential lawsuits had its license revoked by the state attorney general. Then Theobald Lutz, who at first quartered the stallions at his place, soon refused to do so anymore, as it took more time and money to take care of them than he was willing to give. The death of Joseph Boomer in 1890 further deprived the company of one of its major backers. But the company had made a modest annual profit, and in addition to the thousand dollars split among the stockholders at the end, there was another nine hundred dollars from the sale of the two stallions. At a time when money was still scarce, this was a tidy sum for all involved to share.

5. Rosena Haag had been visiting relatives in Wisconsin when she passed away 24 July 1892. She was brought back to Holton, Kansas, and was buried in the Holton Cemetery alongside her husband John Christopher Haag.

6. Osborne County land records show that in October 1893, Henry and Rosie bought the northern half of the northeast quarter of Section 18 in Ross Township from Lew Richardson for $3,100. The pastureland lay a mile north of their home and was part of the original homestead of the Reverend John J. Bowers. There was also a substantial apple orchard that Bowers had first planted on part of the land. In 1904 Rosie mortgaged this land to John Wolfert for $700, paying it back one year later.

7. This autograph album is currently in the possession of the Osborne County Genealogical & Historical Society in Osborne, Kansas. Page 1 reads: "Presented to Alma Ise, by her brother, Charles D. Ise, Sun. Nov. 8th 1891." Alma filled it with autographs and verses from her cousins and closest friends.

8. Scott W. Carney was born in Manhattan, Kansas, in 1867. He went to Downs on 23 April 1888 and established a news and confectionery store, which he ran until 1896 when he was appointed postmaster. Mr. Scott Carney married Minnie Nicholas in 1891 in Colorado Springs, Colorado. He moved there in 1901, returning to Downs in 1904 to open the Carney Clothing Company with his brother, J. B. Carney. He died on 12 October 1936 and was buried in the Downs Cemetery.

Chapter Thirty. Trouble in School and Church

1. Her name was Alma (Allie) Gibson.

2. Anna Jones, the daughter of Wiley and Elizabeth Jones, became the teacher in the Ise school in 1891. The "insurrectionists" that arrayed themselves against her, according to Rosa Ise's notes, were Am Jones, Charles Ise, Bartley Yost, Cramer Boomer, and Ed Heiser.

3. His real name was Cramer Boomer, a son of John Boomer.

4. "George Hunker used to rent the Lutz place after Lutz left, and Ed and Phil Heiser, Frank Boomer, Pete Senti and Nate Winters (a little), and McCormick boys—would meet there, sometimes go over to Whewells, drink beer and play cards, and tell stories and smoke and chew. Bad place."—Rosa Ise notes to John Ise.

5. "The night we went to Joe Coates' place to have our hair clipped with the only clippers then in the country, and when on our return the boys fired off an old army musket right in front of George Sollner's house, and we were chased by the said gentleman on horseback, I did not run two miles through fields, pastures, rivers, creeks, etc., like Nate Winters and some others I could name; no, I hid behind a hedge fence on the Dittman farm and watched the fun at close range."—Bartley Yost in *The Yost Family*, p. 85.

6. A charivari (or shivaree) was a mock celebration accompanied by much discordant sound. On the prairie such a celebration took the form of the young men in the neighborhood hounding a newlywed couple in the middle of the night, whereupon the couple was expected to provide a treat to the celebrators, who more often than not overstayed their welcome.

7. His real name was George Washington Creamer. Creamer was born in August 1828 in Pennsylvania. His first wife, Matilda (born 1829), died in 1895, after which George married again, which places his age at the time of

the charivari at sixty-seven. George and Matilda homesteaded the southwest quarter of Section 8 in Ross Township with their seven children—John, Forrest (died in 1878 of typhoid fever), Robert, William, Rebecca, Frances, and Margaret. George passed away in 1903 and was buried next to Matilda in the Oak Dale Cemetery in Eastern Ross Township.

"The night that we serenaded George Washington Creamer, who had just taken upon himself a second wife at the age of 70 years, I helped to throw two dozen chickens into the kitchen through a broken window, also to try to smoke the old fellow out by stopping up the chimney. I might add that I was also in the brave bunch of fellows to run half a mile, all out of breath, when George Washington appeared in the doorway with a loaded rifle in his hand."—Bartley F. Yost, *The Yost Family* (N.p., 1928), p. 84.

"Afterward, Creamer wanted the names of all the men in the crowd and they gave it to him, all thirty-three of them. Then they had to stay to get him in good humor so he wouldn't arrest them. They then made up enough money (60¢ each) to repair the windows and the wall of the house."—John Ise notes of Nate Winters story.

8. Nathaniel F. Winters was the son of Robert and Catherine Winters. He was born in 1876 in Indiana and went with his parents to Osborne County in 1883. He ran his family's farm and was married to Bertha George in 1901, fathering a son, George. Nate was a member of the Masonic Lodge and the Congregational Church. He died in 1959 and was buried in the Downs Cemetery. Bertha passed away in 1963.

9. Bartley Yost was the son of George and Elizabeth Yost. He was born 20 September 1877 in Seewis, Switzerland. He later worked for the U.S. State Department, working in consulates in such places as Canada and Mexico. He was head of the U.S. Consulate in Berlin when World War I broke out. In 1955 he published a book, *Memoirs of a Consul,* detailing his consulate experiences.

10. His real name was Charles Schmidle. He was licensed in 1893 and served two years—1894 and 1895—at the Rose Valley Church in rural Ross Township.

11. The Reverend H. Mattill was a pioneer minister of the Evangelical Church in Kansas. He was presiding elder when the Kill Creek Evangelical Church in Osborne County was dedicated, at the time the most western church structure in Kansas. He died 23 January 1918 in Berkeley, California.

12. Their real names were Fred Heiser and his younger brothers Edward and Albert. The Heiser family lived in the northeast quarter of Section 24 in Bethany Township, Osborne County. The parents had died and Fred, the eldest, kept the family together. The other children were Lizzie, Lydia, and Phillip.

13. As no family by that name was in the area at this time, "Duffy" is probably an alias. The person's real name remains unknown.

14. Henry Metz (born 1850) and his wife, Amanda (born 1854), had three children—Minnie, Mary, Elizabeth.

Chapter Thirty-one. A Dust Storm

1. It was at the Chicago World's Fair that, for the first and only time, Henry was reunited with his sister Kate and his brother John since Henry and Kate had left New York for Illinois in 1866 (Mary Lindley Wright, *Prairie Legacy* [N.p., 1981], pp. 75-76).

2. "The picket fence was added in 1894."—John Ise notes.

3. In 1894 the Osborne County tax assessment rolls listed the Ise farm as having 184 acres under cultivation, using nine horse-drawn farming implements, and another 90 in pasture. They owned eleven horses, fifteen hogs, and thirty-two head of cattle. In 1895 the farm had grown to 420 total acres, making it the largest in the township. The Ise family made and sold 1,500 pounds of butter. Crop prices were favorable—wheat went for fifty cents a bushel, and corn for forty cents. Cattle sold at three cents a pound, while hogs brought three and a half cents.

4. Frank Harold Ise (nicknamed "Dutch") was the twelfth and last child to be born on the Ise homestead. He came into the world on 5 April 1895.

Chapter Thirty-two. The Darkness Before Dawn

1. H. D. Washburn was born 13 July 1857. He first went to Downs in 1881 having worked on the grading of the railroad farther to the west. He was employed by William C. Huff in his blacksmith shop, and in a short time Washburn had bought it outright. He ran this shop for twelve years before engaging in the harness and implement business with Wiley Jones. His first wife, Nina (born 21 April 1858), passed away in 1888. They had two daughters—Pearl, who was born in 1894 and lived only eight months, and Vina. He also had a daughter, Ruth, by his second wife, Clara Winters. Later he became pastor of a church in Woodston, Kansas, where he died in March 1905. He was buried with his first wife and daughter in the Downs Cemetery.

2. His real name was Charlie Oliver, son of David and Jennie Oliver. He was born 5 April 1874 and passed away on 30 May 1895. Charlie was buried in the Rose Valley Cemetery in northwest Ross Township.

3. Mrs. Ellison's real name was Jane (Jennie) Oliver. She was born Jane Simpson on 8 April 1849 at Bedford, Ireland, and died 2 August 1927 at Alvin, Texas. In 1852 her family emigrated to America, first settling in New York.

They then moved to Michigan and Hebron, Indiana, where Jane married David Oliver. She was buried in the Rose Valley Cemetery.

4. His real name was David Oliver. He was born 24 April 1842 at Hebron, Indiana, where he met and married Jane Simpson on 23 March 1869. At the age of eighteen served in the Indiana Infantry, receiving an honorable discharge in 1865. In 1872 the Olivers moved to Ross Township, Osborne County, Kansas, where they settled on a homestead located in the northern half of Section 7. They had six children—Allen, Edwin, Charles, Joseph, Margaret, and Annette. In 1913 the family removed to Alvin, Texas, where David passed away 28 May 1925. He was buried in the Rose Valley Cemetery.

"Oliver came from Indiana before Ma and before Jones. He had been out buffalo hunting when Jones got there, with Dave George. Lived in a stone dugout—always shabby, although Mrs. Oliver was a nice worker. Not so particular about convenience for his family. She put up with anything when he got stubborn. Kindly, had good horses, good living in some ways, although not a good house. Raised more fruit than the rest of us had. His eyes used to snap in such a kindly way. I remember how he brought us apples. Baertsch had to feed his hogs at night so Oliver's turkeys wouldn't eat the feed. Powerful boys, and rough. Ed Oliver was engaged to Lydia Heiser, but when he got to Waterville he found a showier girl and got engaged to her. She later married a cousin of his. Lydia Heiser then married Hillker, a good man, and they lived at Racine, Wisconsin."—John Ise notes.

5. John Ise broke his arm about 15 September 1896—and broke it again 15 October 1896.

6. The wife of Tommy Maier, her real name was Lisa Maier. Born in Switzerland, she lived a very lonely existence in the hills north of the Ise farm, where it was said that "she was permitted to go to Downs only once in the twenty years she lived there" (Rosa Ise notes). Her family had been friends of Rosie's in Jackson County, Kansas.

7. " 'Herr Je,' is a dialectical abbreviation of 'Herr Jesu!'—Jesus or Lord Jesus."—John Ise notes.

8. Alma and Minnie Ise entered the Kansas State Normal School (now Emporia State University).

Chapter Thirty-three. Better Times

1. William McKinley, twenty-fifth president of the United States (1897–1901).

2. Actually, not one buyer but a number of men formed a board after they had bought the elevator from Henry. Among them were Wiley Jones and John J. Bowers. It then became known as the Farmers' Union Elevator.

3. "1897—We sold the lots in Downs for about what we paid."—Rosa Ise notes to John Ise.

4. A four-wheeled, two-seated pleasure carriage. The Ises bought theirs in 1893.

5. The addition of the summer kitchen in 1896 added an unusual outside feature to the house—a "false front," or free-standing wall above the kitchen door, something usually found only on storefronts. These false fronts were built in order to make the buildings appear larger than they really were.

6. Grand Army of the Republic, an organization of Union Army veterans formed after the Civil War.

7. "Dawn" or "Dawn of Morning."

8. In February Christian Baertsch had become afflicted with a kidney disease. He traveled to Atchison to visit a daughter and to Holton to see a son, returning in July. He was then confined to his bed for four weeks and passed away on 25 August 1897 at the age of sixty-two, his wife and nine children gathered about his bed. The funeral services were held in the Rose Valley schoolhouse in both German and English, and Baertsch was buried in the Rose Valley Cemetery. The funeral procession was said to be the largest ever known in the area, so great was the esteem in which the deceased was held.

9. "Oh, there is Billy."

Chapter Thirty-four. The End of a Brave Fight

1. The Hastings Trail was a well-traveled commercial route between Cawker City and Hastings, Nebraska (the trail ruts started a mile west of Cawker City). One would head north, keeping to the top of the divides, passing through such long-forgotten villages as Salem in Jewell County, Kansas, and current towns such as Red Cloud and Blue Hill in Nebraska, eventually ending up in Hastings. Many freight wagons passed this way throughout the 1870s and 1880s.

2. This is one of many snippets of songs and poems written down in John Ise's notes, usually without a title. On the written manuscript sheet for this lyric the date "1877" is given at the bottom.

3. The Osborne County tax assessment rolls show that in 1900 the Ise farm was a busy and prosperous place. One hundred and eighty-four acres were under cultivation, while another ninety were not. The value of the land was set at three dollars an acre. There were nine horses, sixty head of cattle, and eight-five hogs to take care of. In these later years the Ises had taken to putting half of their land in their eldest son Edward's name, who had an additional one hundred and twenty acres under cultivation and another seventy head of cattle.

4. Dr. F. M. Daily (1855–1912) was a prominent physician and surgeon in Beloit, Kansas. He and his wife, Clare (1857–1938), had six children—Helen, Mattie, Alice, John, Francis, and Paul. He is buried in the St. Johns Cemetery in Beloit.

5. The preacher was the Reverend J. H. Kiplinger, minister at the Rose Valley Church in 1900.

6. Tuesday, 21 November 1900.

Chapter Thirty-five. Rosie and the Children Manage

1. Henry had finally applied for his soldier's pension in 1890 but was rejected as he had no proof that his medical complaints were due to the war. In 1901 an Act of Congress allowed Rosie as a widow of a soldier to collect his pension, which came to eight dollars a month. In 1909 this was raised to twelve dollars, and in 1930 it was set at forty dollars (Department of Veteran's Affairs, Henry Christian Ise, Military Pension File, File No. 738003 [Wichita, Kans.: Department of Veteran's Affairs, 1890–1947]).

2. A farming implement used to stack straw or hay, replacing men with pitchforks. This machine was the forerunner of the threshing machine, which was in turn replaced by the combine.

3. Also called a sulky plow, this enabled the farmer to ride in a seat behind the horses as they pulled the implement along, instead of walking behind them.

4. A Chautauqua was an outdoor assembly held for educational purposes, combining lectures and entertainment, first held at Chautauqua, New York. The Lincoln Park Chautauqua was located on Oak Creek halfway between the towns of Downs and Cawker City. Chautauquas were held there from 1897 through 1914, attracting such speakers as Kansas governors, famous authors, and even presidential candidates.

5. The Kill Creek Evangelical Church was located twenty-four miles southwest of the Ise homestead. It began in 1872 as a Sunday school, and in 1877 the fifty-member congregation built the Little White Church, then the westernmost religious structure between Kansas City and Denver. Services were held there until 1968, when the church merged with two others.

6. "There is one thing that I believe you could put in the book which would add to it, and I think it is due Walt, and that is his leaving for the Philippines, his going around the world, the report that he had been killed and his return home. That could easily be added to some chapter of the book, and I really think it is worth mentioning. You dwell a great deal on the gloomy side of life and if you were to mention these incidents, I would not dwell much on the fact that he was reported dead. You will recall that you and I

were at the University when the papers carried a notice of the insurrection and stated that he and Bachelder had been killed and their bodies carried back into the mountains."—Charles Ise, letter to John Ise, 14 July 1932. John Ise papers, University Archives, University of Kansas (see also Mary Lindley Wright, *Prairie Legacy* [N.p., 1981], pp. 161–71.

7. William C. Quantrill, infamous leader of Confederate guerrilla band during the Civil War. On 21 August 1863 he led four hundred men on a raid of Lawrence, Kansas, in which upwards of one hundred and forty citizens were killed and nearly two hundred buildings were burned.

8. Estelle May Ise attended the college in Manhattan, not Emporia.

Chapter Thirty-six. The Sale, and the End of Pioneering

1. John Kaser, Jr., was born in Goshocton County, Ohio, on 16 April 1851. He moved to Osborne County with his father, John, and stepmother, Mary, in 1870. The Kasers were among the first settlers in the county, taking up residence in Section 21 of Penn Township. John, Jr., married Annette Leaver on 15 September 1874. They had four children—William, Clyde, Lottie, and Louise. John, Jr., became a famous buffalo hunter, working with the likes of Buffalo Bill Cody and Jeff Durfey. He died 31 January 1940 and was buried in the Osborne Cemetery.

2. This species of owl preys mainly on prairie dogs.

3. "Two of the older Schoen boys, Albert and John, Jr., had built a four-wheeled wagon for their black dog, Coalie, and taught him to pull the cart. One day the Ise family, who lived several miles west on Dry Creek, came to visit. They were accompanied by their little crippled boy, John. He was an intelligent lad but because of his affliction could not follow the older children to school. Everyone admired the dog and cart.

"Why don't you give him to John Ise to drive to school?" their father asked.

They did, and that is how this boy was able to start his education. This lad was destined to become a famous author and brilliant professor of Economics at Kansas University. There his forceful personality would be an inspiration to John Schoen's grand- and great-grandchildren as they would study his books or listen to him lecture."—Rose Marie Schoen Dean, *The John Schoen Story* (Beloit, Kans.: Beloit Daily Call, 1962), p. 13.

4. Wilton (Bill) Edgar Bowers (born 1868) was a son of the Reverend John J. Bowers. His wife was Alfaretta Mikesell. Wilton farmed the Ise homestead for eleven years. They had six children—Alice, Arthur, Mabel, Gertrude, Hazel, and Bessie.

Chapter Thirty-eight. The Haag Family and the Early Years in
Kansas

1. Information given here on the George Adam Haag and John Christopher Haag families was copied from the Haag family bible by Rosa Ise in
1909 after her move to Lawrence.

2. For more on Christopher Haag see Chapter 4, n.8.

3. In Mary Lindley Wright, *Prairie Legacy* (N.p., 1981), pp. 146 and 154.
This account by Alma Ise Lindley was written in 1963, some seventy-seven
years after her stay with her grandparents. Rosena Haag, her grandmother,
was sixty years old when Alma visited her.

4. This account has appeared in print twice before, in Charles Robert
Haag, *A Record of the Descendants of John Christopher Haag (1817-1890)* (El Segundo, Calif., 1962), pp. 89-102, and Wright, *Prairie Legacy,* pp. 122-40.

5. Wright, *Prairie Legacy,* p. 123.

6. "Percy says they settled near *Theresa,* which I can't find in the atlas. I
suppose the home was near both places."—John Ise.

The Haags did settle near the town of Theresa, located in Dodge County,
Wisconsin, sixty-three miles northwest of Racine and forty-two miles northwest of Milwaukee. The "Percy" mentioned is Percival David Haag, first
cousin to John Ise and son of George and Frances Haag.

7. John William Haag died 30 November 1852 on the family farm near
Theresa, Wisconsin.

8. Actually three more children were born near Theresa, Wisconsin.
Carl David Eugene Haag, or "Ike," was born 19 November 1853. His nickname was derived from the German pronunciation of Eugene. Rosena Christina Haag, named after her mother and the "Rosie" and "Rosa" of *Sod and
Stubble,* was born 7 October 1855. Wilhelmina Christina Haag, or "Minnie,"
was born 12 September 1857. See also Chapter 10, nn.8 and 5.

9. "Mother always believed in pre-natal influences, although of course
no scientist does now."—John Ise.

10. Rosena Christina (Friehoffer) Haag passed away 24 July 1892 near
Theresa, Wisconsin. She was brought back to Jackson County, Kansas, and
buried in the Holton Cemetery.

11. "This is the way Mother told the story, but Will Haag was inclined to
believe that Grandfather came to Kansas earlier, perhaps 1856 or 1857, 'when
Christ was nine years old.' If he did come when Christ was nine years old that
would have been in 1856. I can't easily believe he would have left his family for
four years but have no way of finding out definitely. Percy Haag says it was
1859."—John Ise.

12. "I have the deed in my strong box."—John Ise.

On record in the Jackson County, Kansas, Register of Deeds office in

Holton, Kansas, as of 7 May 1880, is the following: "Whereas, in pursuance of the Act of Congress approved March 3, 1855, entitled 'An Act in Addition to certain acts, granting Bounty Land to certain Officers and Soldiers who have been engaged in the Military Service of the United States,' there has been deposited in the General Land Office Warrant No. 72391, for 160 acres in favor of Micco Cochookany, minor chief of Sin-ho-he-ithle, Deceased Warrior, Captain Ufanean Micco's Company, Creek Volunteers, Seminole War, with evidence that the same has been duly located upon the North West quarter of Section Twenty-One in Township Six . . . in the District of Lands subject to sale at Kickapoo, Kansas . . . the said Land Returned to the General Land Office by the Surveyor General, the said warrant having been assigned by Louis McIntosh, Guardian of the Said Micco Cochookany, to Christoph Haag, in whose favor said tract had been located.

Given under my hand at the city of Washington the Fifteenth day of September in the year of our Lord one thousand eight hundred and sixty and of the independence of the United States the Eighty fifth.

By the President James Buchanan

Recorded Vol. 451, page 141."

13. George Adam Haag, his grandfather's namesake, was born 3 January 1859 near Theresa, Wisconsin (see Chapter 13, n.4).

14. John Frederick Haag was born 28 March 1861 in Jackson County, Kansas. He stepped on a rusty nail as a boy and suffered medical problems for the rest of his life. A farmer by trade, he married Mathilda Grace Rother (1869–1940) on 14 February 1888. In 1907 they moved to Oklahoma, where he died 22 January 1934 at Weatherford. They were both buried in the Greenwood Cemetery there. John and Mathilda had eight children—John, Walter, Robert, Sophia, Bertha, Anna, Eugene, and Kathryn.

Frederick William Haag, known as "Willie," was born in Jackson County, Kansas, 19 November 1862. Willie was born at midnight, which led to the problem of what day to designate as his birthday. He chose 19 November as two of his brothers also had been born on on that day. A farmer, he was married 24 November 1886 to Lee Jettie Whitfield (1870–1942). He had left Kansas for California on 25 April 1881; he died 7 June 1953 in Rio Bravo, California. Willie and Lee were buried in the Memorial Park in Bakersfield, California. They had seven children—James, George, Rosa, Frank, Carl, Hazel, and Ray.

15. "I appropriated the album when Mother died."—John Ise.

16. "My grandfather states that he heard her say many times that it was at Farrs' that her feet were frozen."—Charles Robert Haag. Robert's grandfather was Frederick William Haag.

17. "This is the way Mother told this story, but I think there may be

some confusion in it. It would sound more reasonable if it had occurred while the family was still in Wisconsin."—John Ise.

18. "Will Haag tell[s] another story, of the time Chris helped take care of the Footes when they had typhoid. According to this story two of the children died, and Chris had to help bury them. There was no funeral."—Charles Robert Haag.

19. Johanna Christina Haag, or "Jennie," was born in Jackson County, Kansas, 18 March 1864 (see Chapter 13, n.4).

20. "My grandfather, F. W. Haag, remembered this, although he was only three years old. He was sleeping upstairs and looked out of the window to see what all the excitement was about."—Charles Robert Haag.

21. "Chris was married 4 May 1872."—Charles Robert Haag.

22. "My grandfather, F. W. Haag, said that there were pegs rather than ladders. He thought the shanty was probably 12 feet by 18. Later, an addition was built on the east side of it."—Charles Robert Haag.

23. Henry Albert Haag was born in Jackson County, Kansas, 6 March 1869. He passed away 1 June 1870, and was buried in the Holton Cemetery.

24. Anna Maria Haag, or "Mary," was born 20 March 1866 in Jackson County, Kansas. On 19 May 1874 she came out to Osborne County, Kansas, and lived with her sister Rosa Ise for three years. When she became ill the doctor was uncertain what her disease was. A leg was amputated, but it did no good. Mary died of what is now known to be bone cancer 4 May 1884. She was buried in the Holton Cemetery.

25. "Will Haag tells a different story of Henry Ise's first trip to Holton. Will says Christ, who had moved out to Downs in 1872, when he was married, and knew Pa out there, wanted him to marry his sister Rosena, and took him to Holton in the fall of 1872 to see if he couldn't arrange it."—John Ise. "Will" was William Edward Haag, a grandson of the Christopher Haag mentioned here.

"My grandfather, F. W. Haag, thought that Will's story was less probable than the first account."—Charles Robert Haag.

26. "Mary now has it."—John Ise. "Mary" was his sister, Mary Alice Ise.

27. "The 'scuttle-box,' I have now. I think the yellow roses may well be the ancestors of the yellow roses that were planted on 'Coalie's' grave, and of some yellow roses that I have in my yard now."—John Ise.

For more on Coalie see Chapter 36, n.3.

28. For a translation, see Chapter 2, n.1.

29. Rosa Ise's memory may not have been serving her well here, as the town of Glen Elder in Mitchell County, Kansas, was first known as West Hampton. She may have confused it with the town of Havensville in eastern Pottawatomie County, Kansas, near which she and Henry spent their first night during the trip west.

30. "In Mother's lifetime four of the friends who seemed to her so rich and fortunate when she was a little girl lost everything they had and had to depend on some kind of charity."—John Ise.

Chapter Thirty-nine. Henry Ise and the Eisenmanger Family

1. Alma Ise Lindley, in Mary Lindley Wright, *Prairie Legacy* (N.p., 1981), p. 7.

2. Most of the early genealogy for the Eisenmangers comes from a notarized family tree that Alma Ise Lindley had made in Germany in 1905. However, the tree also lists Georg and Johanna's first child as being born in 1827, and there is no mention of a child being born out of wedlock. It is not known if this is an error or not.

3. In the notarized family tree of the Eisenmangers her name was listed as "Susanna Dorothea, born Zeller, in Pfitzhof." However, in *Prairie Legacy*, Alma Ise Lindley and her daughter Mary Lindley Wright both listed her as Johanna Klumpf, which is the name used in this text.

4. Georg Christoph (Chris) was born 2 August 1827; Johann Georg (John), born 8 February 1833; Ludwig Friedrich (Fred), 23 March 1835; Luise Katherina (Katherine), 10 May 1838; Christoph Heinrich (Henry), 29 April 1841; and Friedrich Karl (Carl), 18 September 1844.

5. Wright, *Prairie Legacy*, p. 7.

6. The children of John and Magdalena were John, Henry, Charles, Magdalena, Lydia, George, Sarah, and Mary.

7. Their names were Walter and Mary Ann.

8. The children of Fred and Margaretha were Margaretha Marie (Mary), Margaret, Kathyrn (Kate), Louisa, Charles, Joanna (Tillie), William (Jack), and Wolpurgis (Rose).

9. Alma Ise Lindley, in Wright, *Prairie Legacy*, p. 4.

10. For the rest of Kate's story see Chapter 10, n.3.

11. Wright, *Prairie Legacy*, p. 7.

12. Alma Ise Lindley, in Wright, *Prairie Legacy*, p. 8. In *Sod & Stubble*, Henry is portrayed as the youngest son leaving his home in Germany instead of Carl.

13. Alma Ise Lindley, in Wright, *Prairie Legacy*, p. 8.

14. The children of Carl and Margaretha were Heinrich (Andy), Louisa, Henry (Carl), William (George), and Louis (Christy).

15. Brigadier General J. N. Reece, *Report of the Adjutant General of the State of Illinois, Volume I* (Springfield, Ill.: Phillips Bros., State Printers, 1900), p. 509.

16. *Muster and Descriptive Roll of Company H, 10th Infantry Regiment of Illinois Volunteers* (N.p., 1861), p. 89.

17. *Report of the Adjutant General*, ppg. 509–11. Company H suffered more casualties in the Civil War than any other company in the 10th Illinois Volunteer Infantry.

18. Alma Ise Lindley, in Wright, *Prairie Legacy*, p. 21.

19. Ibid., p. 26.

20. Ibid., p. 24.

21. Ibid., p. 144.

22. Ibid., p. 8.

23. Ibid., p. 20.

24. Ibid.

25. On 18 July 1900 Henry Ise wrote out a single-page biography of his life, complete with names and dates, which can be found in the John Ise papers, University Archives, University of Kansas, Lawrence.

26. In Wright, *Prairie Legacy*, p. 112. These letters from Henry to Rosa were found in 1955 by John Ise and sent around to various members of the Ise and Haag families. This story of Chris talking Henry into writing Rosa a letter seems to reinforce the impression given elsewhere in the text that Chris was the instigator of Henry and Rosa coming together.

Chapter Forty. The Writing of *Sod and Stubble*

1. Alma Ise Lindley, Mary Lindley Wright, *Prairie Legacy* (N.p., 1981), p. xiv.

2. Interview with Harold Dwight Hampton by Von Rothenberger, February 1994.

3. William Allen White to John Ise, 8 February 1933, John Ise papers, University Archives, University of Kansas, Lawrence.

4. C. Gibson Scheaffer to John Ise, 3 May 1933, John Ise papers, University Archives, University of Kansas, Lawrence.

5. Mari Sandoz's book, *Old Jules*, was published in 1935. In notes for talks he gave after the publication of his book, John cited Sandoz as an example of the problems faced by a writer when writing a book. John himself was no doubt influenced in keeping the content of his own work relatively clean by the fact that Rosa would be reading the manuscript.

6. Everett E. Hale to John Ise, 3 August 1933, John Ise papers, University Archives, University of Kansas, Lawrence.

7. Charles B. Blanchard to John Ise, 12 May 1934, John Ise papers, University Archives, University of Kansas, Lawrence.

8. Mathilde Weil to John Ise, 29 July 1935, John Ise papers, University Archives, University of Kansas, Lawrence.

9. Mathilde Weil to John Ise, 14 August, 18 October 1935, John Ise papers, University Archives, University of Kansas, Lawrence.

10. During the summer of 1928 John Ise visited Ruth Ruede of Osborne, who had in her possession letters sent by her brother Howard from his homestead in central Osborne County back to his parents in Pennsylvania. Dating from 1877 and 1878, they spoke eloquently of the everyday battle of the homesteader, and John undertook the task of editing them into a readable manuscript. They were an interesting contrast to John's experience, for while Henry Ise's claim rested on secondary river-bottom land, Howard Ruede had arrived late and had to settle on land in the hills even less suited for crops, and where water was difficult to obtain.

11. *Sod-House Days* was initially accepted for publication by Columbia University Press in November 1933, but because of the limited titles that press was publishing at the moment, Dr. Ise was told that it would be two more years before a final contract for publication would be sent. He waited on them, and in November 1935, a contract was signed.

12. Rufus Rockwell Wilson to John Ise, 1 May 1936, John Ise papers, University Archives, University of Kansas, Lawrence.

13. Rufus Rockwell Wilson to John Ise, 1 May 1936, John Ise papers, University Archives, University of Kansas, Lawrence.

14. Rufus Rockwell Wilson to John Ise, 6 November 1936, John Ise papers, University Archives, University of Kansas, Lawrence.

15. Rufus Rockwell Wilson to John Ise, 23 November 1936, John Ise papers, University Archives, University of Kansas, Lawrence.

16. Rufus Rockwell Wilson to John Ise, 3 November 1938, John Ise papers, University Archives, University of Kansas, Lawrence.

17. Alma Ise Lindley to Max Goheen, 11 November 1973, in possession of Max Goheen.

Chapter Forty-one. After *Sod and Stubble:* Of Rosa and the Children

1. Alma Ise Lindley to Max Goheen, 22 June 1973, in possession of Max Goheen.

2. Mary Lindley Wright, *Prairie Legacy* (N.p., 1981), p. 100.

3. *San Diego Union,* 13 December 1974.

4. Alma Ise Lindley, in Wright, *Prairie Legacy,* p. 58.

5. Charles Robert Haag, *A Record of the Descendants of John Christopher Haag (1817–1890)* (El Segundo, Calif., 1962), p. 34.

6. Alma Ise Lindley, in Wright, *Prairie Legacy,* p. 59.

7. *Downs News,* 30 May 1907.

8. Haag, *Descendants of John Christopher Haag,* p. 37.

9. Alma Ise Lindley, in Wright, *Prairie Legacy,* pp. 79–80. The operation was performed at Stormont Hospital in Topeka.

10. Felix served as commandant of the Norfolk (Va.) Naval Yard during World War II; see ibid., p. 256.

11. Haag, *Descendants of John Christopher Haag,* p. 39.

12. Alma Ise Lindley, in Wright, *Prairie Legacy,* p. 60.

Bibliography

Newspapers (all Kansas unless otherwise noted)

Atchison Daily Globe. 1894.
Beloit Daily Call. 1951.
Bull City Post. 1880.
Cawker City Public Record. 1892.
Cawker City Sentinel. 1872.
Downs Chief. 1883–1887.
Downs News. 1889–1965.
Downs News and Times. 1917–1949.
Downs Times. 1886–1915.
Marshalltown Times-Republican (Iowa). 1921.
Osborne County Farmer. 1879–1936.
San Diego Union (California). 1974.
Smith County Pioneer. 1908.

Published Sources

Andreas, A. A. *History of Kansas.* 2 vols. Chicago, 1883.
Biography of State Government Officials. Madison, Wisc., 1890.
Dean, Rose Marie Schoen. *The John Schoen Story.* Beloit, Kans.: Beloit Daily Call, 1962.
Emigh, Tula Draher. *The Story of Lincoln Park.* Cawker City, Kans.: Cawker City Ledger, 1958.
Enoch, Gladys Buck. *Osborne County Revisited.* N.p., 1971.
Haag, Charles Robert. *A Record of the Descendants of John Christopher Haag (1817–1890).* El Segundo, Calif., 1962.

Hurt, R. Douglas. *American Farm Tools: From Hand-Power to Steam-Power.* Manhattan, Kans.: Sunflower University Press, 1982.

McStay, Esther. *Wiley Wilson Jones: His Children and Their Descendants.* N.p., 1968.

Miller, Darrell, ed. *Pioneer Plows and Steel Rails.* Downs, Kans.: Downs News and Times, 1961.

Minear, Mildred. *Original Land Owners of Osborne County, Kansas.* Osborne, Kans.: Osborne County Farmer, 1979.

Muster and Descriptive Roll of Company B, 10th Infantry Regiment of Illinois Volunteers. Springfield, Ill.: n.p., 1861.

Osborne County Genealogical and Historical Society. *Osborne County, Kansas, 1870–1930.* 2 vols. Osborne, Kans.: Osborne County Farmer, 1981.

_____. *The People Came.* Osborne, Kans.: Osborne County Farmer, 1977.

Plat Book of Osborne County, Kansas. Philadelphia: Northwest Publishing Company, 1900.

Reece, J. N. *Report of the Adjutant General of the State of Illinois, Volume 1.* Springfield, Ill.: Phillips Bros., State Printers, 1900.

Rothenberger, Von. *Osborne County in Maps.* Osborne, Kans.: n.p., 1984.

Schell, Dorothy Dean Viets. *A Viets Genealogy: Dr. John Viets and His Descendants.* Baltimore, Md.: Gateway Press, 1990.

Standard Atlas of Osborne County, Kansas. Chicago: George A. Ogle and Company, 1917.

Stephenson, John C. *Downs Did It.* Osborne, Kans.: Osborne County Farmer, 1978.

_____. *Downs: The First One Hundred Years.* Osborne, Kans.: Osborne County Farmer, 1977.

United States, Department of Agriculture, Soil Conservation Service. *Soil Survey of Osborne County, Kansas.* Washington, D.C., 1977.

United States Postal Department. *Record of United States Postmasters, Volume 40.* Washington, D.C., 1879.

Wolf, Esther Akens. *Book of Bower(s).* Agra, Kans.: Agra Star, 1950.

Wright, Mary Lindley. *Prairie Legacy.* N.p., 1981.

Yost, Bartley F. *The Yost Family.* N.p., 1928.

Unpublished Sources

Brown County, Kansas. Letters of Administration, Case Number 574. Clerk of the District Court, Hiawatha, Kansas, 1883.

Clydesdale and Percheron Horse Company. Minutes, 1886–1892. John Ise papers. University Archives, University of Kansas, Lawrence.

Hampton, Harold Dwight. Notes of interview with Von Rothenberger, February 1994. In the possession of the author.

Ise, Henry Christian. Military Pension File. File No. 378003. Wichita, Kansas, Department of Veterans Affairs, 1890–1947.

Ise, John. "Breaking Sod—The Story of Pioneer Life in Kansas." John Ise papers, University Archives, University of Kansas, Lawrence.

————. Letters, 1928–1940. John Ise papers, University Archives, University of Kansas, Lawrence.

————. "Mother's Recollections of Her Early Life." John Ise papers. University Archives, University of Kansas, Lawrence.

————. "Prairie Pioneers." John Ise papers. University Archives, University of Kansas, Lawrence.

Ise, Rosa. Notes, 1924–1928. John Ise papers, University Archives, University of Kansas, Lawrence.

Ise Auction Sale Book. Auctioneer's listing of items and winning bidders, 7 March 1909. John Ise papers. University Archives, University of Kansas, Lawrence.

Kansas State Agricultural Census. Mitchell County. 1880.

————. Osborne County. 1875–1915.

Lindley, Alma Ise. Letters to Max Goheen. In the possession of Max Goheen, 1973.

Osborne County, Kansas. Court Records. Clerk of the District Court Office, 1876–1900.

————. Land Records. Register of Deeds Office, 1871–1965.

————. Real Estate Tax Assessment Rolls. County Clerk Office, 1872–1910.

————. Real Estate Tax Rolls. County Clerk Office, 1872–1910.

Rose Vale Grange. Minutes, 1874–1877. Historical Society of the Downs Carnegie Library, Downs, Kansas.

United States, Bureau of the Census. Mitchell County, Kansas. Washington, D.C., 1870–1900.

————. Osborne County, Kansas. Washington, D.C., 1870–1900.

Wells, F. M. Recollections. John Ise papers, University Archives, University of Kansas, Lawrence.

Index

439